I0753212

HISTORIC PHOTOS OF
WASHINGTON D.C. MONUMENTS

TEXT AND CAPTIONS BY TRACEY GOLD BENNETT

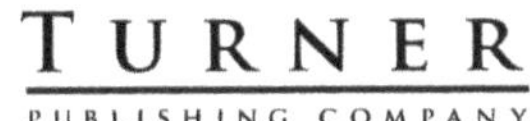

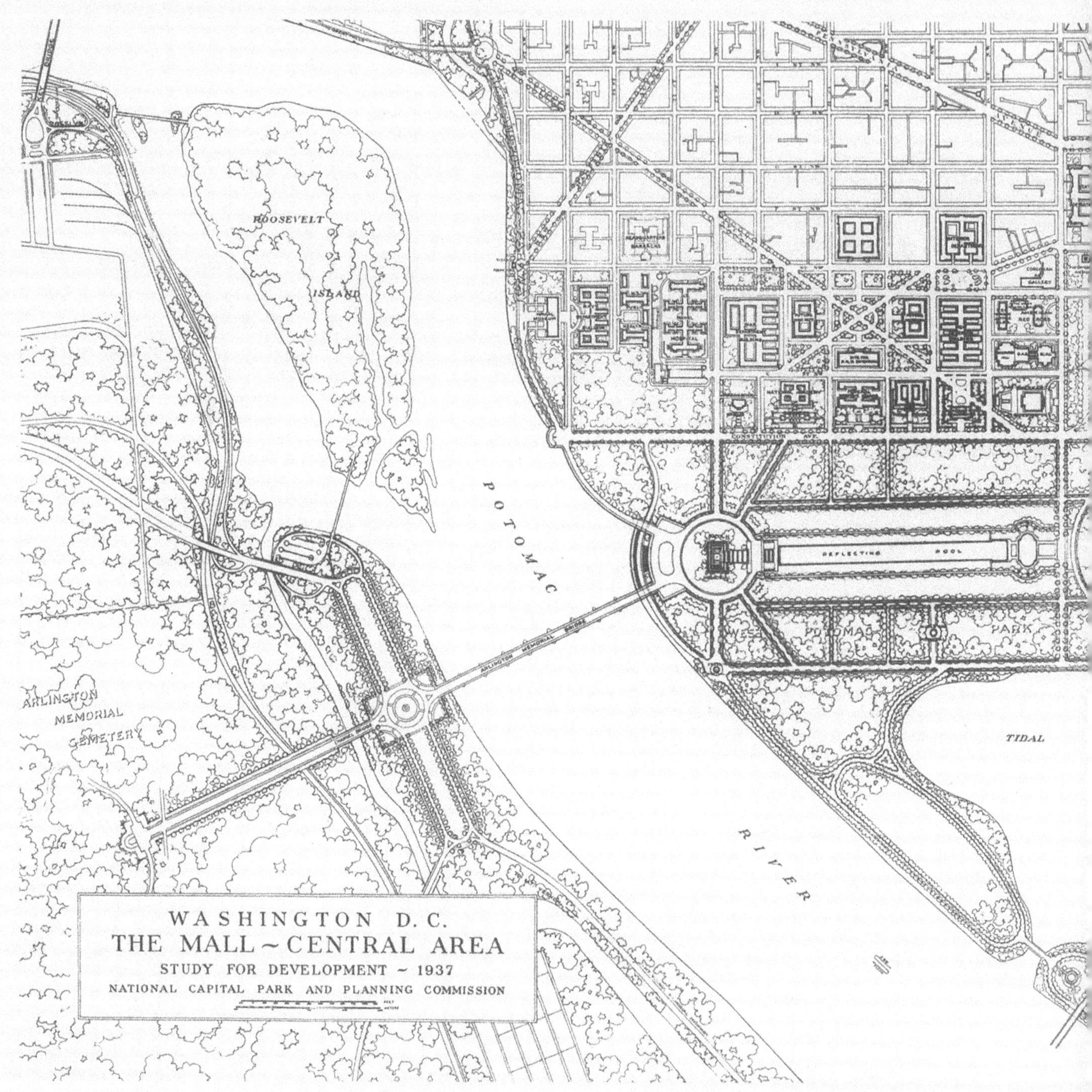

A close inspection of this 1937 National Park and Planning Commission drawing of the National Mall shows parts of Virginia, including the Key Bridge that connects Georgetown and Arlington. Arlington National Cemetery is also visible.

HISTORIC PHOTOS OF
WASHINGTON D.C. MONUMENTS

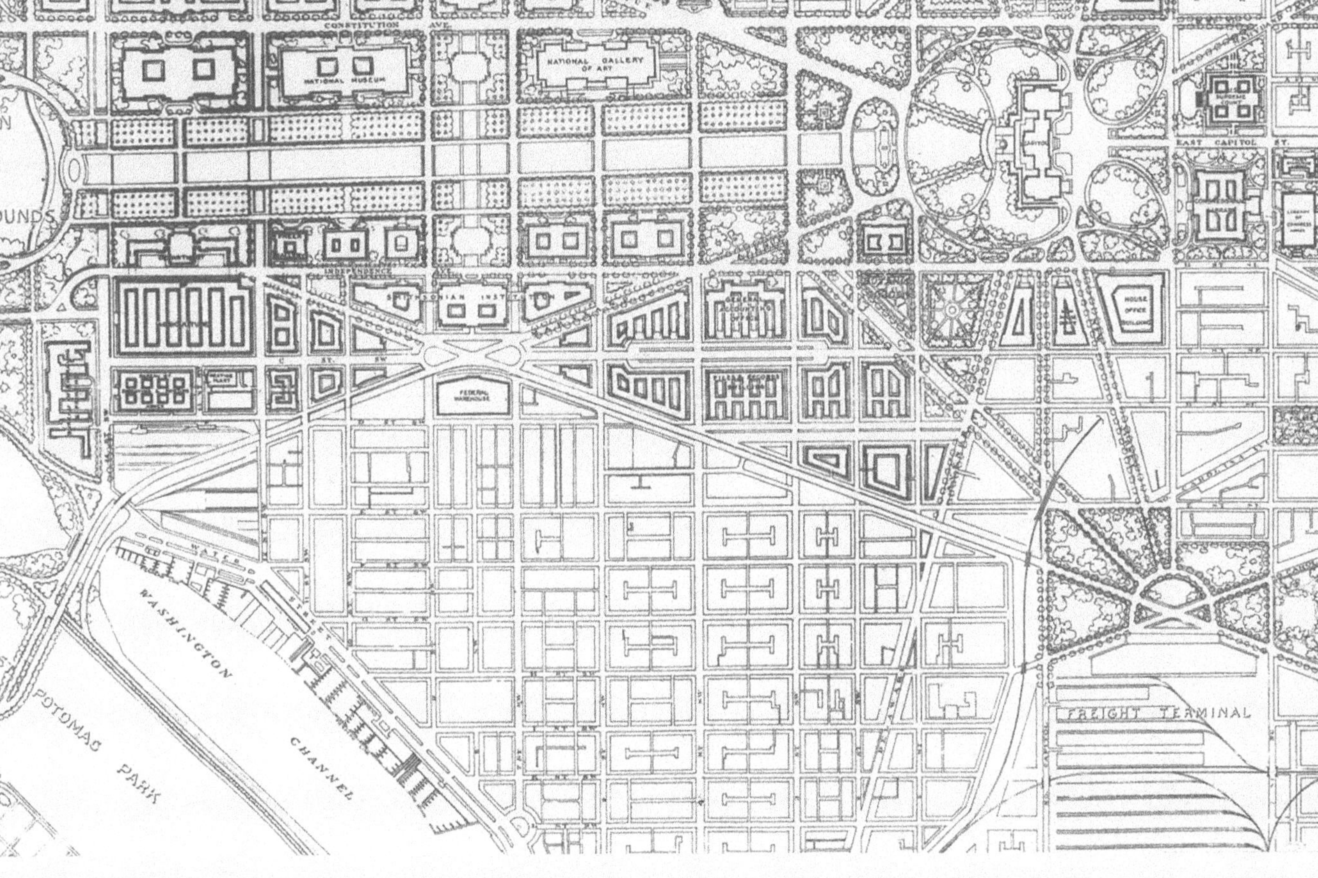

Turner Publishing Company
4507 Charlotte Avenue • Suite 100
Nashville, Tennessee 37209
(615) 255-2665

www.turnerpublishing.com

Historic Photos of Washington D.C. Monuments

Library of Congress Control Number: 2008904907

ISBN: 978-1-59652-505-4

ISBN: 978-1-68442-073-5 (hc)

Printed in the United States of America

09 10 11 12 13 14 15 16—0 9 8 7 6 5 4 3 2 1

Contents

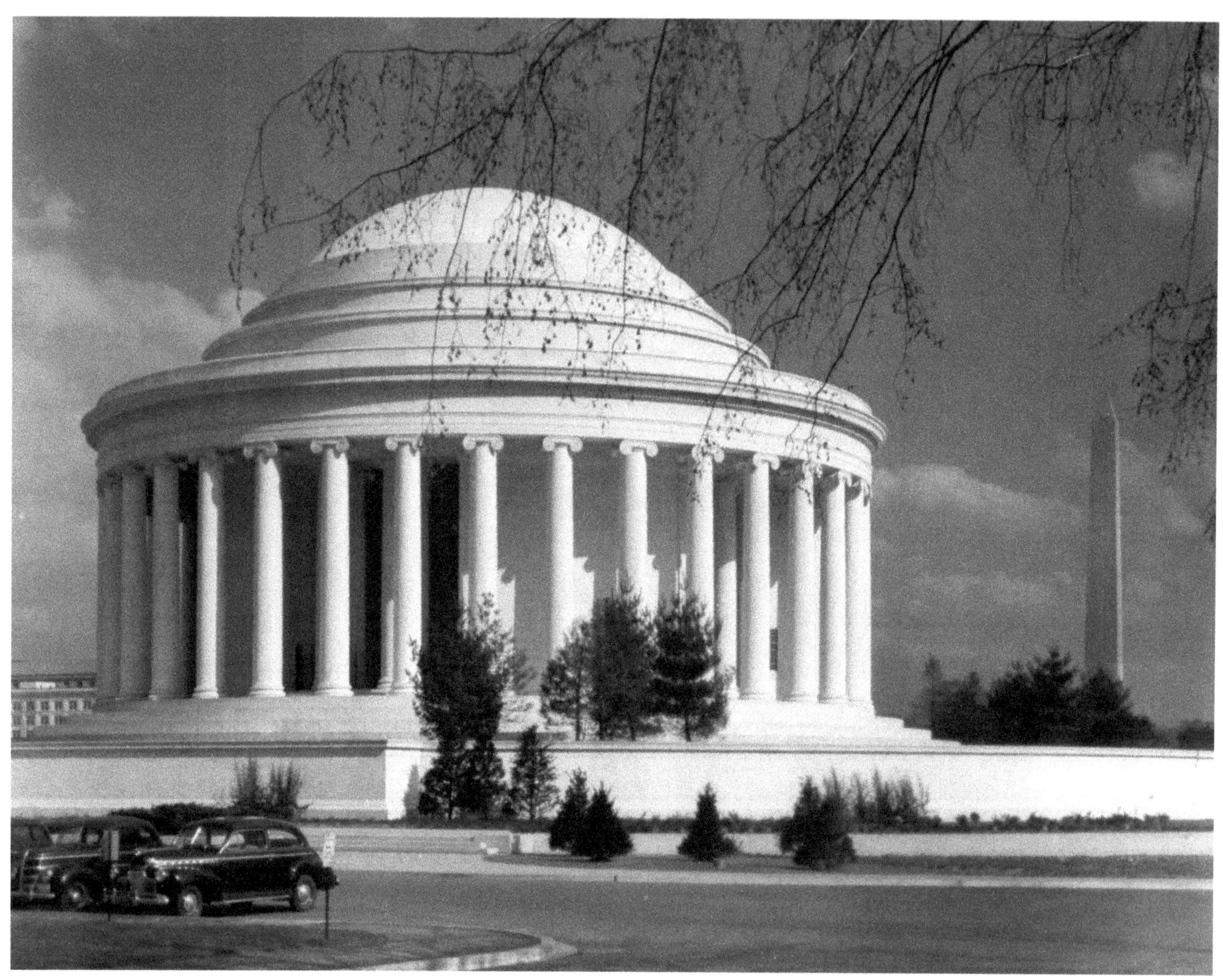

Two Presidents remembered. President and elder statesman Thomas Jefferson's legacy is forever symbolized by the Jefferson Memorial while the Washington Monument honors the nation's first president, George Washington.

Acknowledgments

This volume, *Historic Photos of Washington D.C. Monuments,* is the result of the cooperation and efforts of many individuals, organizations, and corporations. It is with great thanks that we acknowledge the valuable contribution of the following for their generous support:

The United States Department of Defense
The Library of Congress
The National Archives
The Smithsonian Institution

This book would not have been possible were it not for the support and assistance of Turner Publishing and Michael McCalip for bringing me on to write this book. A billion thank yous to Christina Huffines and Mike Pentecost for all of their hard work on this manuscript. The Turner editorial team proves a three-cord strand is better than one. Special thanks goes to The Poor Clares of Perpetual Adoration, Carolyn Love, Olachi Onyewu, Sabrina Dames Crutchfield, Nizam and Vida Ali, and Saidu Koroma for your encouragement and support.

With the exception of touching up imperfections that have accrued with the passage of time and cropping where necessary, no changes have been made. The focus and clarity of many images are limited by the technology and the ability of the photographer at the time they were taken.

Preface

Why do people love Washington, D.C., so much? Ask this question on a local street in the nation's capital and you're likely to get a range of generic responses, including great neighborhoods and walking trails, to more specific answers such as shopping at Eastern Market on Saturdays. But undoubtedly, among the top answers will be because of the monuments, memorials, museums, and national park attractions that are available. In fact, subtracting the cost of lunch and metro fare for an entire day, visiting this nation's top attractions is absolutely free.

This book will briefly examine a number of significant monuments, memorials, and historic sites through black-and-white photographs spanning a century and a half. The people who are being memorialized, the architects and artists behind the structures, and accompanying historical facts are included in photo captions.

The power of photographs is that they are less subjective than words in their treatment of history. Although the photographer can make subjective decisions regarding subject matter and how to capture and present it, photographs seldom interpret the past to the extent textual histories can. For this reason, photography is uniquely positioned to offer an original, untainted look at the past, allowing the viewer to learn for himself what the world was like a century or more ago.

Each of the chapters in *Historic Photos of Washington D.C. Monuments* contains photographs (some old, some more recent) which depict how time has affected some of this country's greatest treasures. Beginning with some of the earliest known photographs of Washington, D.C.'s, monuments, the first section records photographs of the Washington Monument from its construction in the mid-1800s to more recent times in the twentieth century. The second section, the Jefferson Memorial, depicts the memorial beginning with its construction in the 1930s. Section Three explores the Lincoln Memorial from 1911, when Congress approved the bill for the structure, to the 1960s, a decade of protests, rallies, and speeches, many of which took place at the memorial. The last section covers several monuments and memorials throughout Washington, D.C., from the 1800s to recent times.

From the Vietnam Memorial to the Franklin Delano Roosevelt Memorial to the Arlington Bridge that connects the Lincoln Memorial and Arlington House (the former residence of Confederate general Robert E. Lee), this book introduces readers to both prominent and obscure monuments in photographs primarily culled from the archives of the Library of Congress, the National Archives, and the Smithsonian Institution. Some monuments readers may have already visited but may want to return to after exploring this material. Other structures receiving significantly less foot traffic—but ones that are no less significant—are also remembered in *Historic Photos of Washington D.C. Monuments.* Armed with snippets of information about all of these sites and with curiosity piqued, it is hoped that readers will visit these hallowed places and see for themselves why people love Washington, D.C.

—Tracey Gold Bennett

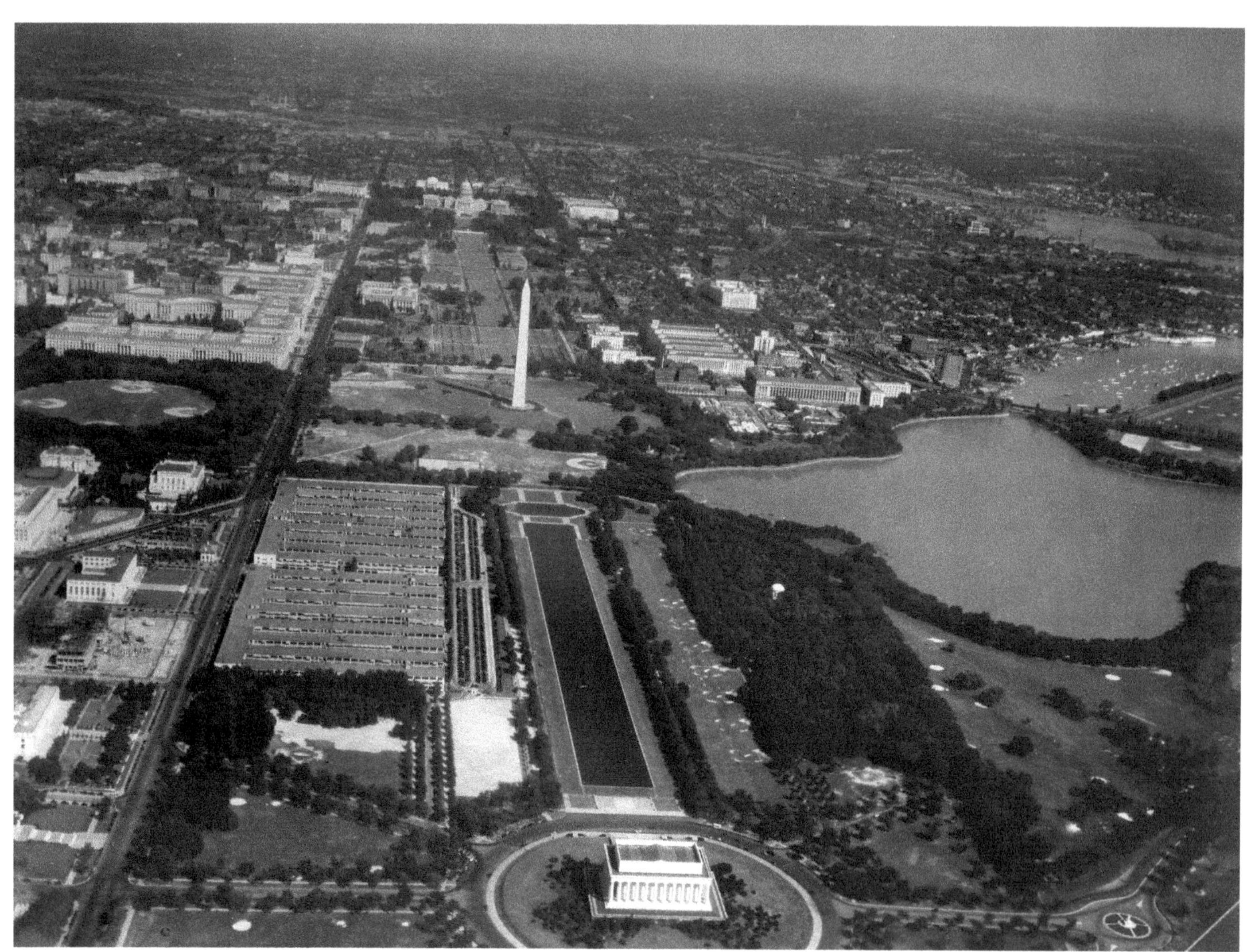

A bird's-eye panorama of one of the most historically engaging cities in the world—Washington, D.C.

The Washington Monument

(1848–1979)

The Washington Monument can be seen from many vantage points around the city and is one of the most easily identifiable masonry structures in the world. Built to honor Revolutionary War hero and first president George Washington, the monument's design plan was initially quite elaborate before it was paired down to the design we know today.

Located on the National Mall, its formidable reflection visible in the Reflecting Pool, the towering obelisk draws more than a million visitors annually. Created from 36,000 masonry blocks towering 555 feet 5 inches high and weighing nearly 100,000 tons, the monument's construction was a nearly impossible undertaking that spanned four decades.

In fact, the project, which broke ground in 1848, took so long to complete that architect Robert Mills would not live long enough to see his vision completely erected in 1884. He died 30 years earlier in 1855. Though the last stone was laid in 1884, the monument did not officially open to the public until October 9, 1888.

Why did it take so long to build this marble, granite, and sandstone monument? Two reasons: funding was depleted and the Civil War began. The Washington National Monument Society, organized by former president James Madison in 1833, spearheaded the project, selecting Robert Mills among a group of architects vying for the project. The price tag was $1,187,710. When funds ran out in 1854 and with the advent of the Civil War in 1861, construction would halt and not resume for 25 years.

Because Washington, D.C., is the nexus from which critical policy decisions radiate that affect the nation and the world, the city and its magnificent structures have more than once been targeted by terrorists. On February 16, 1965, members of the Black Liberation Front and Montreal Separatist Party were arrested for their plan to bomb the Washington Monument. In 1982, a nuclear weapons protestor also threatened to detonate explosives at the monument.

In 1999, the Washington Monument was covered in scaffolding and underwent a $10 million restoration led by architect Michael Graves. The grand reopening ceremony in 2001 was reminiscent of the elaborate day-long dedication of the monument in 1885. Today, the monument remains the site of national events, concerts, and celebrations, perhaps most notably the annual Independence Day commemoration, which includes a magnificent fireworks display.

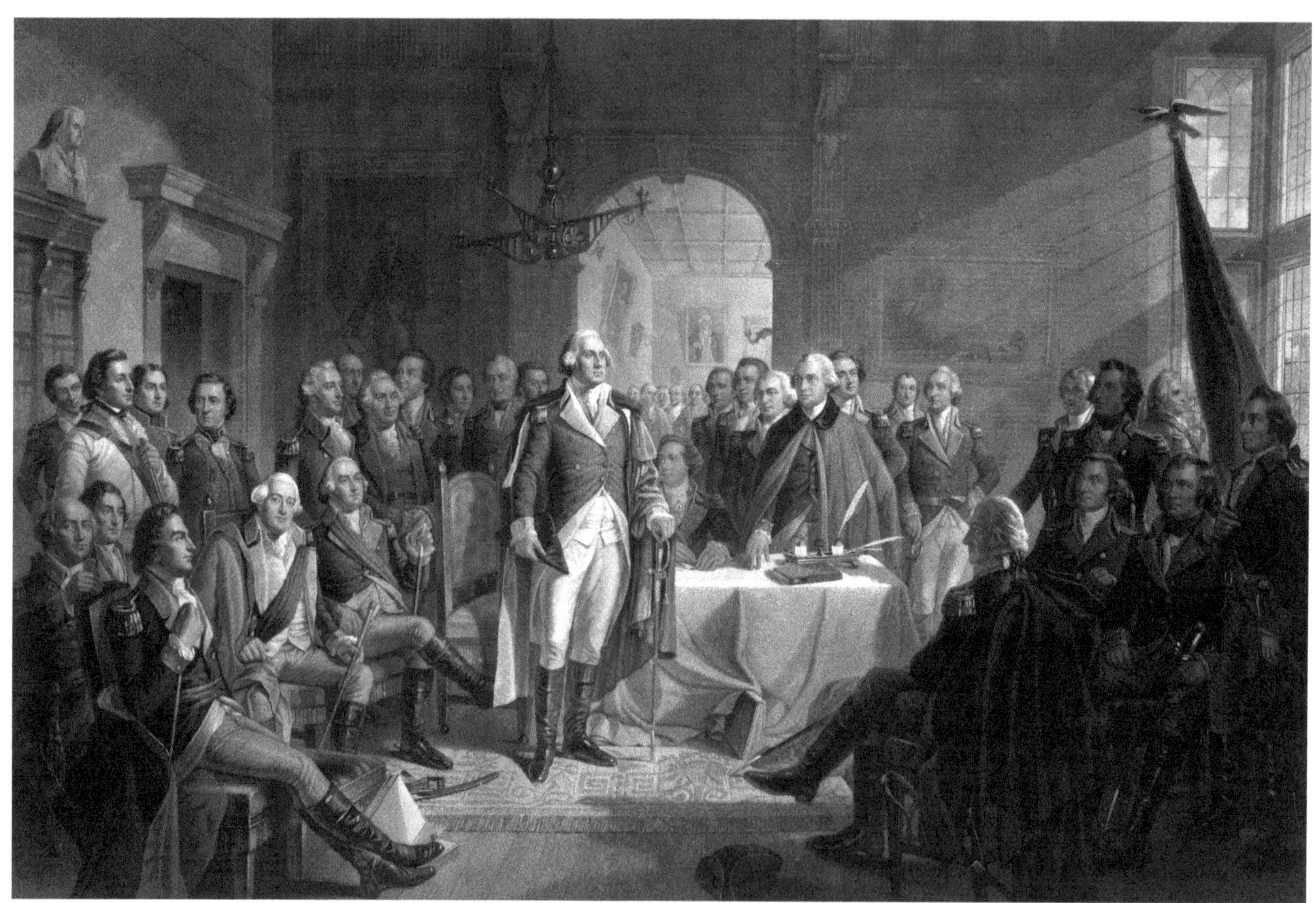

George Washington's role in the Revolutionary War was one of the reasons a monument was built to honor the first president. This A. H. Ritchie print from around 1870 depicts then General George Washington and other Revolutionary War generals gathered in a large room.

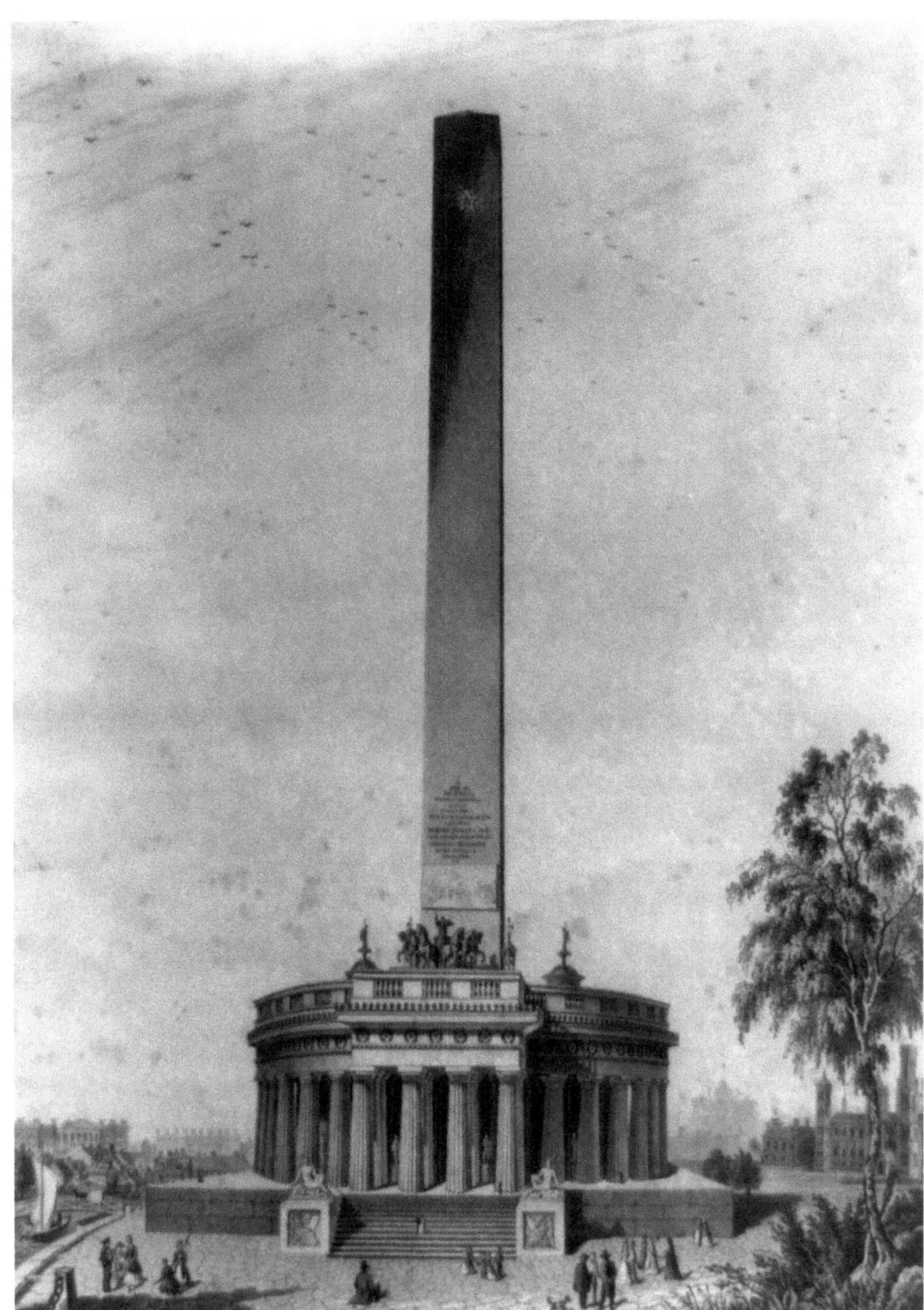

This sketch of the original monument design shows the round of columns at the base. The peak of the monument was almost flat.

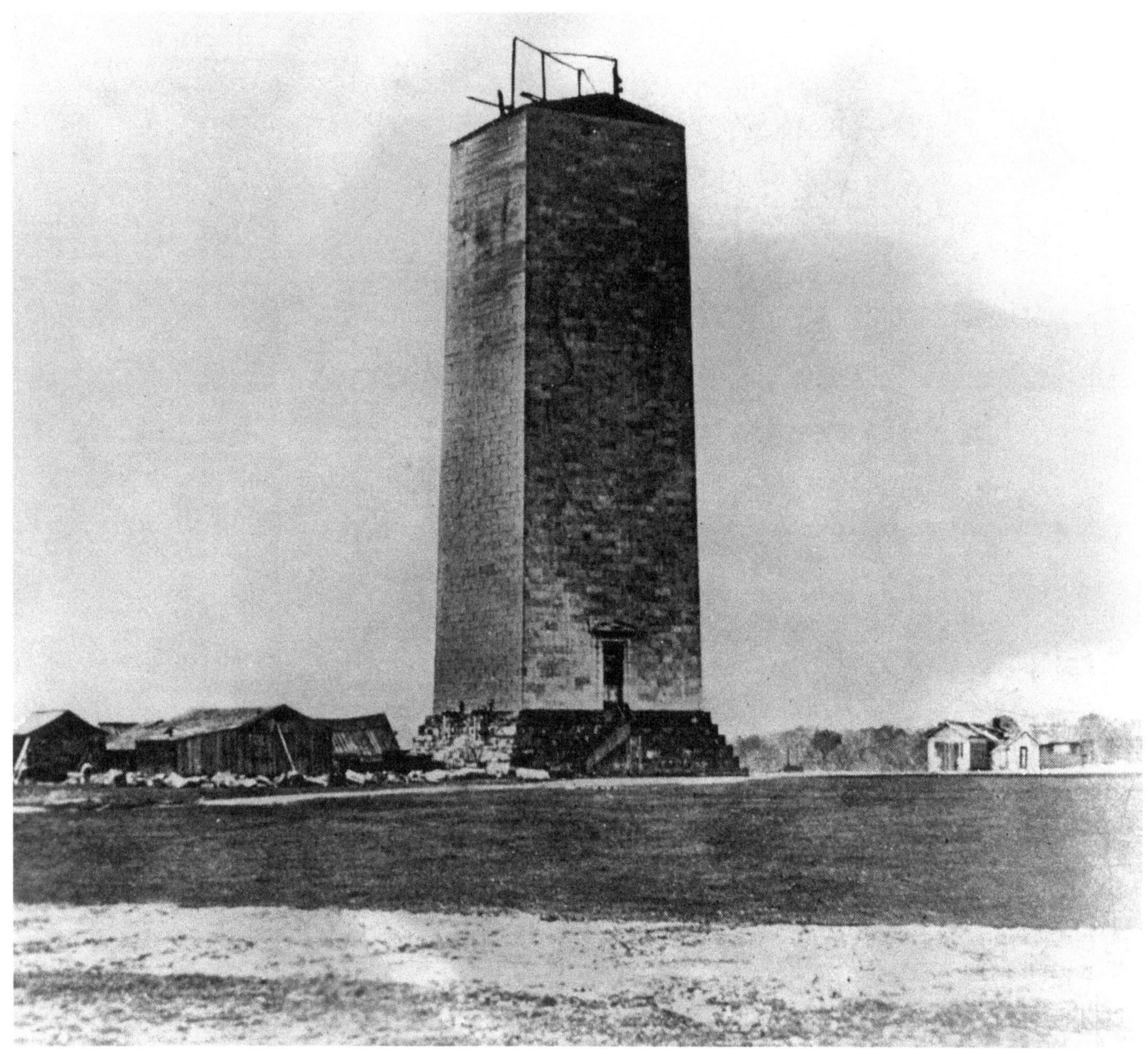

Robert Mills, the architect who designed the Washington Monument, passed away before he could see the monument realized. Money woes forced the project to stop for two decades at the stage seen in this photograph, taken by Mathew Brady around 1860. Initially, Mills' Egyptian obelisk design was much more grandiose and 5 feet taller than the 555-foot final design. In his original plan, the base of the monument would have consisted of 32 Roman columns in a circular design, with a porch for visitors.

Incomplete. That's how the Washington Monument looked for some 25 years after construction began, as shown in this 1860 photo. Building of the monument was interrupted by the Civil War and funding shortfalls. When work resumed, building materials were procured from a different quarry. Two colors of stone on the monument's edifice are evidence of the halted construction.

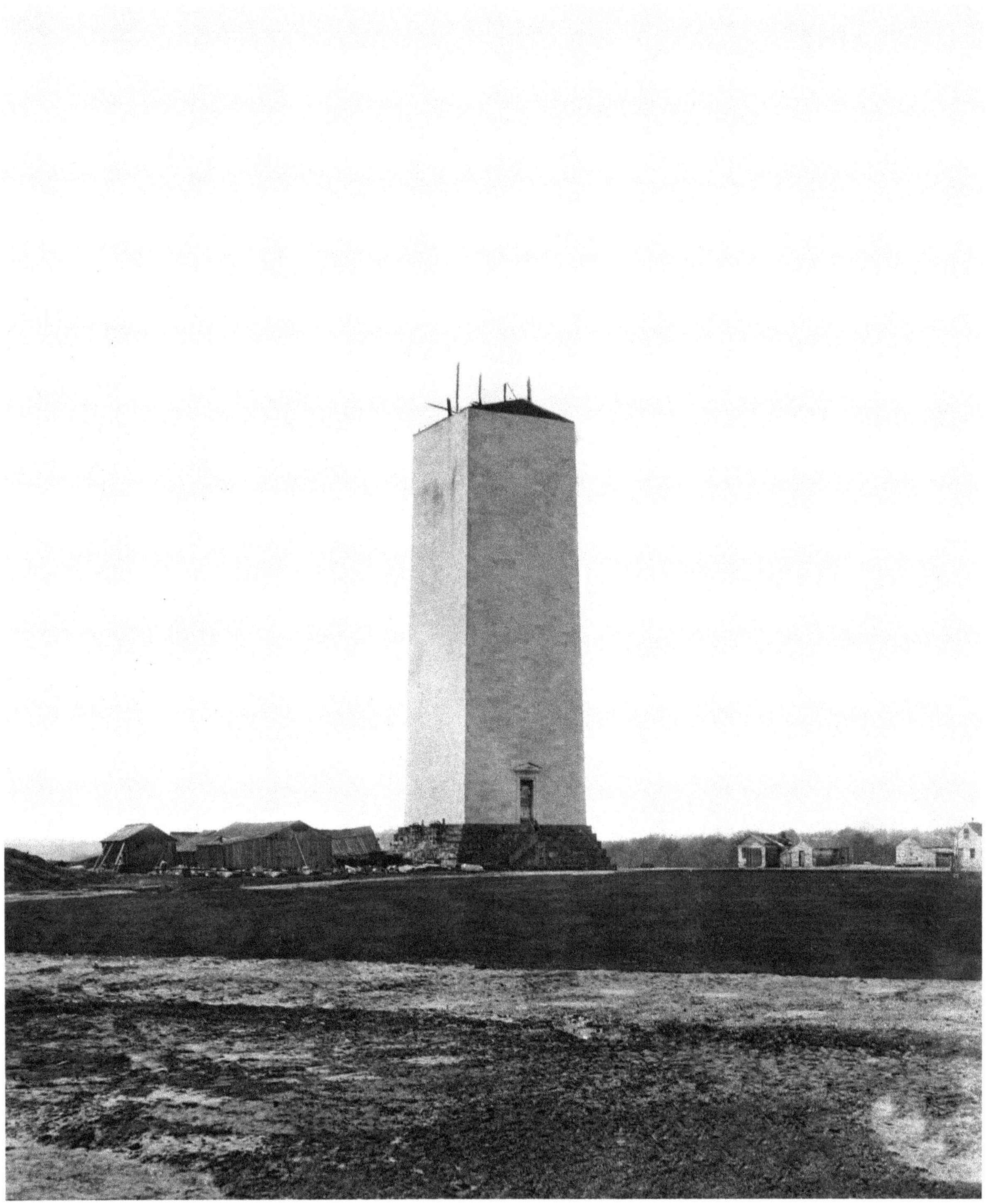

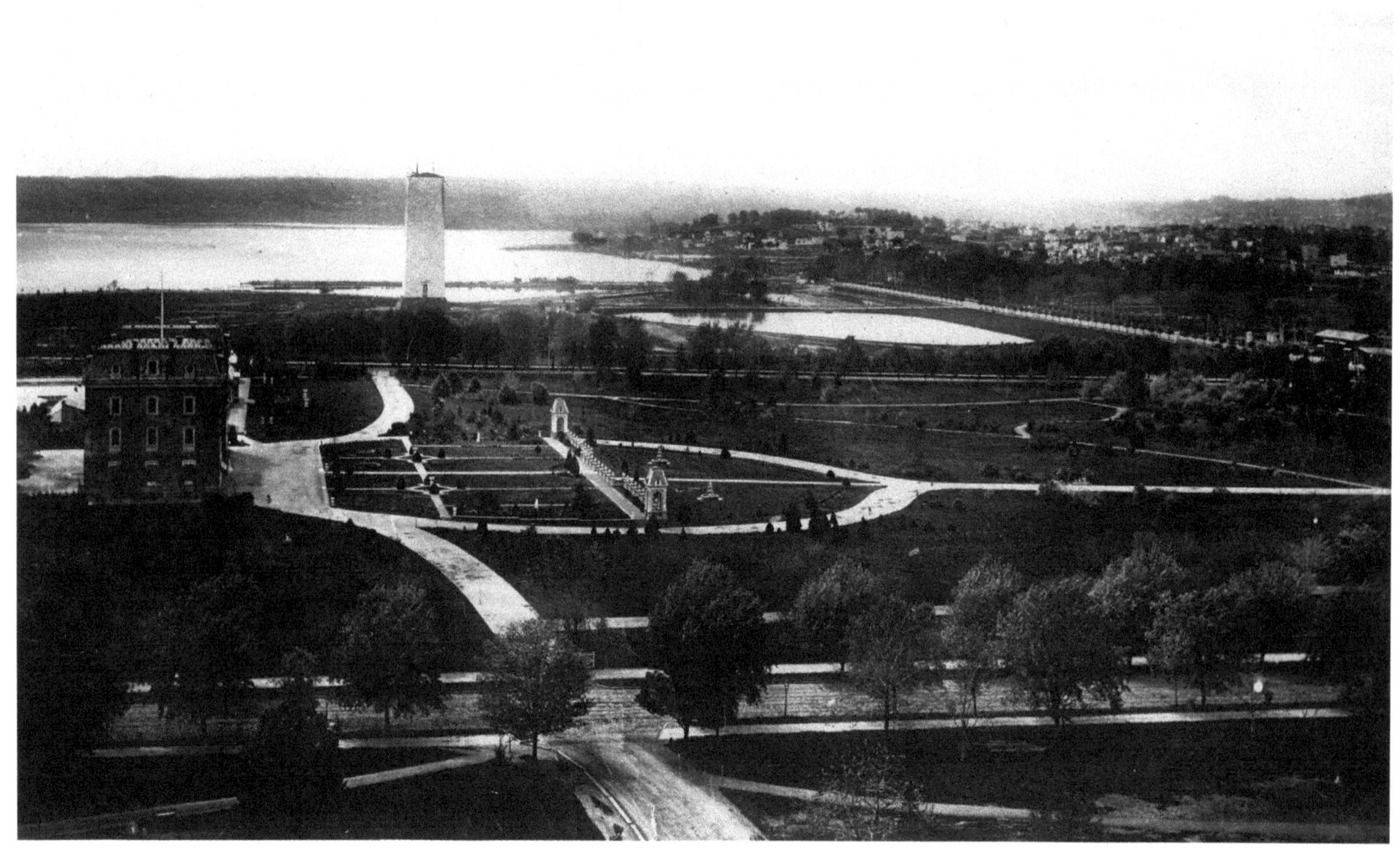

Roof top shot of the Washington Monument foundation construction.

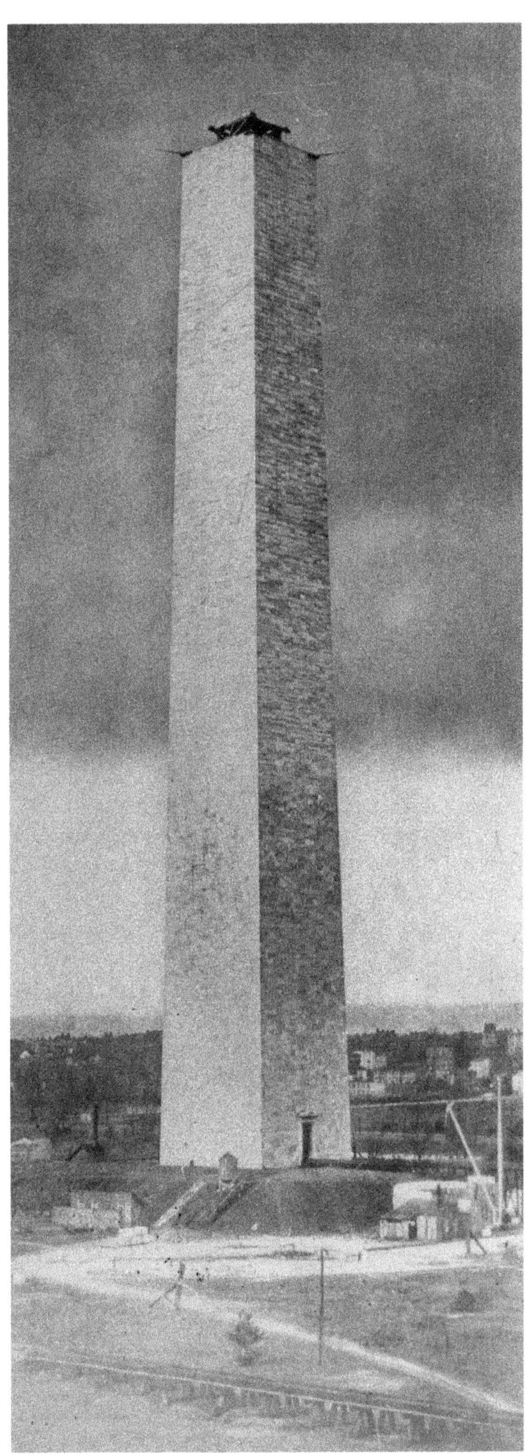

Because of the exorbitant expense associated with his first plan, Mills scaled back his design, eliminated the columns, and fashioned a small, pyramid-like aluminum cap for the top of the monument. This photograph shows an almost fully constructed monument.

The *New York Times* reported on the completion of the monument on December 6, 1884: "The Washington Monument was completed this afternoon by setting in place the marble capstone and its pyramidal apex of aluminum." The following day, December 7, the headline in the *New York Times* read: "Setting the Capstone; the Washington Monument Finished at Last. The American Flag Floating 600 Feet Above the Ground, Fifty Feet Above the Top of the Obelisk."

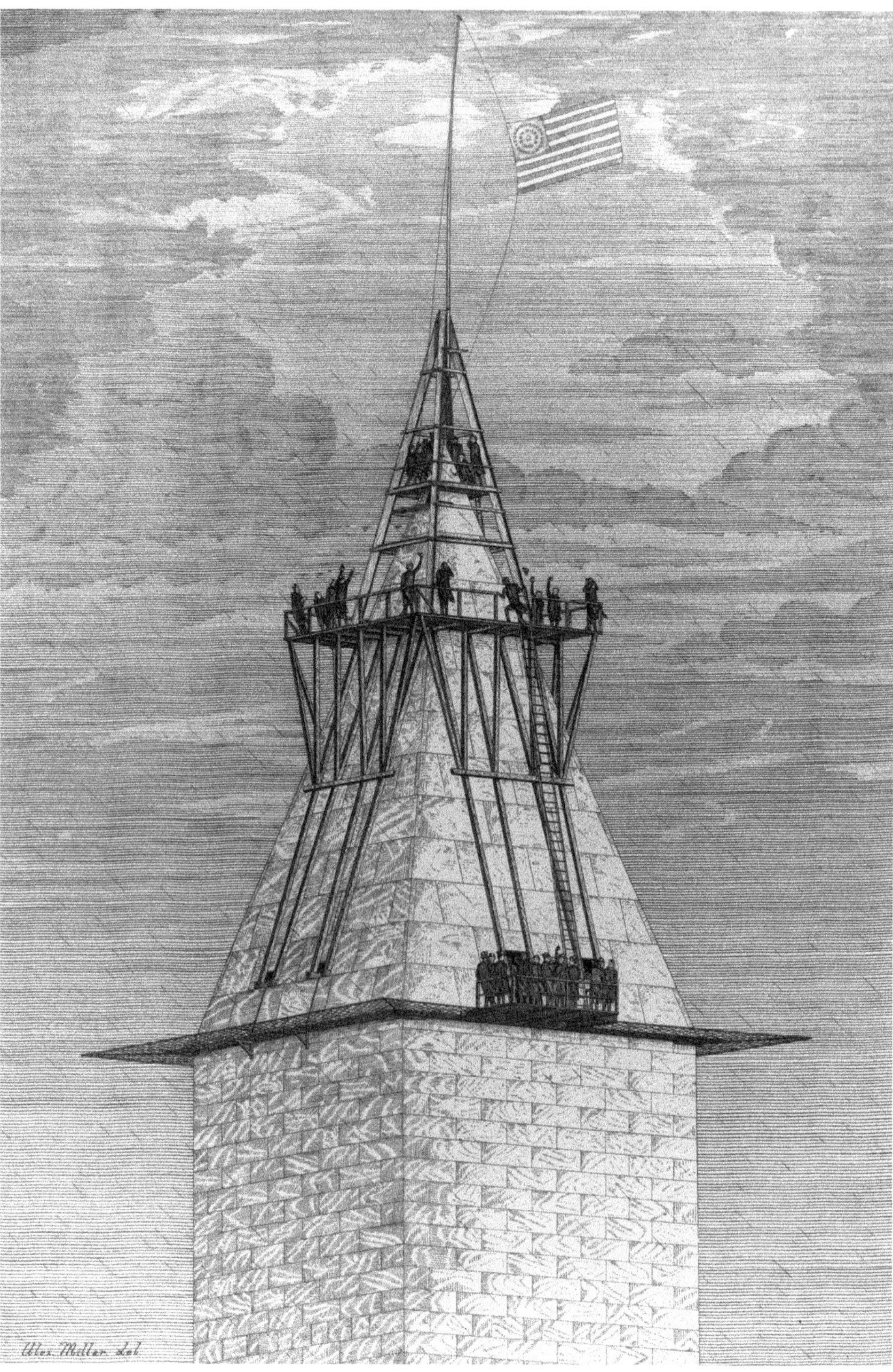

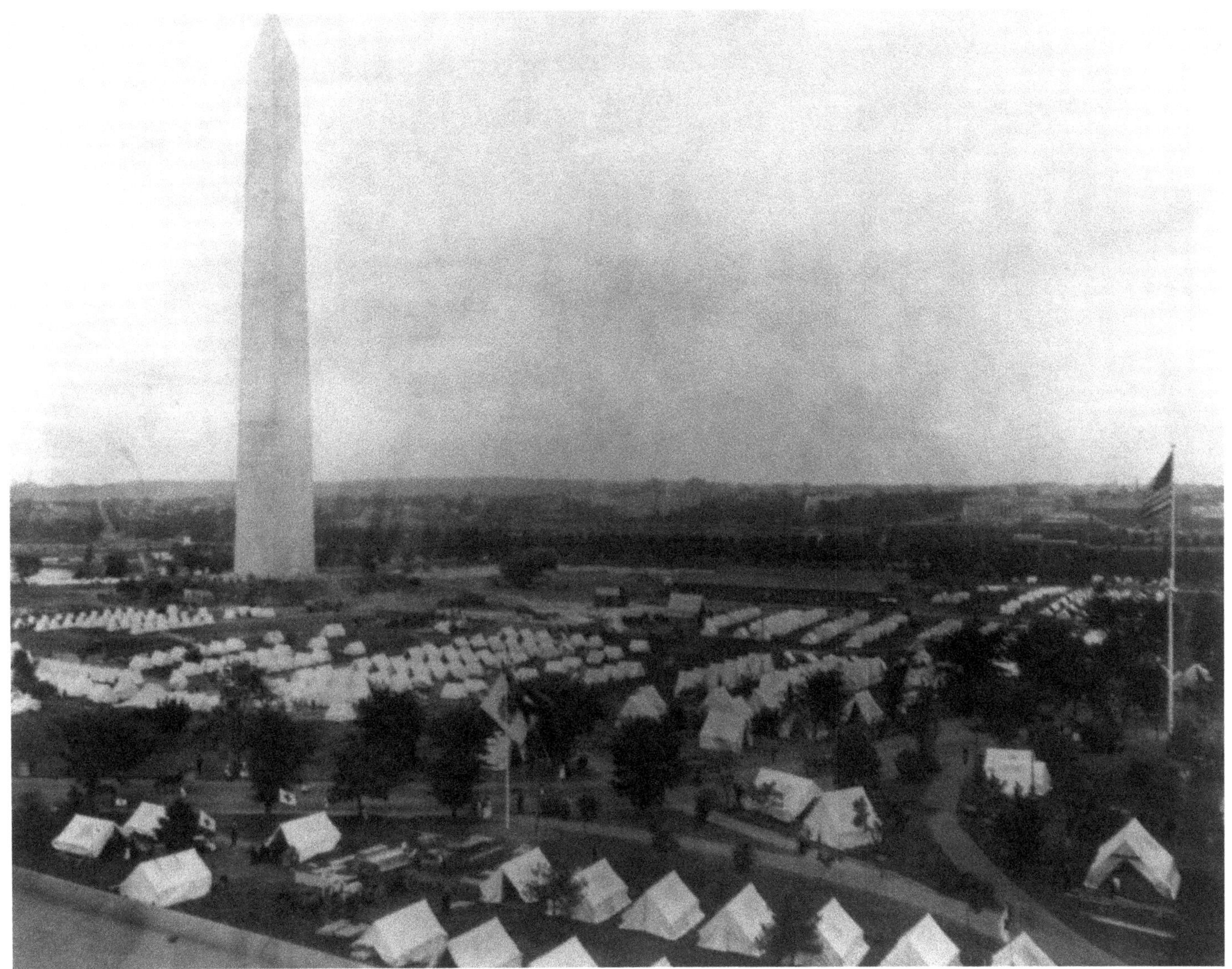

The surrounding grounds of the Washington Monument were home to Camp George in 1887. This photo shows a bird's-eye view of the veterans' tents, which were assembled around the monument.

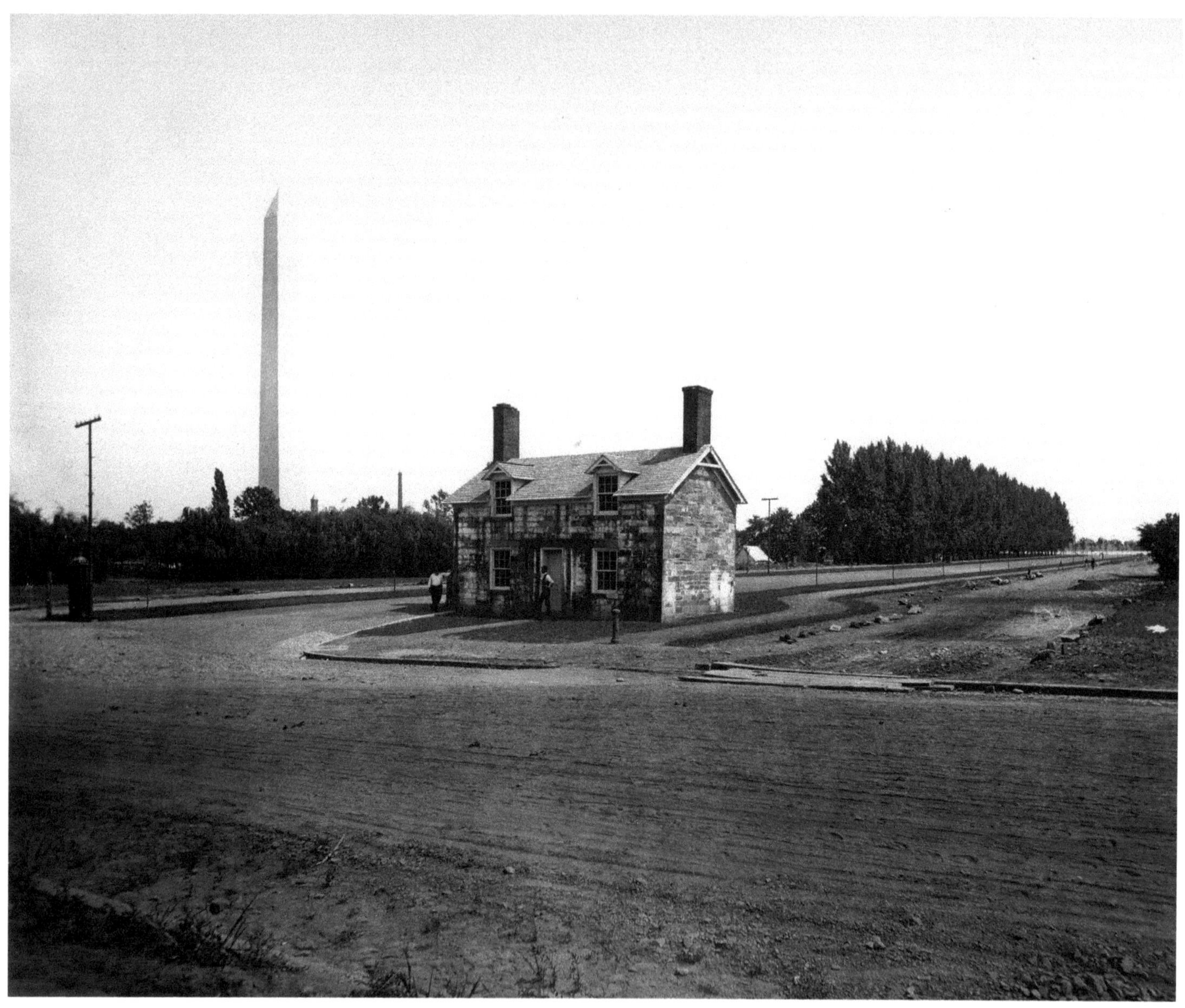

When Constitution Avenue was a canal, the Lock House was located at the western end of the canal at the tributary where the Tiber Creek emptied into the Potomac River. In the 1800s boats could sail right up to the house on what is now 17th Street and Constitution Avenue, NW.

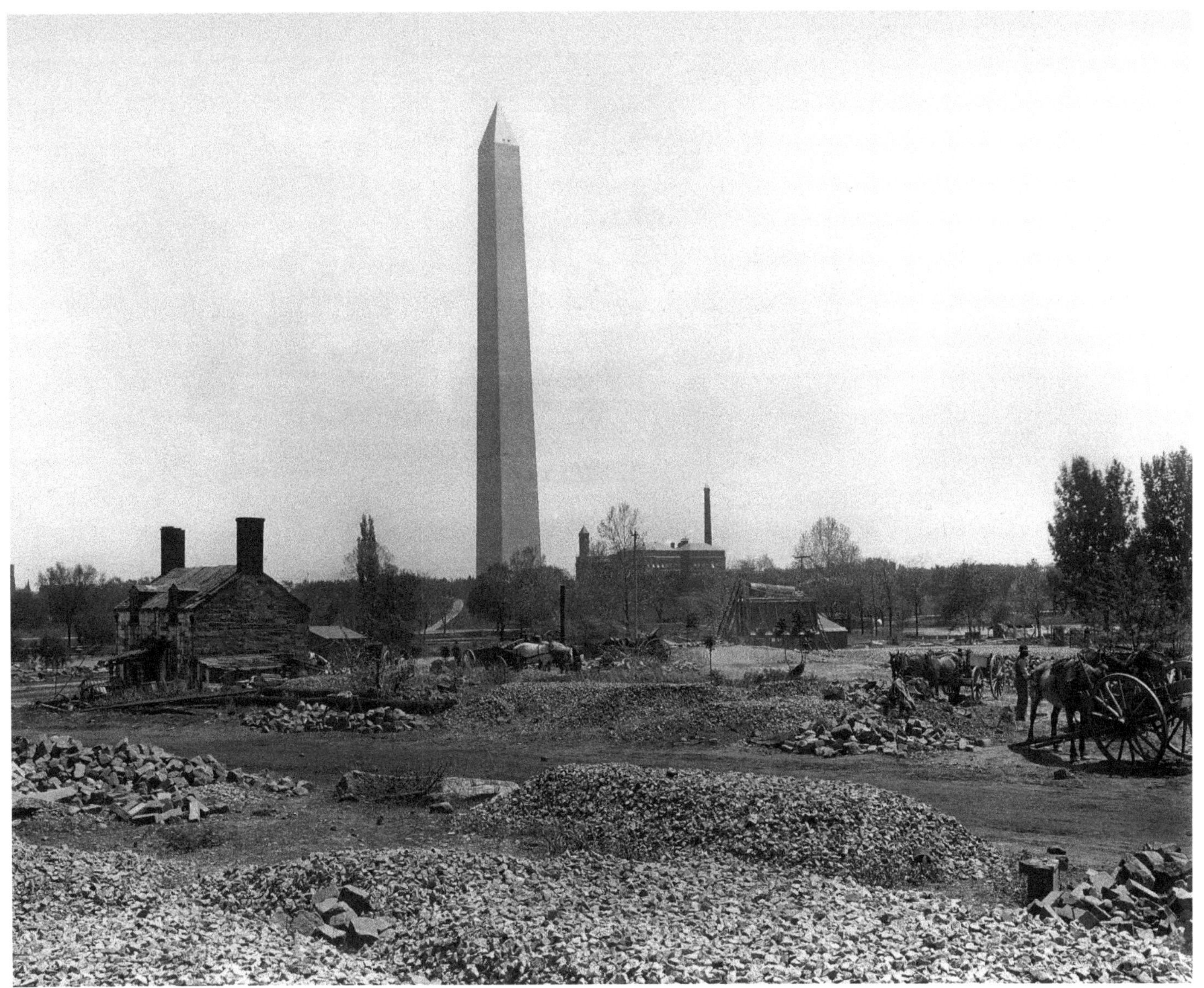

The Lock House was constructed in 1833 when the C&O Canal Extension was finished. The new monument towers over the old canal district.

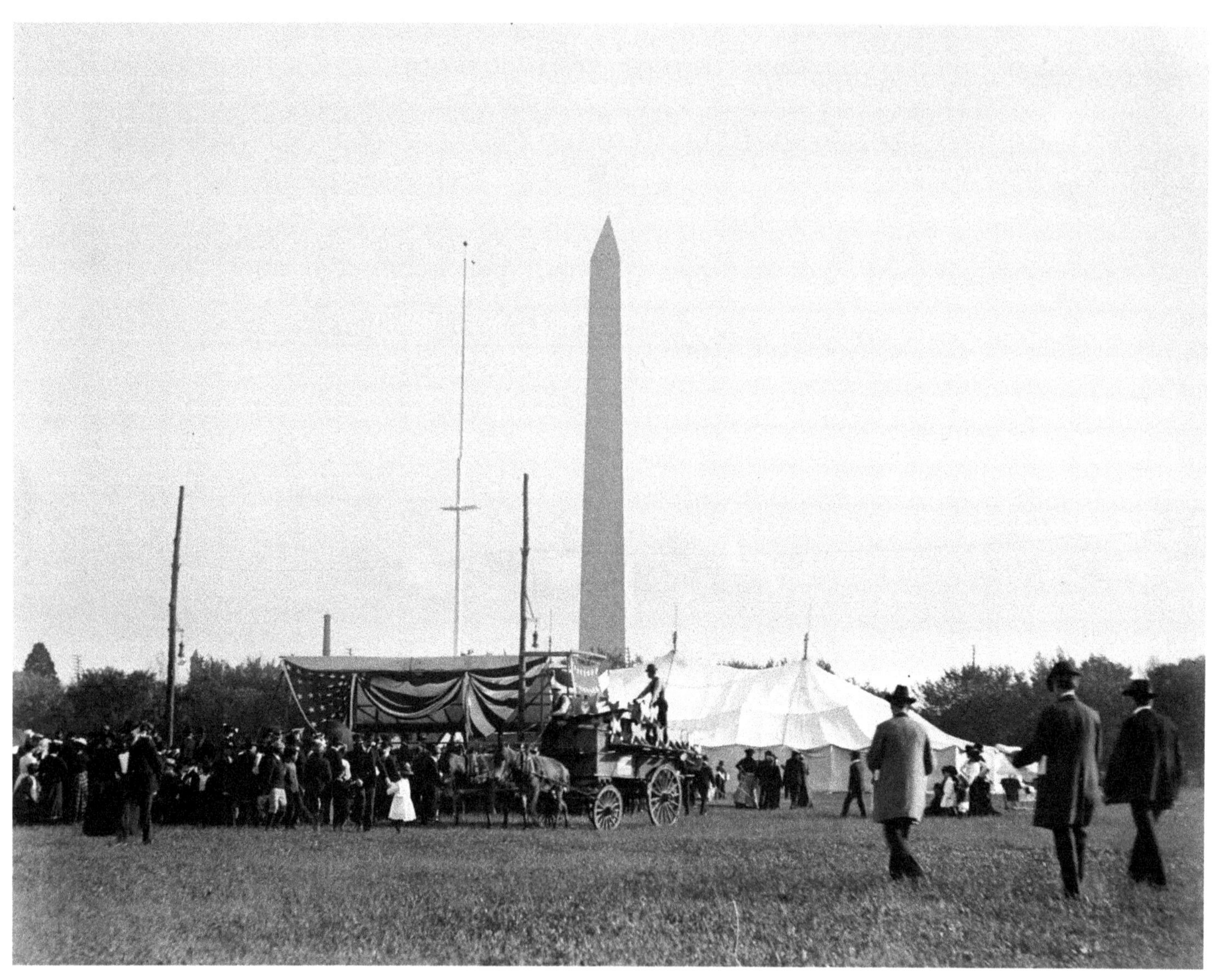

Here, crowds are assembling for dedication exercises during the 1902 opening of Camp Roosevelt. Secretary Hay delivered the dedication remarks.

Recorded in the early 1900s, this image shows four people at the Tidal Basin taking in the sight of what was at that time the tallest structure in the world.

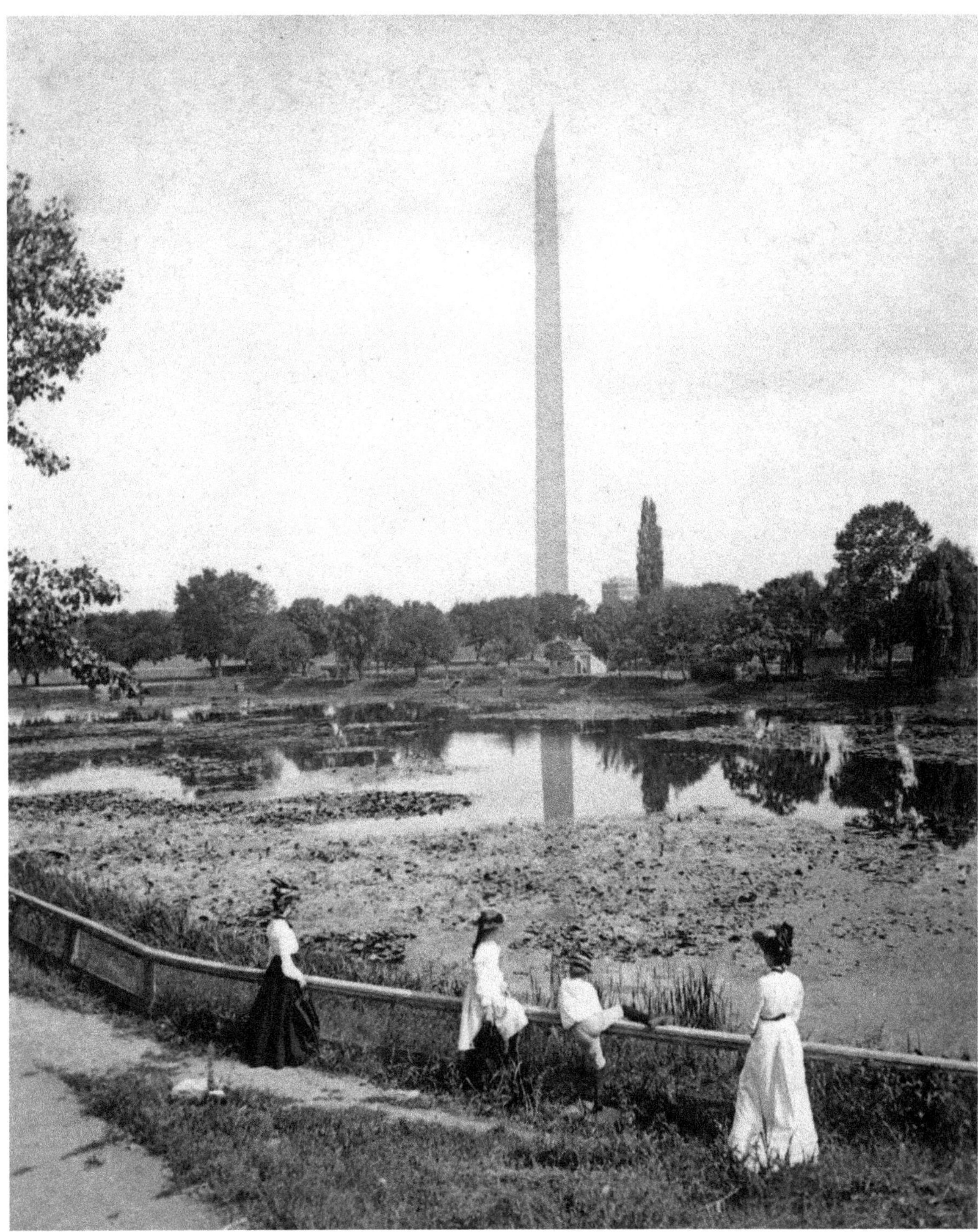

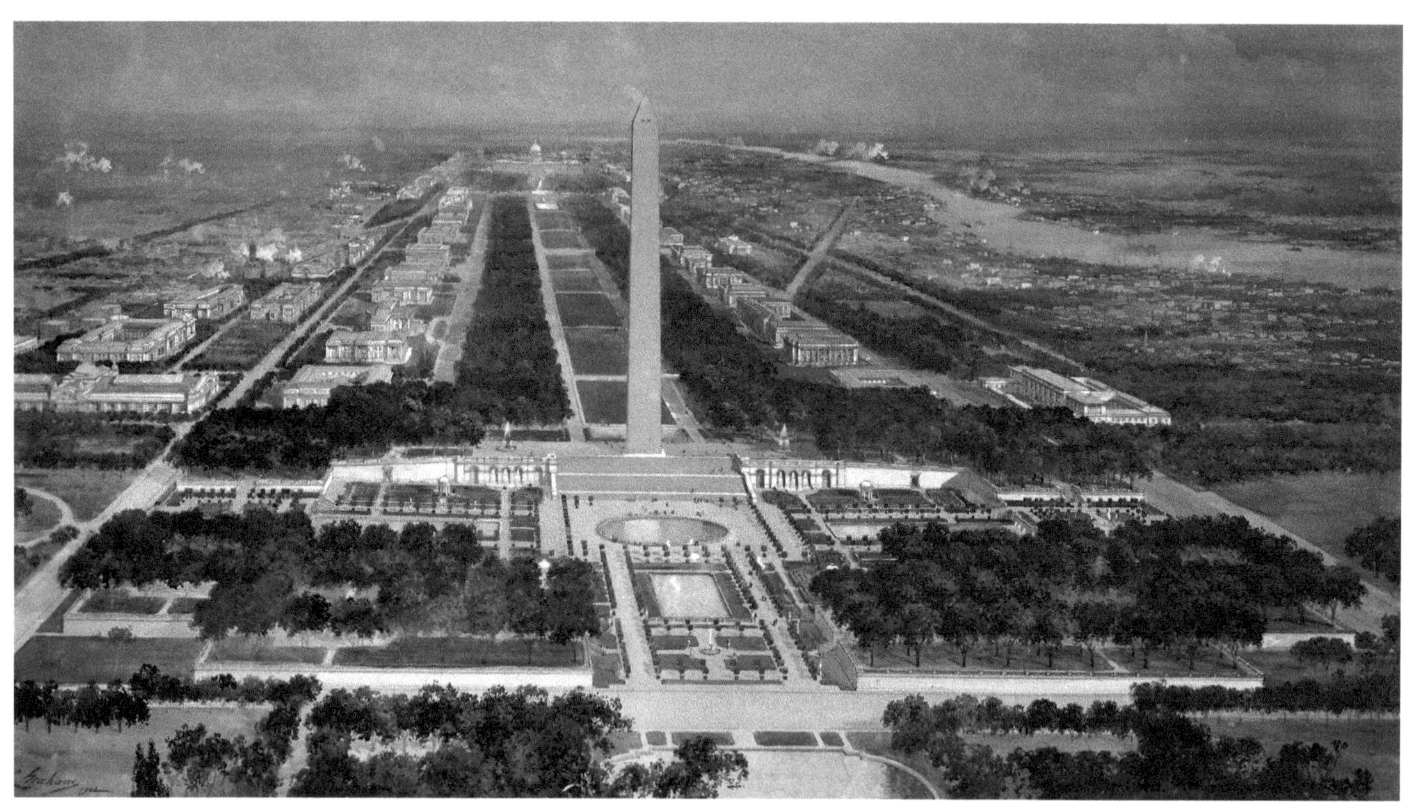

A 1902 aerial view of Washington, D.C., as Pierre L'Enfant might have imagined it. Born in 1752, L'Enfant had honed his artistic skills in Paris at the Royal Academy of Painting and Sculpture. He would later use those skills in planning the complex aesthetics and infrastructure of Washington, D.C. Despite being a Frenchman, L'Enfant had an early allegiance to this country, and in 1776 he joined the Continental army and helped fight for independence from England. L'Enfant was honored with the rank of Major in the Army Corps of Engineers for his efforts.

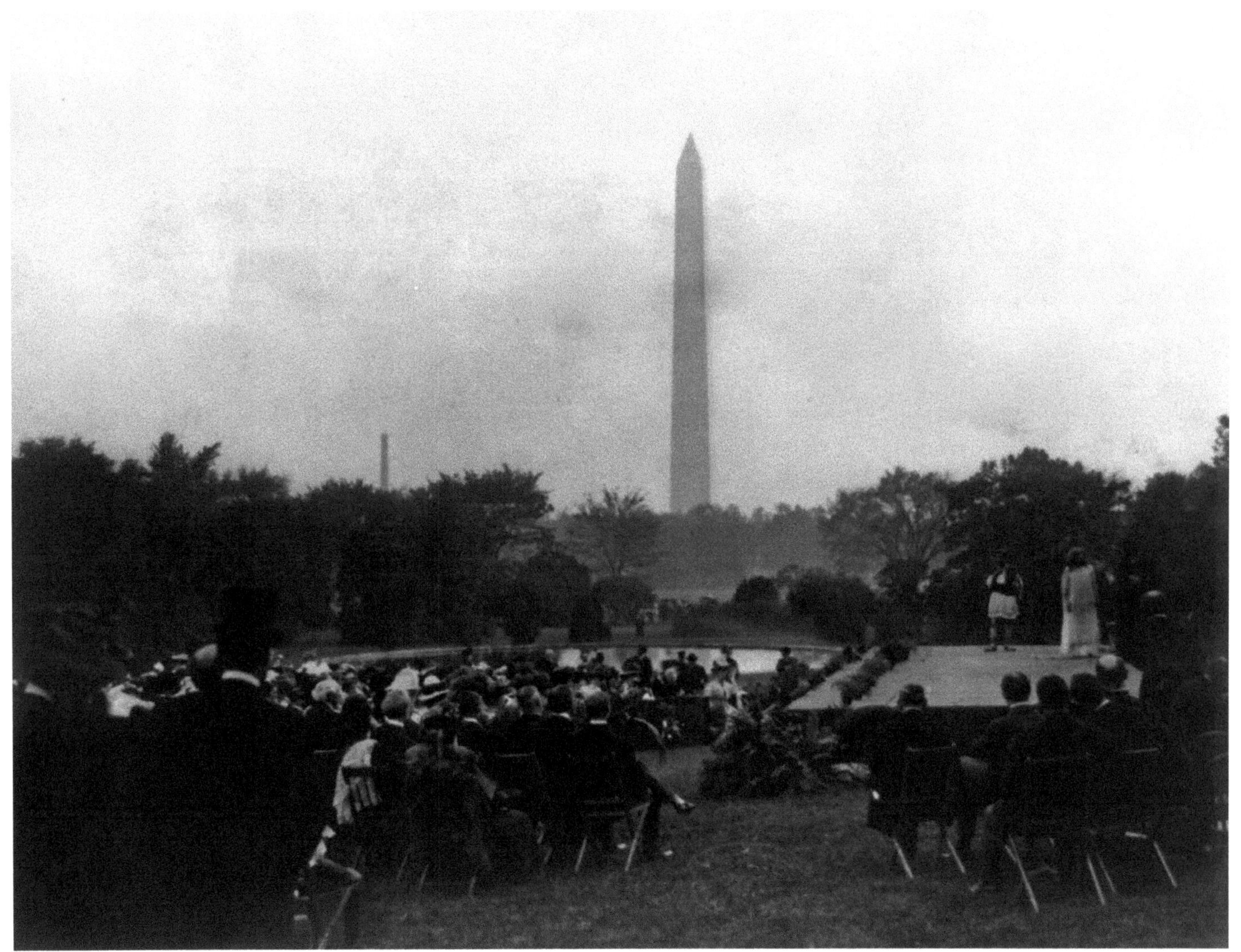

In this 1908 photograph, an audience takes in a performance at the Sylvan Theatre on the monument grounds. The amphitheater, situated on the National Mall adjacent to the monument, still features events today, including military band concerts. President Theodore Roosevelt and other government officials attended this event.

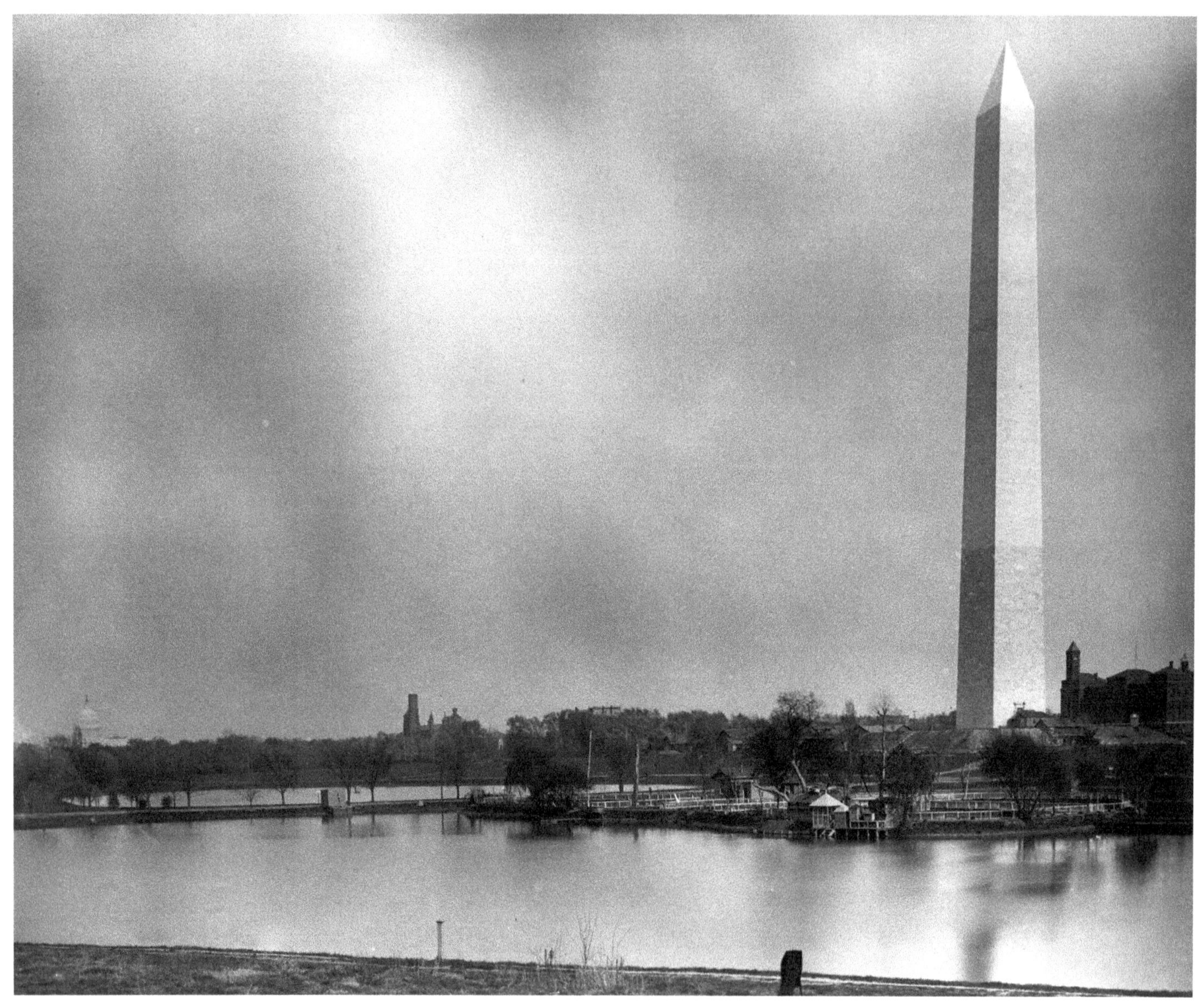

A 1908 scene from Arlington Cemetery with a view of Washington, D.C., across the Potomac. Both the monument and the nation's capitol are visible.

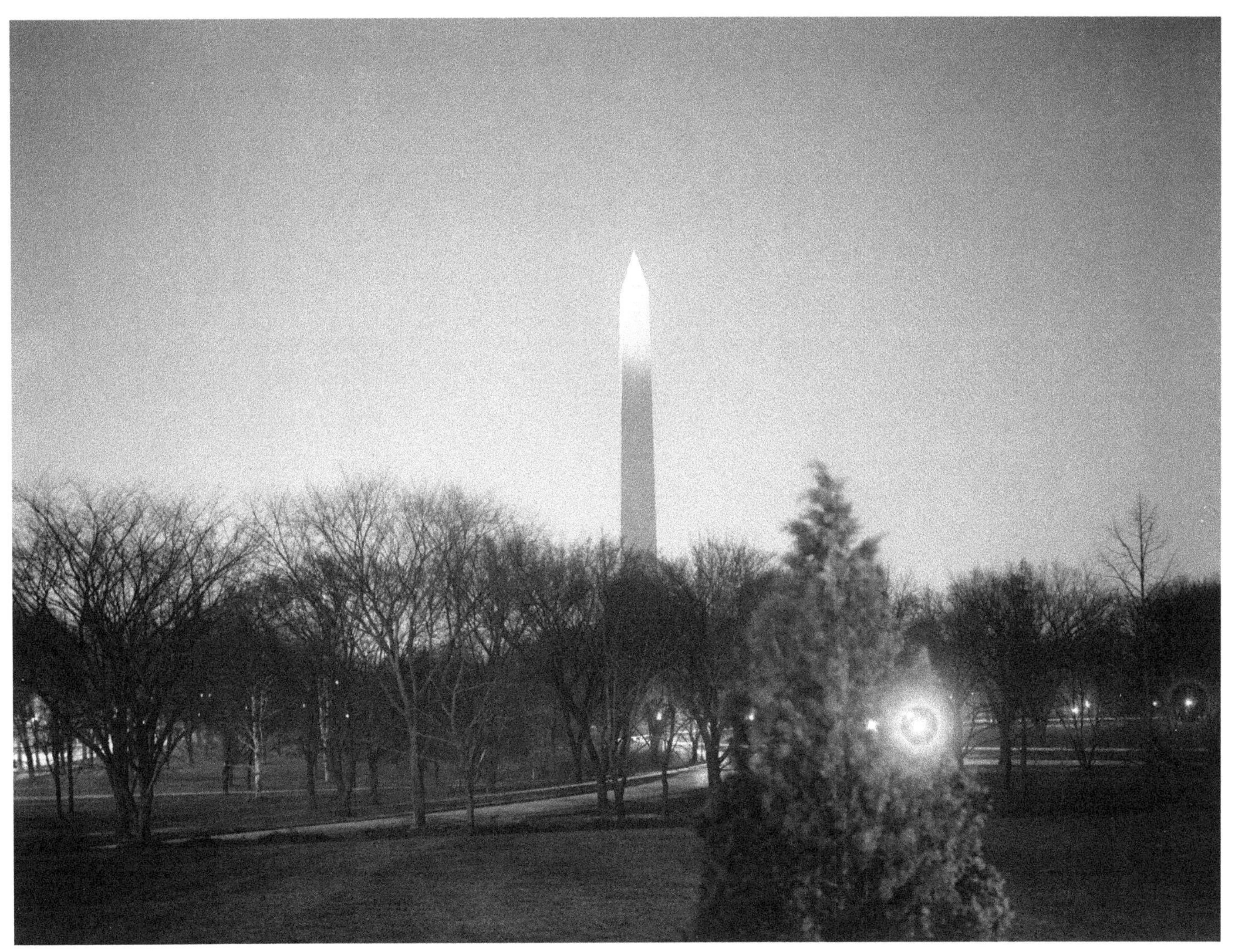

Towering above the trees, the Washington Monument stands in the distance in the early 1900s.

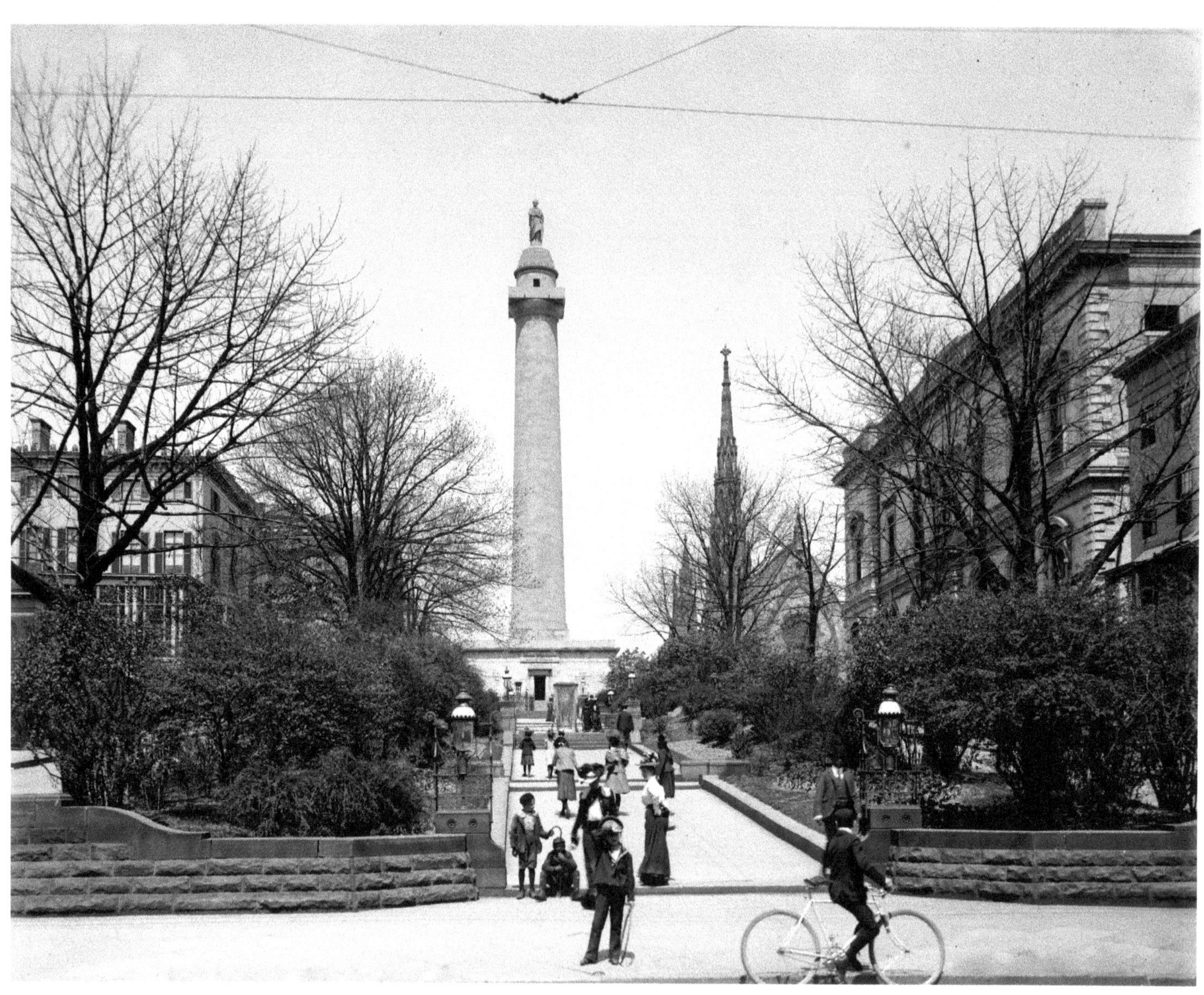

The Washington Monument doesn't hold the distinction as the first monument honoring President George Washington. The Washington Monument at 600 N. Charles Street in Baltimore, also designed by architect and engineer Robert Mills, is much more demure than the monument in D.C.

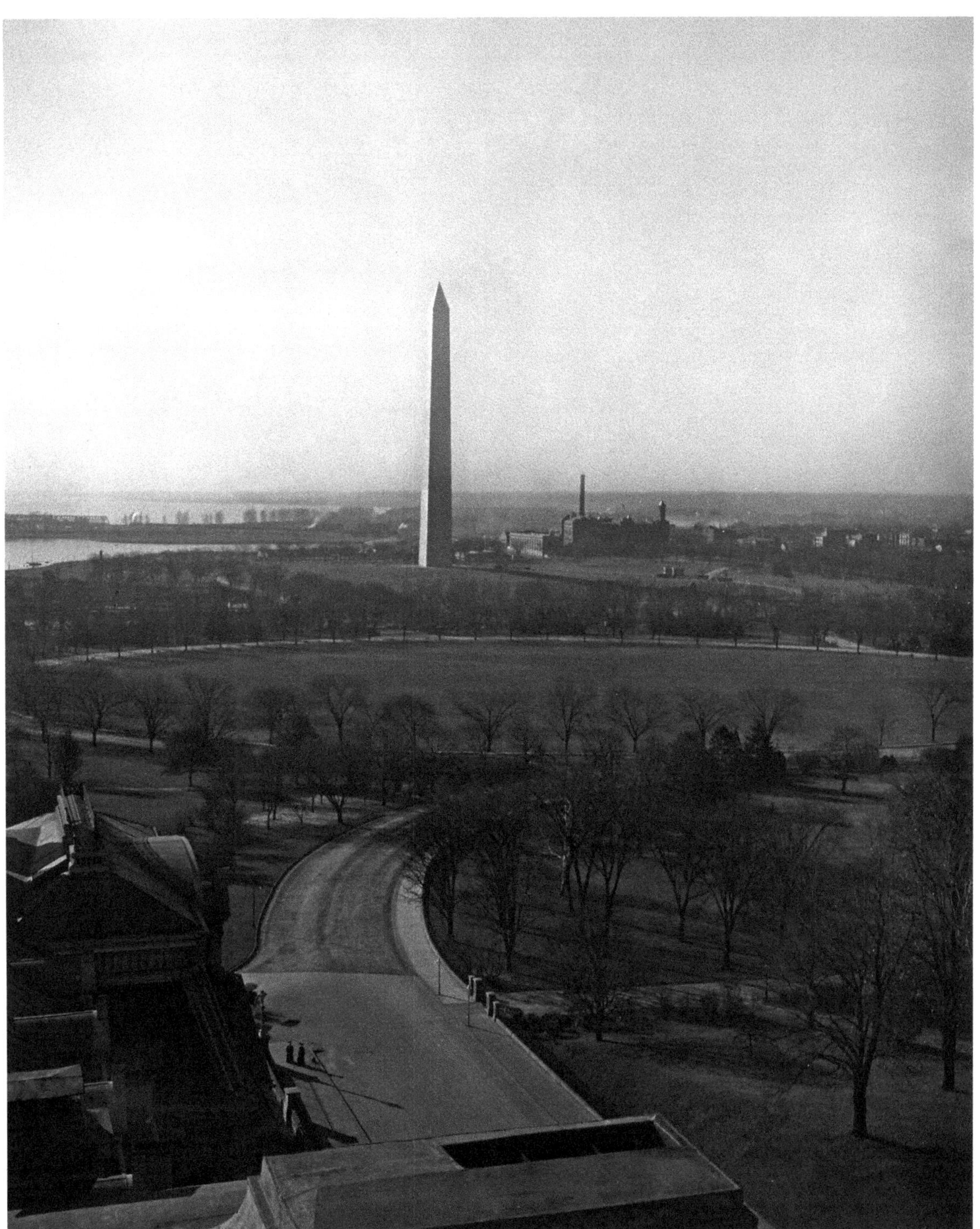

A steam engine chugs by the Washington Monument. At lower left, two women stand on an empty street near a buggy and lamppost.

In this 1919 view of the Washington Monument and its grounds, it appears that the more than 555-foot-tall structure can almost touch the clouds. In fact, on some cloudy days, it can indeed. The monument remains the world's tallest free-standing stone monolith to this day.

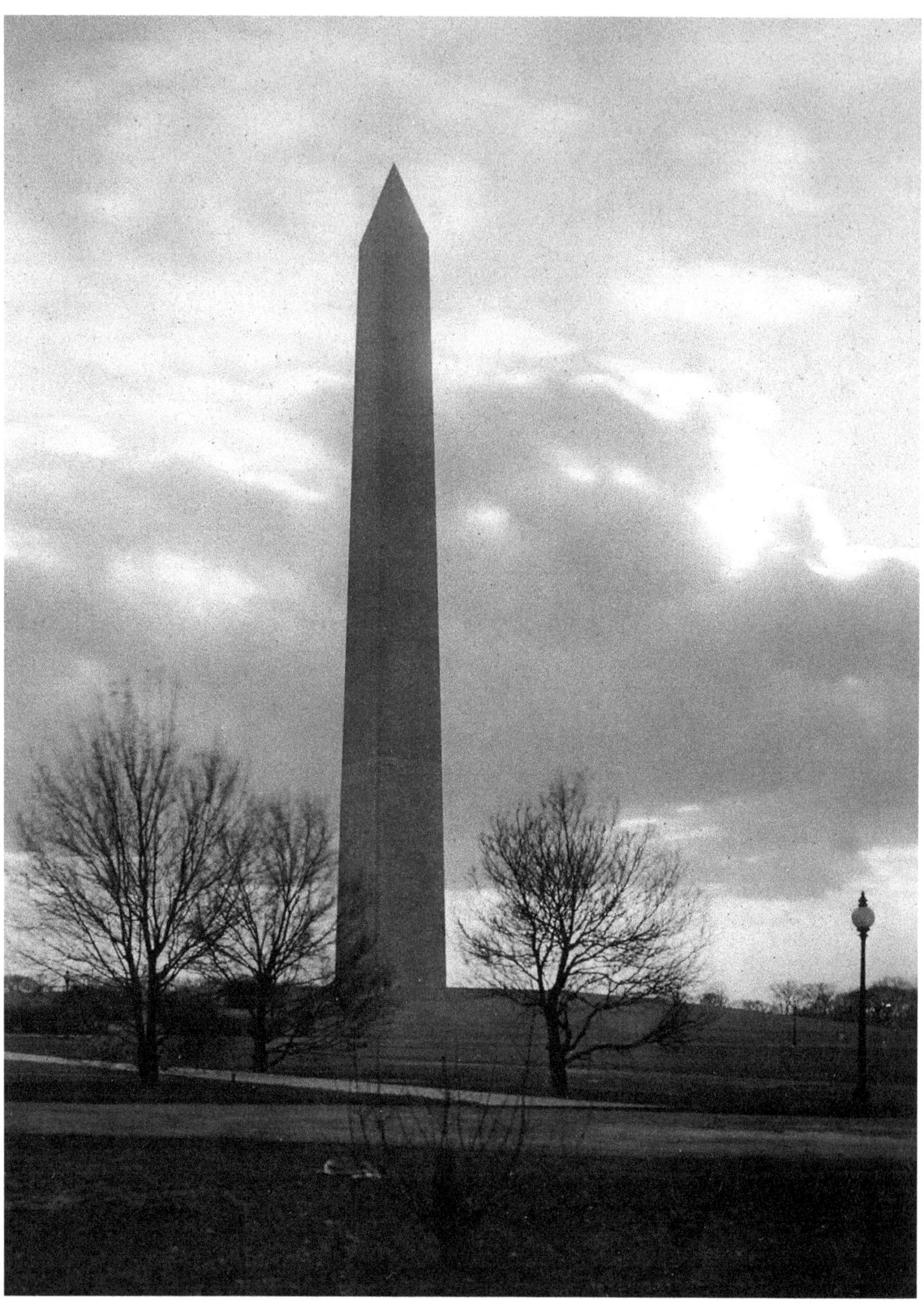

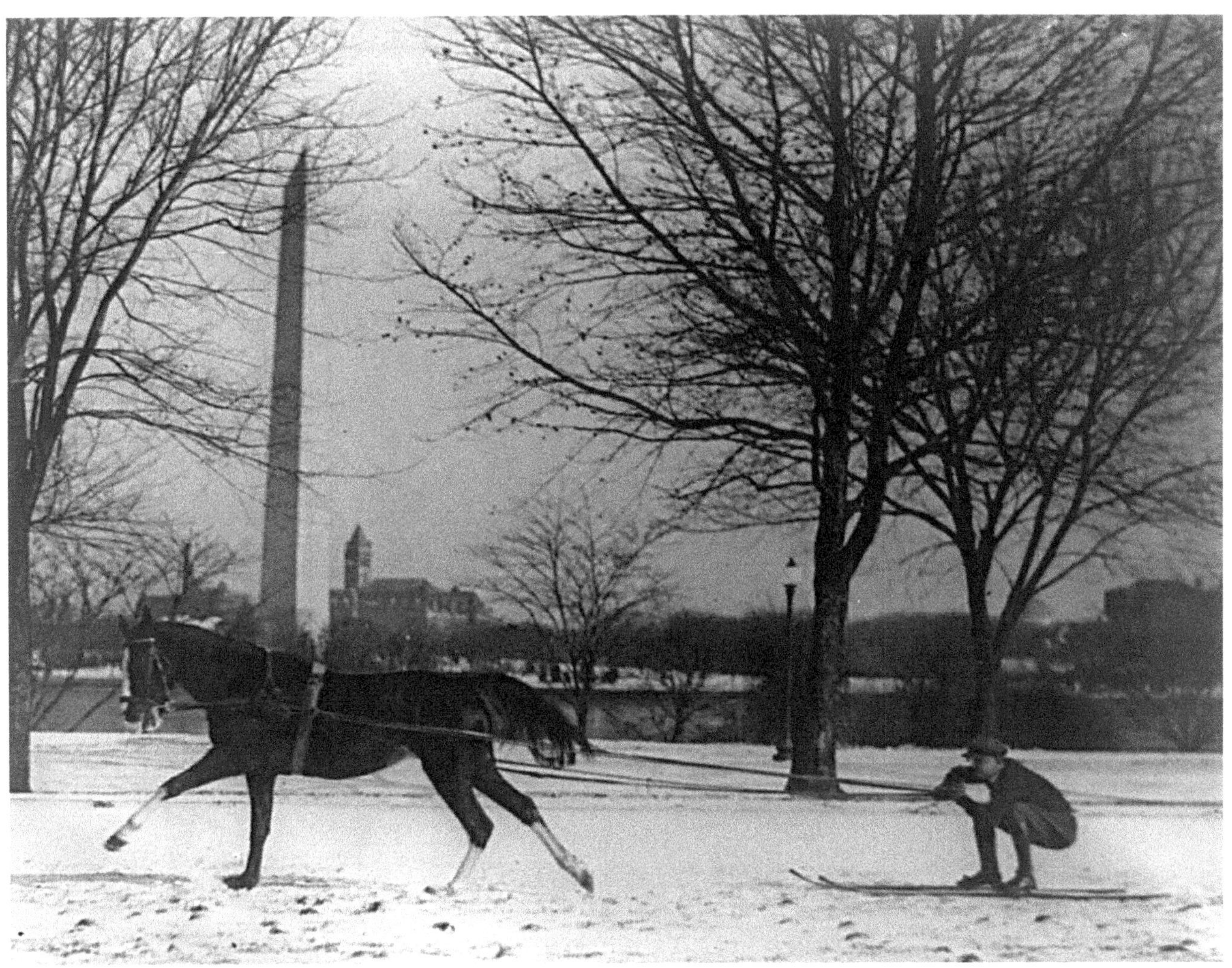

On this snowy day in Washington, D.C., a man on skis is being pulled by a horse. The Washington Monument is the backdrop in this 1919 photograph.

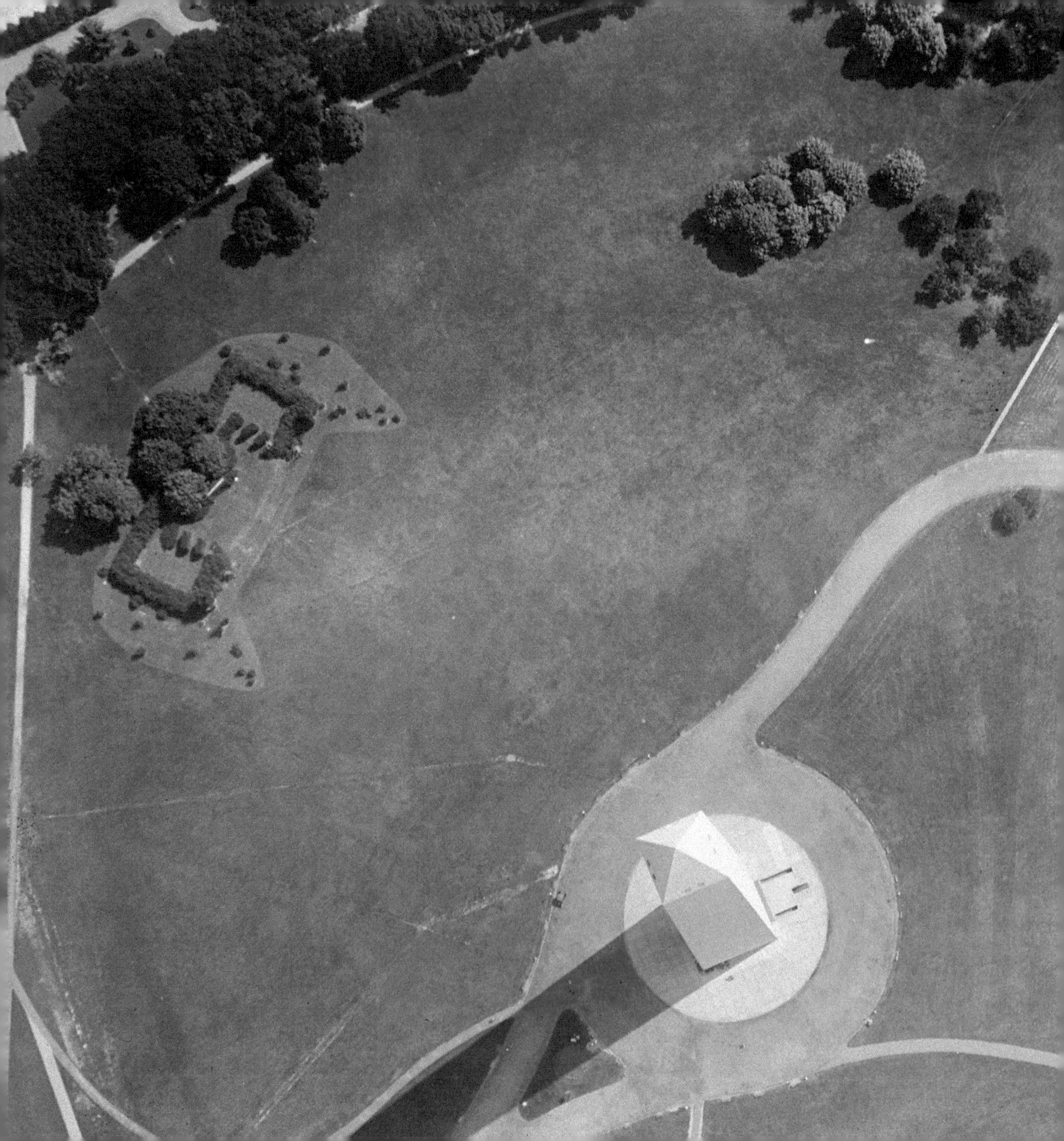

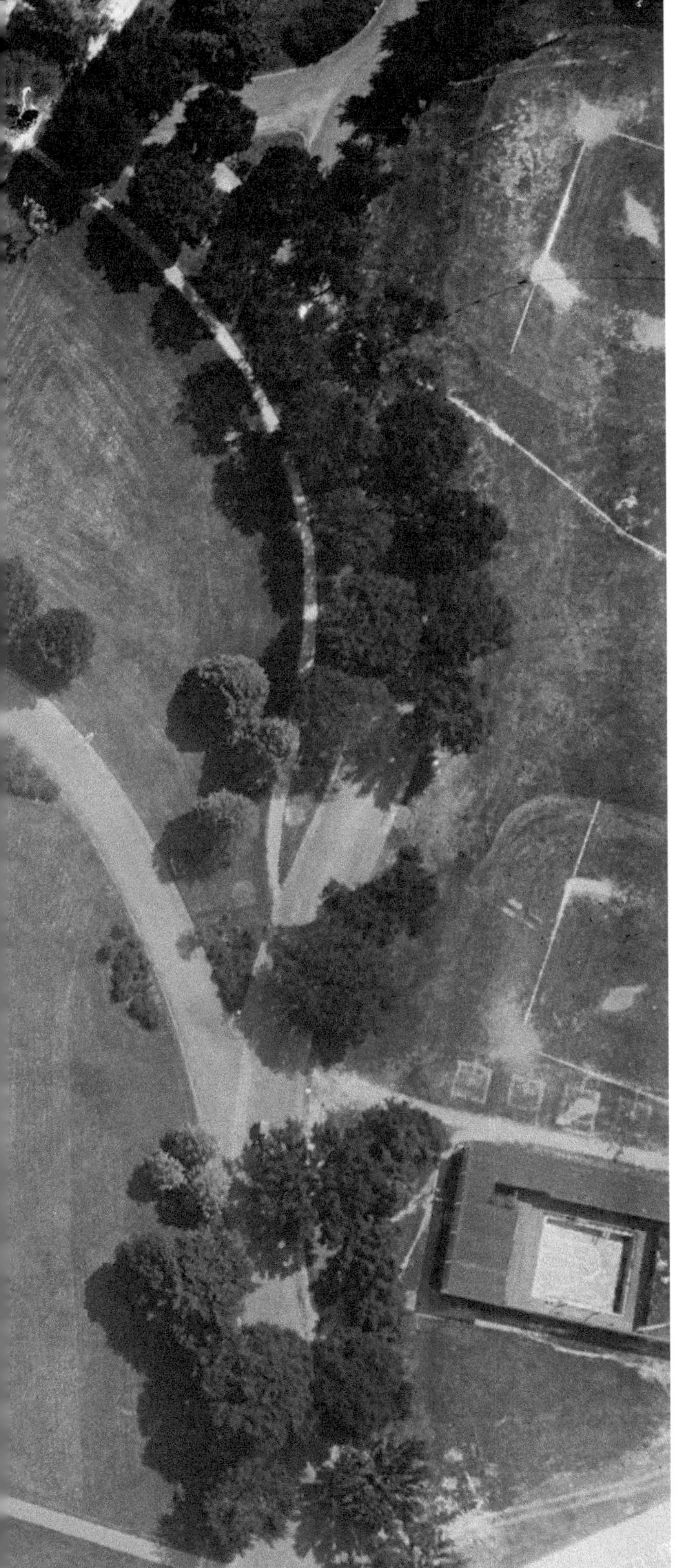

Pictured is a unique aerial view of the Washington Monument in 1919.

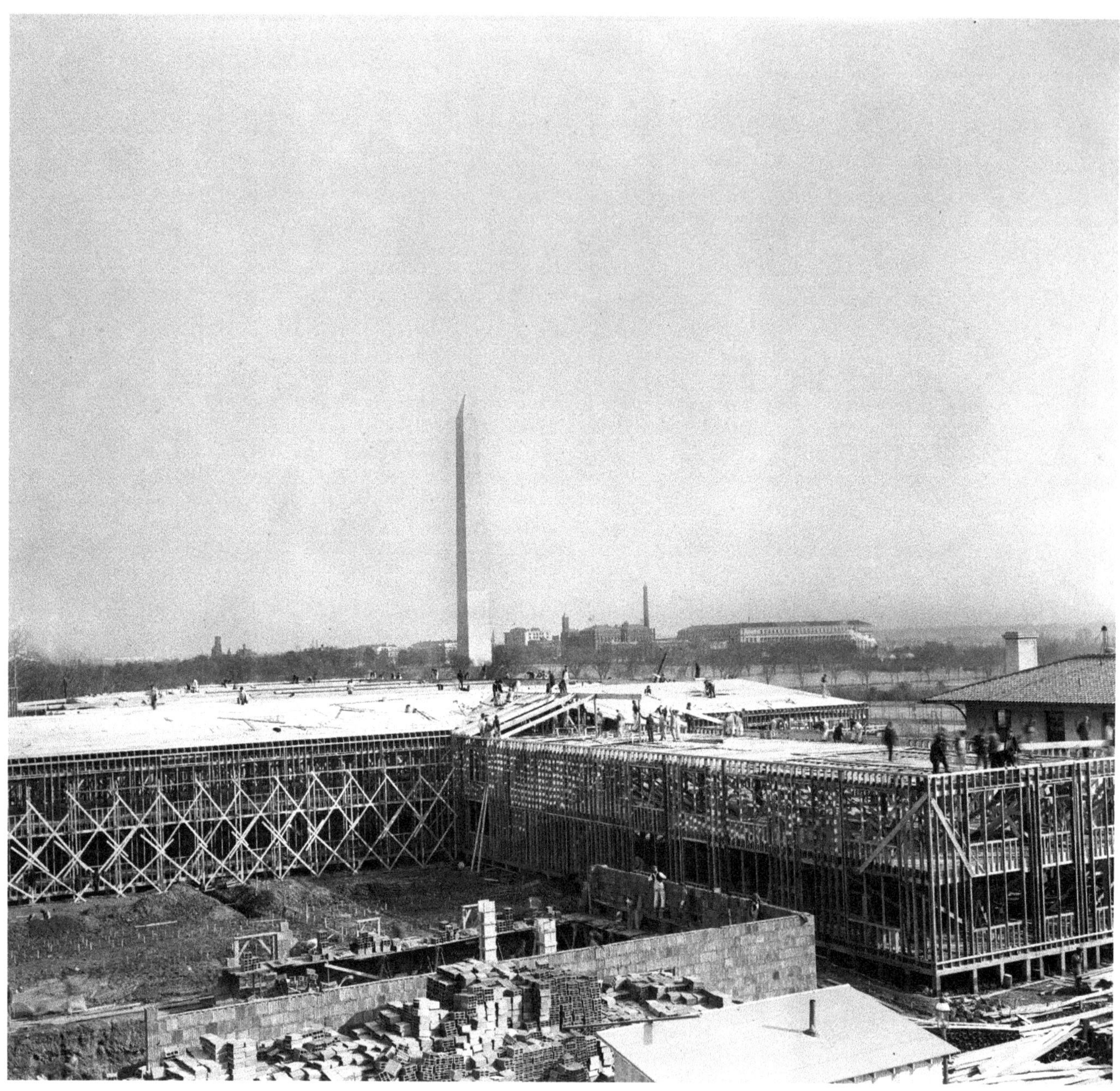

Construction of a government building is under way with the Washington Monument visible in the background. The monument remains the tallest structure in the city and until 1887 was the tallest in the world. That year, the Eiffel Tower surpassed the monument and claimed the record.

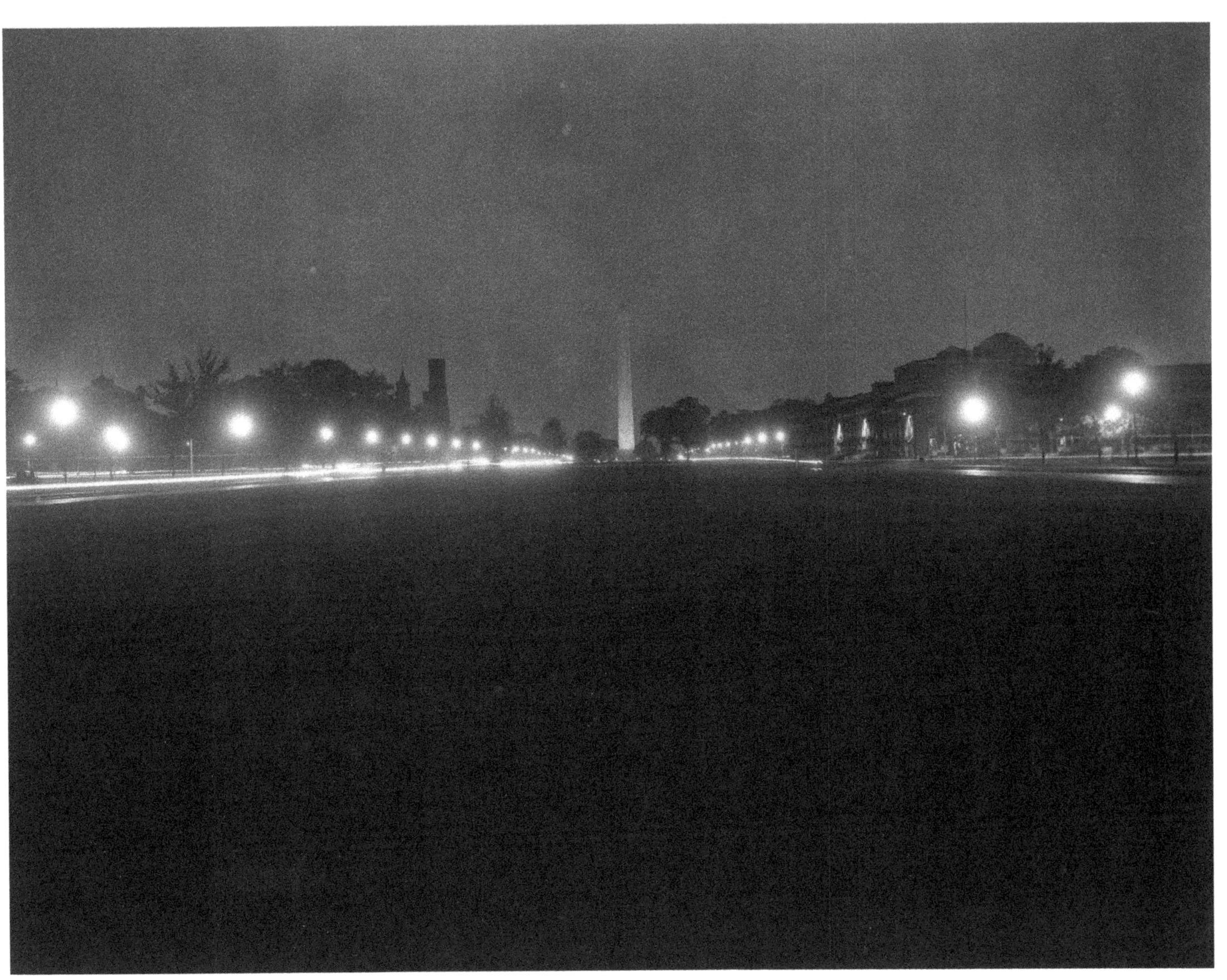

In this nighttime scene, rows of electric lights illuminate the Washington Monument and surrounding buildings.

This undated army signal corps photograph shows a night view of the monument and grounds covered with tents and lights and bustling with activity, all of which suggest a military camp. At different times, both Camp George and Camp Roosevelt used the Washington Monument grounds for operations. This photograph most likely depicts Camp Roosevelt.

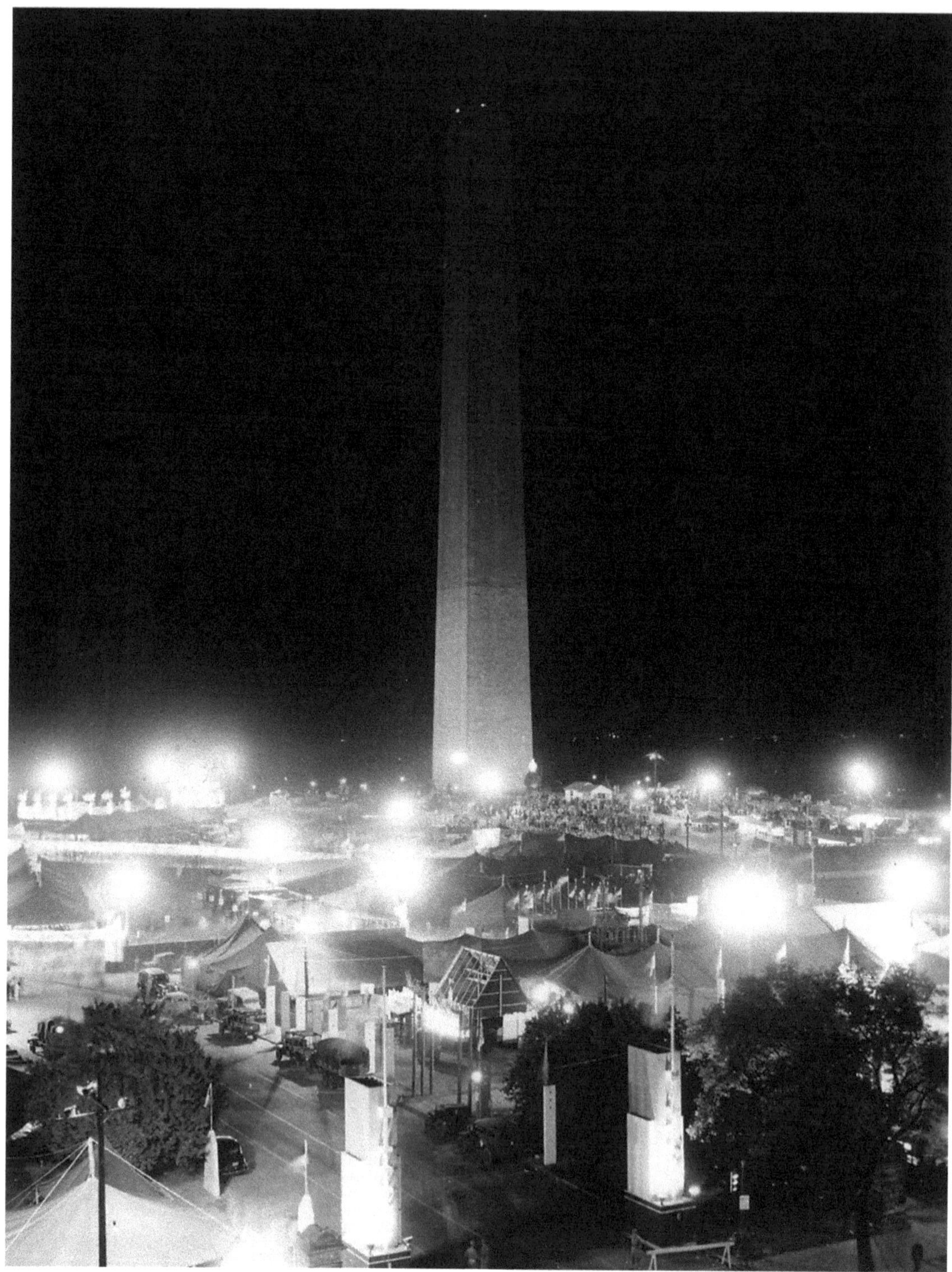

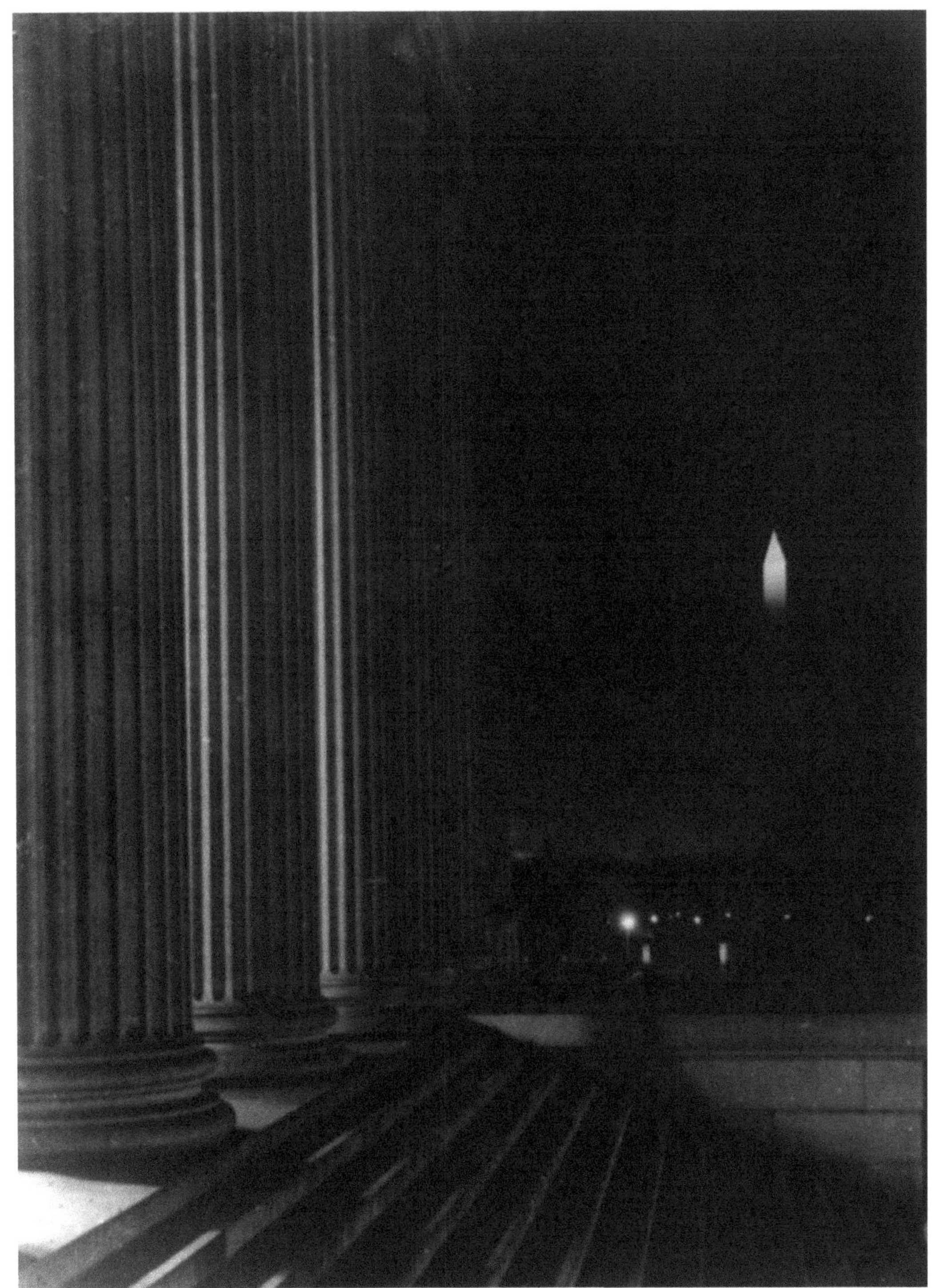

This photo was shot at night on December 28, 1920. The Department of Treasury stairs and columns are prominent in the foreground, while the monument stands in proximity. The Department of Treasury manages government finances and also prints paper money and mints coins.

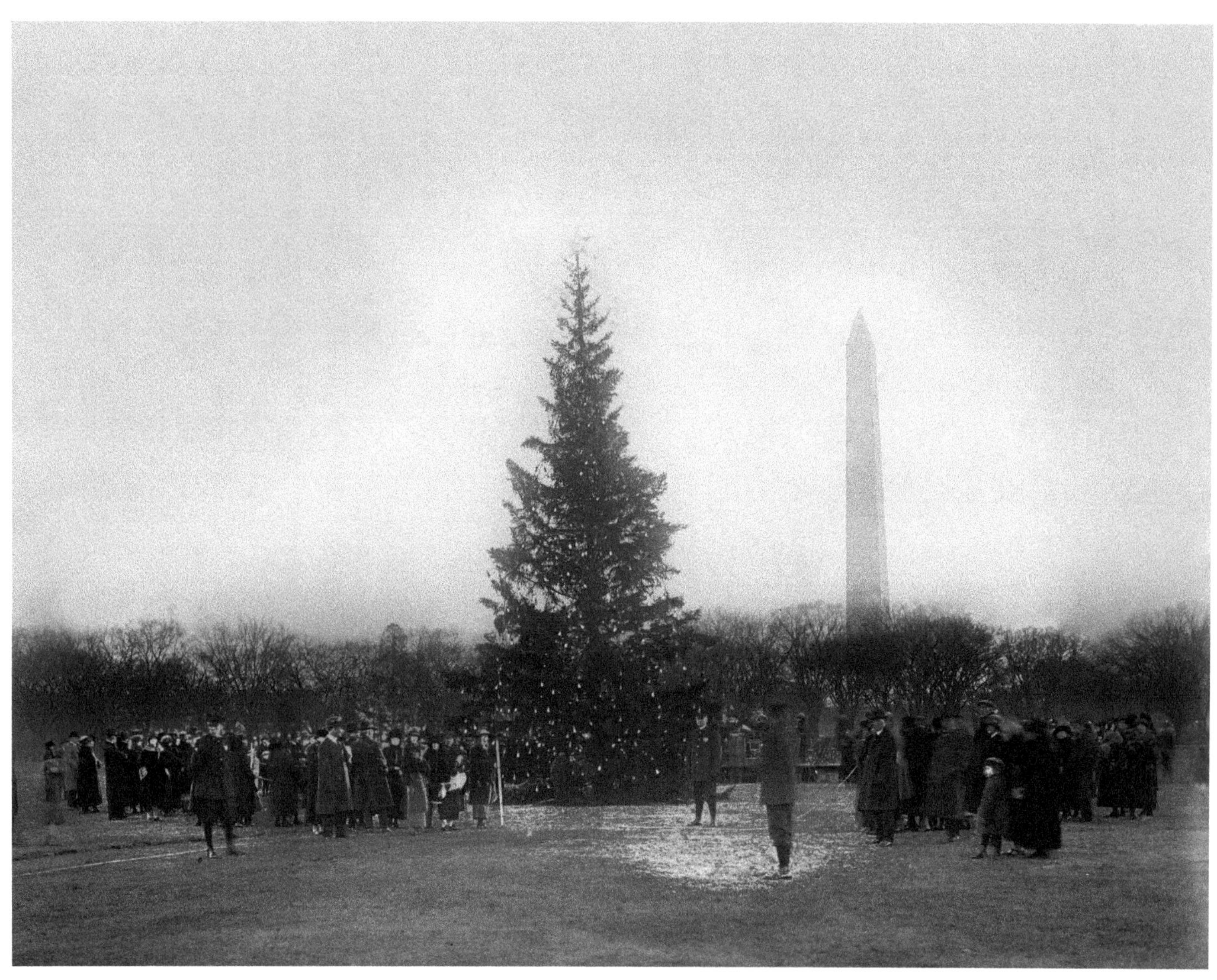

The lighting of the National Christmas Tree on the Ellipse has been a time-honored tradition since November 1923. With the Washington Monument in the background presiding over the event, onlookers gather for the illumination ceremony.

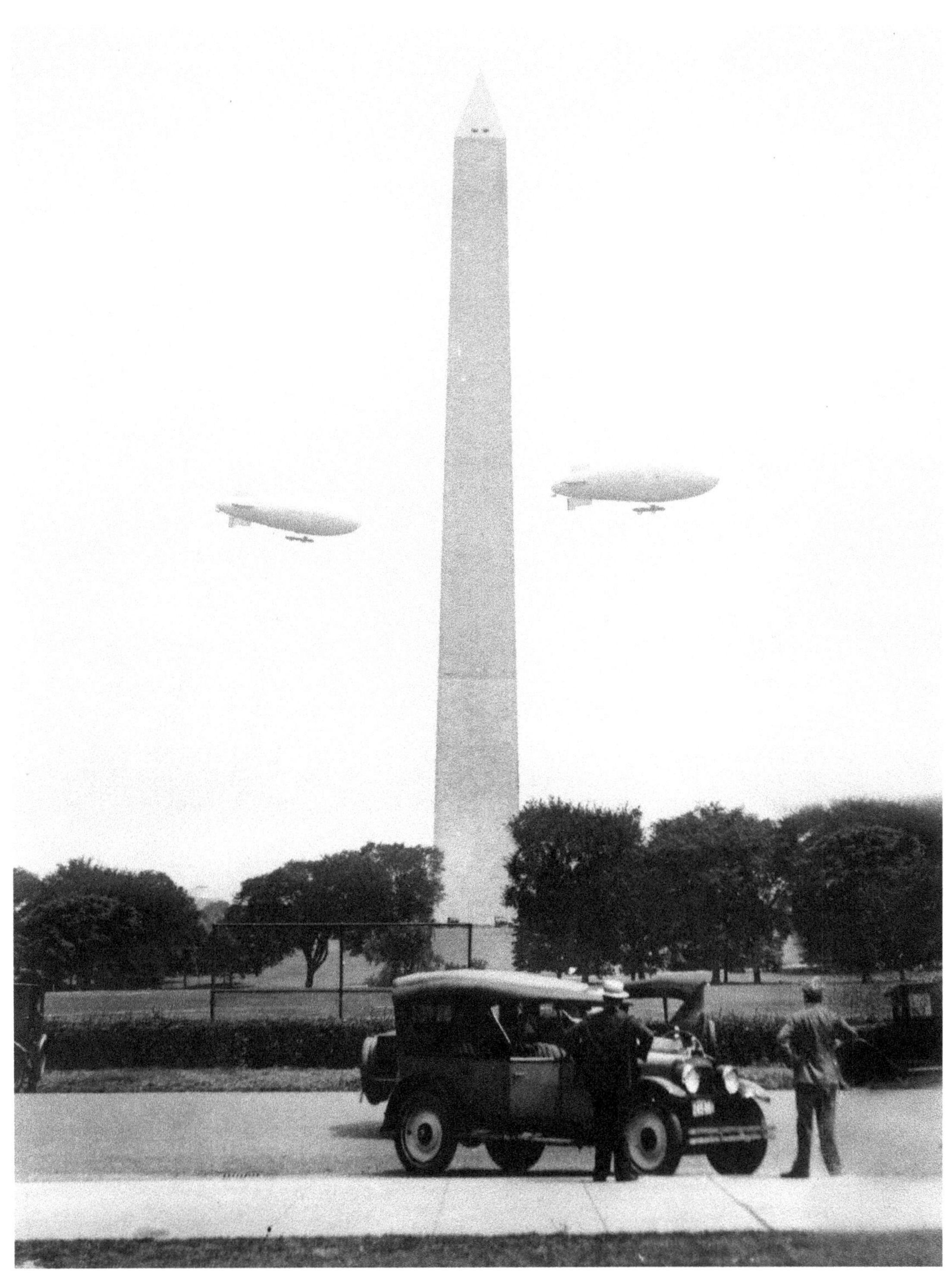

Onlookers focus their attention on blimps flying over the Washington Monument. The army blimps T.C. 5 and T.C. 9, which originated at Fort Langley in Virginia, were participating in practice maneuvers. The navy also used blimps for observation. Following World War I, the army discontinued its use of these airships.

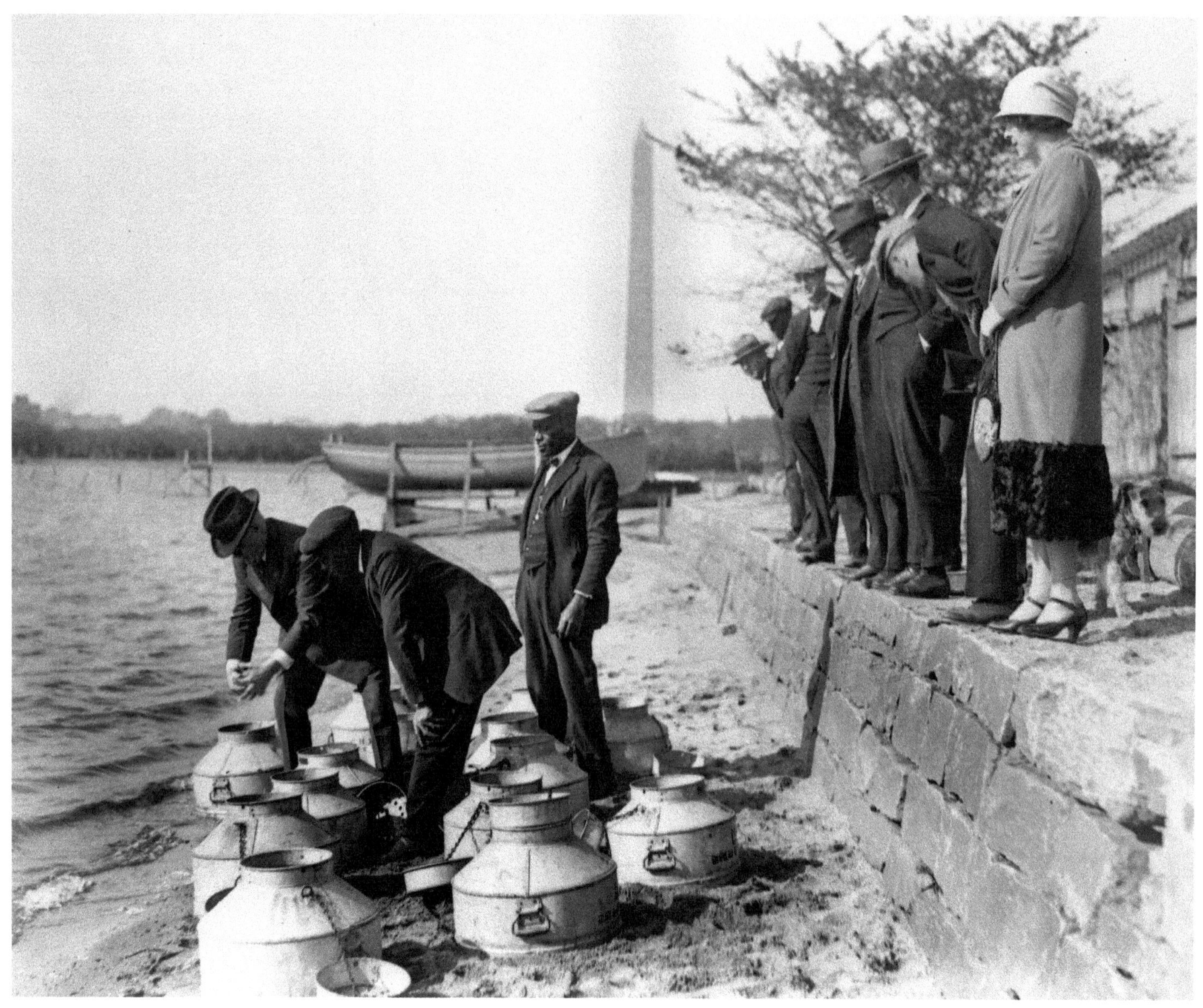

Workers stock fish in the Potomac River at the Tidal Basin as United States Fisheries Commissioner Henry O'Malley looks on. The Washington Monument serves as a backdrop for this photo (ca. 1920s).

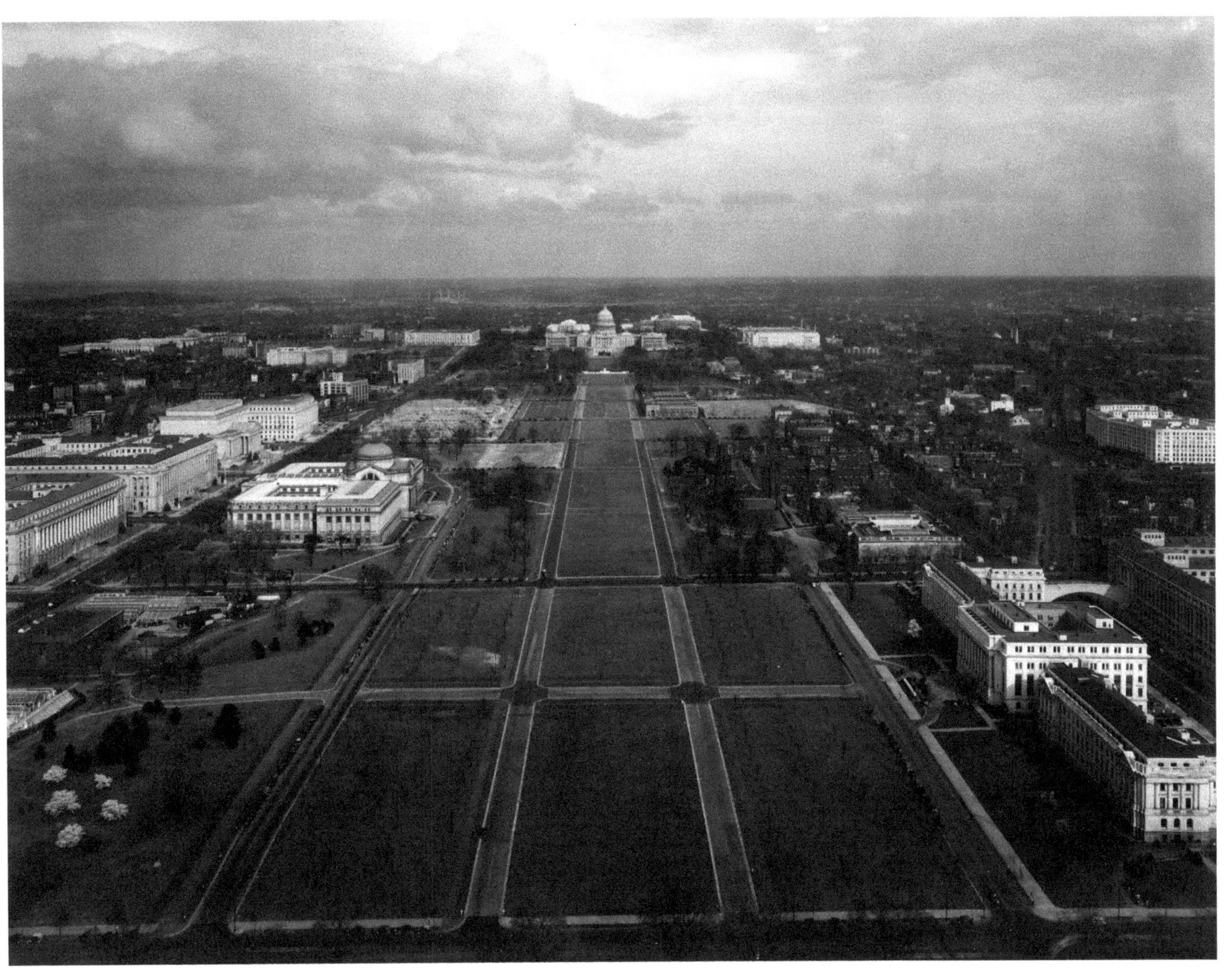

A view of the National Mall and the U.S. Capitol in winter from the Washington Monument's observation deck. The Smithsonian Institution is also visible in this view.

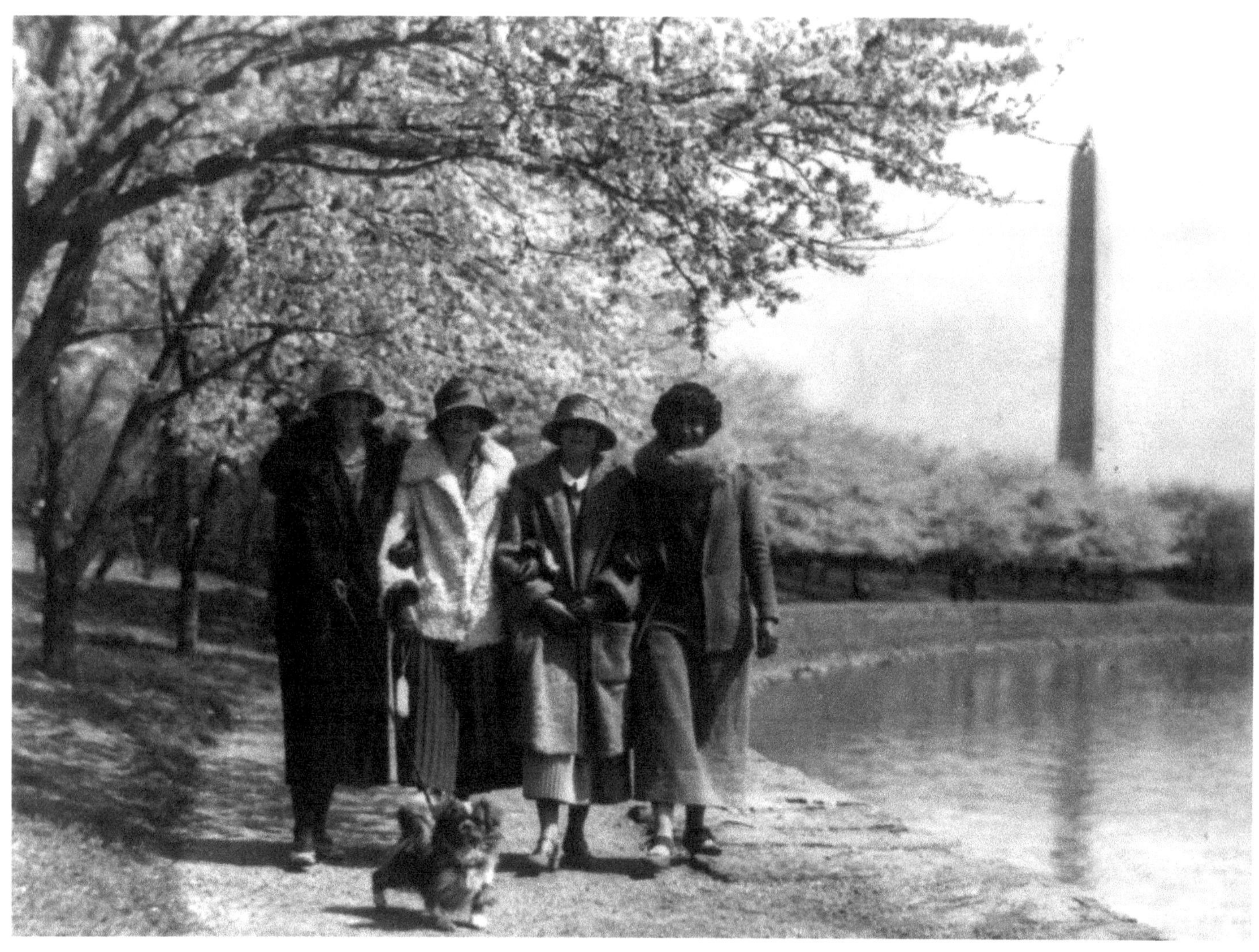

Aside from the period dress, this scene is not much different from what one might see today during cherry blossom season. Here, debutantes take a leisurely stroll along the pink-and-white cherry blossom–lined Tidal Basin. The Washington Monument can be seen in the distance high above the cloud-like cherry blossom trees. This photo of socialites Emma Stitt, Virginia Edwards, Cecil Jones, and Alice Milburn is believed to have been taken in the 1920s.

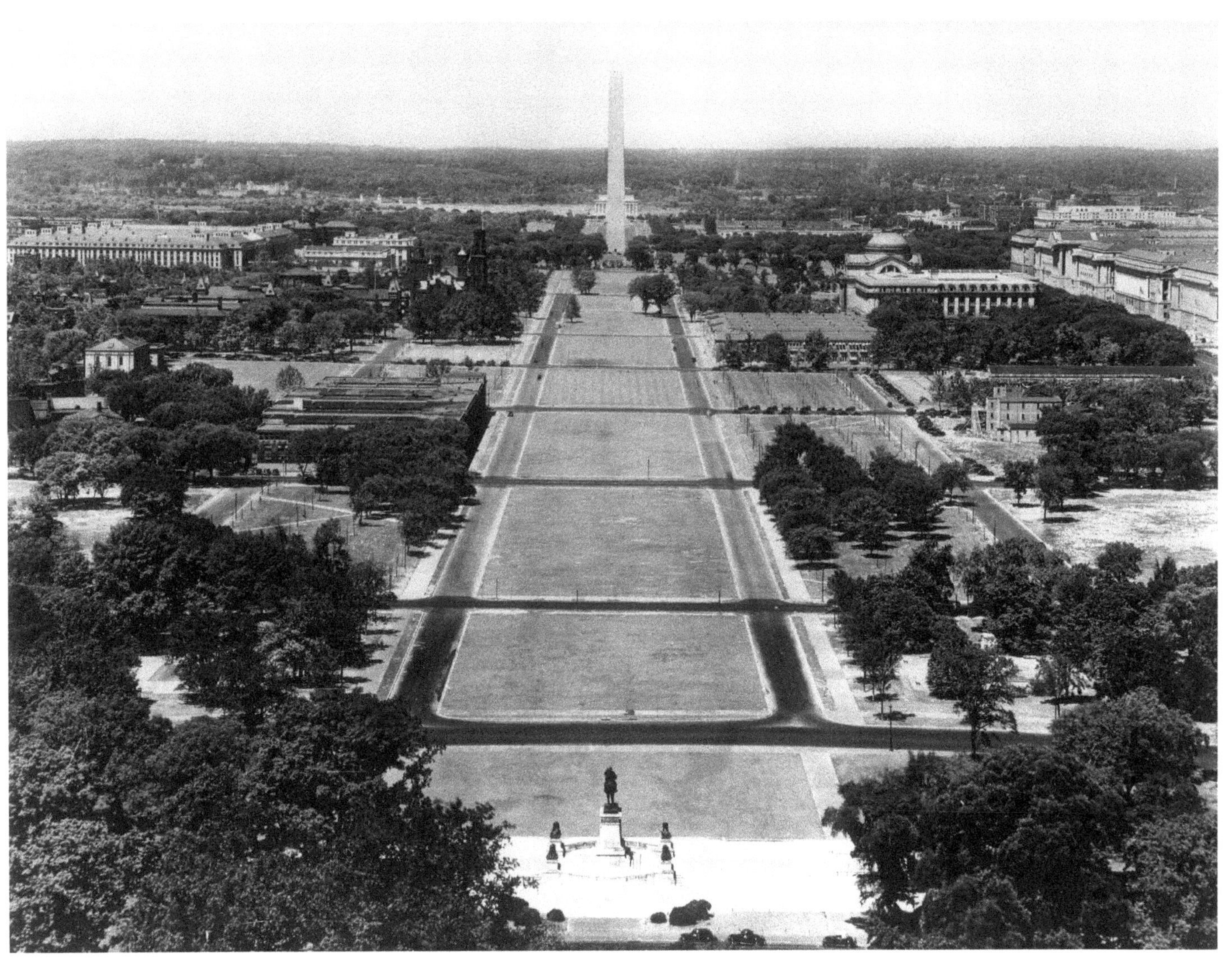

Here is a view of the Washington Monument taken from the Capitol. Lush foliage surrounds the Ulysses S. Grant Memorial at lower center.

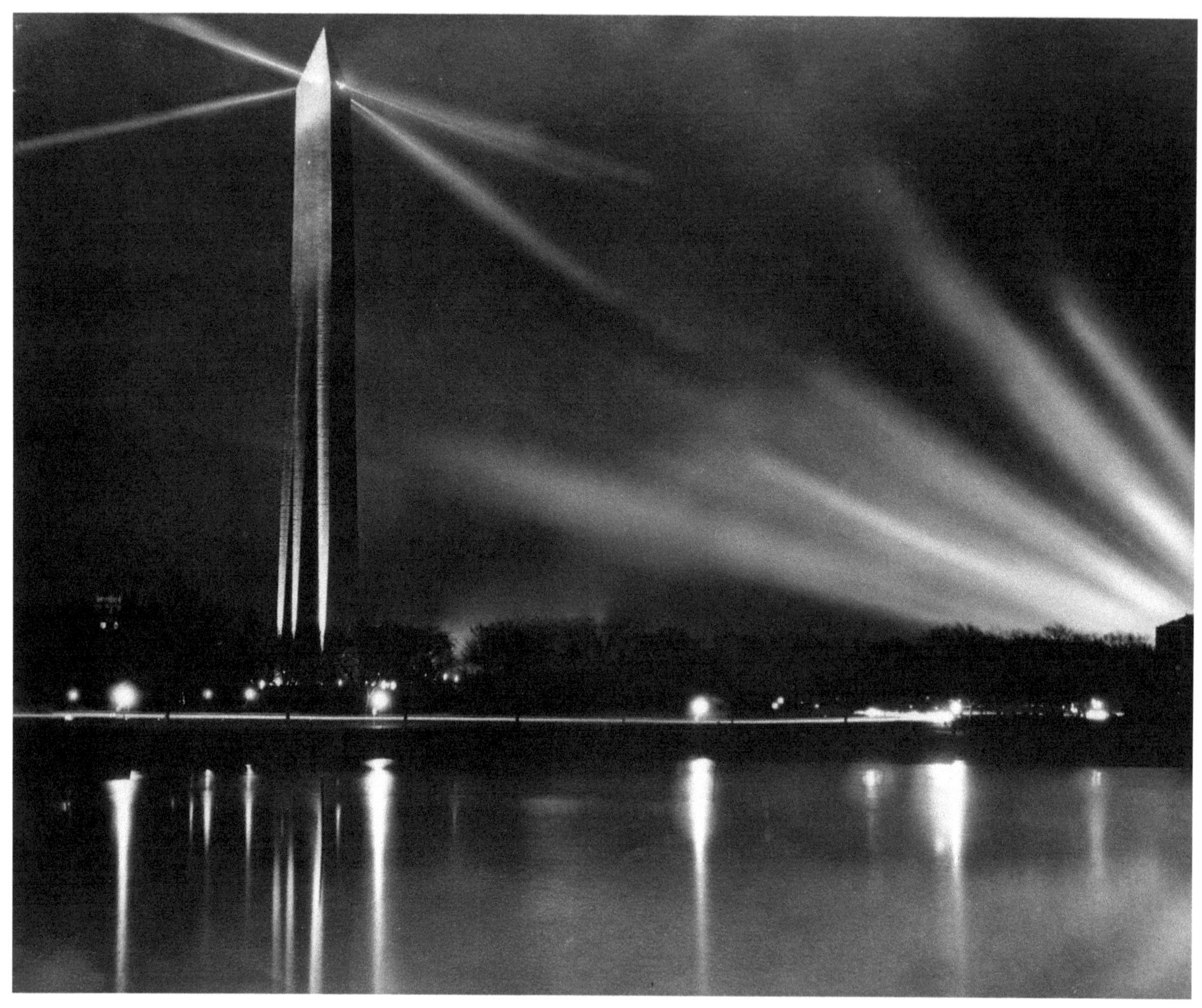

Taken in 1931, this U.S. Army Photographic Agency photo depicts a simply spectacular night view of the Washington Monument.

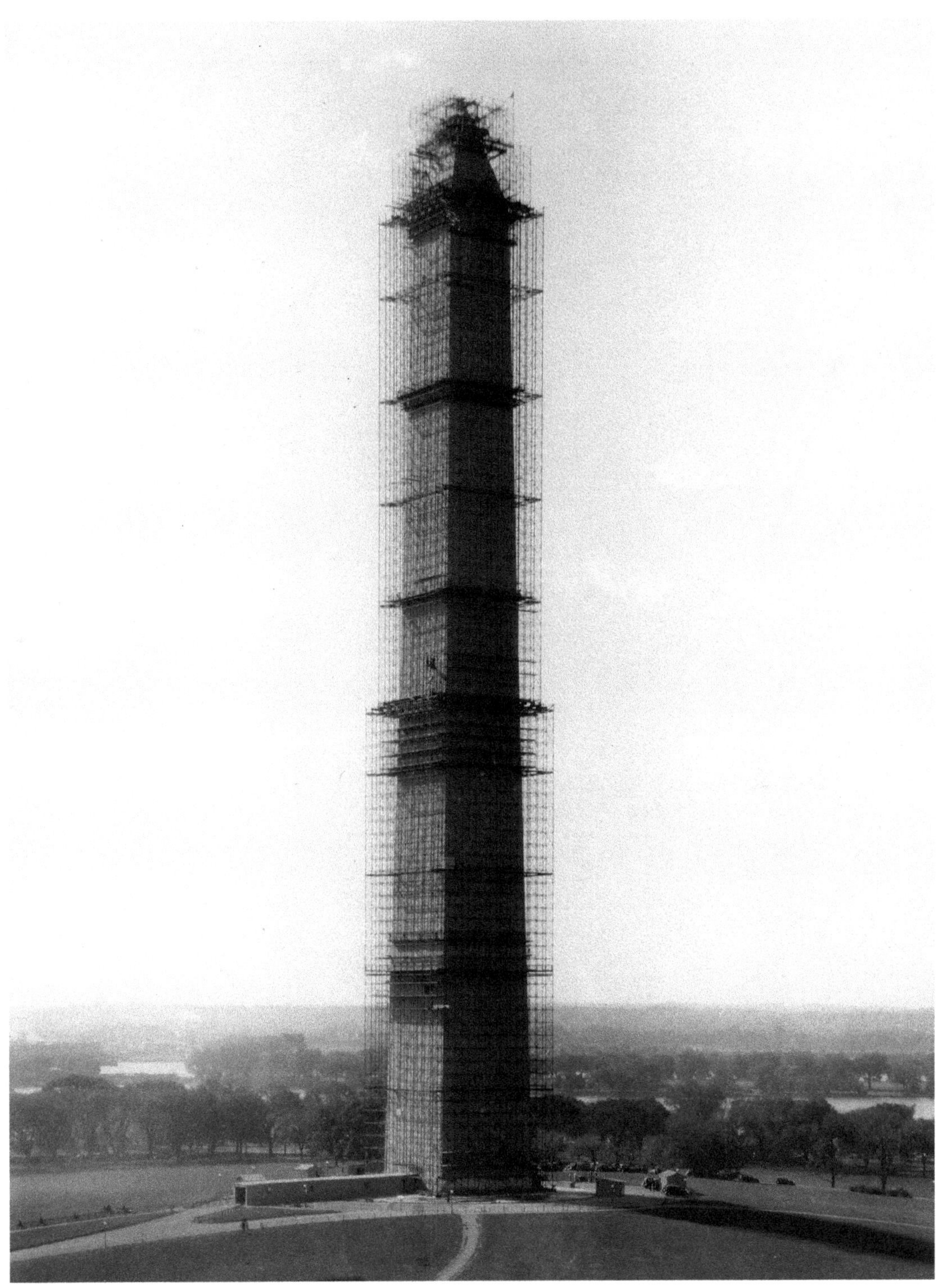

Time and the elements adversely affect the facade of the Washington Monument. Here in 1934, the 50-year-old monument is covered with scaffolding so that nearly 50,000 linear feet of mortar could be replaced by engineers.

Though no longer visible to the public, the Latin phrase "Laus Deo" is inscribed on the interior of the four-sided cap of the Washington Monument. Translated, it means "Praise to God."

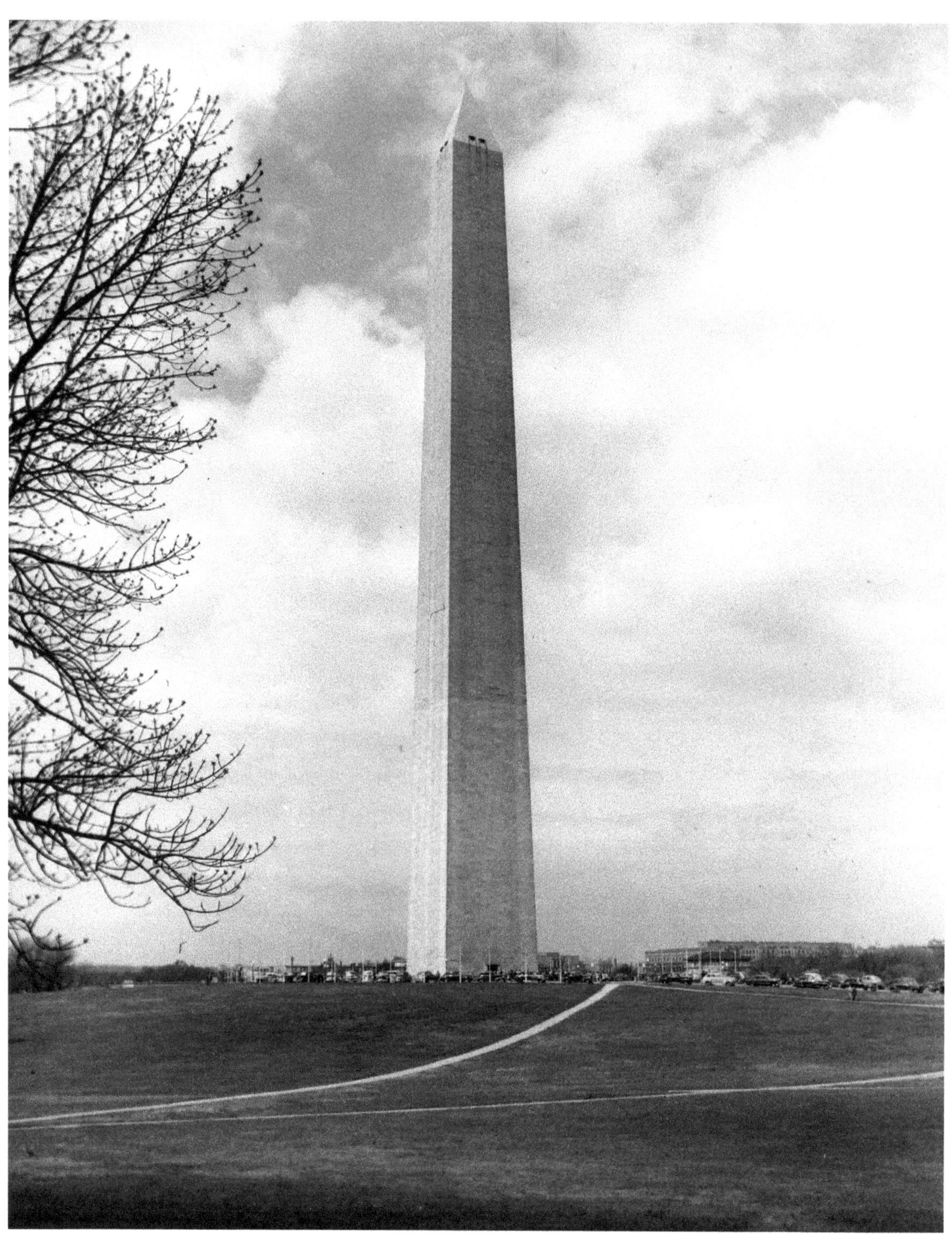

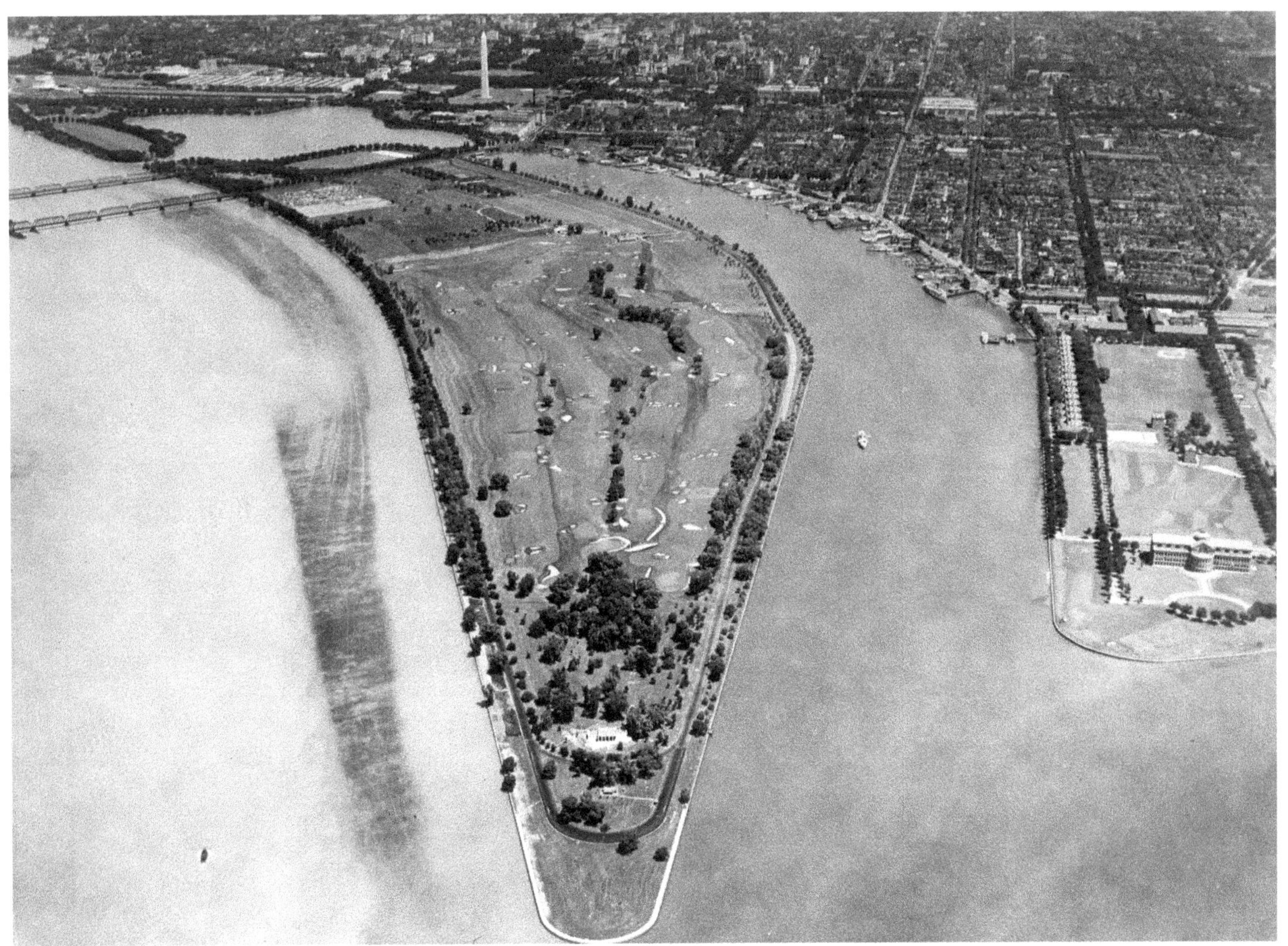

Golf enthusiasts, novices, and idle onlookers alike enjoy East Potomac Golf Club and Park, which provided a relaxing, bucolic respite in the heart of a bustling city driven by politics and government. This 1935 photo looking north toward the Mall boasts an aerial view of Hains Point and the government-run driving range.

One of the nicest things about going to the top of the monument is peering out the windows and trying to locate various parts of the city. The view spans all the way to Maryland and Virginia. Taken on a snowy day, this 1939 photo looking west shows the Washington Monument and cars parked along the Mall.

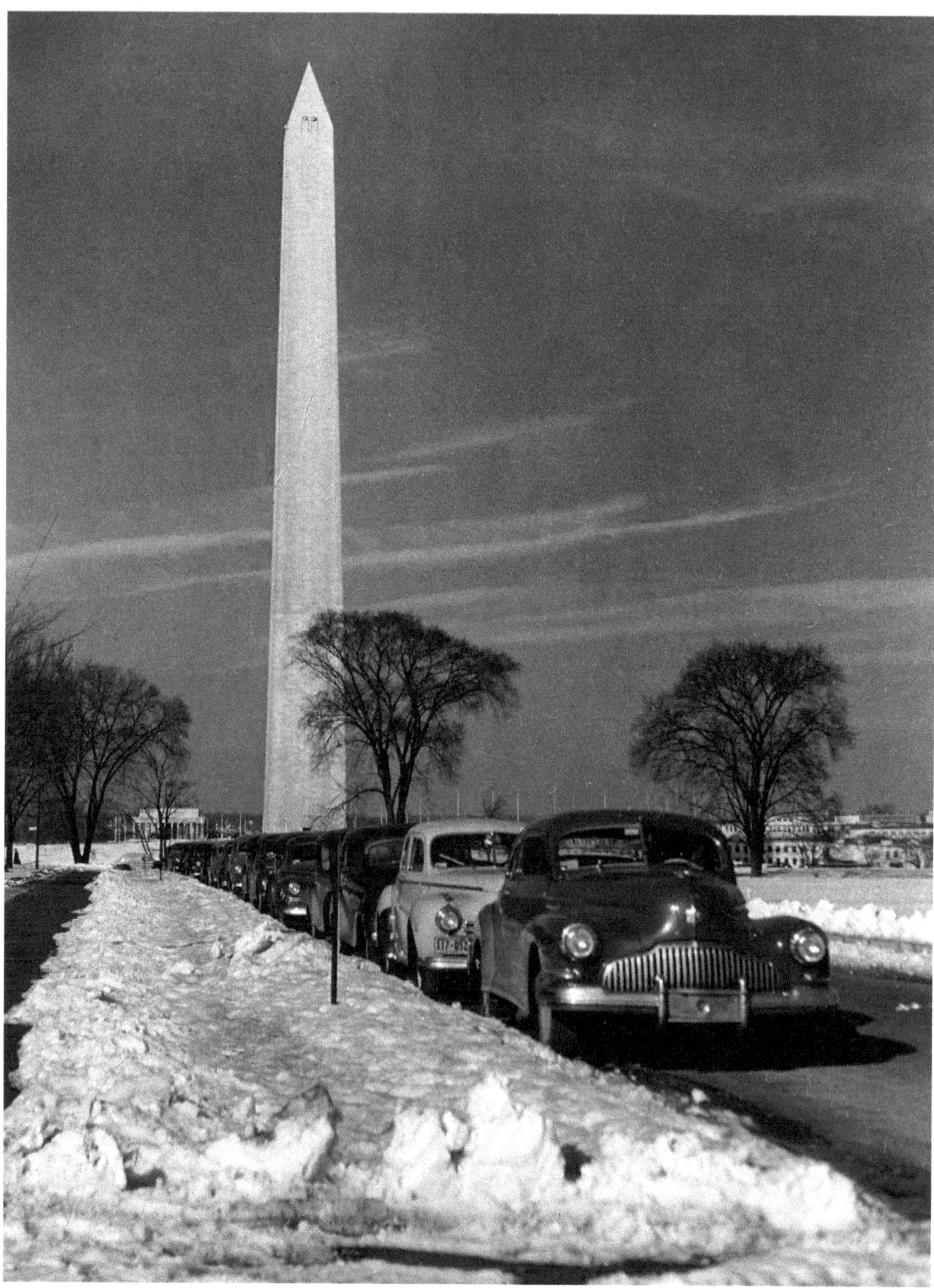

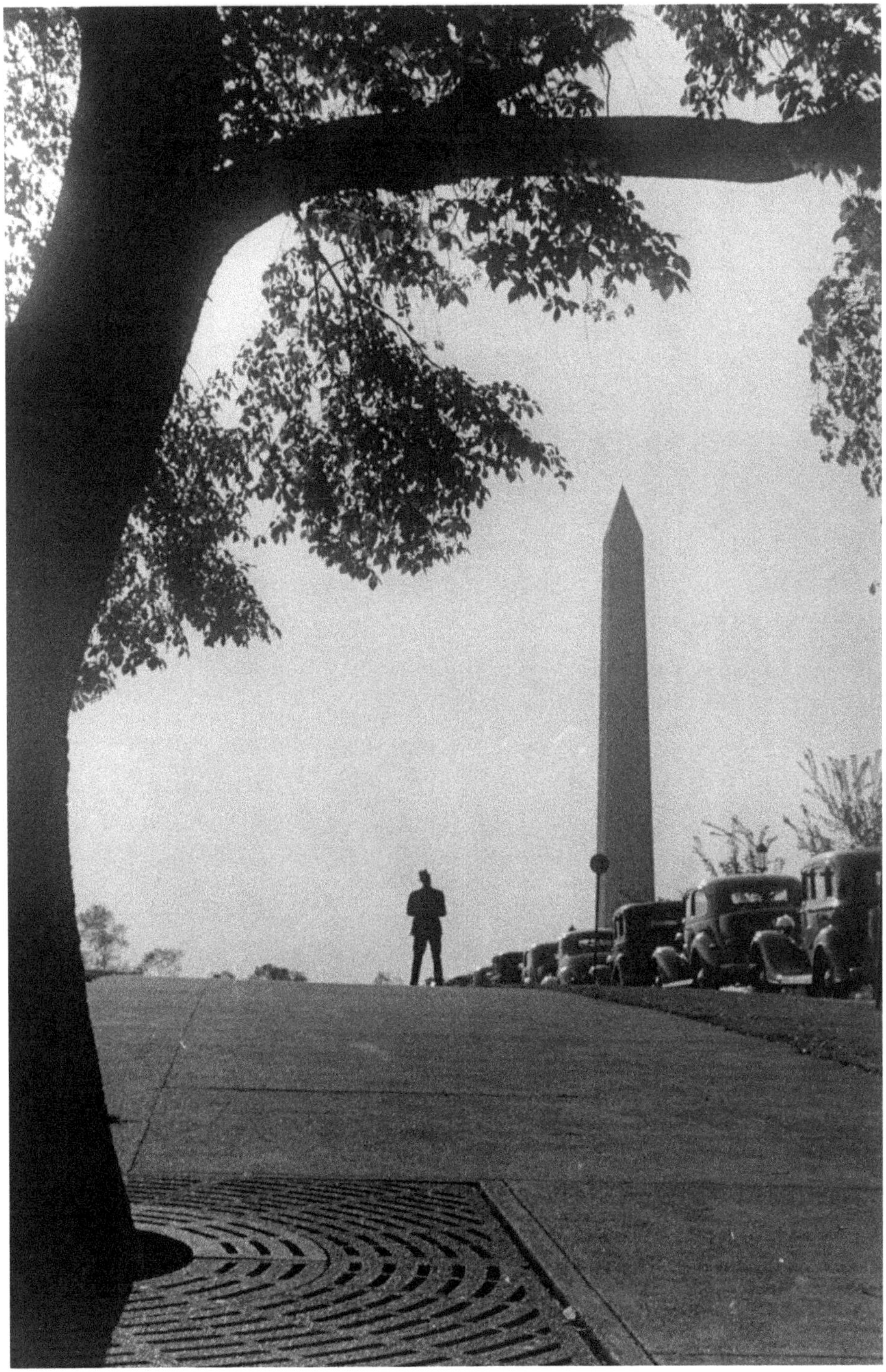

On a sunny day, a man's silhouette is visible near the Washington Monument. His pose suggests he is gazing upward toward the monument in reflective contemplation.

Visitors attend an event on the grounds of the Washington Monument, with the American flag in clear view. The monument was dedicated on February 21, 1885. There are now 50 flags circling the monument. Each flag represents a state in the United States.

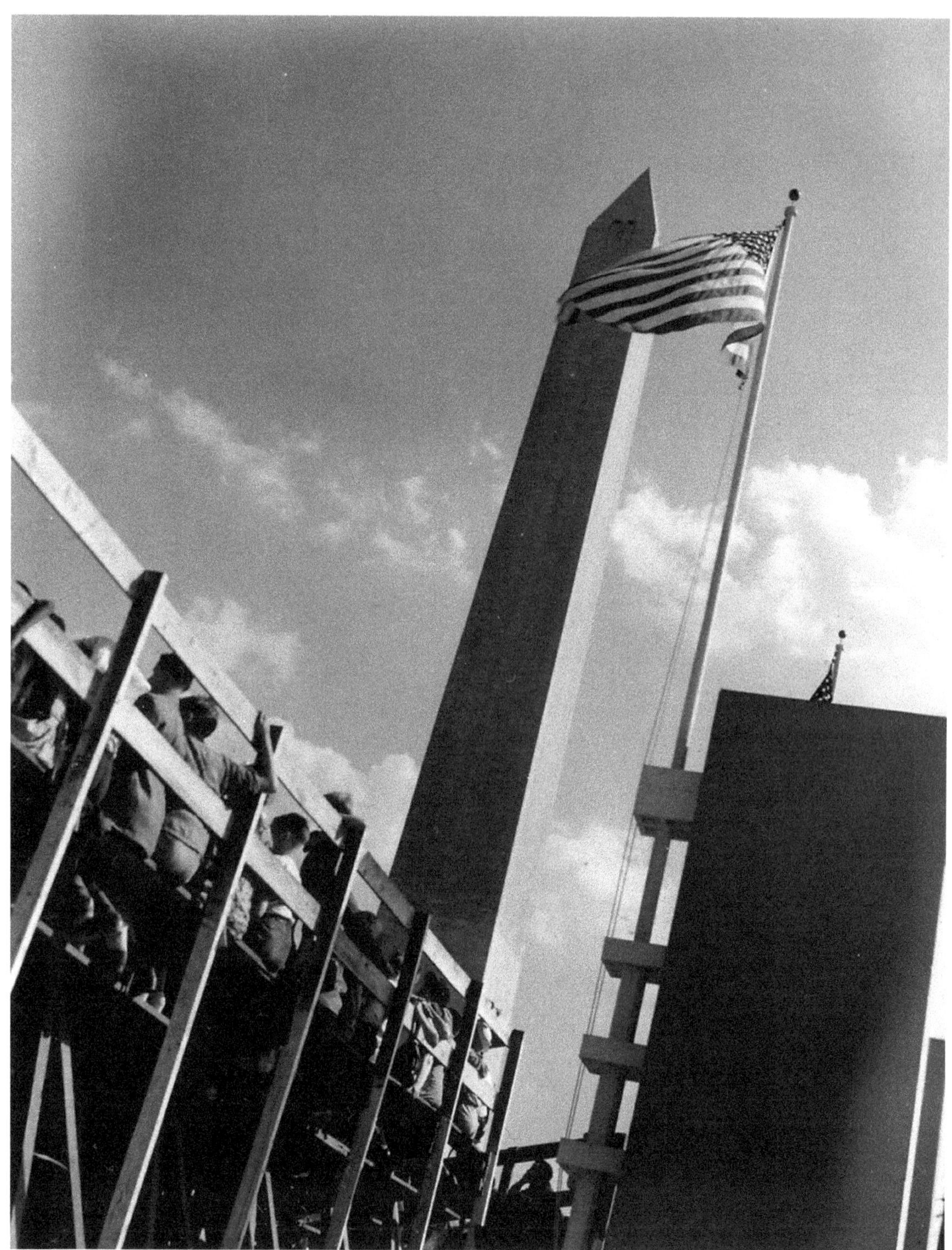

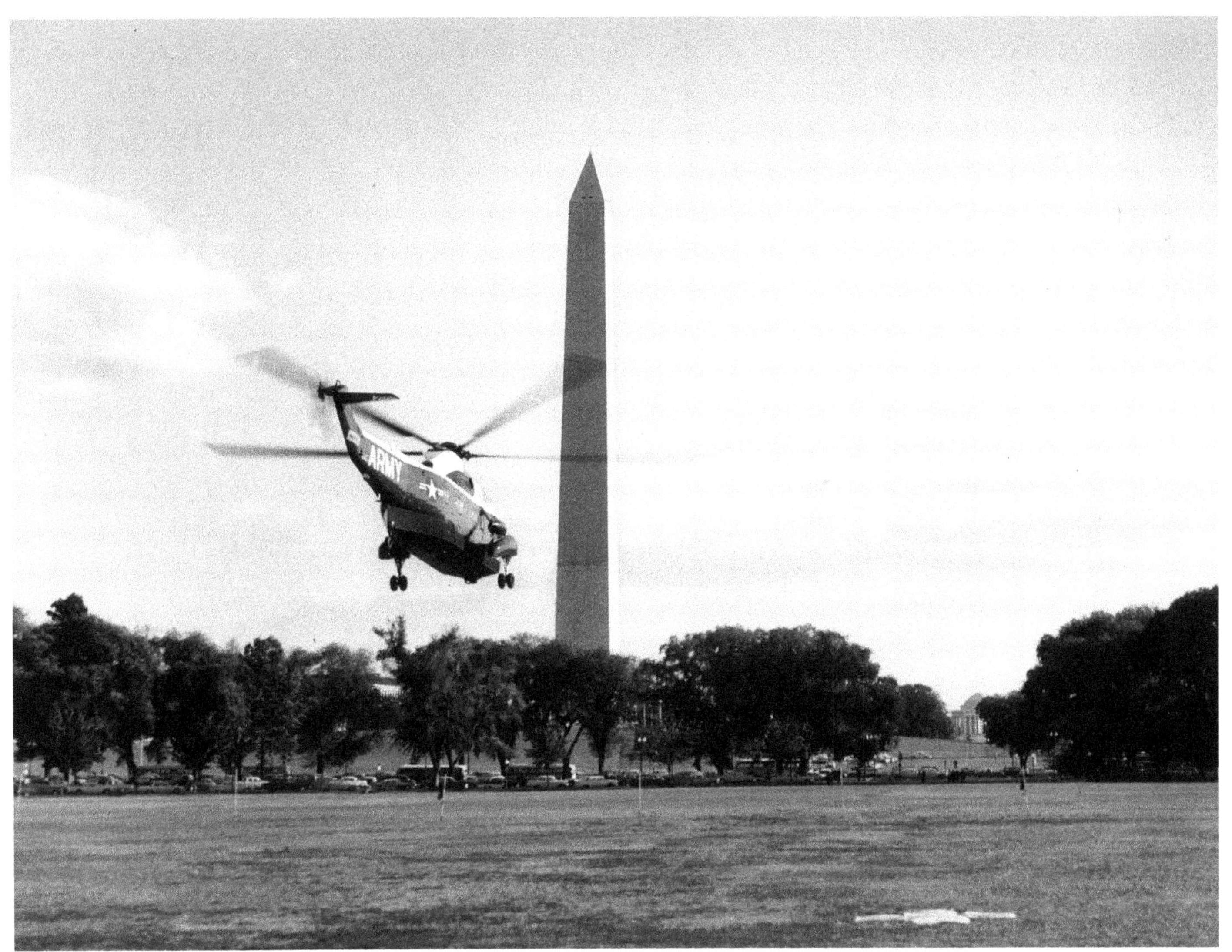

An army helicopter hovers near the ground by the Washington Monument. Peering through the trees is the Jefferson Memorial.

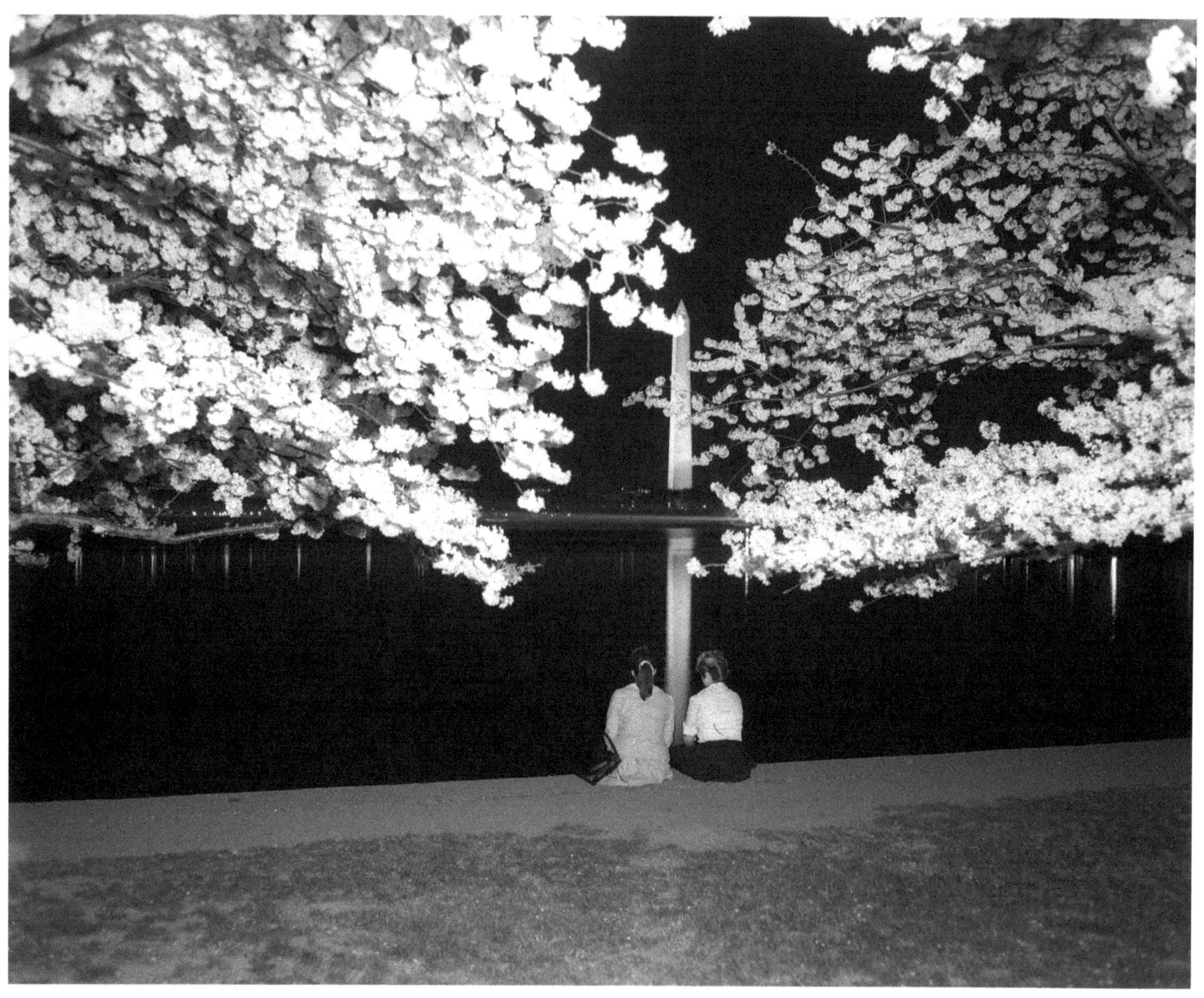

In 1912, Washington, D.C., received 3,000 cherry blossom trees as a gift from Japan. In 1915, the United States reciprocated and gave dogwood trees to Japan. This photo captures two women beholding one of the most spectacular sights in the city—the Washington Monument and its reflection on the Potomac River.

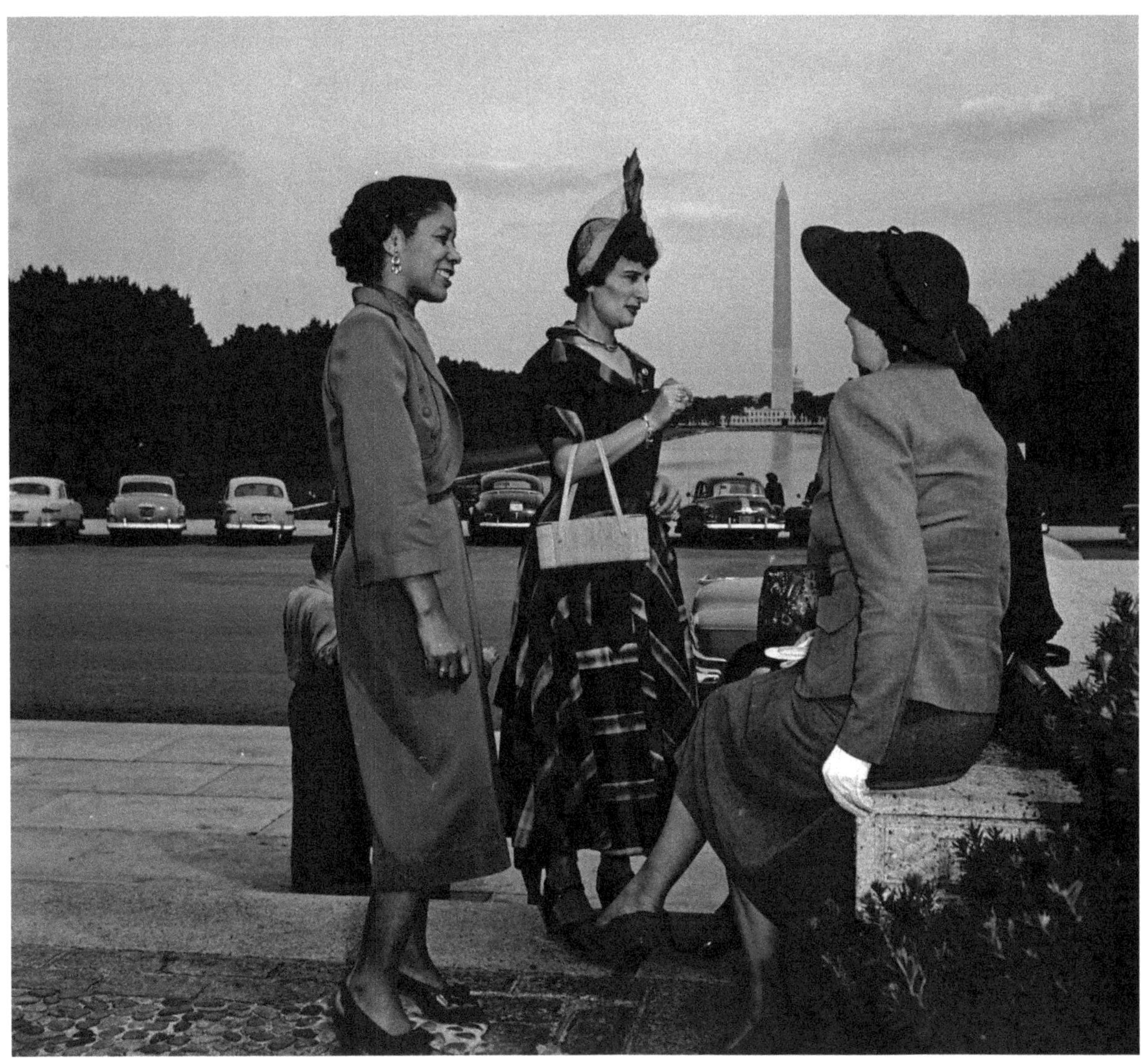

This photo titled "Gold Star Wives" comes from the Addison Scurlock collection at the Smithsonian. Gold Star Wives of America is an organization for widows who lost their husbands in military active duty or from service-related disabilities. The organization was founded in 1945.

Following Spread: Independence Day in Washington, D.C., is always marked with an elaborate fireworks display, concerts, vendors, and other attractions on the grounds of the Washington Monument. One of the great things about living in Washington, D.C., is watching the fireworks from home. The view from houses in Capitol Hill is wonderful because of their proximity to the National Mall.

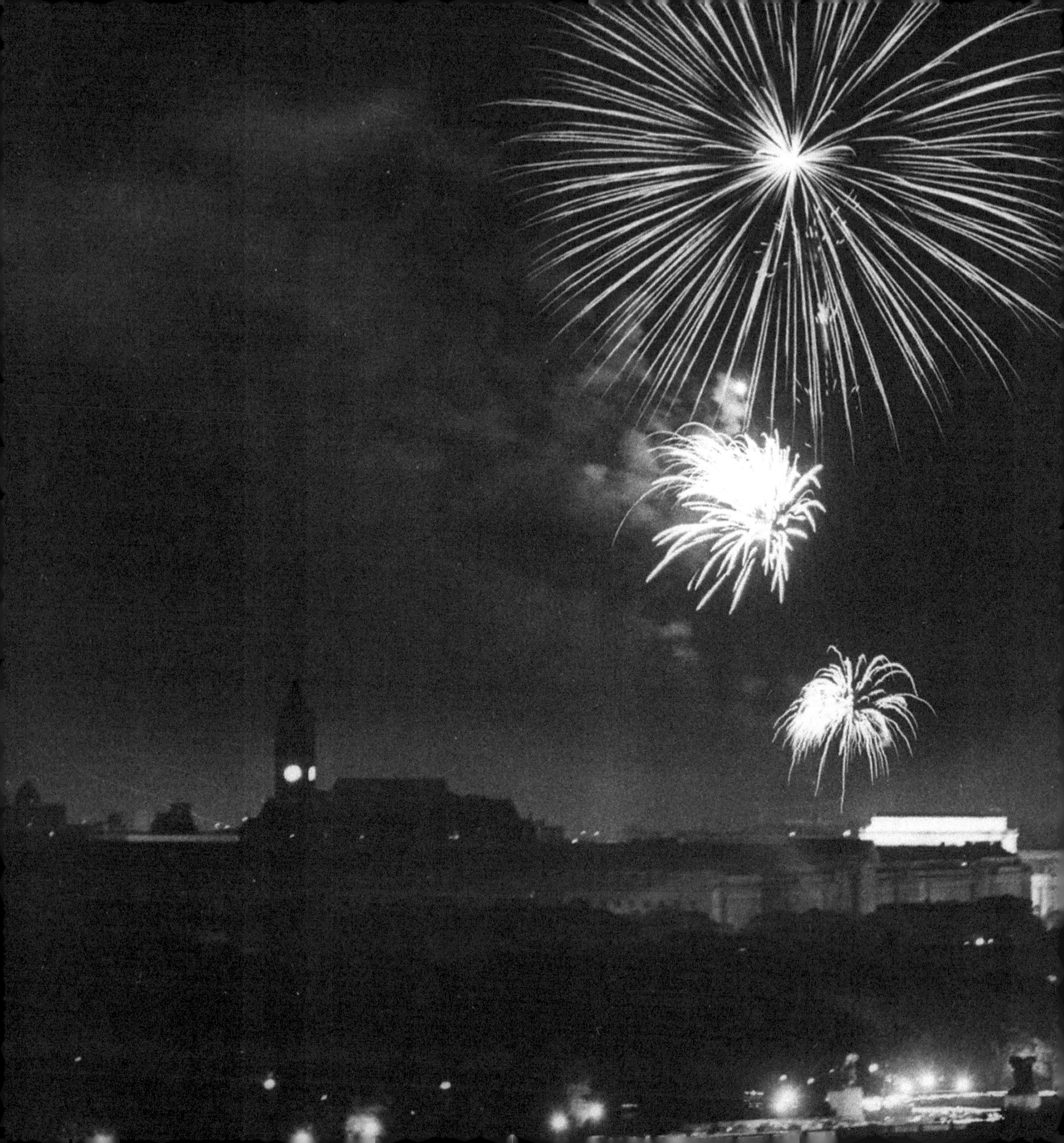

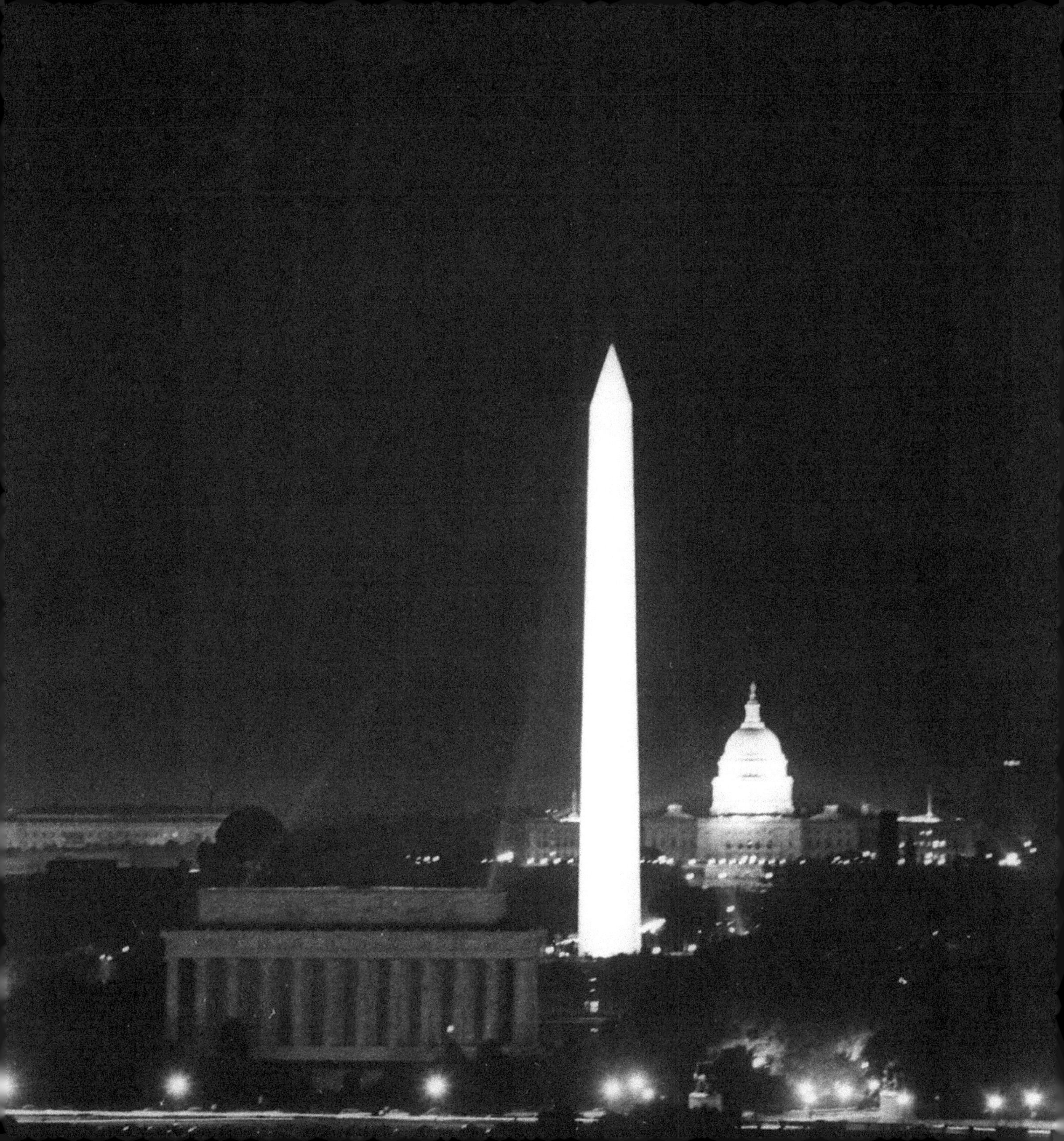

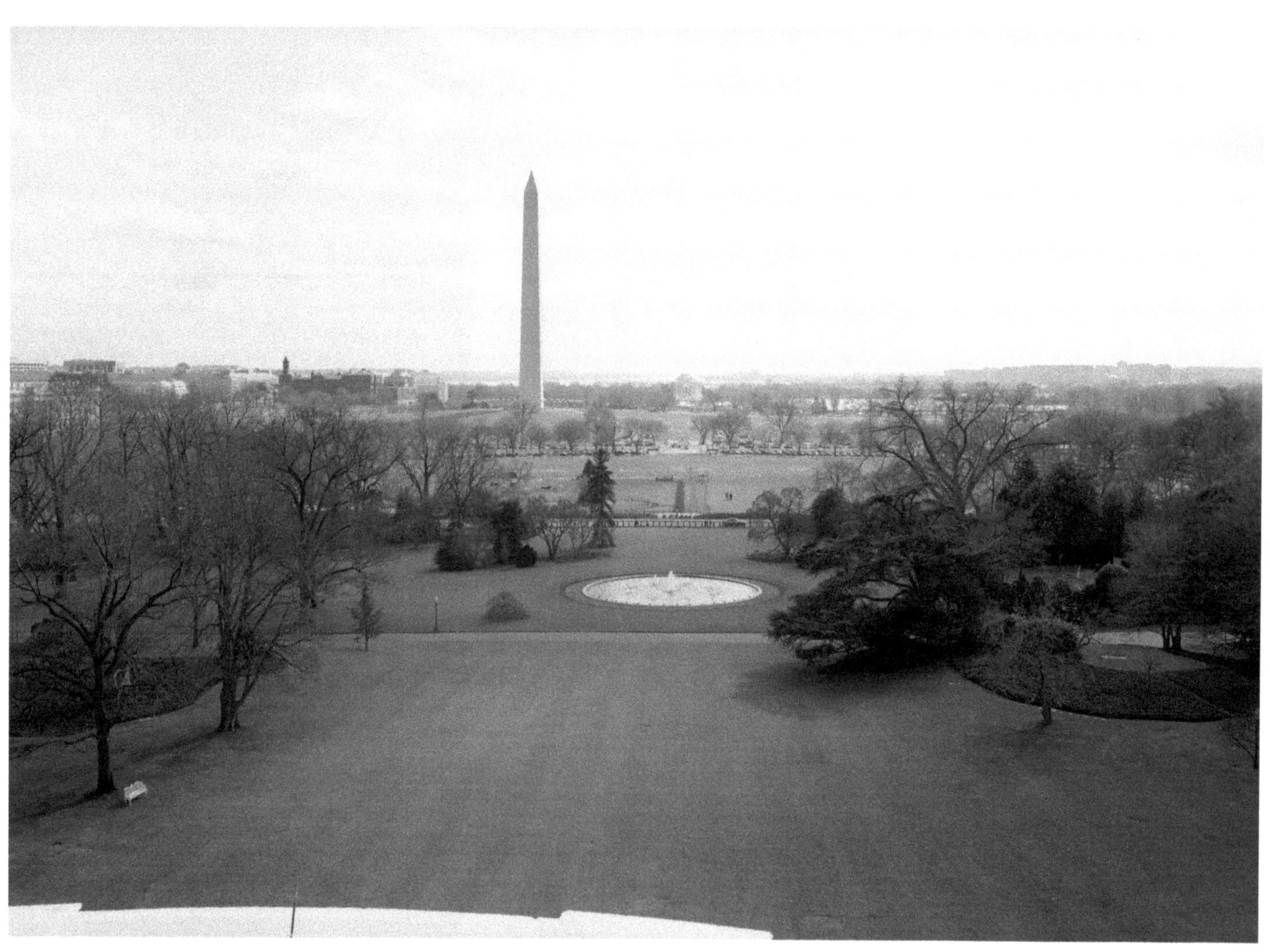

United States presidents and their families have an extraordinary view of the monument from the White House south portico. Abbie Rowe shot this photo in 1949 for the National Capital Parks Interior Department.

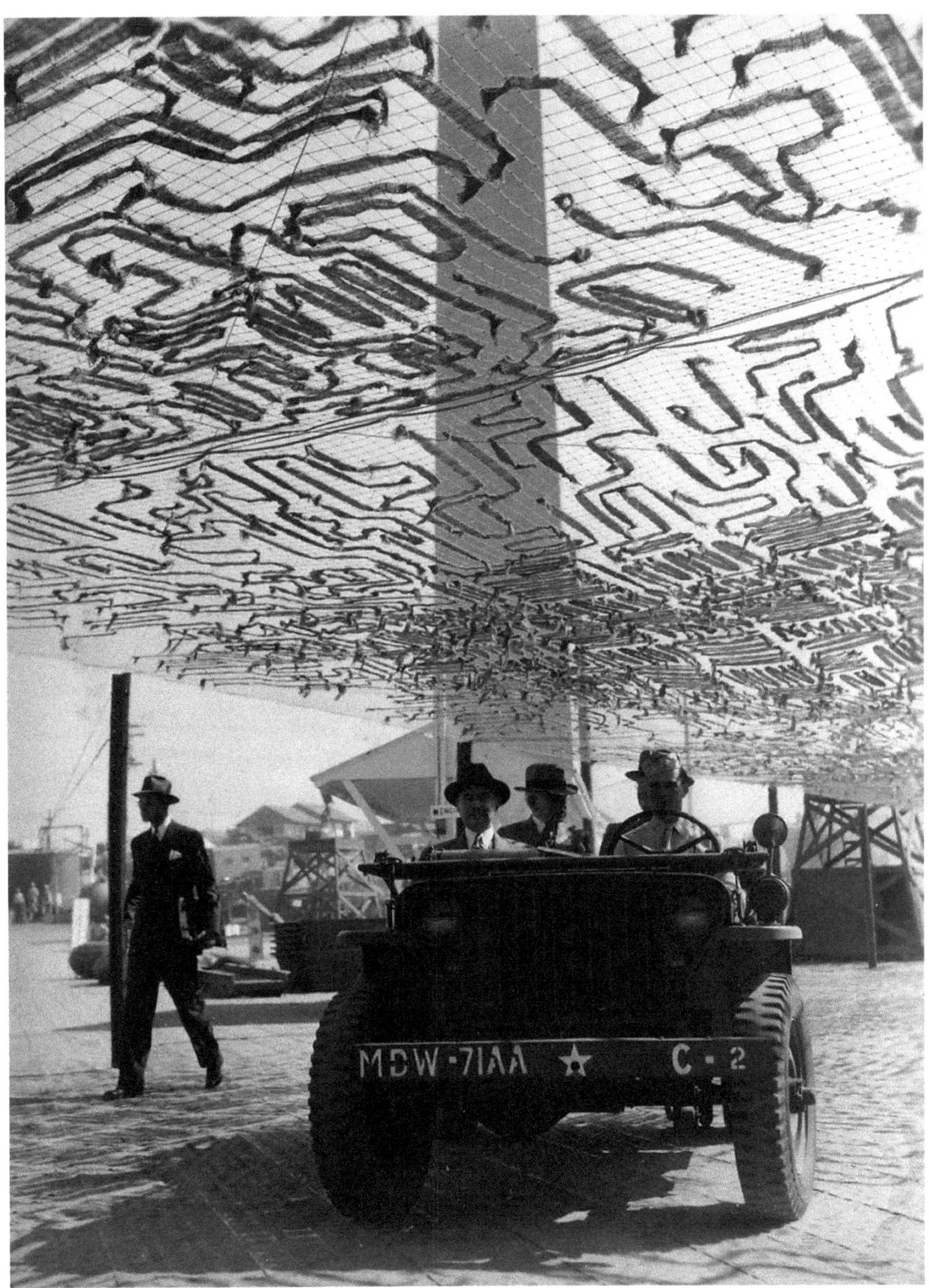

Security in the city has increased significantly since the September 11, 2001, terrorist attacks. Still, the monument, like many other structures in Washington, D.C., is a prime target for terrorists. In 1965 a bomb plot was foiled, but in 1982, law enforcement authorities were held at bay while a nuclear arms protestor threatened to blow up the monument from his van. Norman Mayer reportedly told police he had explosives in the van. Meanwhile, eight people were stuck in the monument, but they were released hours later during the incident. The standoff lasted ten hours and ended tragically with the U.S. Park Police being forced to shoot and kill Mayer. No explosives were found. Camouflage netting shrouds the monument in this war-era scene from the 1940s.

Robert Mills, architect, engineer, and designer of the Washington Monument, is buried here in Congressional Cemetery. His headstone reads:

Robert Mills
(1781-1855)
First Federal Architect
whose influence
moulded
our architecture
and whose genius
gave us the
Washington Monument
The Treasury Building
The Old Patent Office
and the
Old Post Office

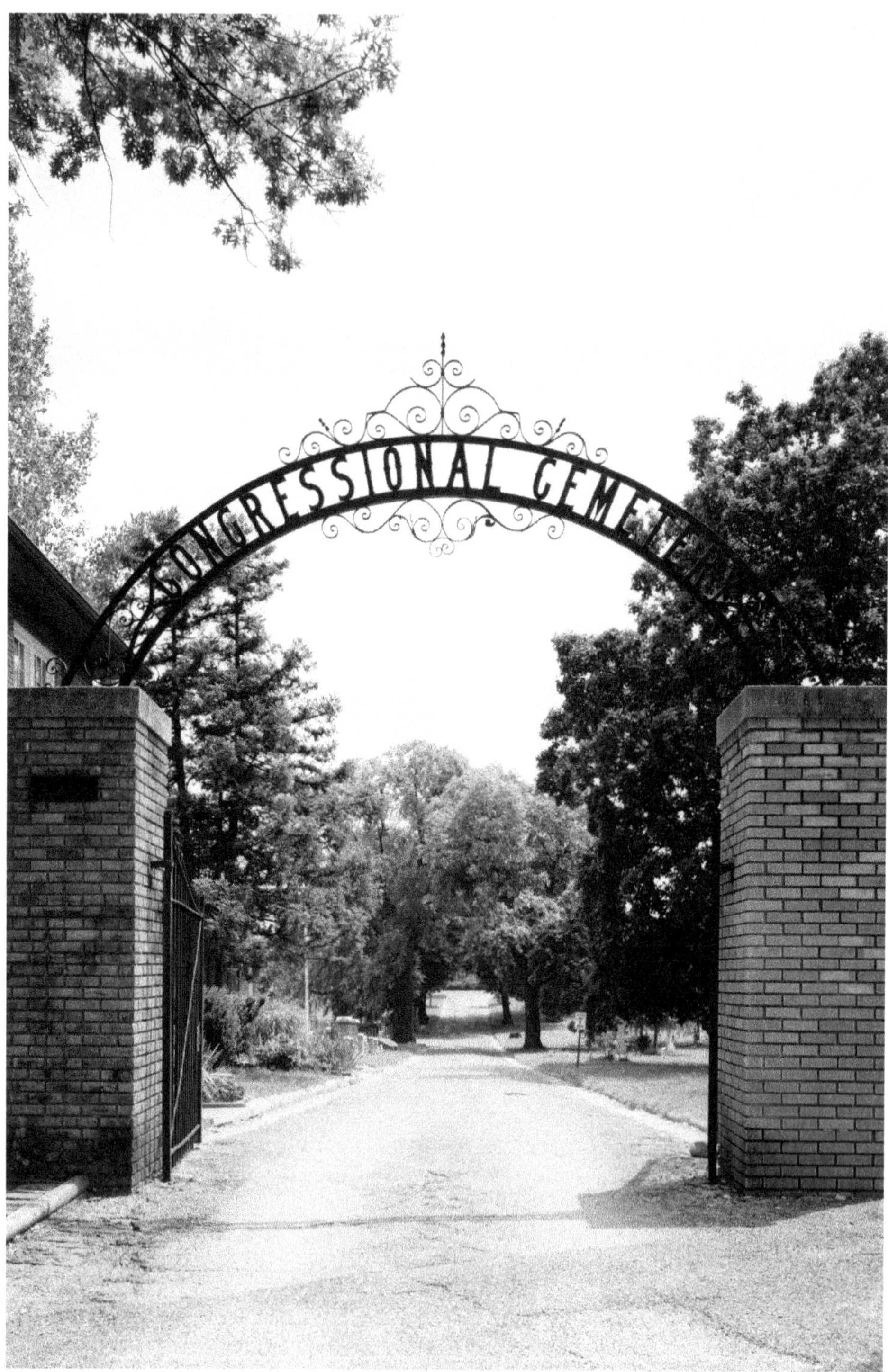

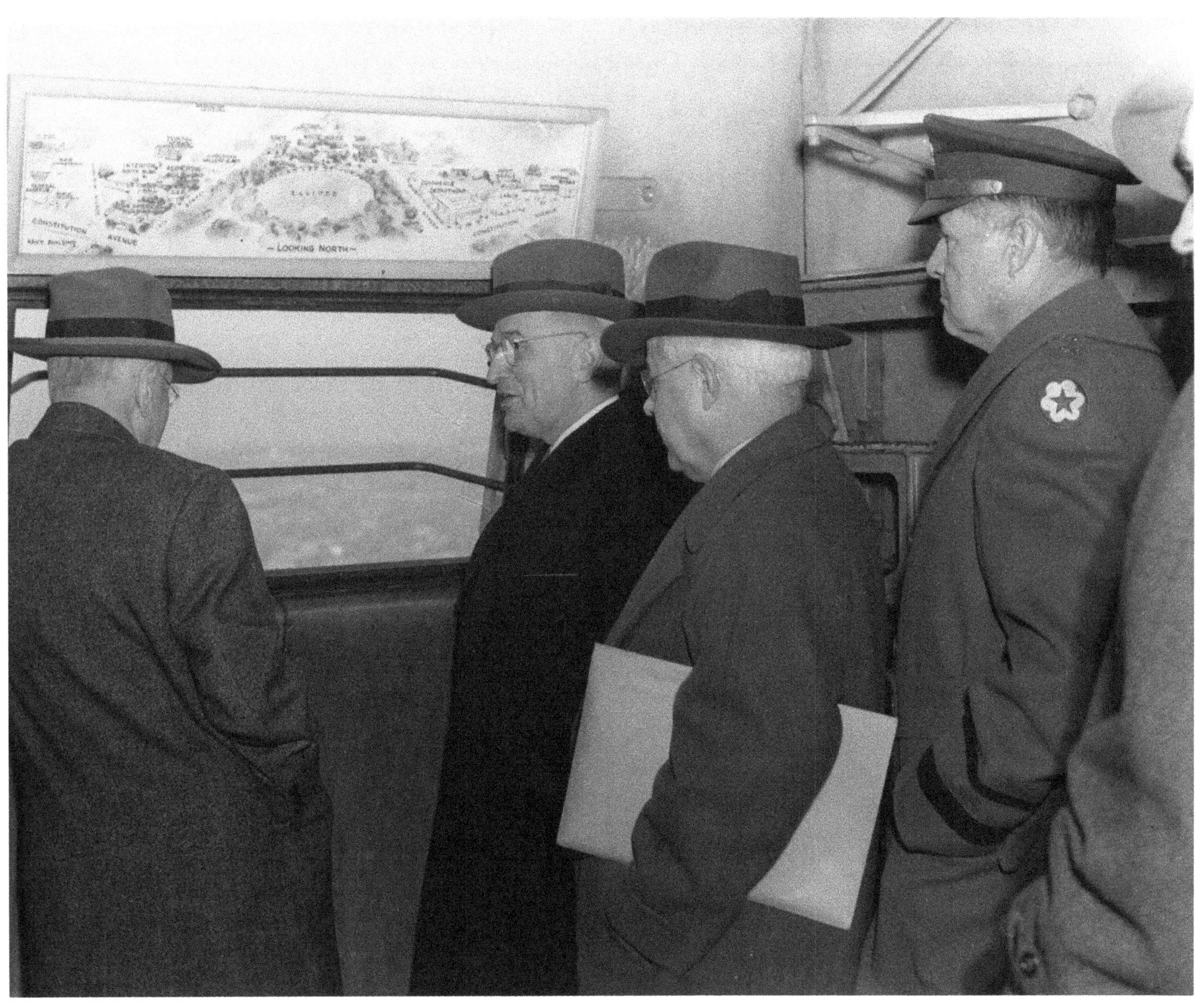

President Harry Truman and guests tour the Washington Monument on January 14, 1946. Here the group looks out of an observation window inside the monument.

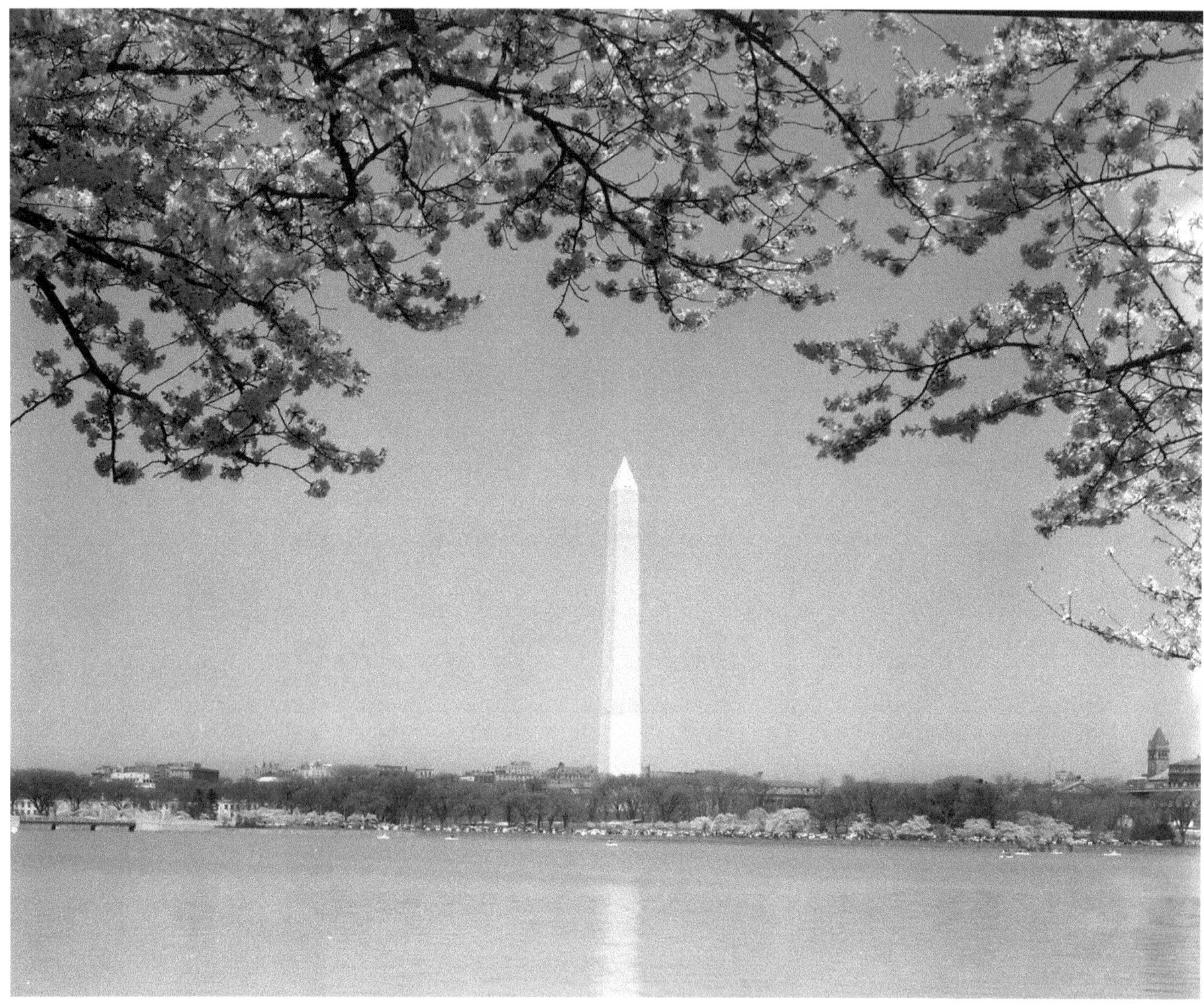

The Empire State Building has one, and so does the Statue of Liberty. The observation deck at the top of the Washington Monument also boasts one: a spectacular view. On a clear day, spectators can see up to 25 miles away. The U.S. Capitol and Kennedy Center are just two of the sites visible from the deck. This photograph displays the Tidal Basin during spring, evidenced by the cherry trees in bloom.

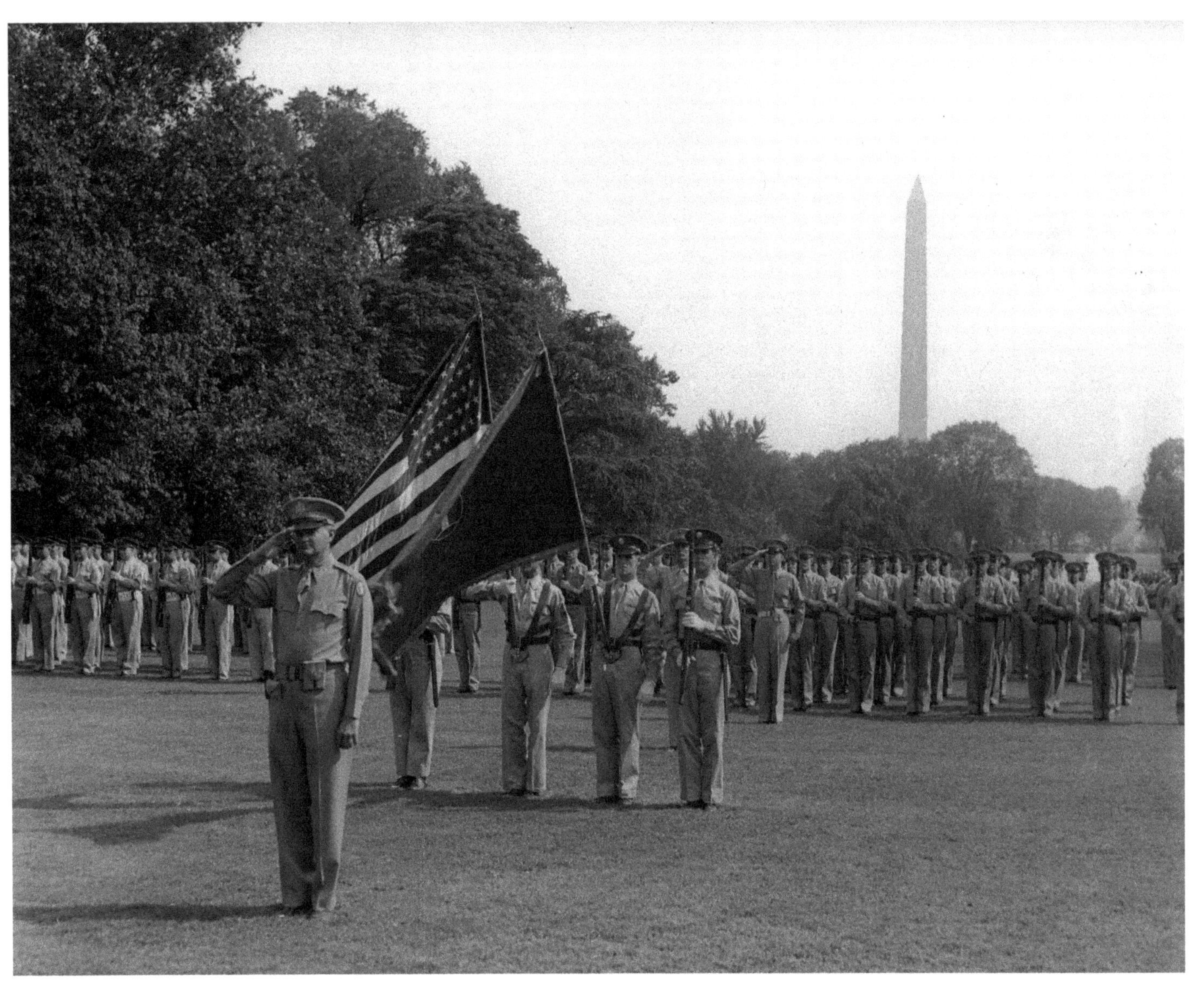

Men in uniform salute on the grounds of the Washington Monument.

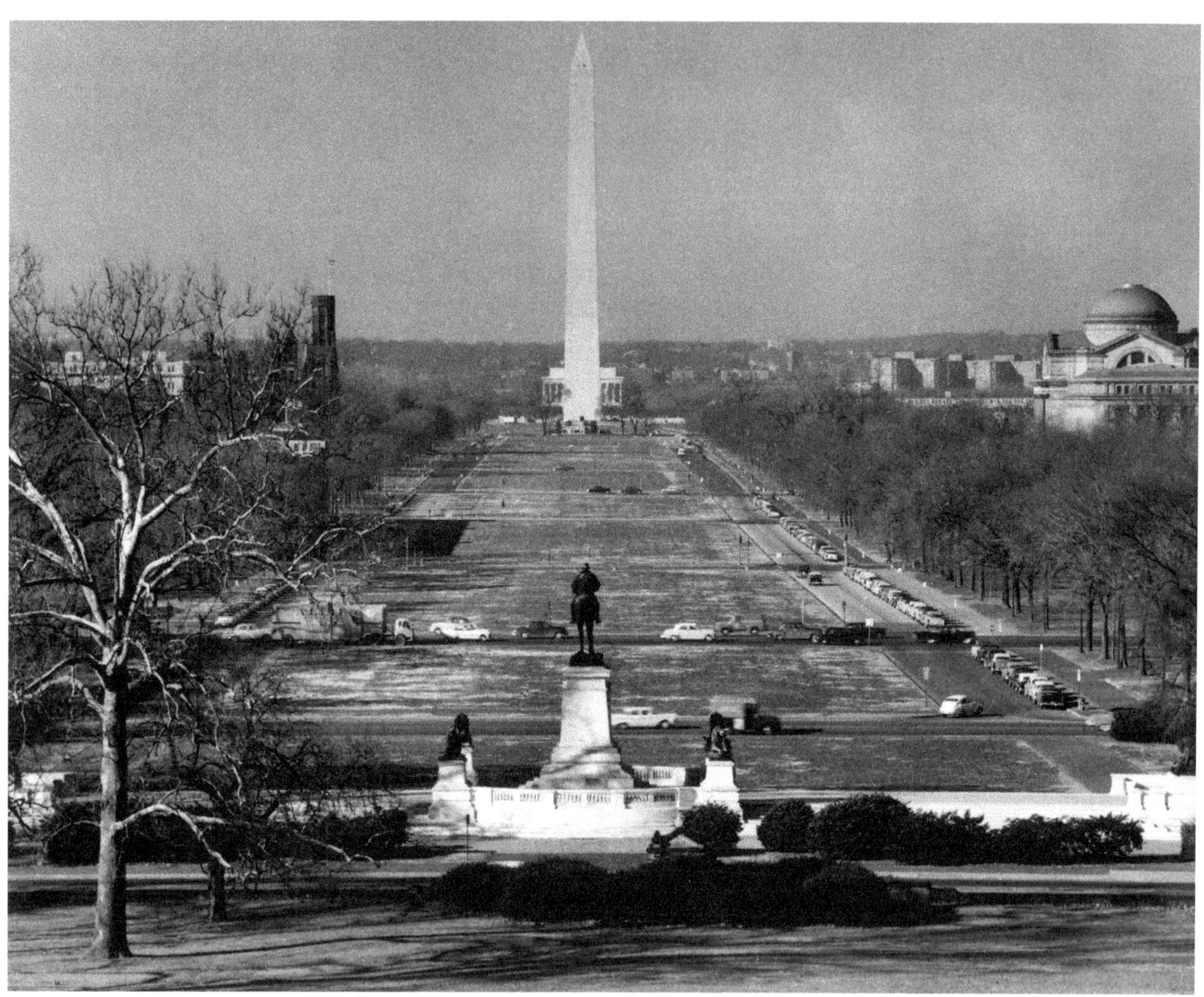

A view of the monument and surrounding grounds is shown in this image. Building materials came not only from two quarries but from several states. Inside the Washington Monument, there are 190 commemorative stones, some of which identify the origins of the building materials. The plaques were donated by organizations including the Association of Oldest Inhabitants of Washington, the Association of Journeymen Stonecutters of Philadelphia, the American Whig Society, the American Medical Association, the Addisonian Literary Society, and the Alexandria Library in Egypt, among many others.

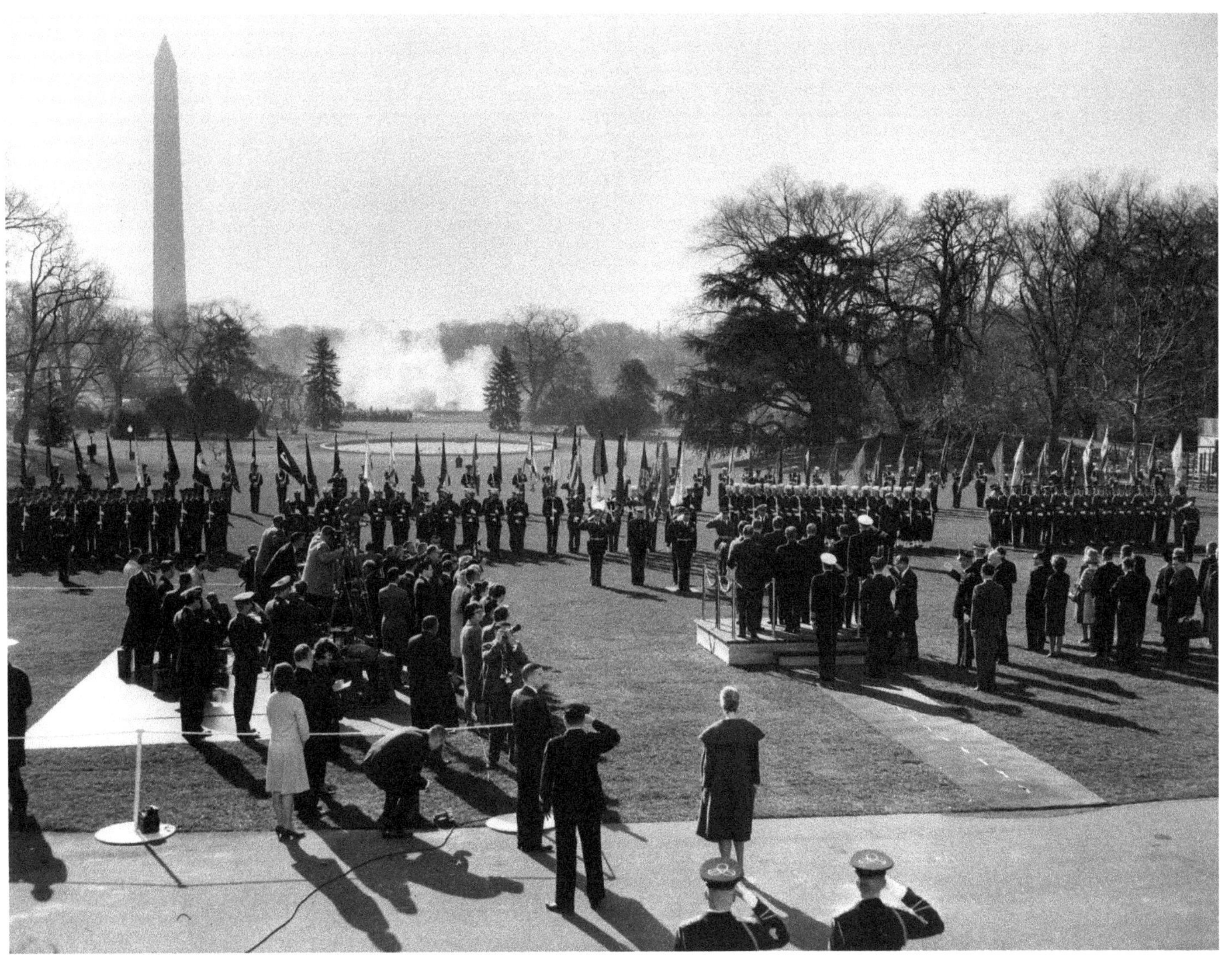

On July 3, 1948, President Harry Truman attends the Washington Monument centennial ceremonies. Military bands are poised to perform at the monument's 100th birthday. The president makes his remarks as seen in this photograph.

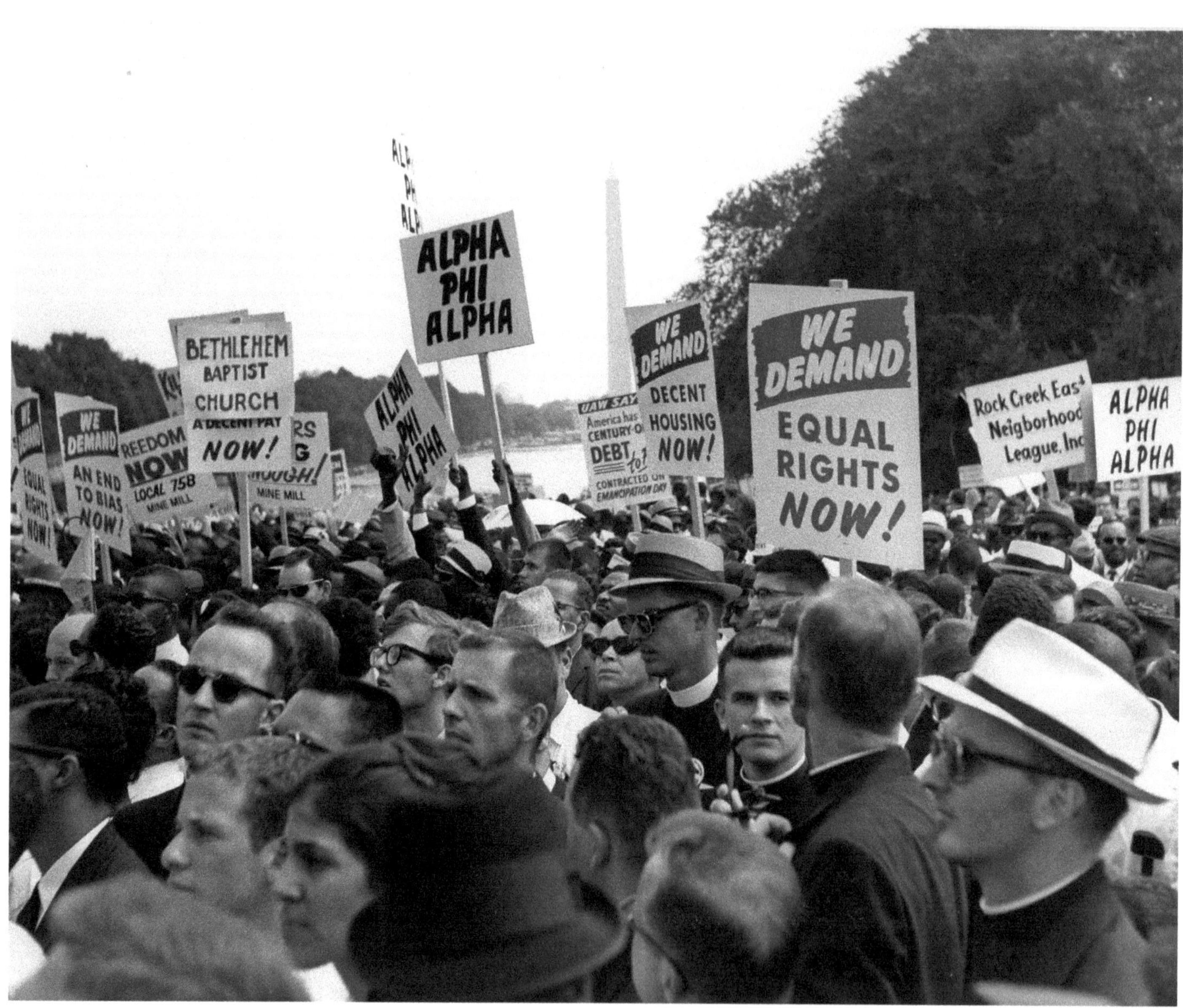

This photo, taken on August 28, 1963, shows a mass of protestors waving signs in the March on Washington for Jobs and Freedom. The signs display slogans such as "We March for Integrated Schools Now" and "We Demand Voting Rights Now."

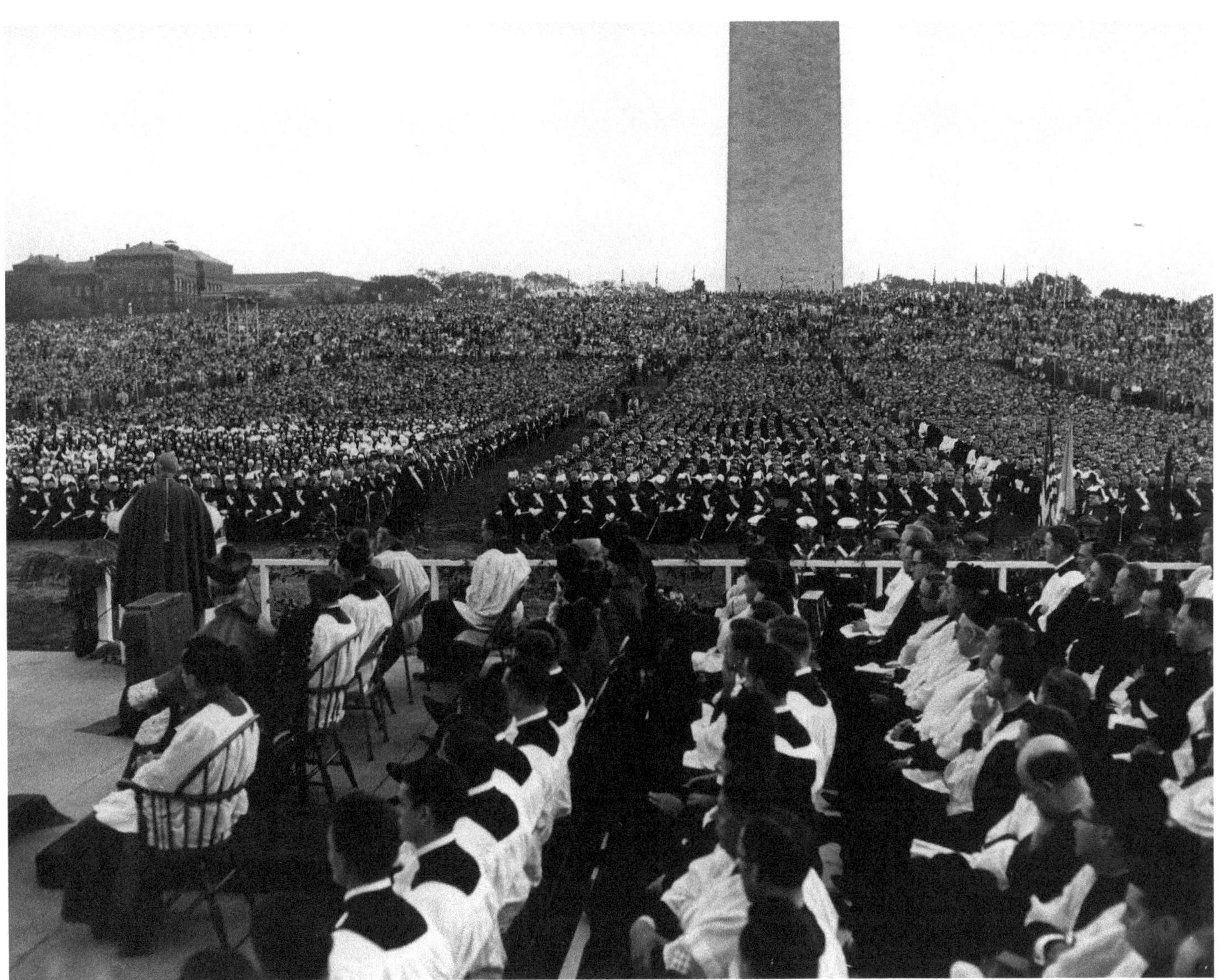

A gathering of Catholics on the monument grounds. In this image, Pope John Paul II offers Mass before 175,000 people on the Washington Mall, at the end of his first visit to the United States as pope. During the 1979 visit, sharpshooters were stationed at the top of the monument to protect the pope as his motorcade made its way through the city.

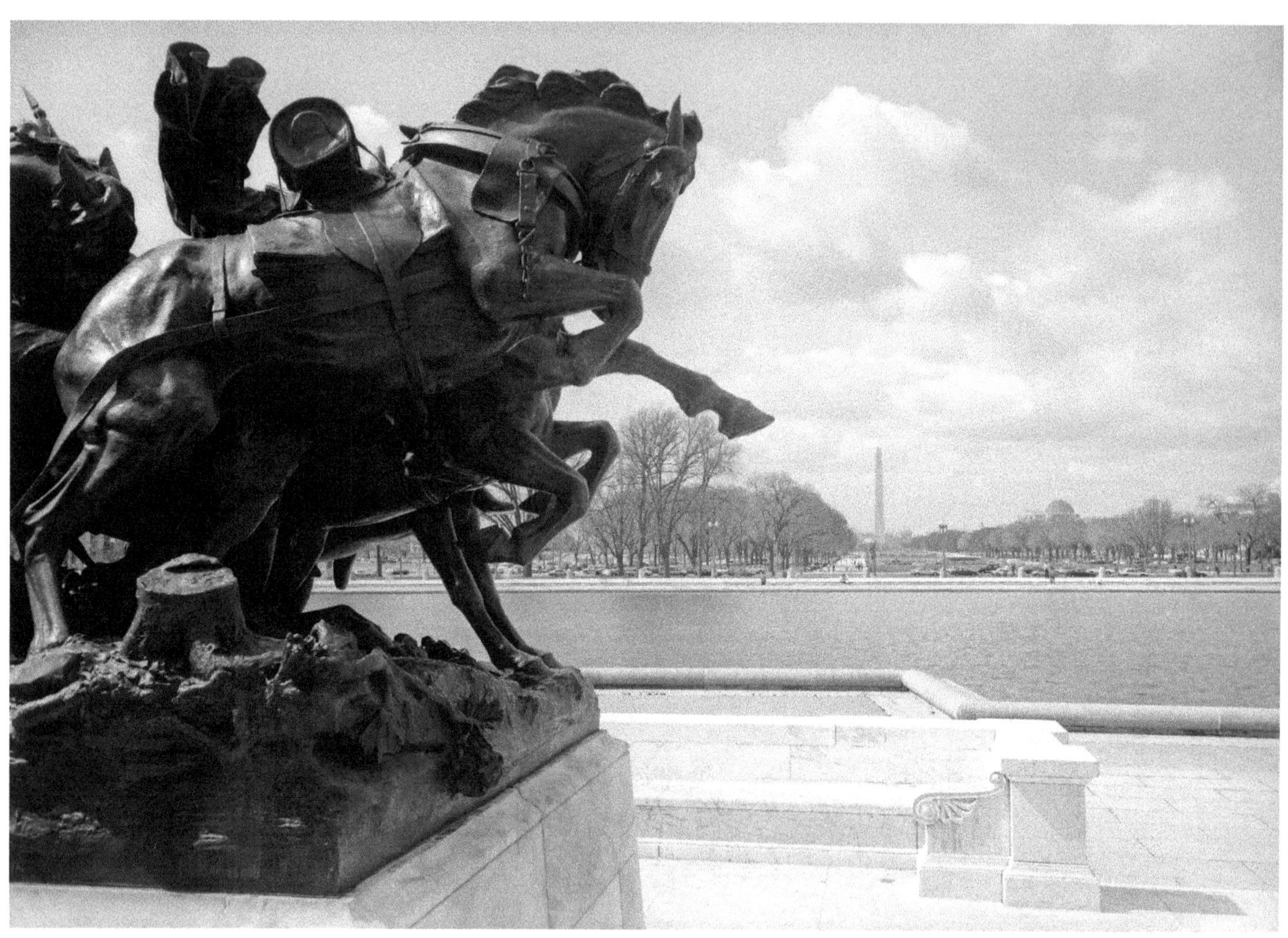

Pictured here is a view of the Mall looking west toward the monument.

The Jefferson Memorial

(1934–1970)

In 1935, architect John Russell Pope was charged with a daunting challenge: drafting and designing a grand monument to honor Thomas Jefferson, a monument equal to the Lincoln Memorial and Washington Monument in scale yet sufficient to honor the third president, draftsman of the Declaration of Independence, former governor of Virginia, congressional representative, and much more.

To the casual observer, it appears Jefferson's background, travels, and penchant for Greek and Roman architecture were exactly what Columbia graduate John Russell Pope pondered when he conceived the neoclassical stone monument. Jefferson himself was a lover of architecture and designed his beloved home, Monticello, the Virginia State Capitol, and the original buildings of the University of Virginia. "Architecture is my delight, and putting up and pulling down, one of my favorite amusements," Jefferson told a Monticello visitor in 1809.

Beginning in 1784, Thomas Jefferson spent a significant amount of time in Europe. In May of that year, President John Adams appointed Jefferson minister to France, and two months later, Jefferson, accompanied by his daughter Patsy and administrative staff, went to Paris. In 1787, Jefferson made his way through the South of France and northern Italy. It is likely that Pope, who honed his craft in the late 1800s at the American Academy in Rome and later at École des Beaux-Arts in Paris, considered Jefferson's life in Europe as he conceived a design for the memorial.

Pope's own time in Rome influenced his design style. The Jefferson Memorial, Temple of the Scottish Rite, and the West Building of the National Gallery of Art are Pope's best-known structures, and all, particularly the Jefferson Memorial, feature Romanesque elements resembling the famous Pantheon in Rome.

The Jefferson Memorial, which cost $3,192,312 to construct, was built by Philadelphia contractor John McShain. The ground breaking for the memorial was December 15, 1938, and the cornerstone was laid November 15, 1939, by President Franklin Delano Roosevelt. The dedication was held four years later in 1943. Like Robert Mills, visionary of the Washington Monument, Pope did not live to see the memorial completed. He died in of cancer on August 27, 1937, one year before the Jefferson Memorial ground breaking.

This early photograph taken from the Washington Monument features a view of the land where the Jefferson Memorial will be built.

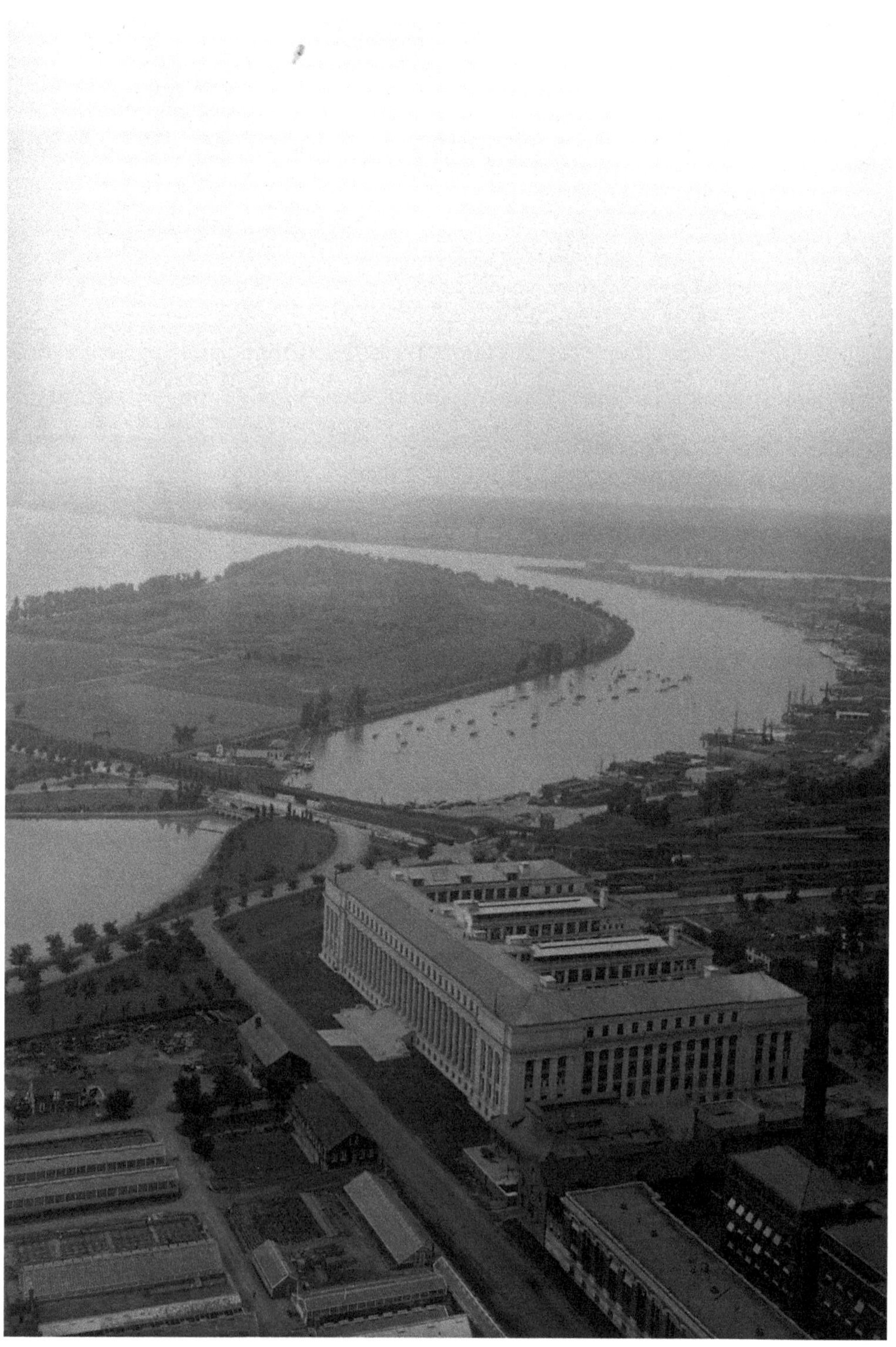

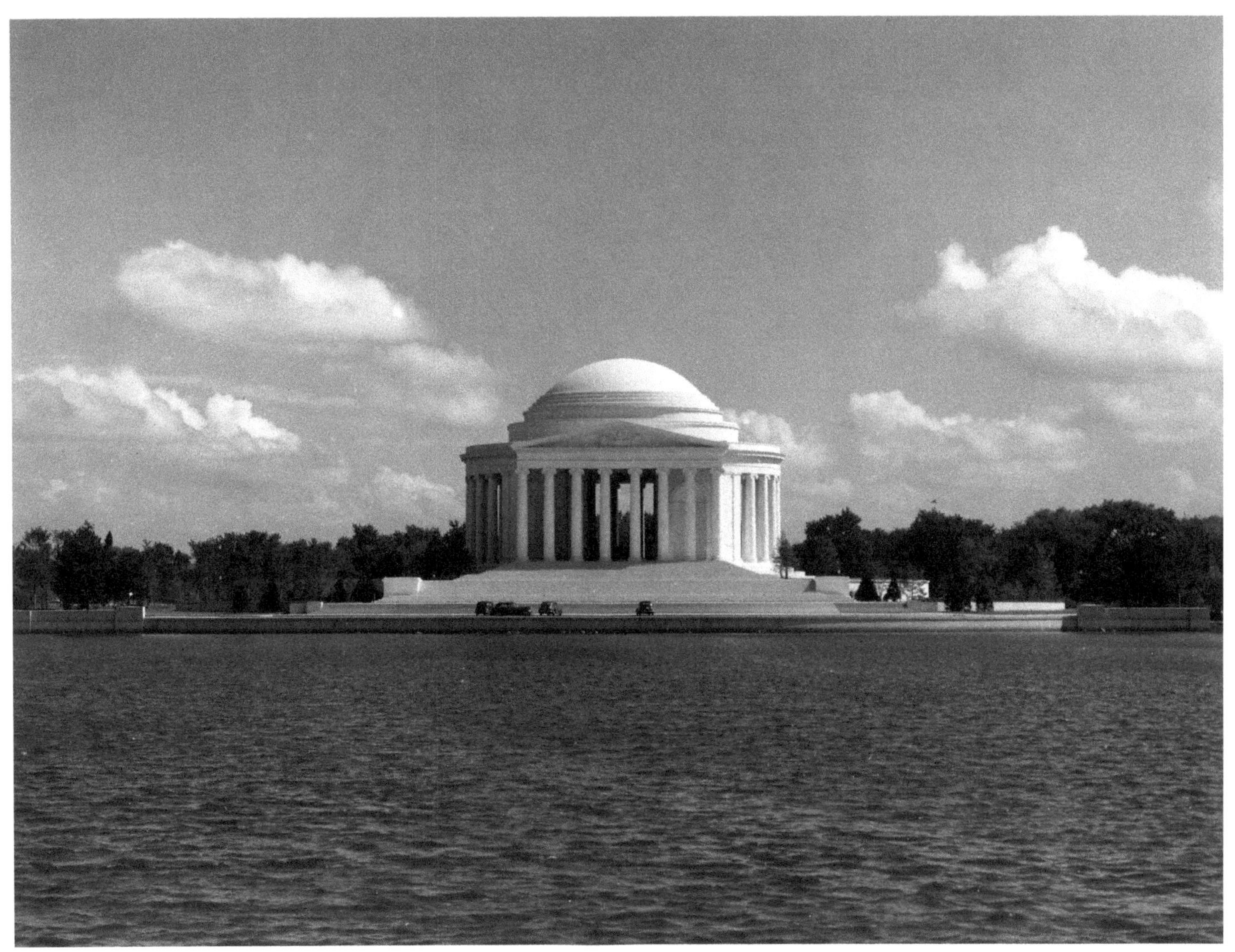

In June of 1934, Congress passed an act to build a memorial to the third president. Three years later the south bank of the Tidal Basin was chosen as the site for the marble memorial.

It would take an entire week or longer to tour every building in Washington, D.C., designed by architect John Russell Pope. Born in New York and educated in New York, Rome, and Paris, Pope's refined style and influence on architecture in Washington, D.C., is obvious. From Ionic columns to the use of massive domes and rotundas, Pope is one of the key figures responsible for the "look" of Washington. But not everyone enjoyed Pope's Beaux-Arts style. Steven McLeod Bedford, in his book *John Russell Pope: Architect of an Empire,* writes about a 1937 conversation between President Franklin Roosevelt and architect Frank Lloyd Wright, in which Wright criticized the style of architecture in Washington: "Frank [Roosevelt], you ought to get up out of that chair and see what they are doing to your city here, miles and miles of Ionic and Corinthian columns." Other noteworthy buildings in Washington designed by Pope include the Daughters of the American Revolution's Constitution Hall and the National Archives building.

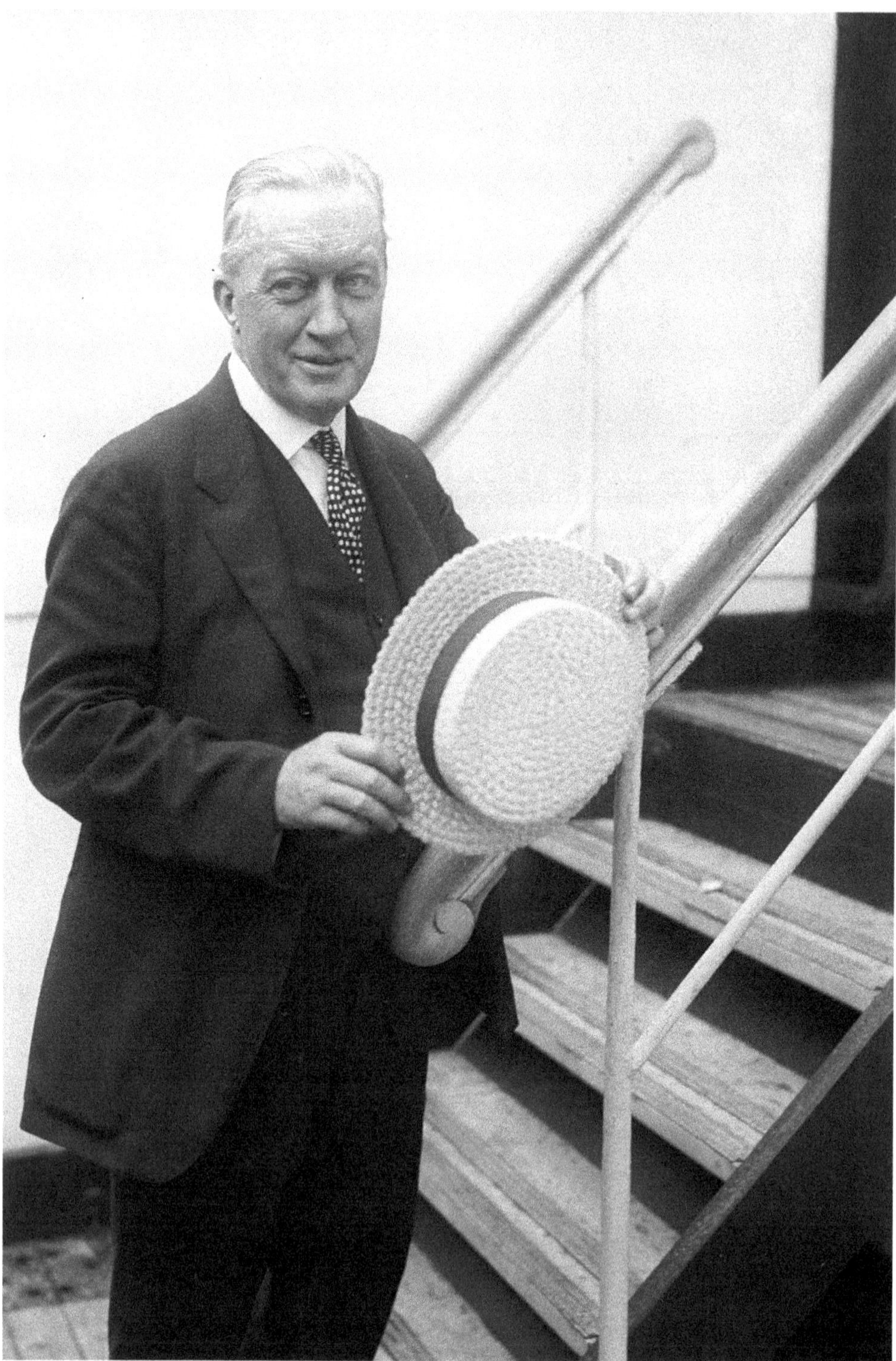

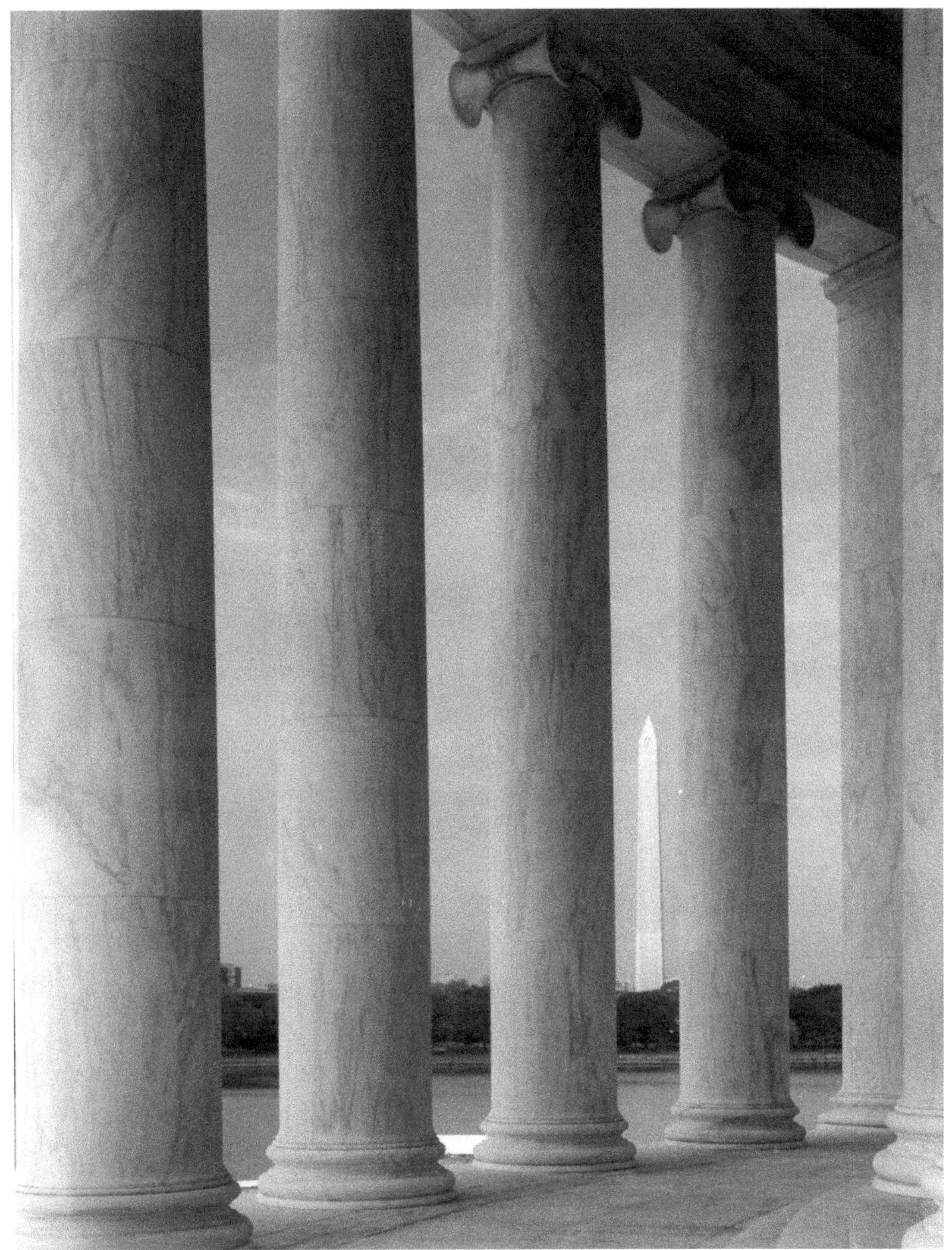

John Russell Pope's signature columns dwarf the Washington Monument in this image taken on October 1, 1941. The monument peers through the columns from a distance.

Photographer Oscar Seidenberg captured this placid view of the Jefferson Memorial across the Potomac River.

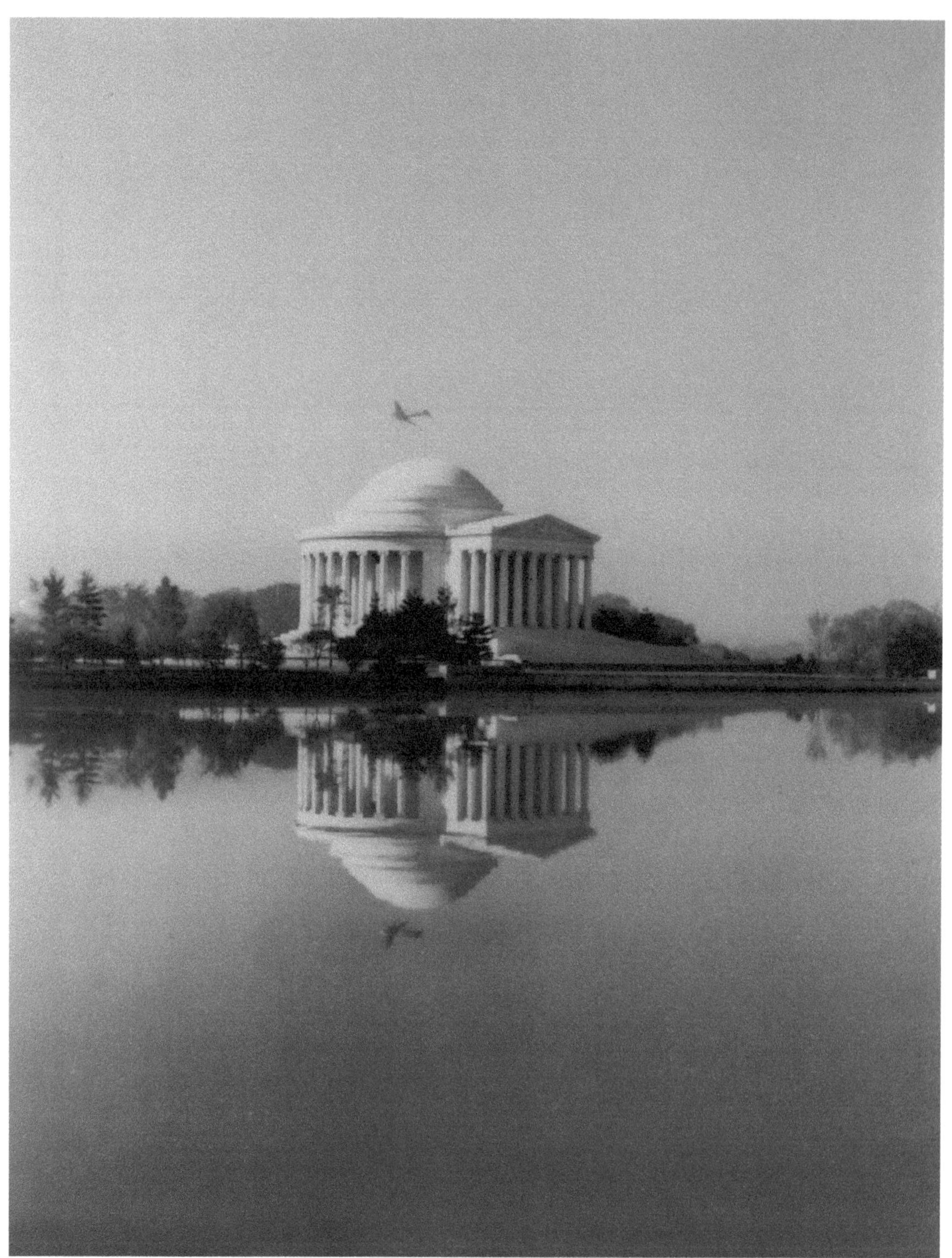

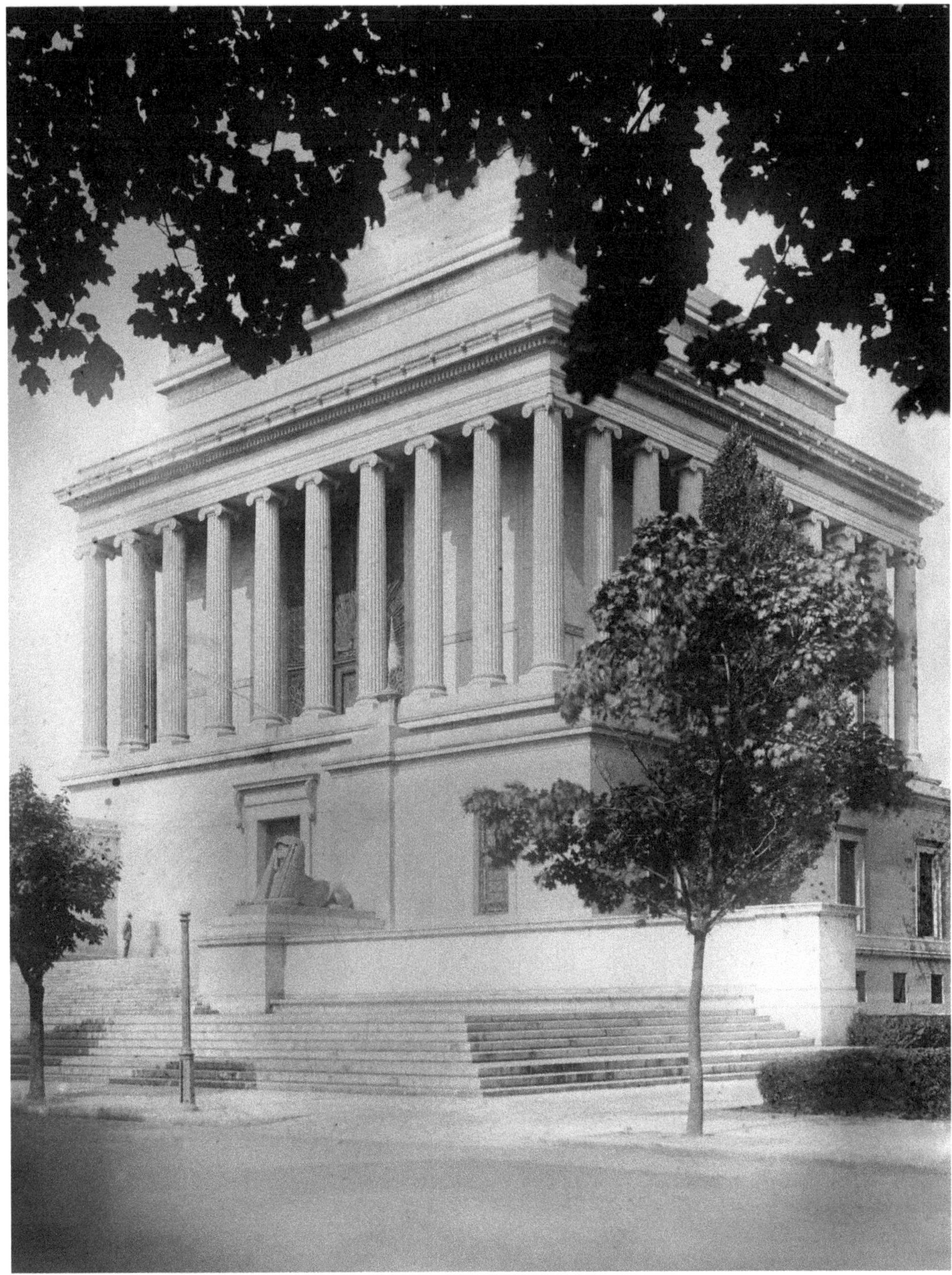

Temple of the Scottish Rite, located at 1733 Sixteenth Street NW, Washington, D.C., opened in 1915. John Russell Pope also designed this elaborate building, which, like the Jefferson Memorial, features Ionic columns.

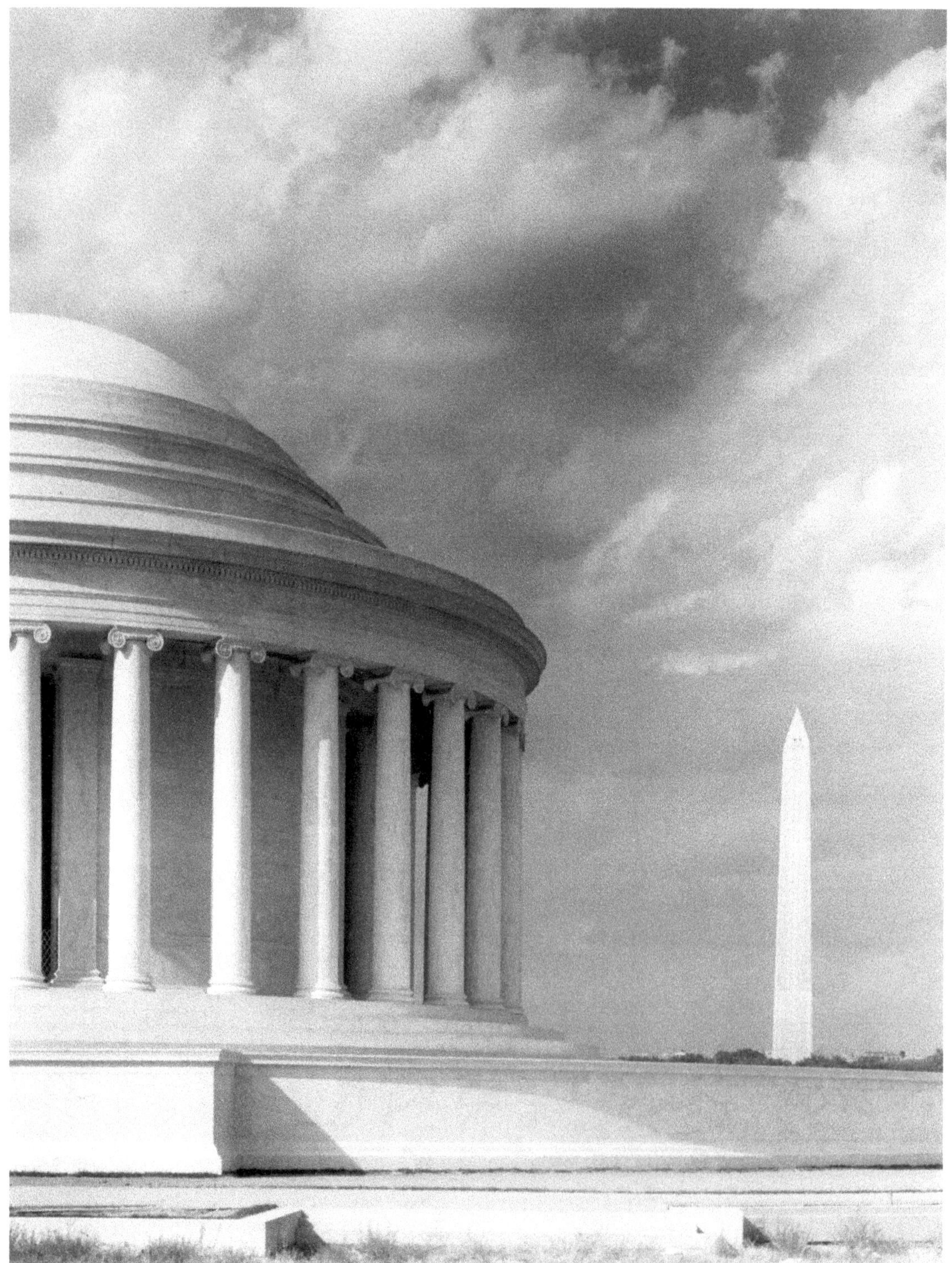

Storms appear to be brewing in this October 1, 1941, photograph of the Jefferson Memorial and Washington Monument. More recently, another storm has surged in. Concerns have been raised over the "sinking" of the monument's seawall. A 2008 study by the National Park Service concludes that repairs are needed.

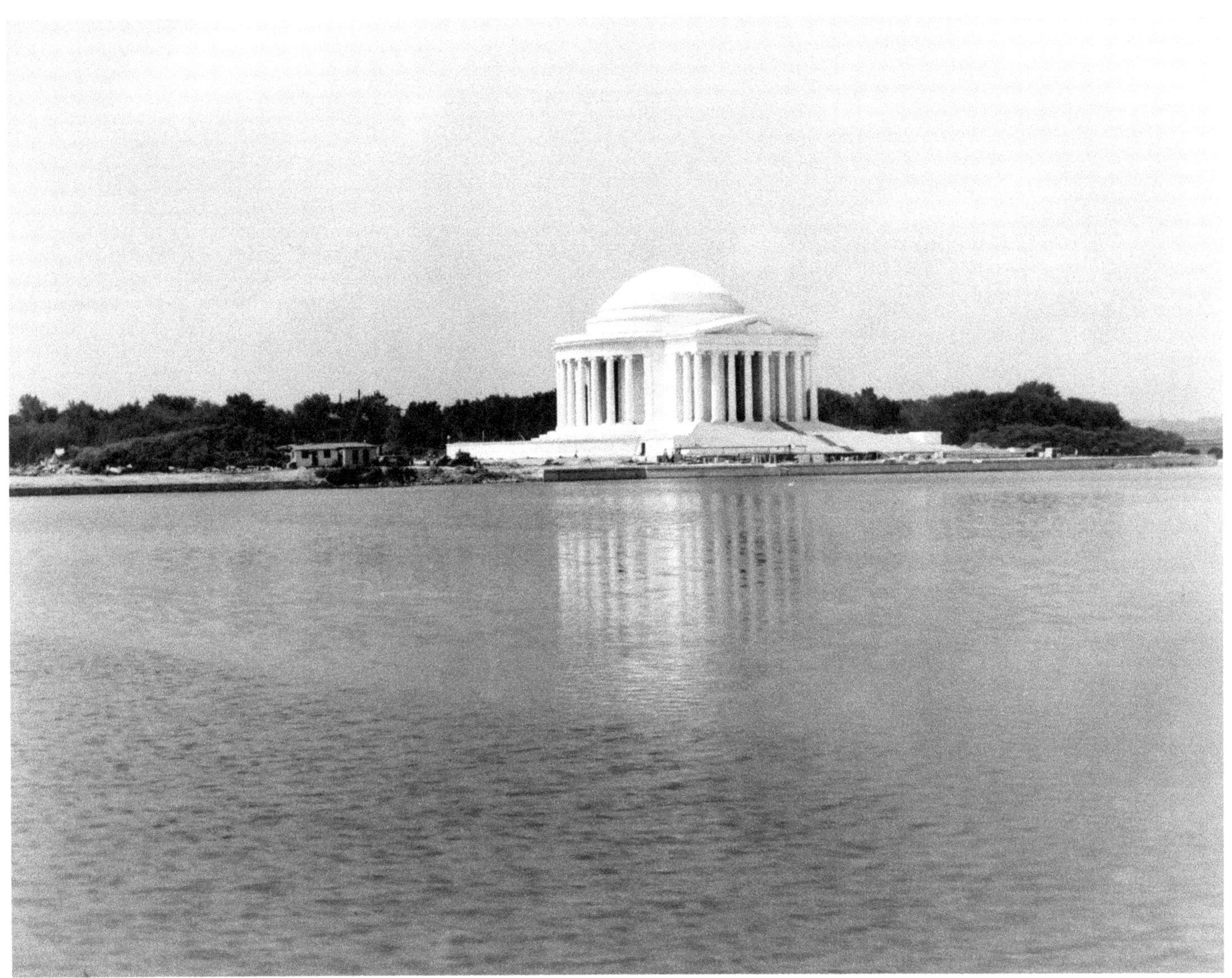

The majestic exterior of the Jefferson Memorial can best be described as an open monument of alabaster marble. Twenty-six columns wrap around the structure, with the roof pristine and domed. The front stairs ascend to the portico, which is fronted with eight columns. Once inside, visitors are met with a bronze statue of the elder statesman.

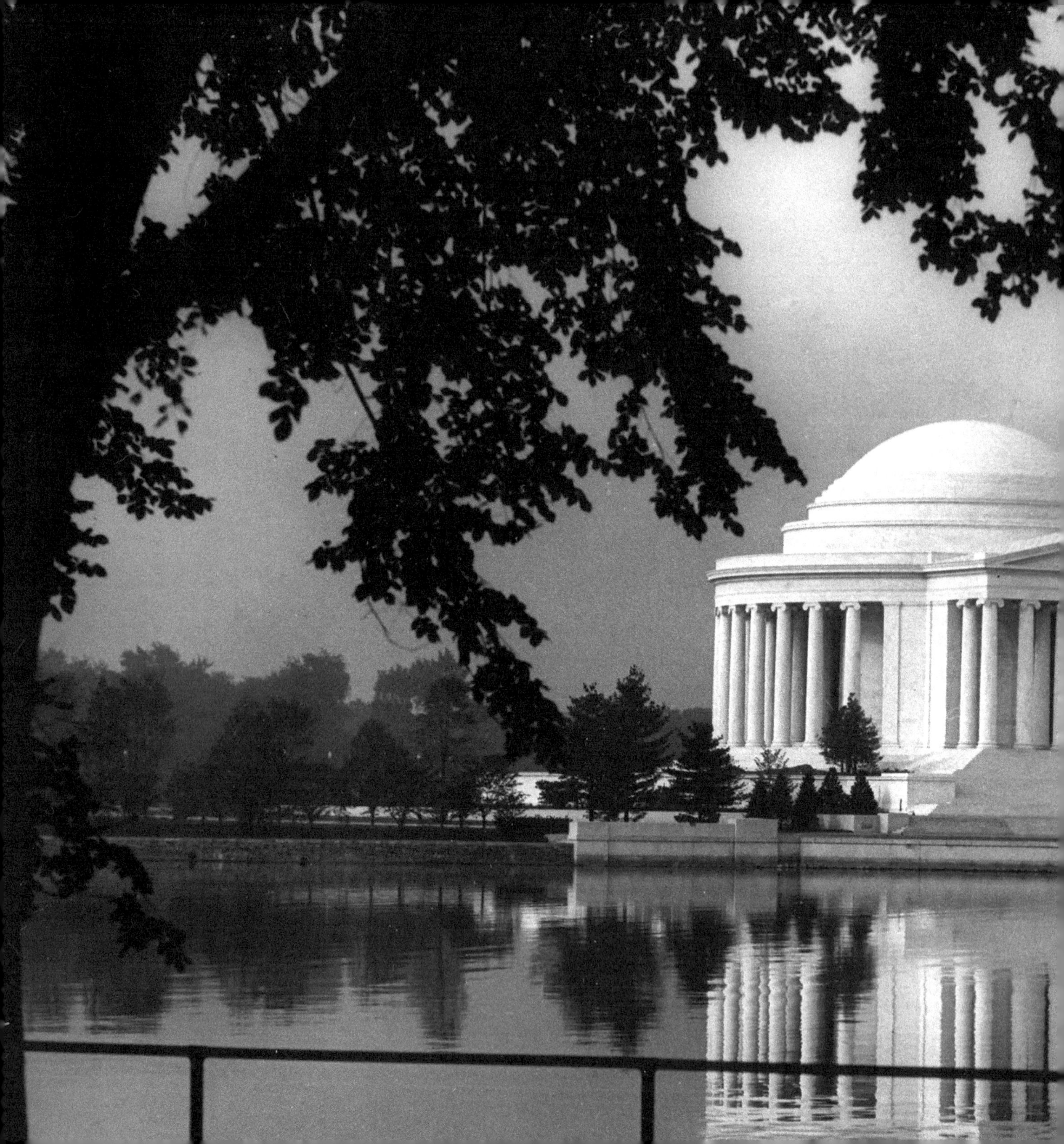

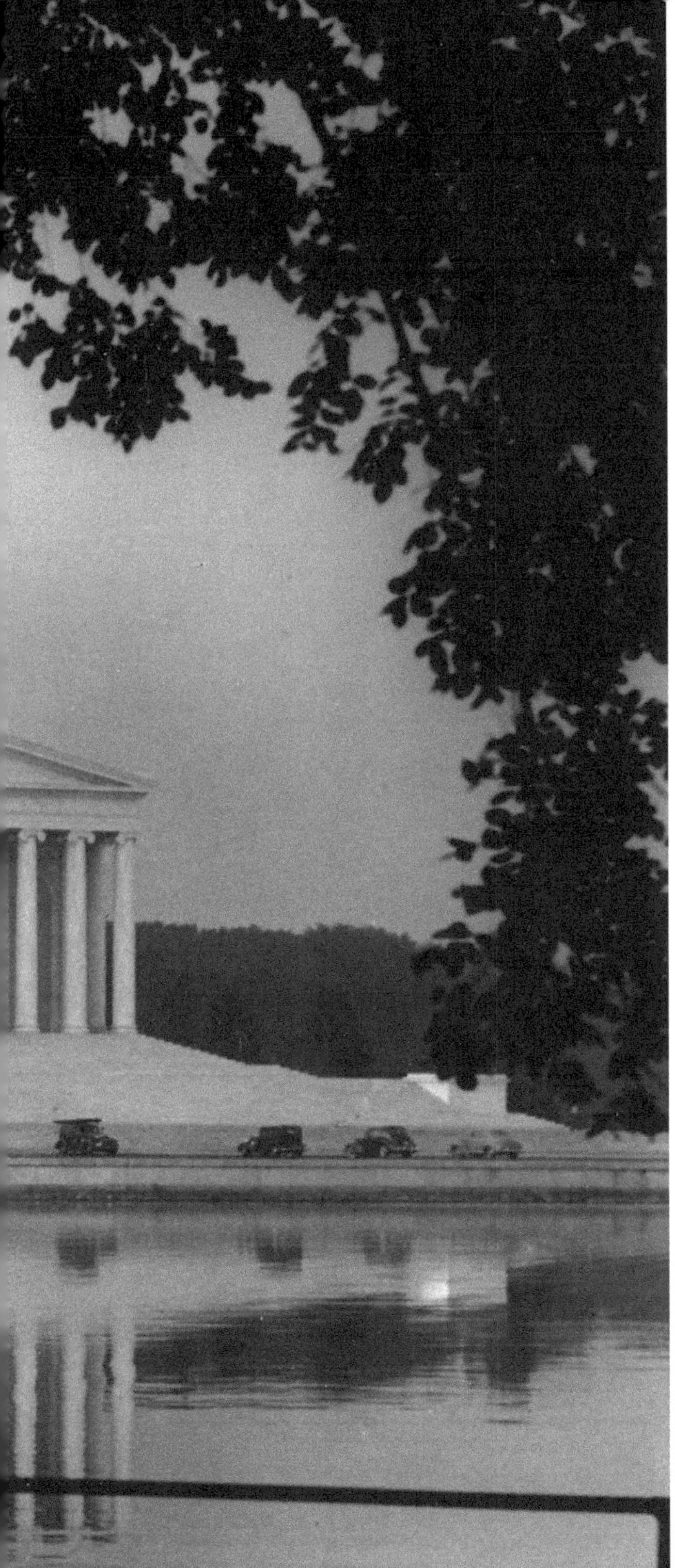

On April 17, 1943, this photograph of the Jefferson Memorial was shot from the northwest.

Pomp, circumstance, and massive crowds characterize this scene on April 13, 1943, the day the Jefferson Memorial was dedicated.

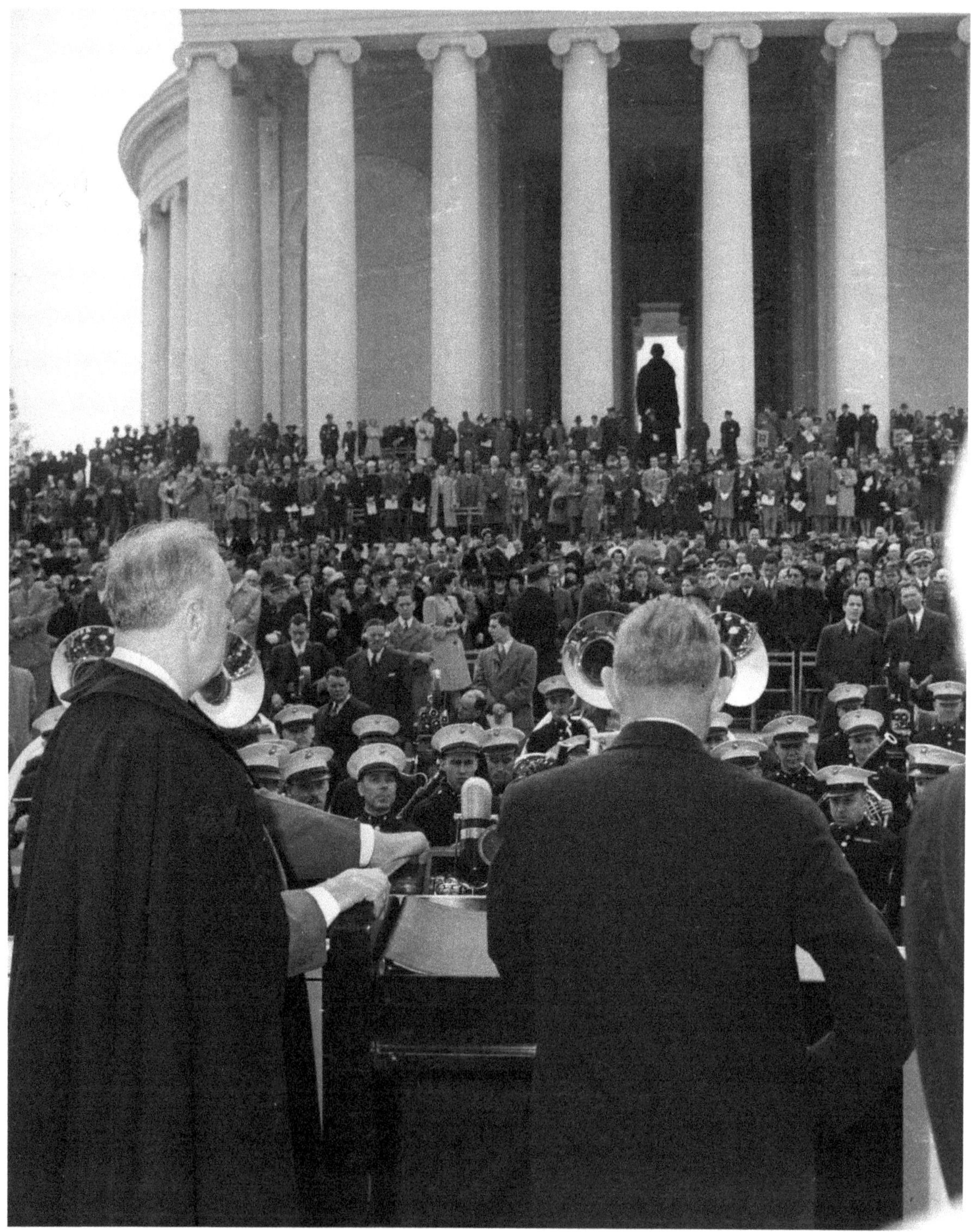

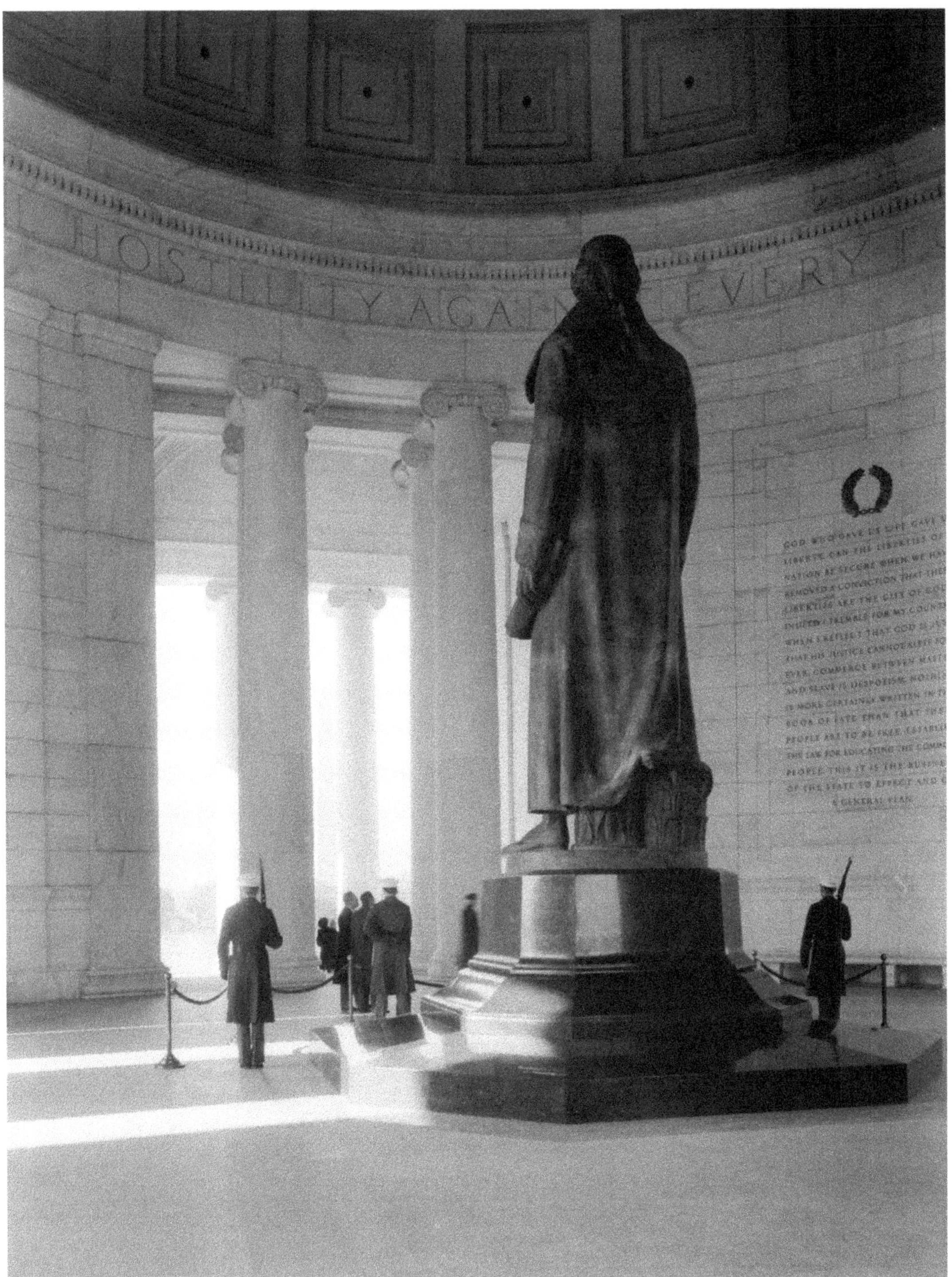

Guards flank Jefferson's statue inside the memorial rotunda, a few days after dedication ceremonies in 1943.

A night view of the Jefferson Memorial interior is as breathtaking today as it was in 1943. The 19-foot-high, 5-ton bronze statue looks toward the White House. Rudolph Evans was the sculptor.

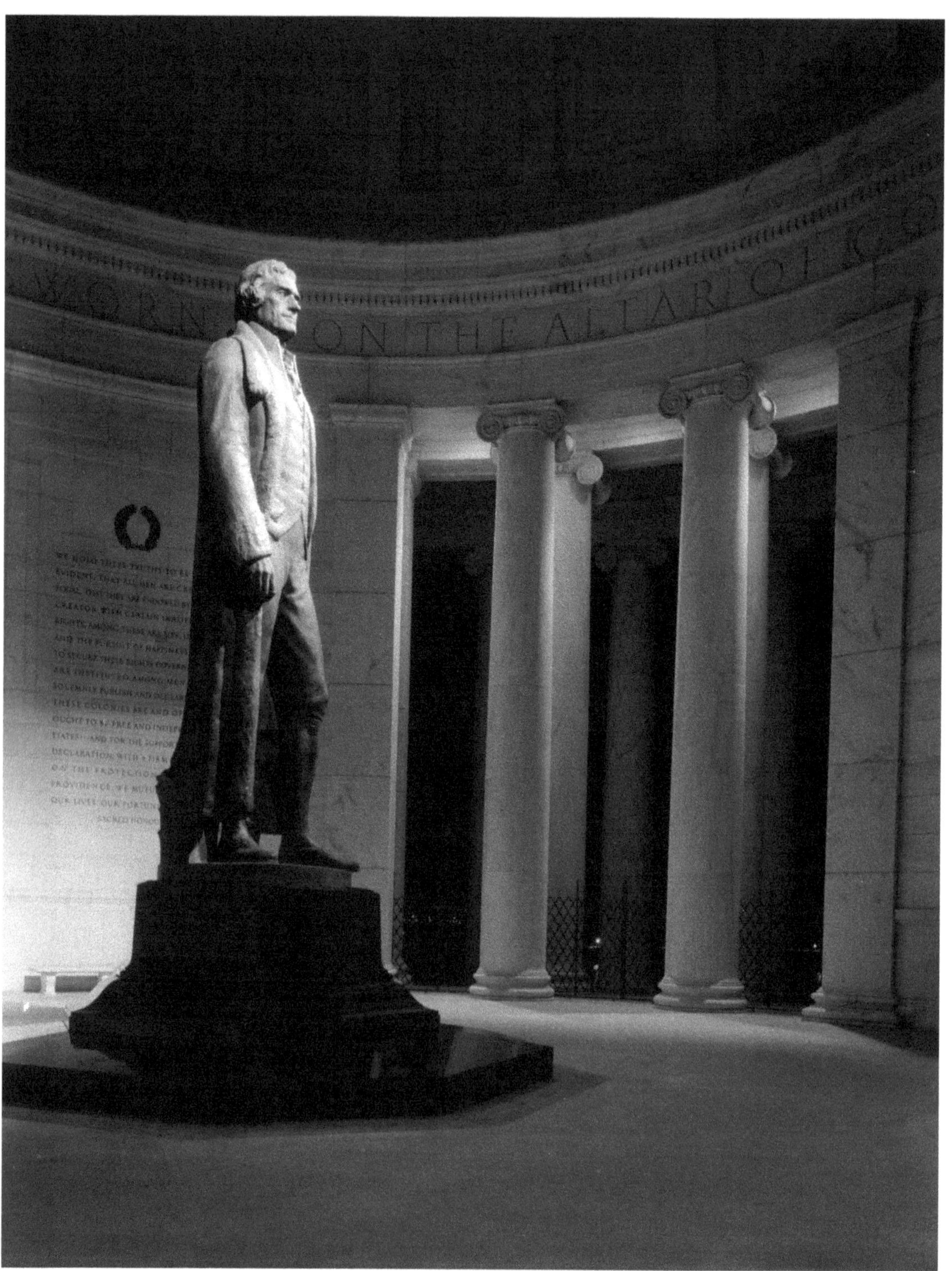

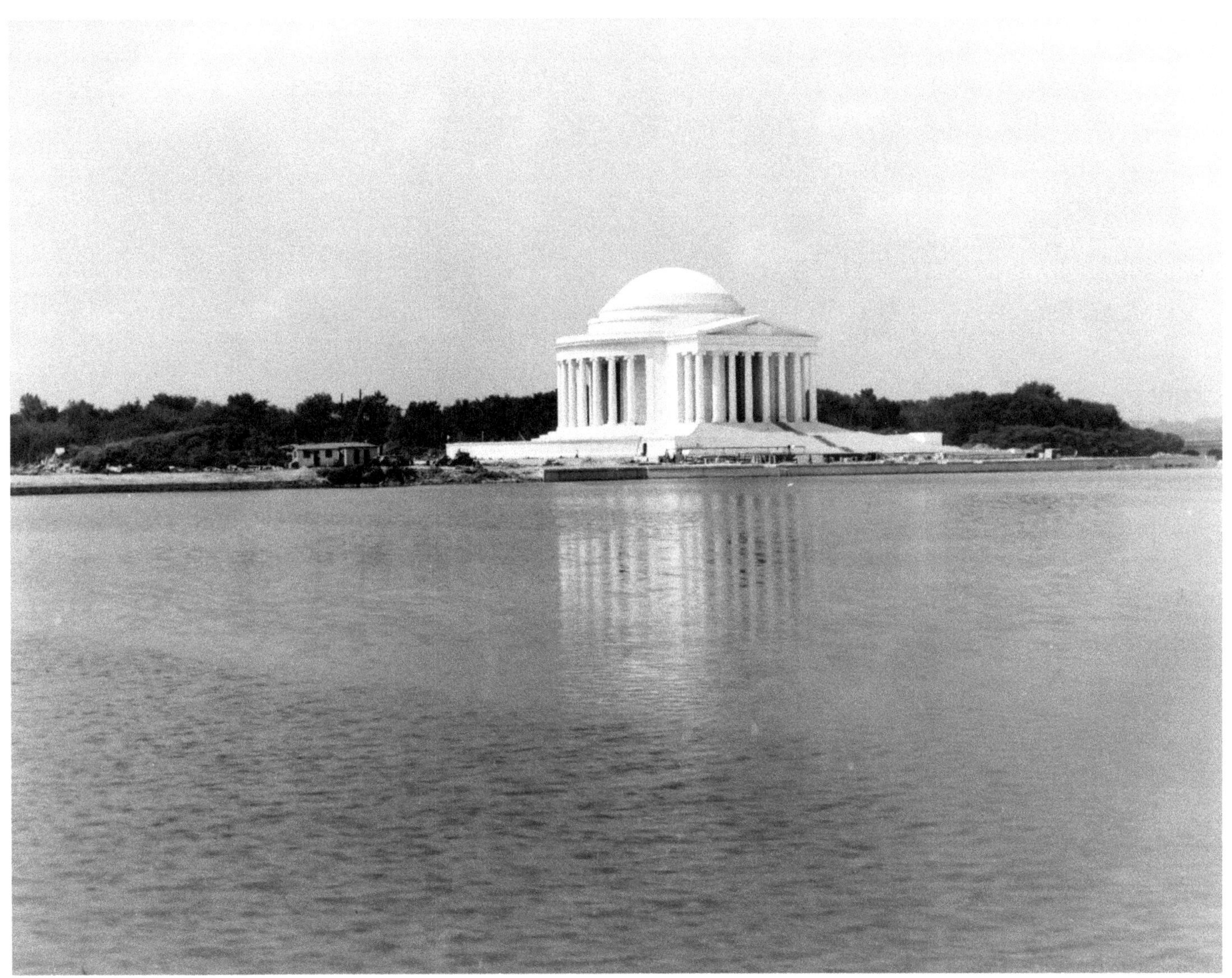

After John Russell Pope died of cancer in his home state of New York in 1937, architects continued to move forward with his monumental vision. Daniel P. Higgins and Otto R. Eggers stepped in and completed the project. Here, the Jefferson Memorial's reflection is cast upon the Potomac River.

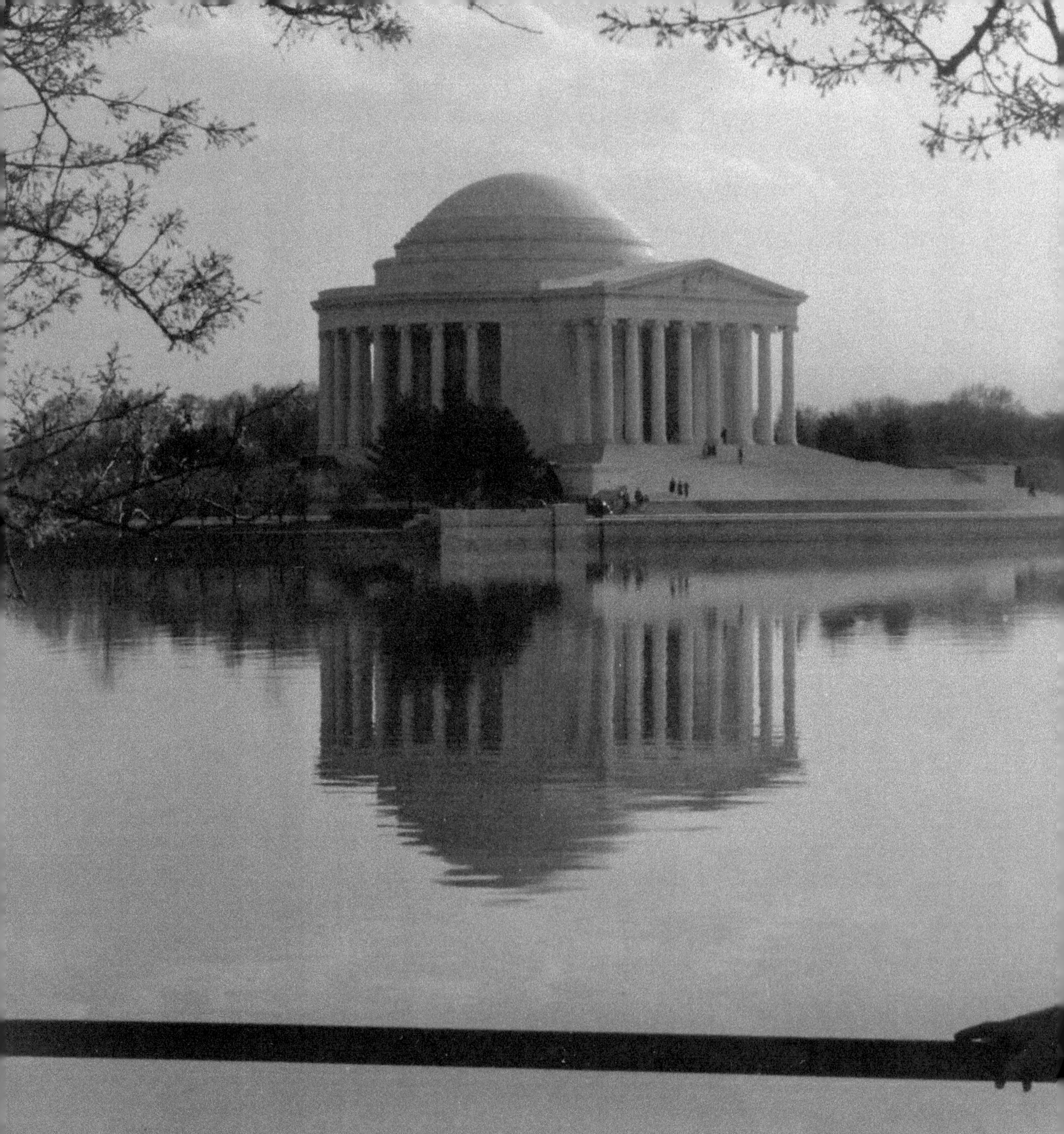

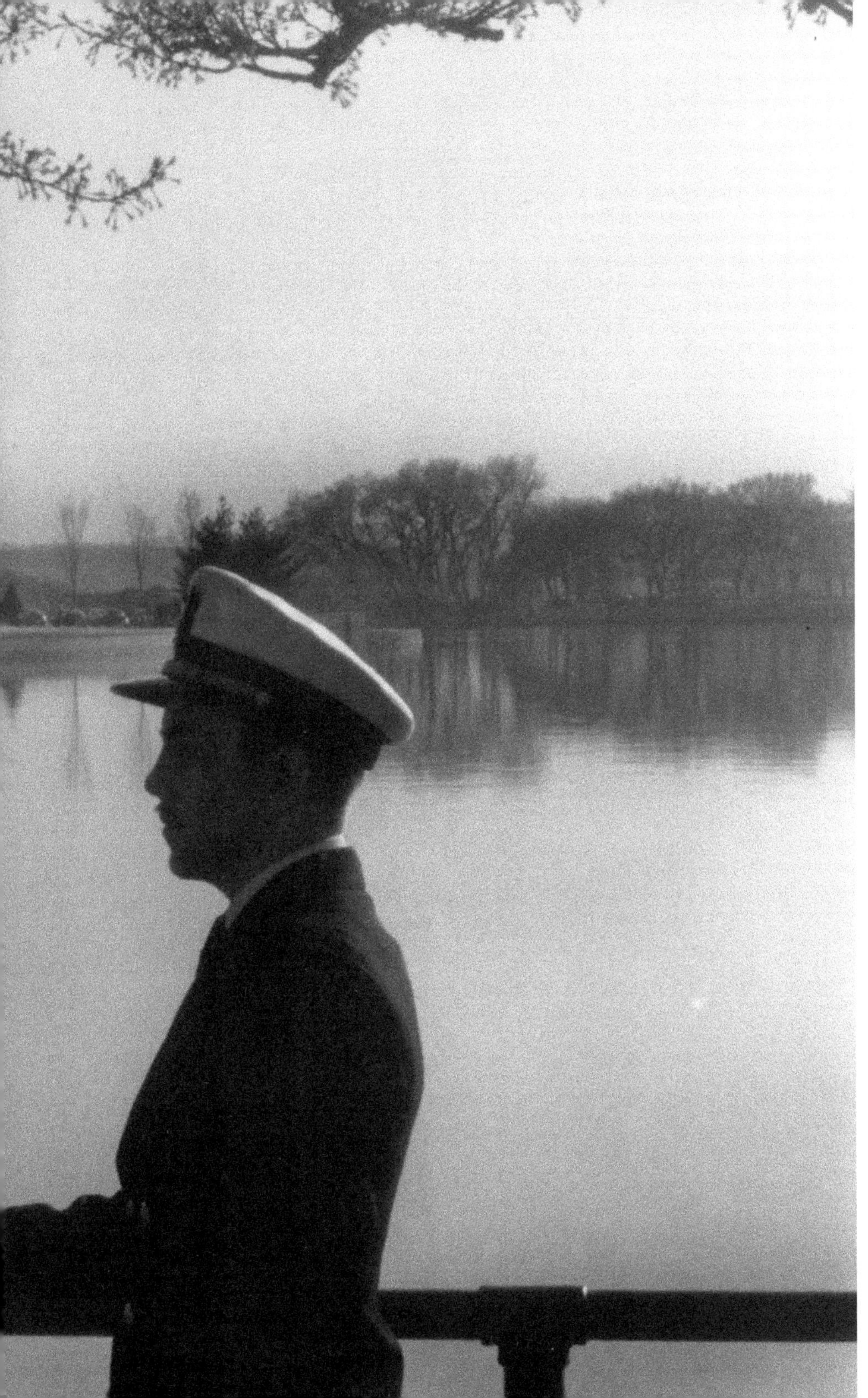

One service member poses here in spring of 1943, with the Jefferson Memorial and its reflection in the Potomac composing the image's background.

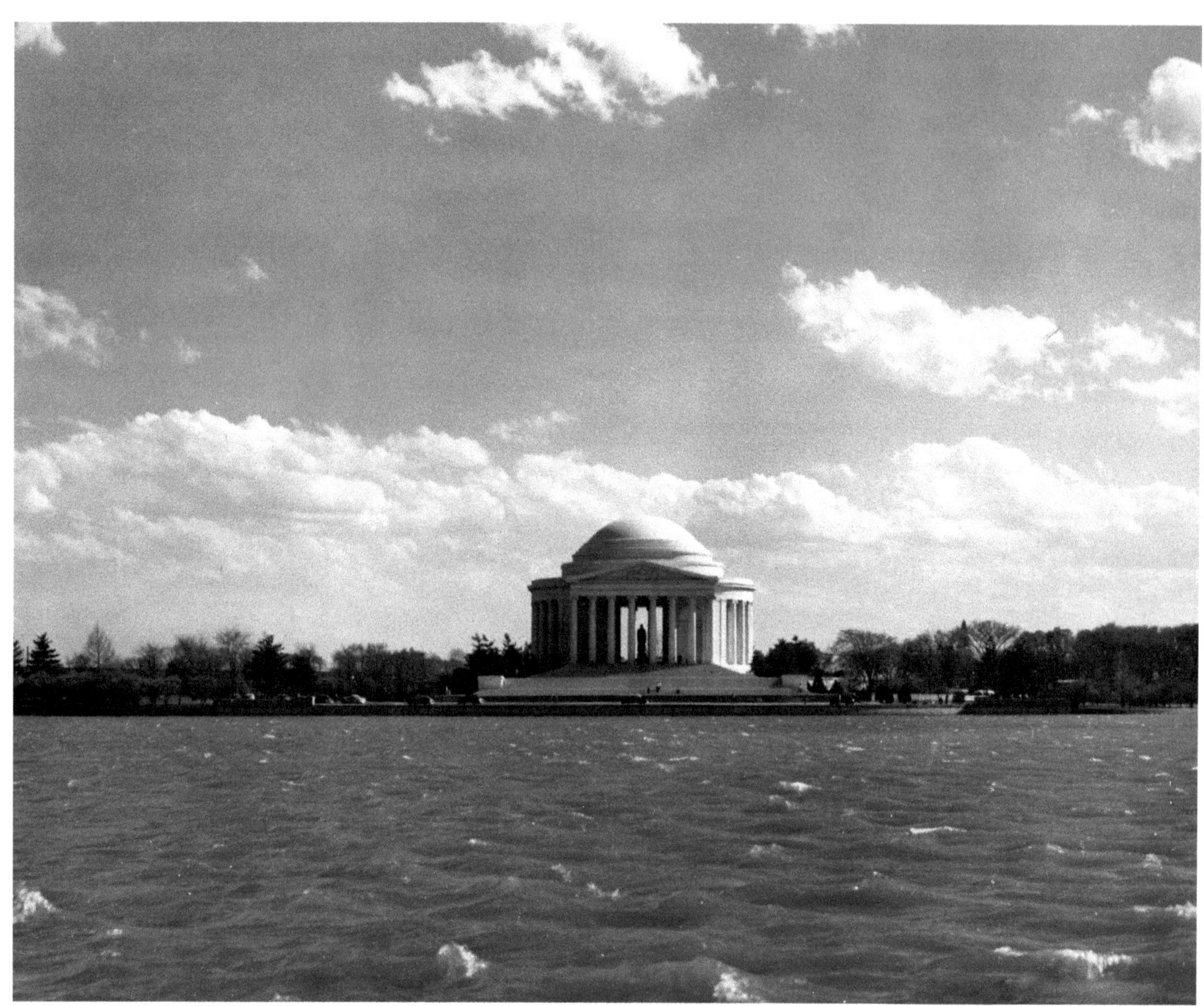

The Jefferson Memorial provides a backdrop for the choppy waters of the Potomac River.

Inside the Jefferson Memorial, a gentleman in period dress portrays Thomas Jefferson as he stands beside the statue bearing the third president's likeness. The inscription on the wall is taken from a letter Jefferson wrote to historian Samuel Kercheval.

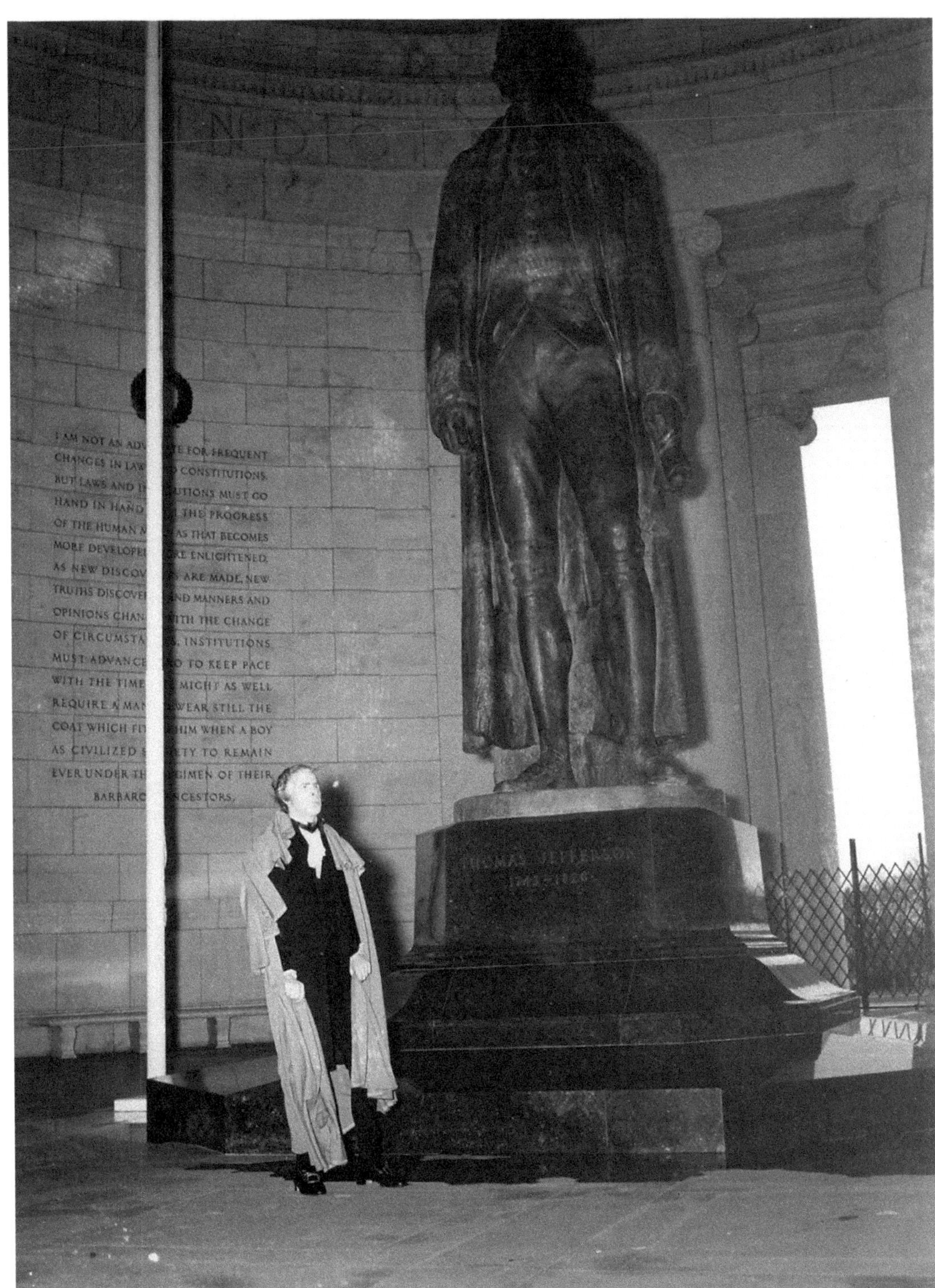

Revolutionary War reenactors stand guard at the Jefferson Memorial while members of the modern-day military stand watch near the statue of Thomas Jefferson. The Revolutionary War began in 1775. Thomas Jefferson authored the Declaration of Independence, and it was ratified by Congress on July 4, 1776, putting King George III on notice that 13 American colonies were free from British rule.

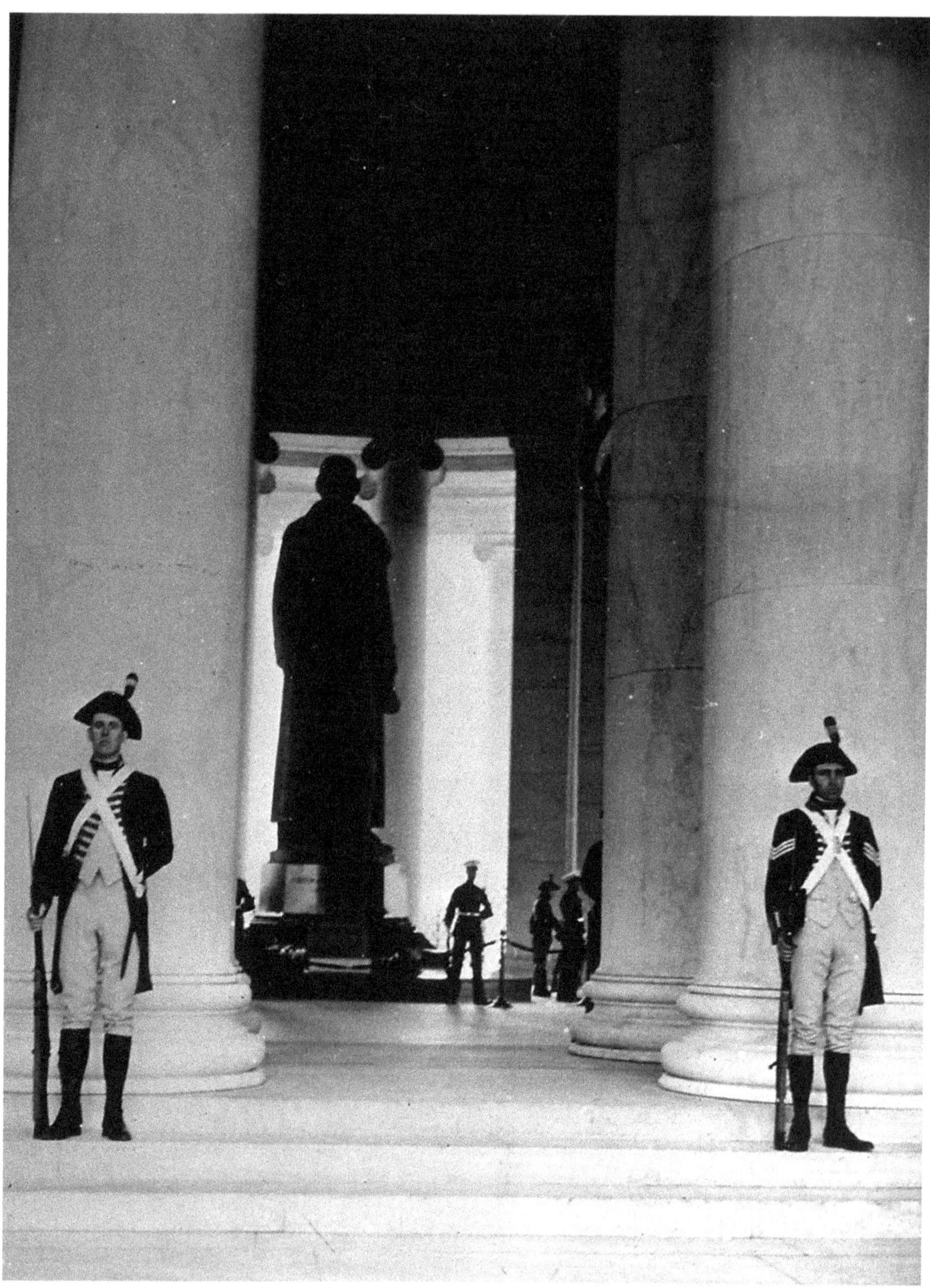

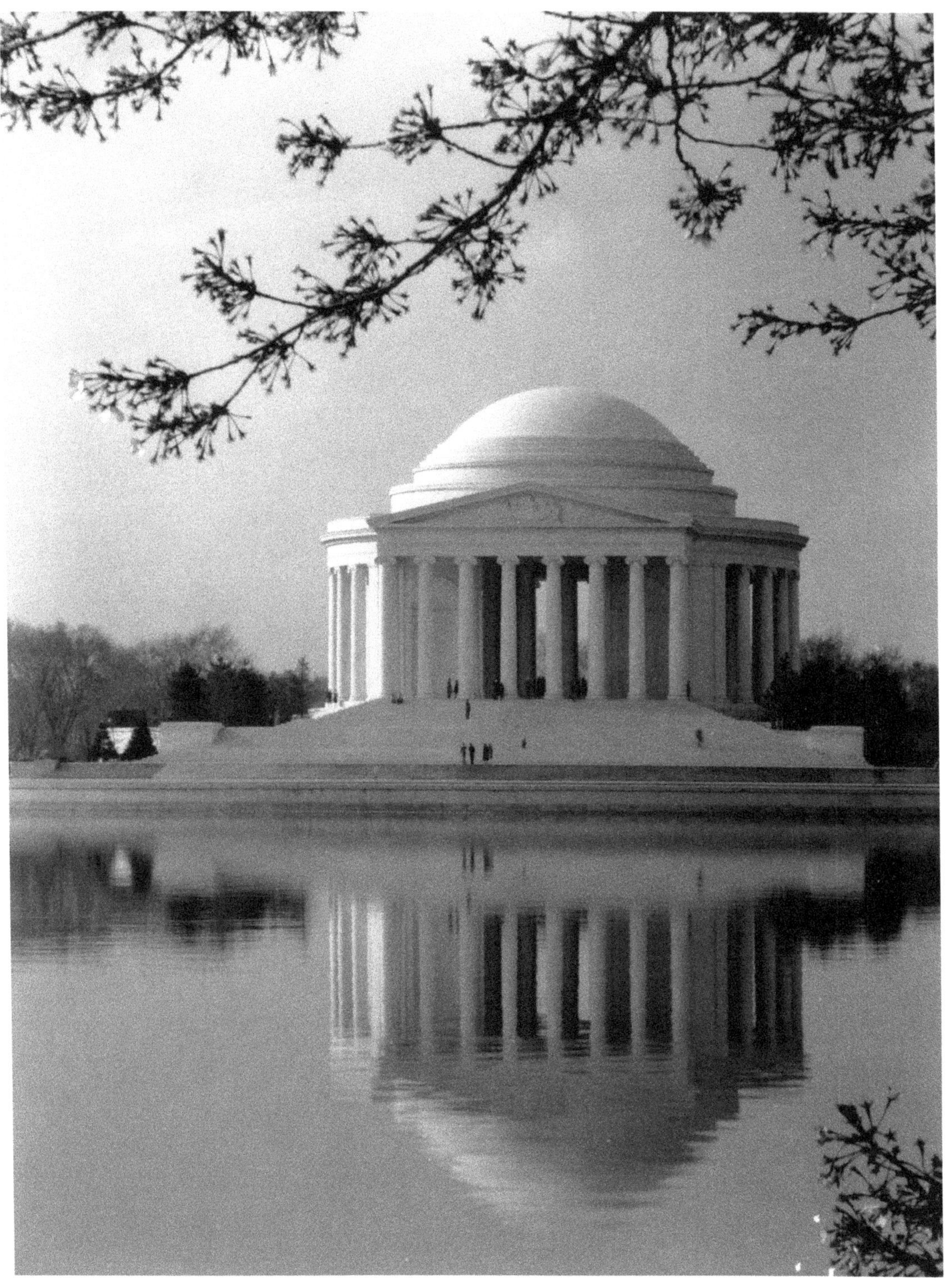

According to National Park Service records, some of the cherry blossom trees needed to be cleared in order to build the Jefferson Memorial. This caused quite a stir among preservationists in 1938. In fact, a group of women chained themselves together near the trees to try to stop the workers from clearing the memorial site. The removed trees were replaced on the south of the Tidal Basin to complement the Jefferson Memorial.

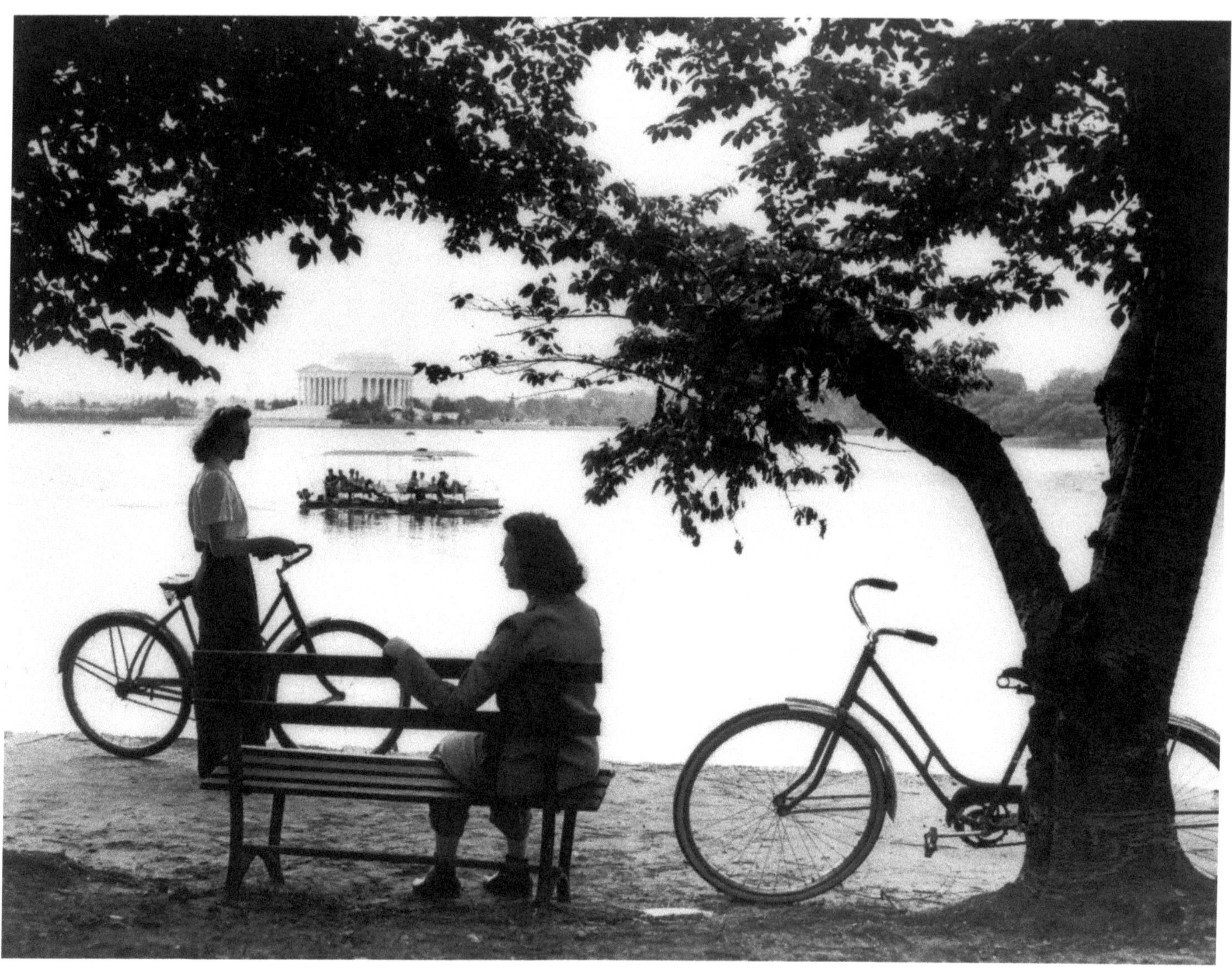

On May 13, 1945, these two young women take a break from cycling near the Tidal Basin. Boaters and the Jefferson Memorial can be seen in the distance. That same year World War II ended.

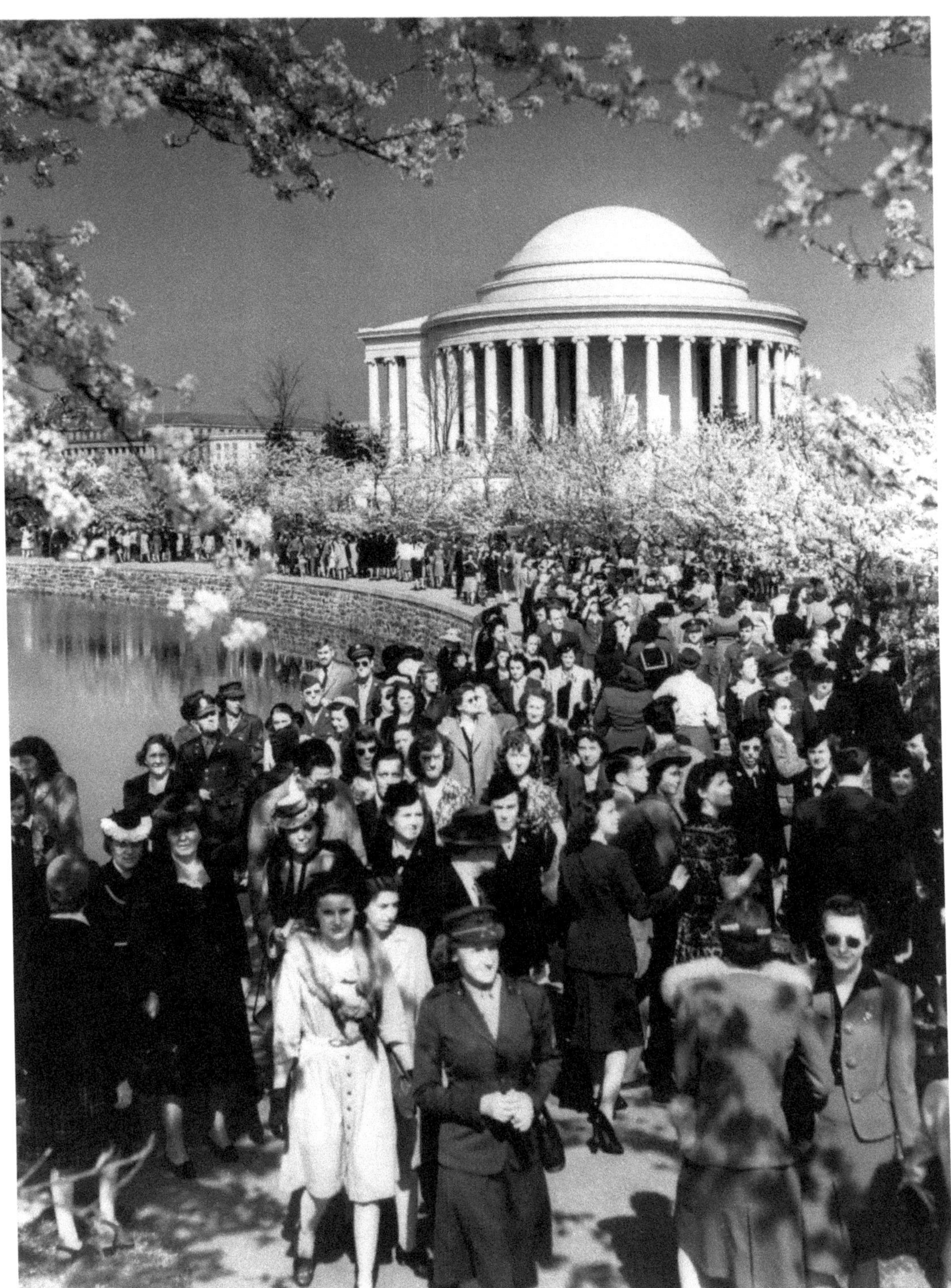

This was the scene near the Jefferson Memorial on March 25, 1945, as visitors flooded the Tidal Basin in an effort to view the cherry blossoms.

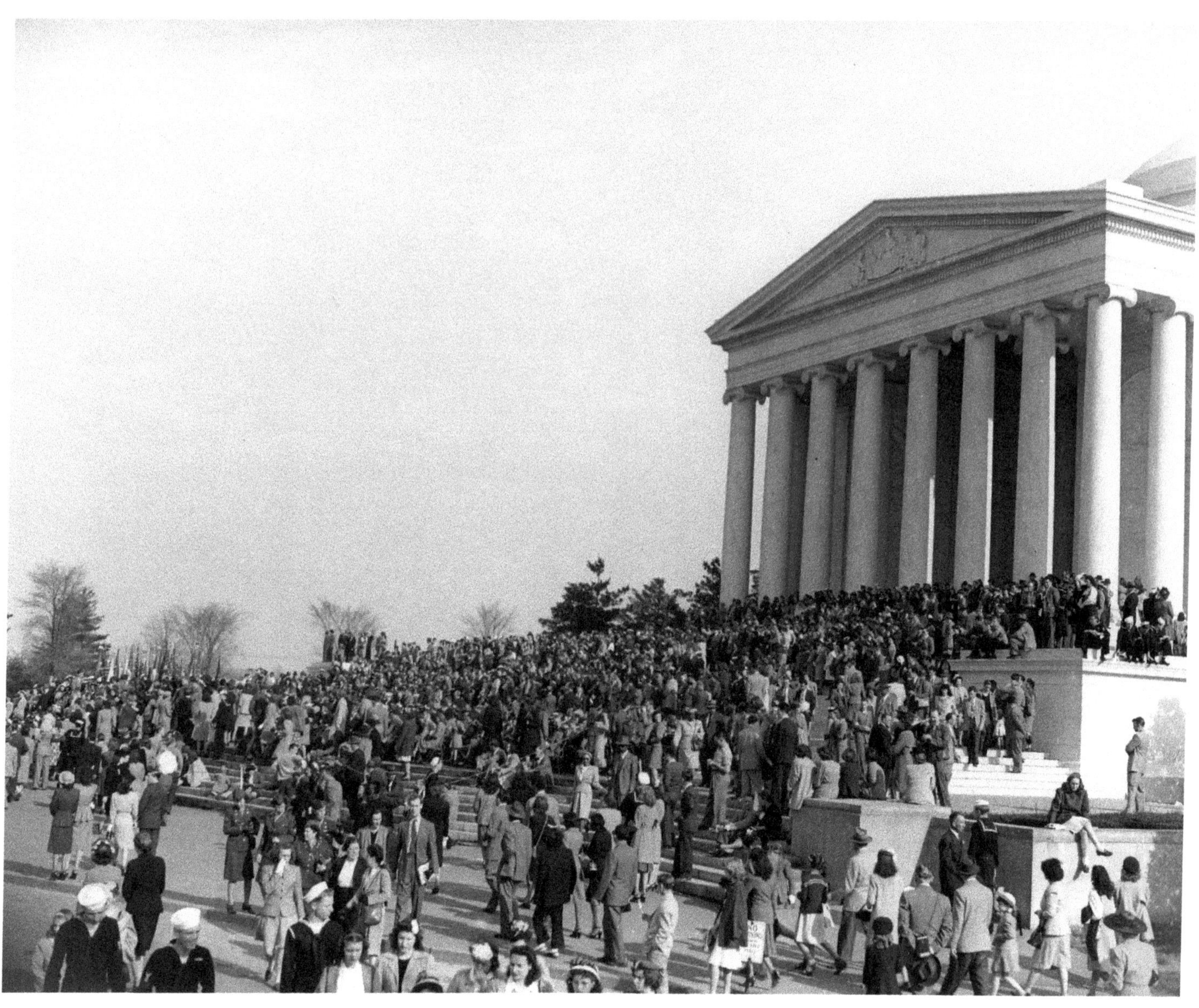

This 1940s photograph captures military men and women as well as other visitors gathering on the steps of the Jefferson Memorial.

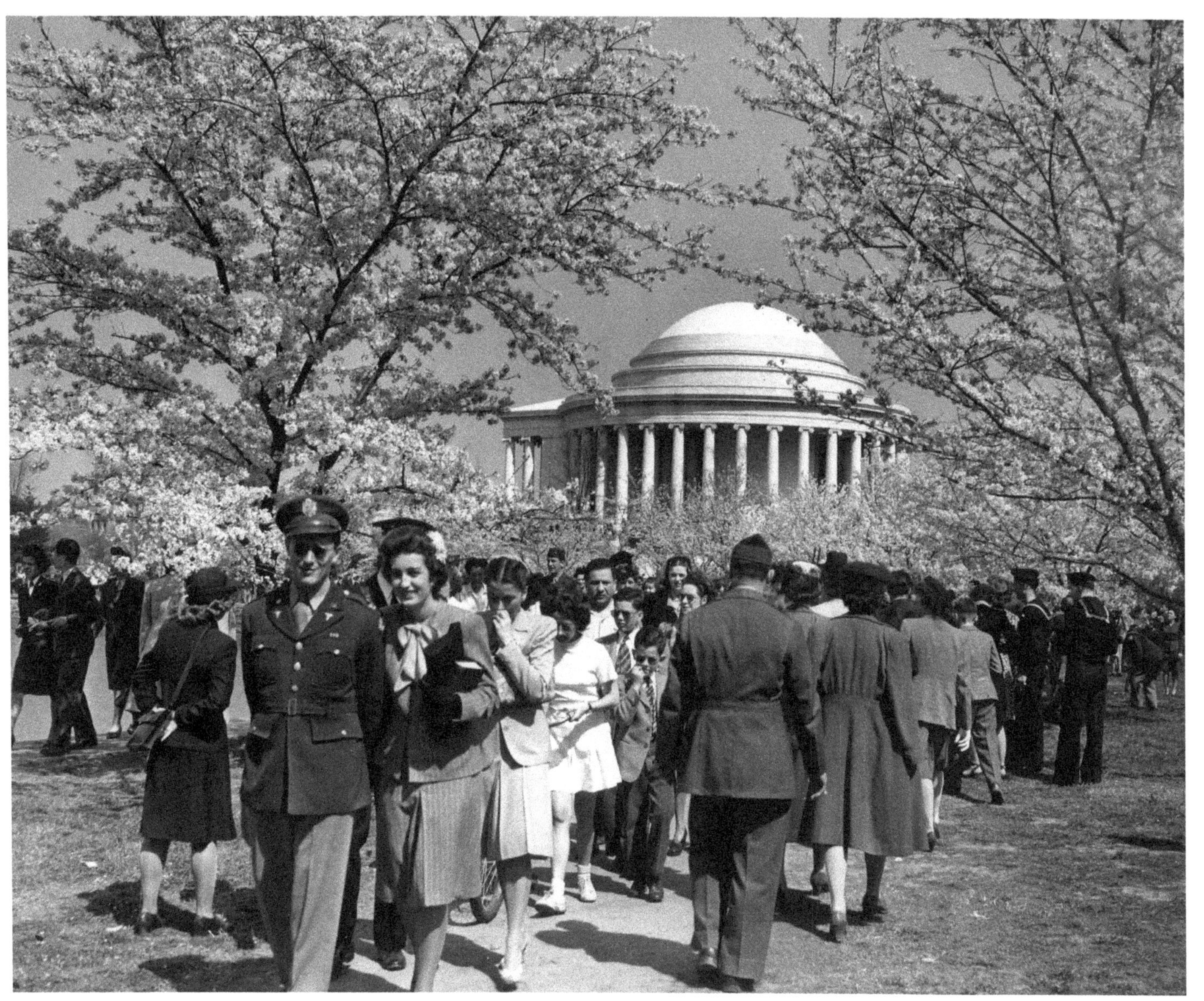

Visitors, including several service members, enjoy the cherry blossoms along the Tidal Basin.

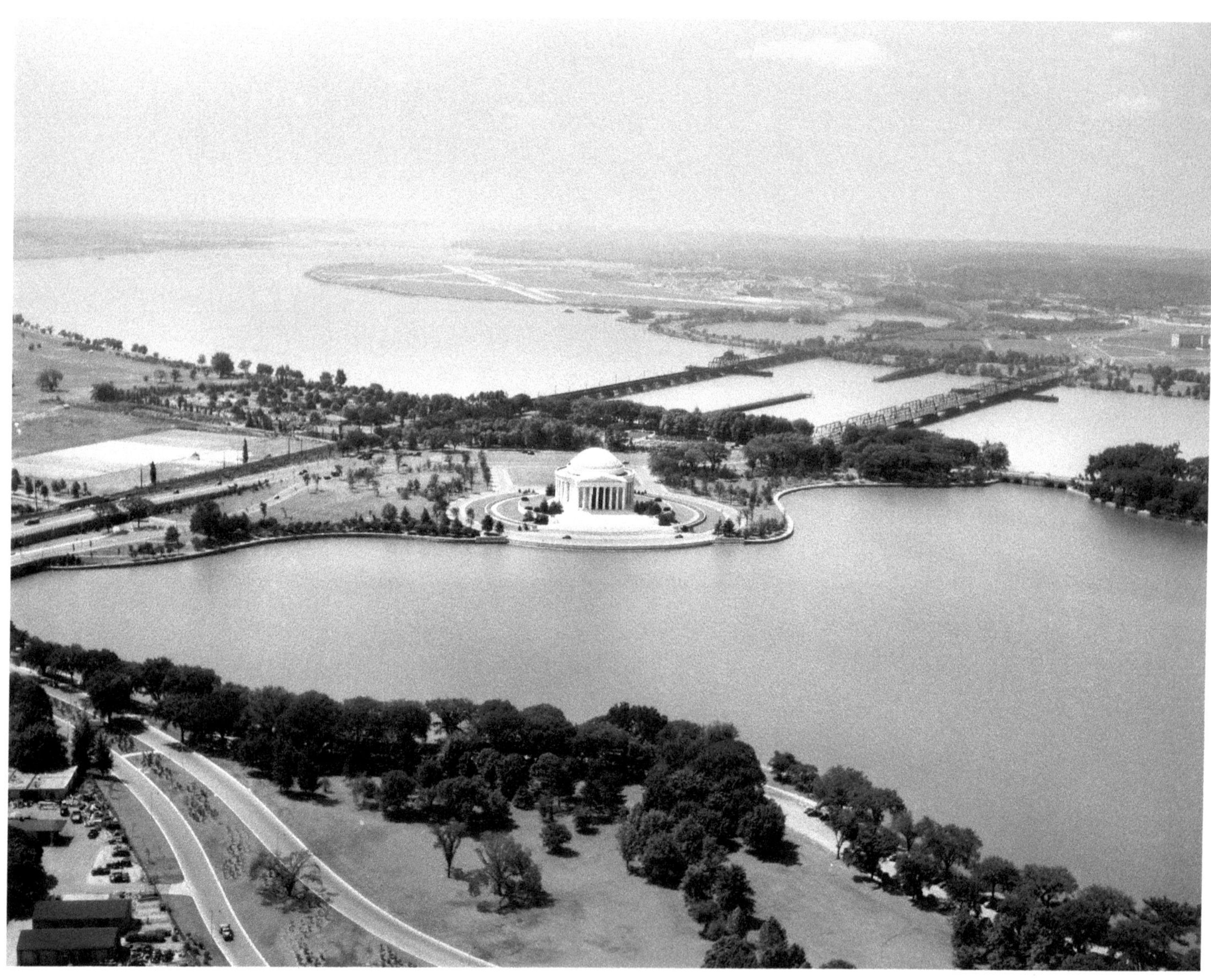

Situated at the southernmost edge of the Potomac River Tidal Basin, the Jefferson Memorial rests south of the White House. Pictured is a bird's-eye view of the Jefferson Memorial taken in 1945 from the Washington Monument.

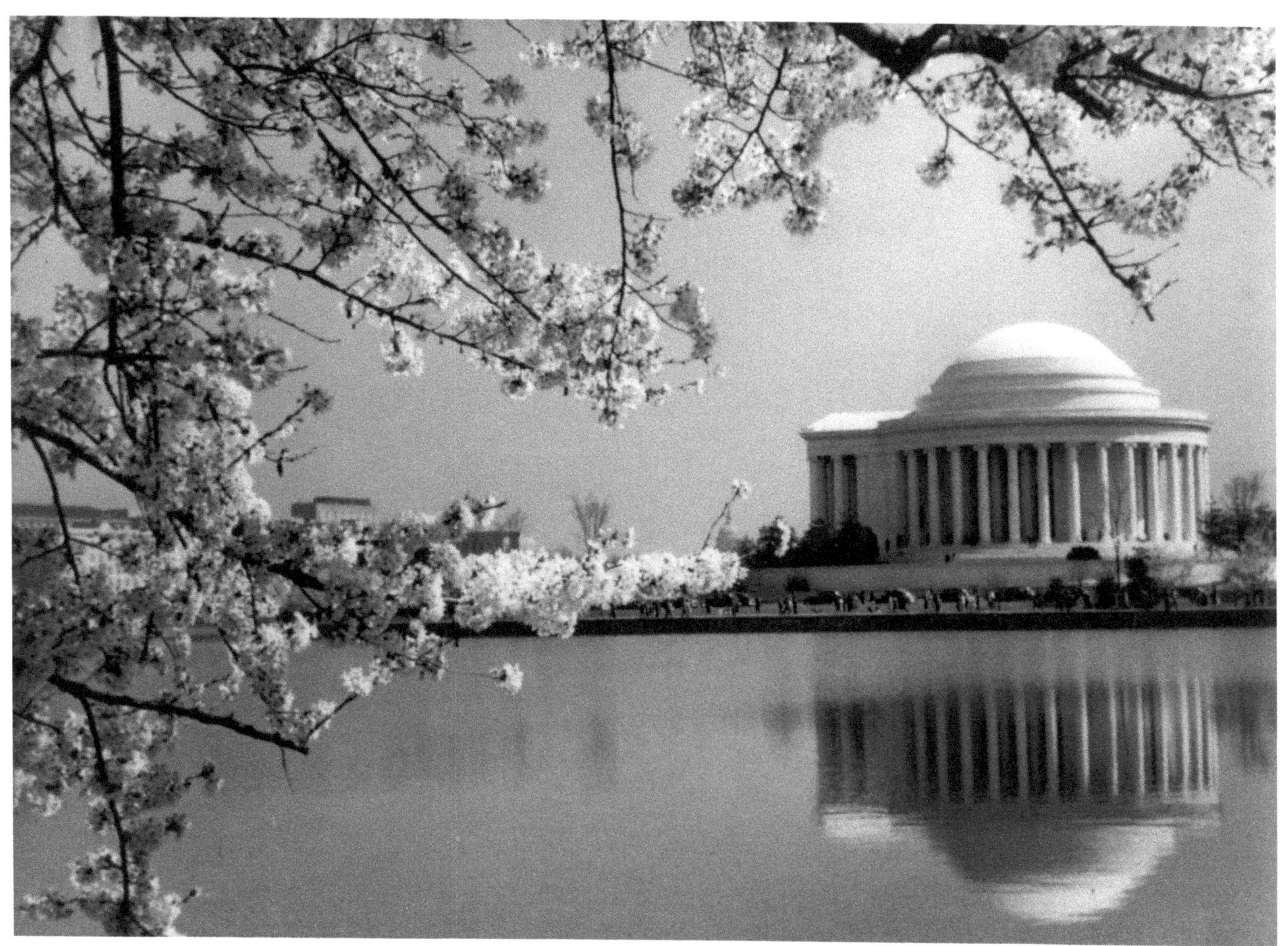

On Valentine's Day in 1912, the SS *Awa Maru* transported 3,020 cherry blossom trees from Yokohama, Japan. The ship docked in Seattle, Washington, and the trees were then delivered by train to Washington, D.C.

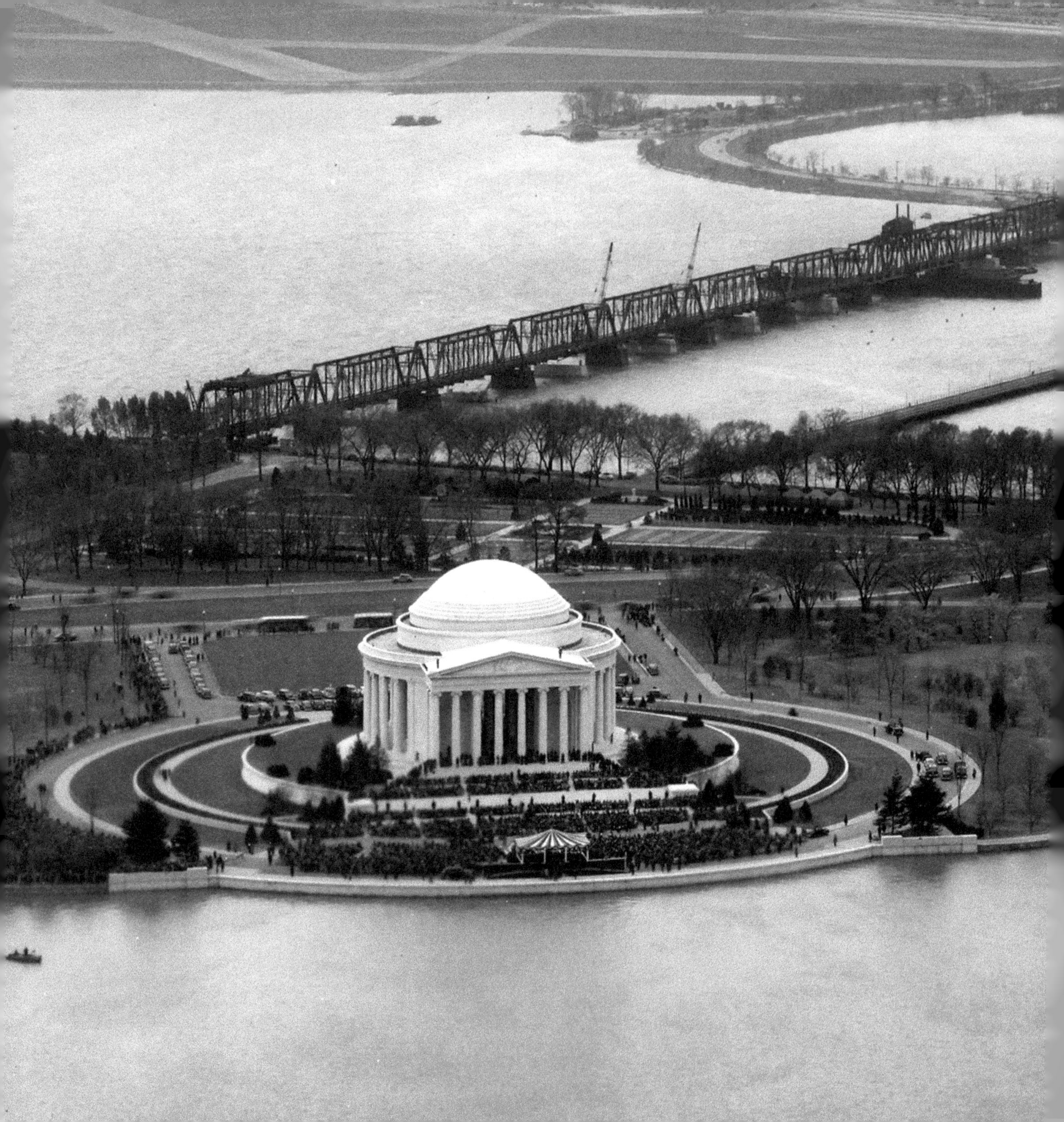

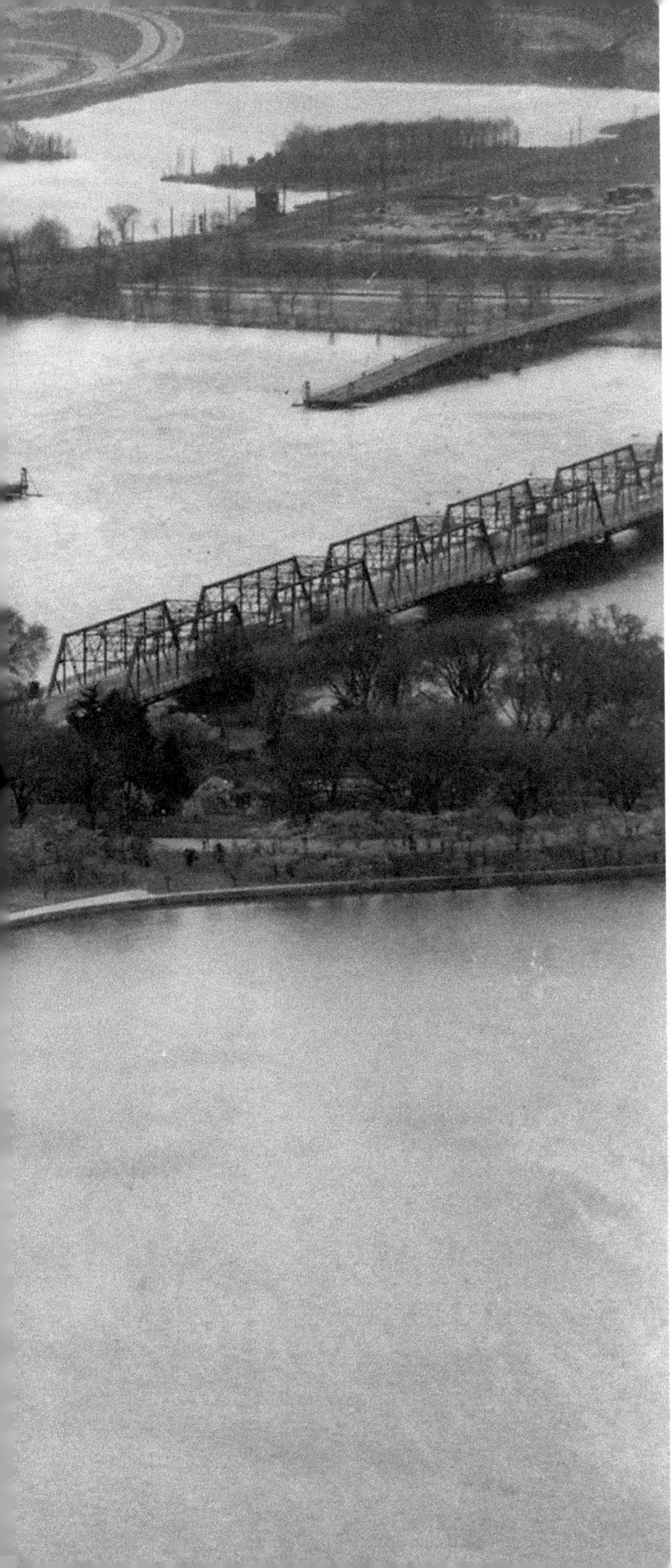

Eighteen acres constituting the Jefferson Memorial site, as well as views of the Potomac River Tidal Basin and Virginia, are pictured in this photo taken by the Department of Defense on June 11, 1953. Ten days later, John F. Kennedy and Jacqueline Bouvier were engaged. They married in September of 1953, becoming president and first lady eight years later.

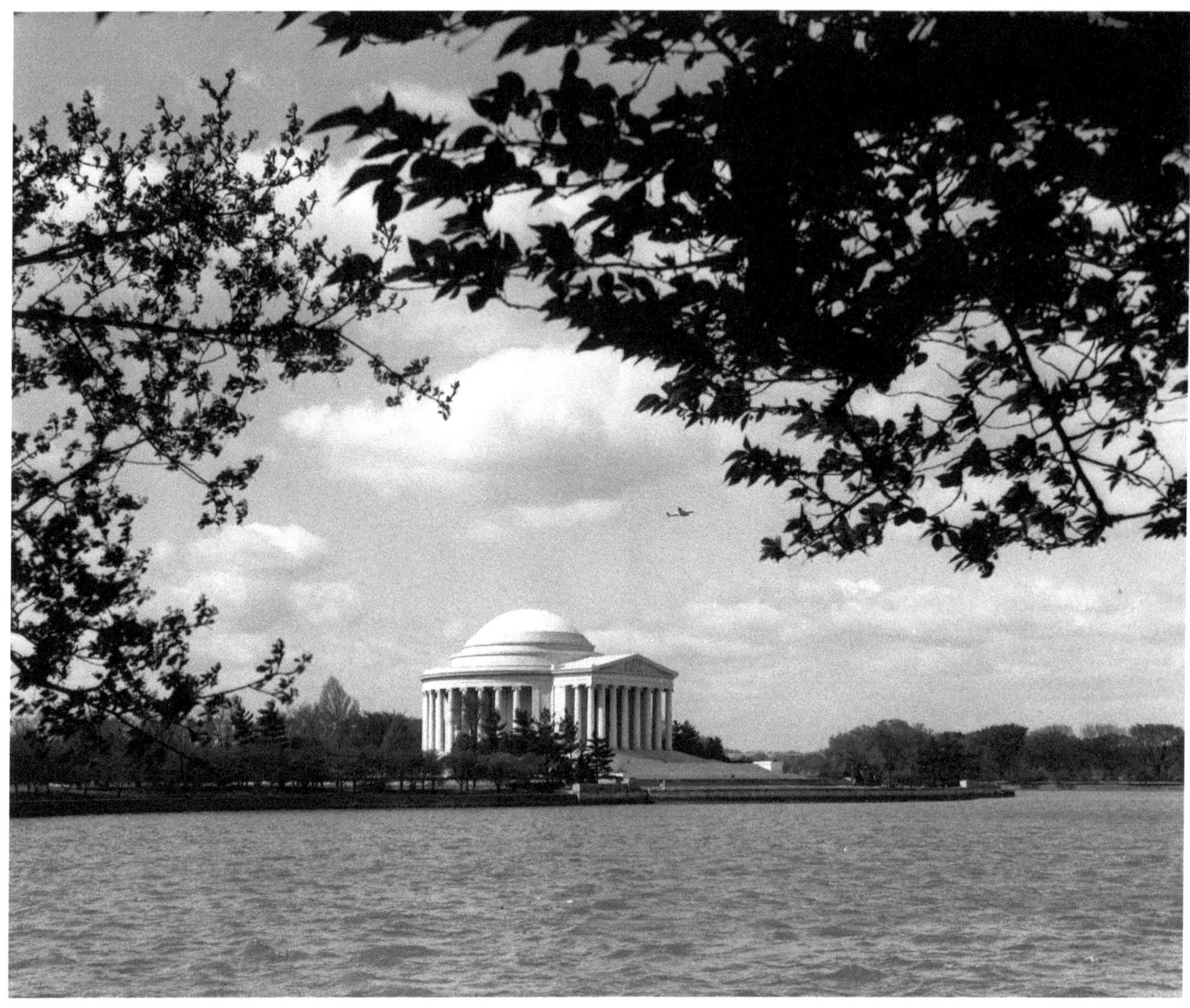

There's nothing better on a clear day than to rent a paddle boat and take it to the edge of the Jefferson Memorial, a time-honored Washington, D.C., pastime.

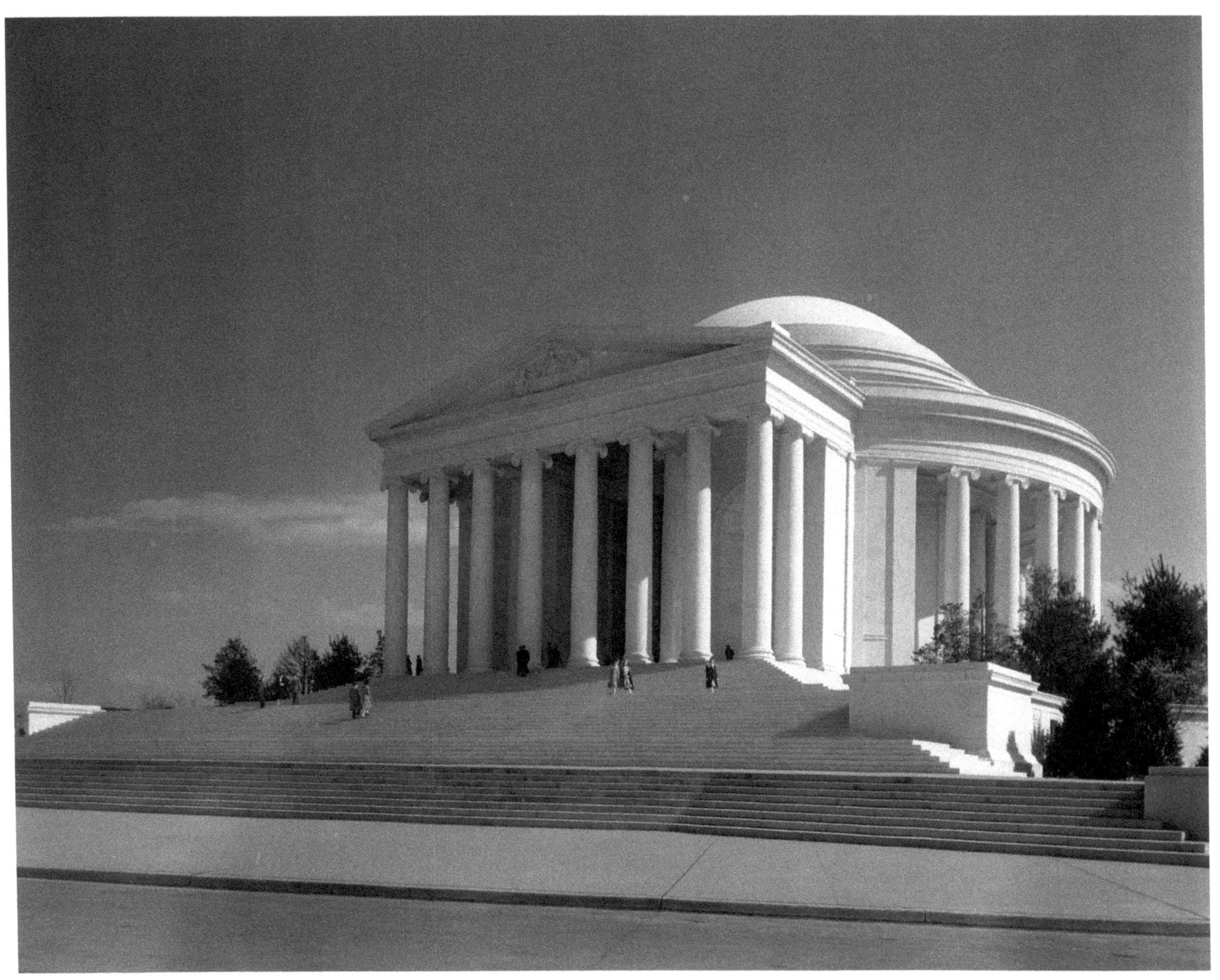

This impressive photograph of the Jefferson Memorial facade was taken from the northwest in 1943. The statue of Thomas Jefferson, originally plaster, would be replaced with a bronze statue after World War II.

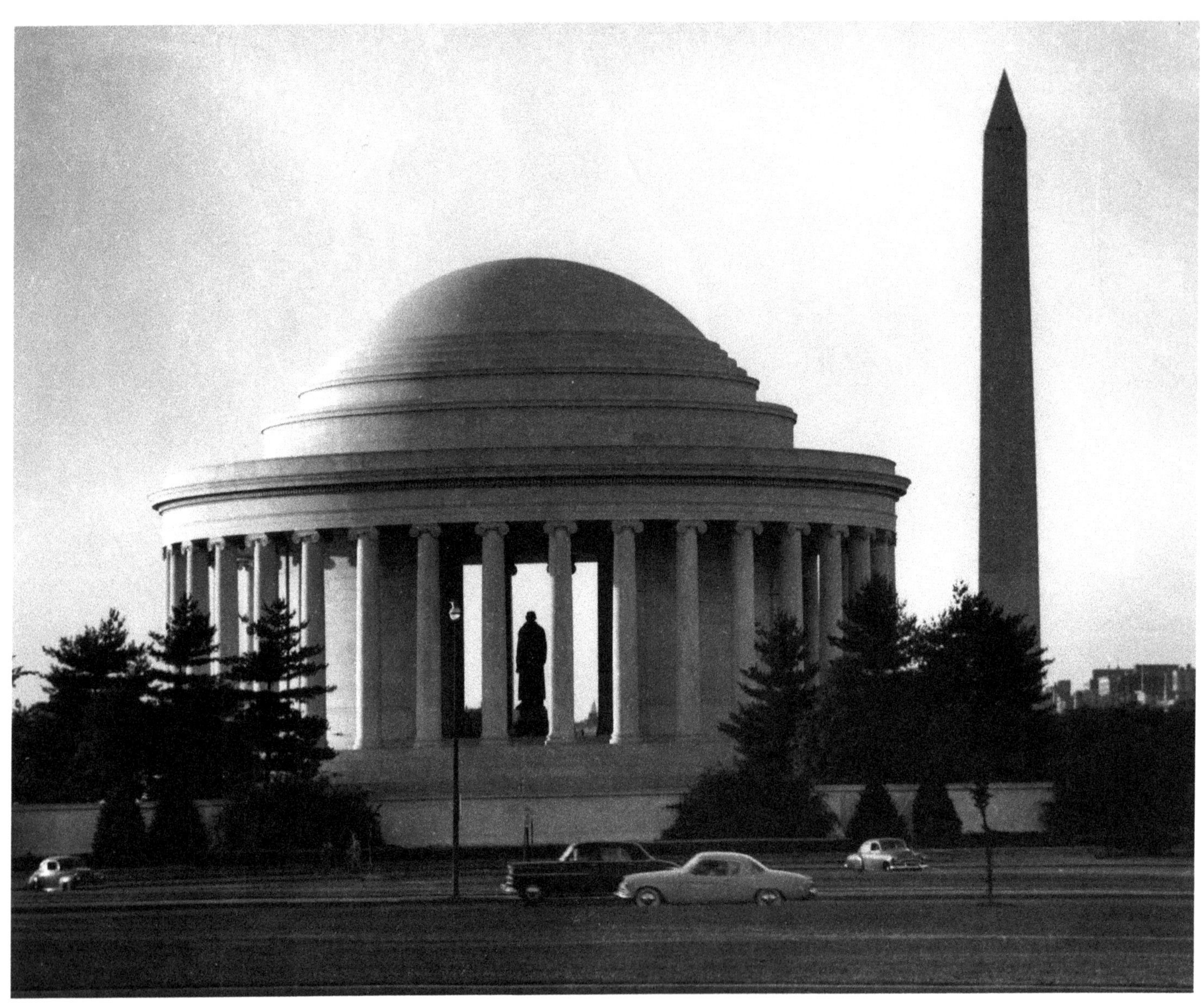

Side by side: The Jefferson Memorial and Washington Monument dominate this image. The Jefferson statue is seen directly in the center of the memorial columns.

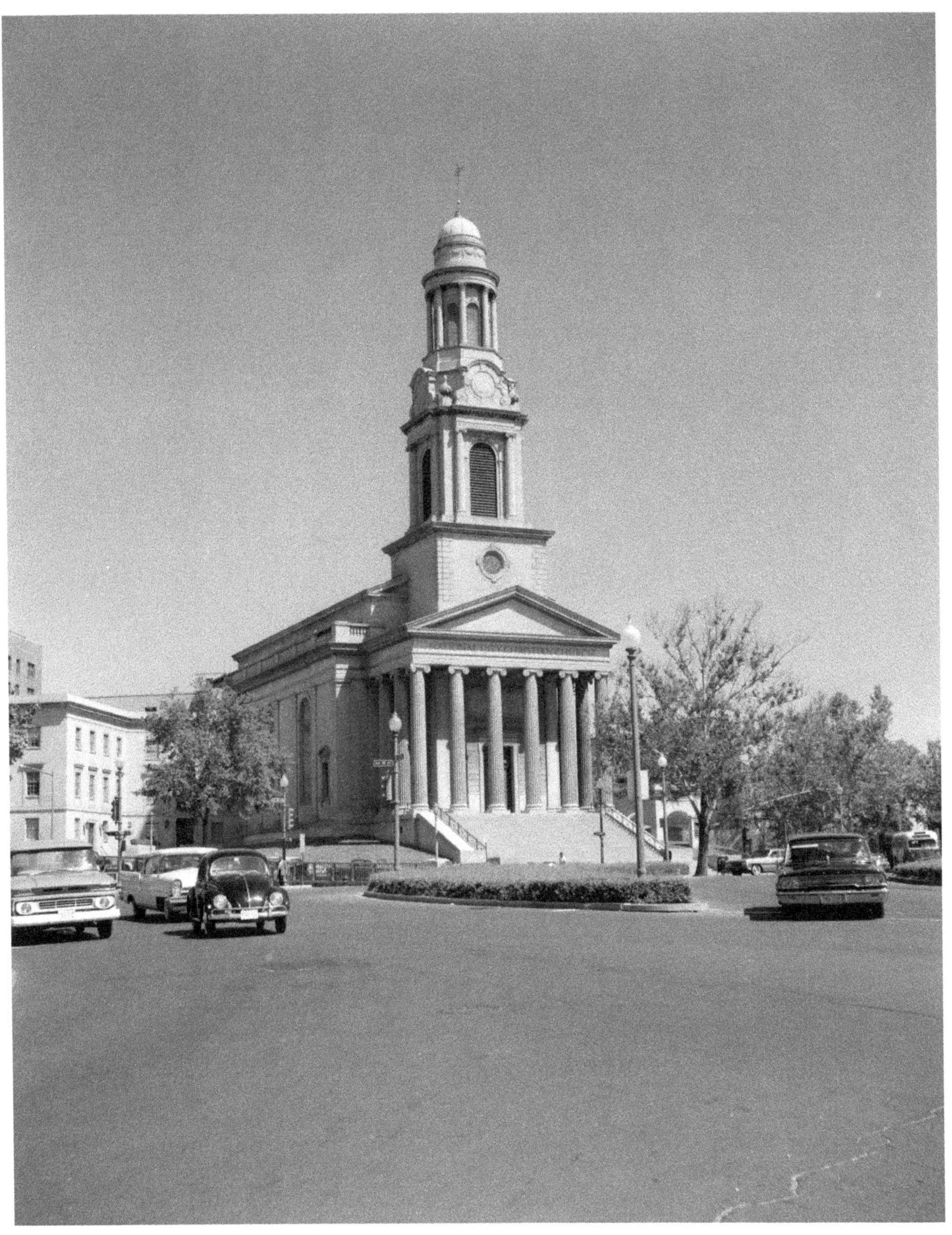

Pictured here is the National City Christian Church, designed by John Russell Pope. In 1919 Pastor Earle Wilfley appealed for donations to fund a new church building, and three Thomas Circle lots were purchased. By 1929 the National City Christian Church had acquired enough funding to break ground. The building was completed in 1930; however, the Great Depression would impair the parishioners' ability to honor their funding pledges.

This photograph of the interior offers a closer view of the marble used in the construction of the Jefferson Memorial. The domed ceiling is an etched geometric design. Visible behind Jefferson's statue are volutes, the spiral fixtures decorating the top of each column. In 1961 the effects of time set in, and one of the volutes cracked and needed to be restored. Similar damage happened again in 1990.

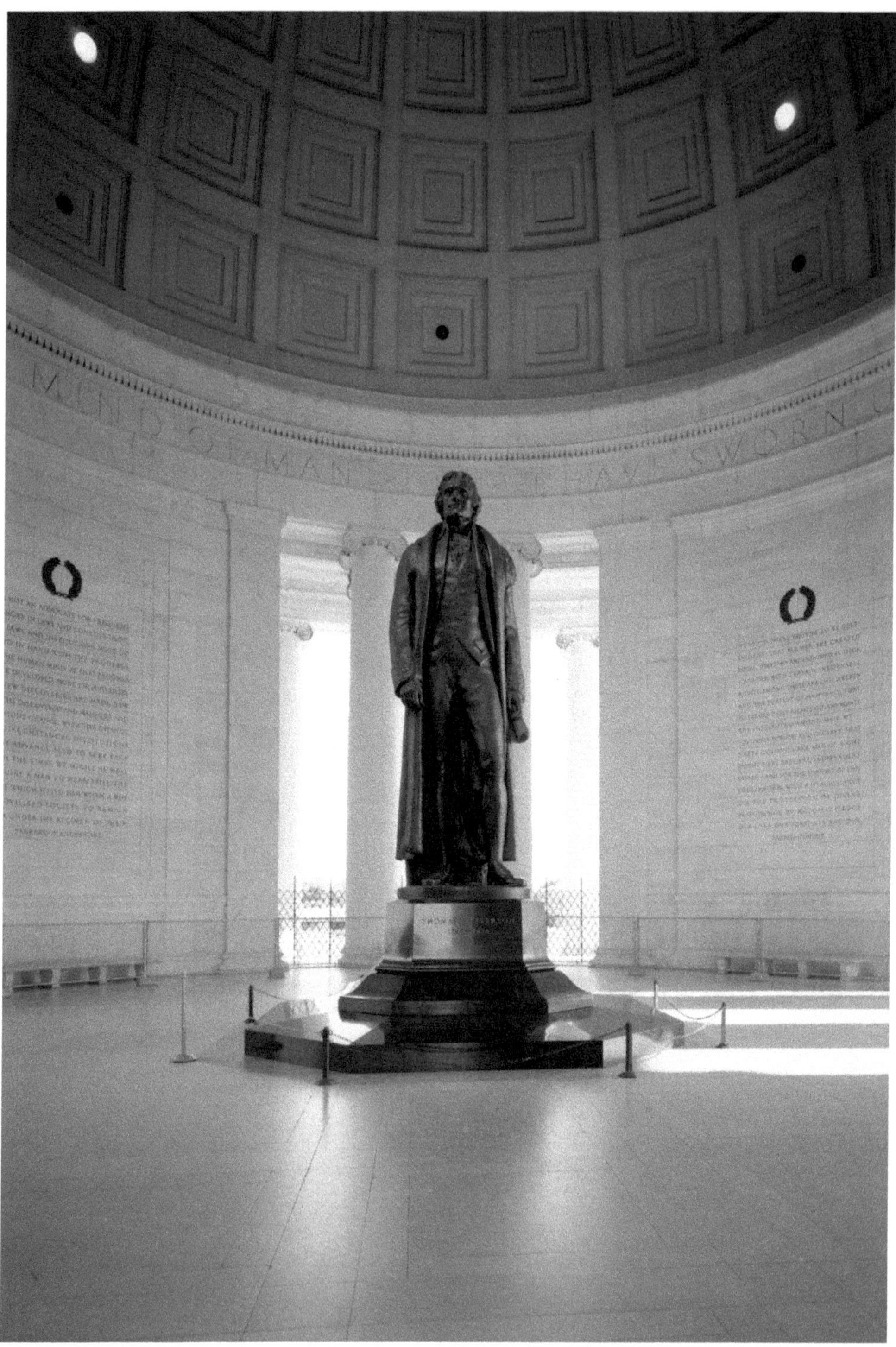

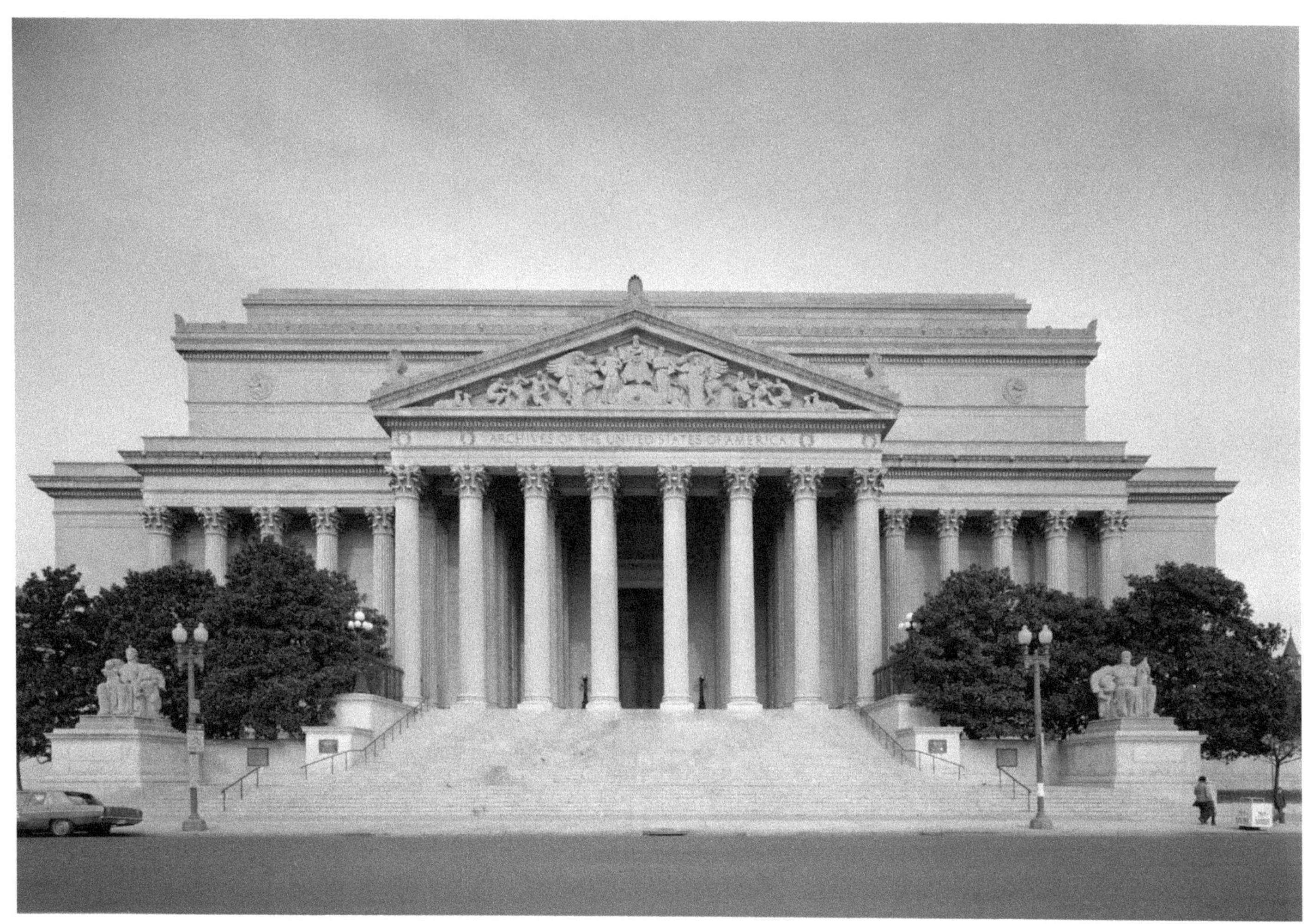

More than 9 billion pages of text, 20 million photos, and several hundred thousand reels of film are housed at the National Archives and Records Administration. The Declaration of Independence, United States Constitution, and Bill of Rights are among the records preserved there. As early as 1791, Thomas Jefferson talked about the need to have such a repository for documents: "Time and accident are committing daily havoc on the originals deposited in our public offices." More than a century later, John Russell Pope would become the architect for both the Jefferson Memorial and the National Archives, where the Declaration of Independence—which Jefferson authored—would be preserved.

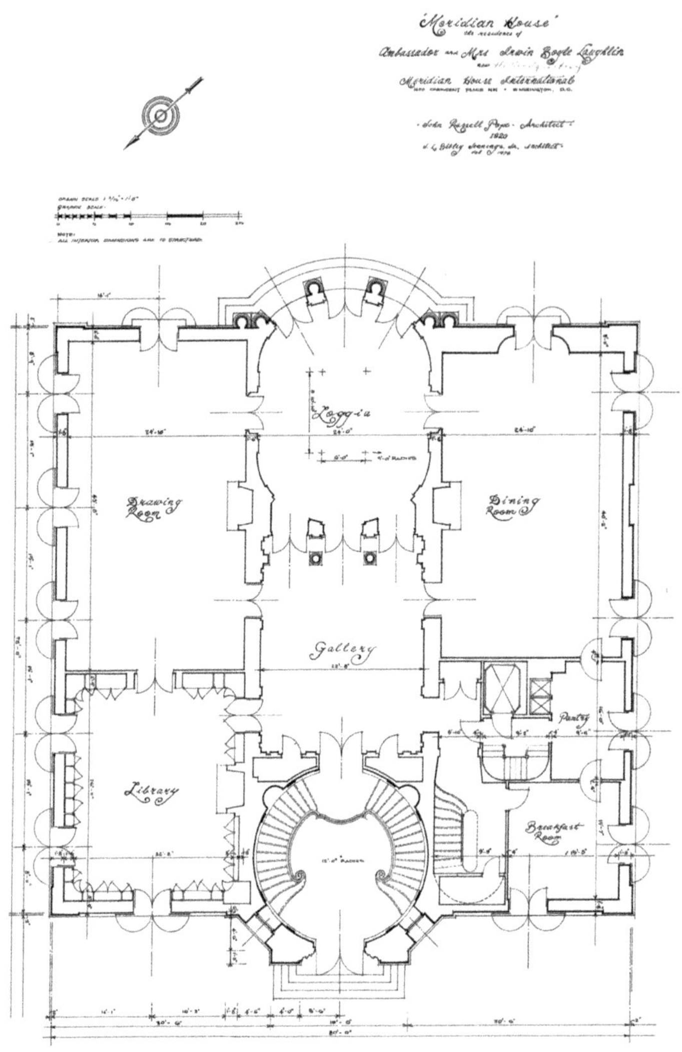

Pictured here is the floor plan of 1630 Crescent Place, designed by John Russell Pope and built by diplomatic ambassador Irwin Boyle Laughlin in 1919. The prominent family of Katherine Meyer Graham, publisher of the *Washington Post*, were the next owners of this property. Graham, then Katherine Meyer, grew up in this house, which is close to 16th Street and within walking distance of Meridian Hill Park and the historic Adams Morgan neighborhood. Added to the National Historic Register in 1973, Meridian House is now Meridian International Center, a nonprofit whose mission is to strengthen international understanding. Pope also designed the White-Meyer House located next door at 1624 Crescent Place.

THE LINCOLN MEMORIAL

(1911–1970)

In his design of the sixteenth president's memorial, architect Henry Bacon employed the use of Greek structural influence. Bacon's memorial is a departure from the Roman influence used by Jefferson Memorial architect John Russell Pope some years later. Instead, the Temple of Zeus is thought to have been Bacon's muse when he sketched plans for the Lincoln Memorial.

Constructed between 1914 and 1922, the nearly 100-foot-tall, 190-foot-long, and 119-foot-wide structure took eight years to build. Its 36 ornate columns, each 44 feet tall and 23 feet in circumference, represent the 36 states in the Union and Confederacy at Lincoln's death, with 2 additional columns standing in front of Lincoln's statue. Engraved on the interior walls are the Gettysburg Address and Lincoln's second inaugural address. The focal point inside the memorial is not the marble etchings or painter Jules Guerin's murals—center stage is Daniel Chester French's imposing 19-foot-tall seated sculpture of Abraham Lincoln. The massive sculpture weighs 175 tons. The entire project cost nearly $3 million.

Freedom is an ever-present theme of the Lincoln Memorial, beginning with the leader after whom the memorial is named. President Abraham Lincoln is best known for his role in leading the country during the Civil War, presenting his Gettysburg Address, and freeing slaves with the Emancipation Proclamation. Historically, groups seeking racial equality, jobs, and social parity have made a pilgrimage to the monument. One of the most prolific marches was the 1963 March on Washington for Jobs and Freedom led by Dr. Martin Luther King, Jr., the preeminent civil rights leader. There, Dr. King delivered his "I Have a Dream" speech. The gathering drew more than 200,000 people and was the catalyst for the 1964 Civil Rights Act and the Voting Rights Act of 1965.

President Warren Harding dedicated the Lincoln Memorial on May 30, 1922. The inscription on the wall behind the statue of Lincoln reads, "In this temple, as in the hearts of the people for whom he saved the union, the memory of Abraham Lincoln is enshrined forever."

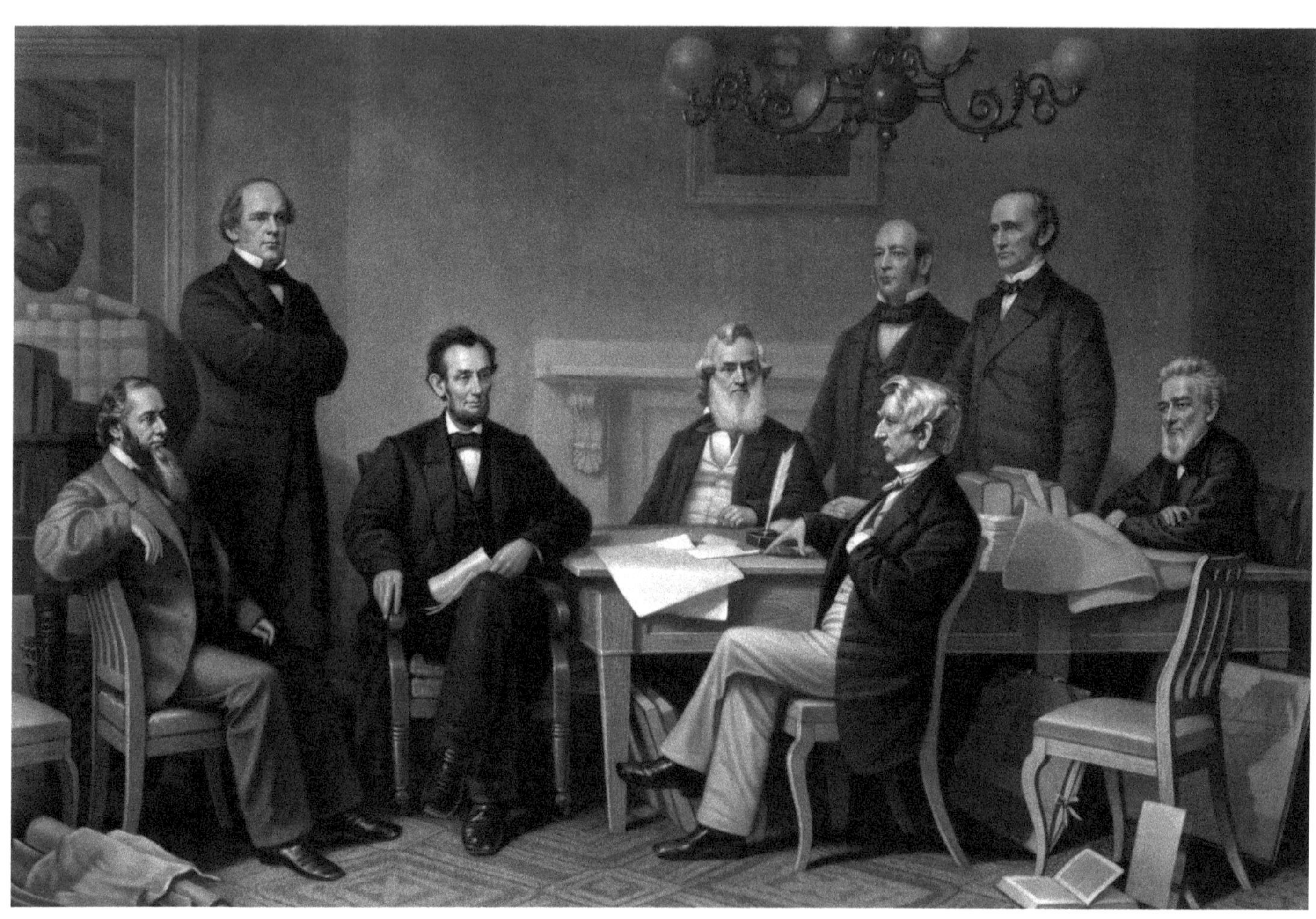

This artistic interpretation is of the first reading of the Emancipation Proclamation before the Cabinet, painted by F. B. Carpenter and engraved by A. H. Ritchie. This print shows Abraham Lincoln seated at the table with members of his Cabinet, July 22, 1862.

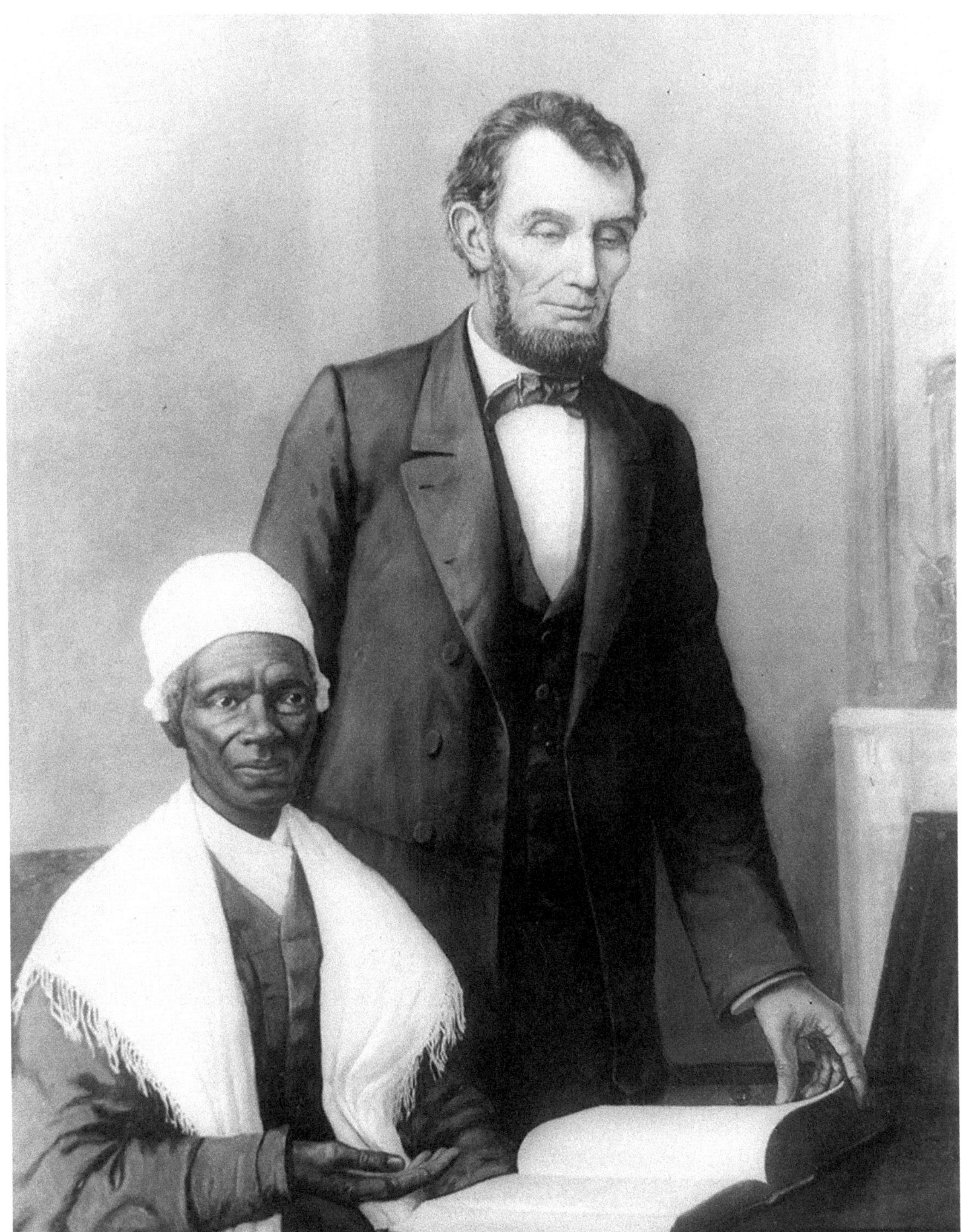

Lincoln met with abolitionist Sojourner Truth on October 19, 1864, at the White House. A significant character behind the scenes of the Civil War, Sojourner Truth actively recruited African-American soldiers and supported them by providing supplies such as food and clothing.

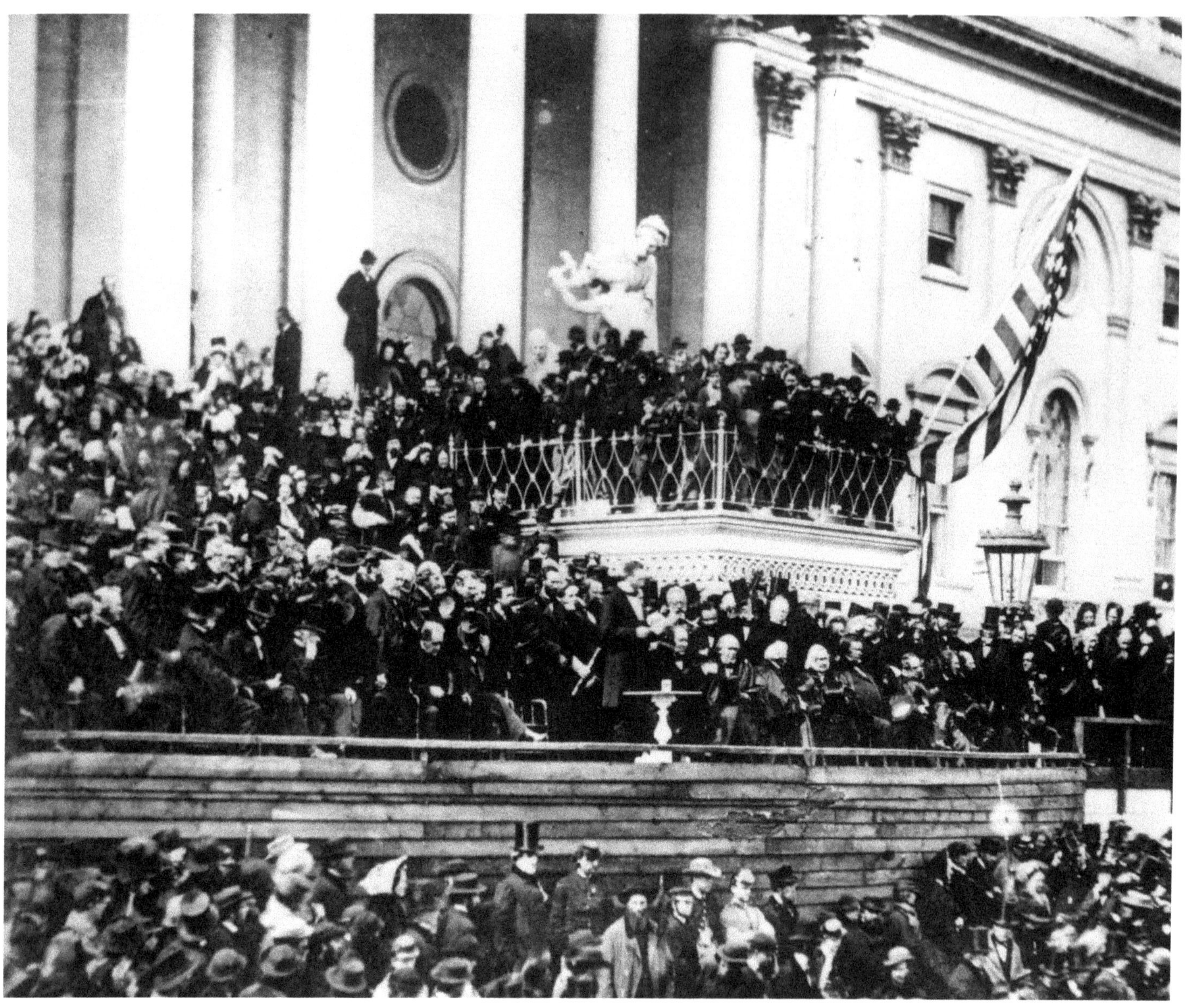

In 1865, Lincoln presents his second inaugural address in front of crowds at the Capitol, only two years before the Lincoln Memorial would be proposed and almost 60 years before the memorial would finally be dedicated.

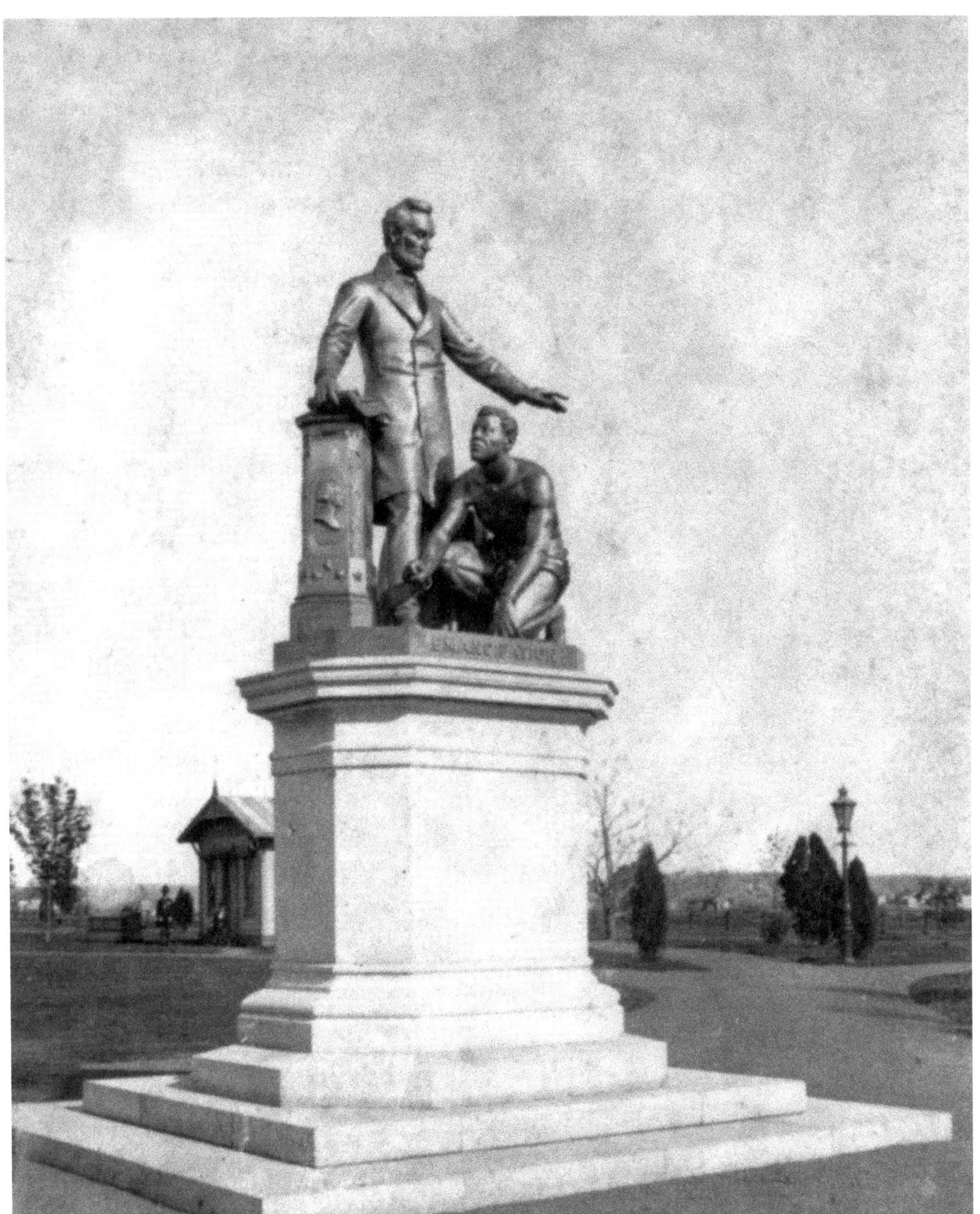

Touted as the original Lincoln Memorial, the Emancipation Memorial, located in Lincoln Park on Capitol Hill, depicts Abraham Lincoln setting an African slave free. Designed by artist Thomas Ball, the monument was erected in the neighborhood park in 1876.

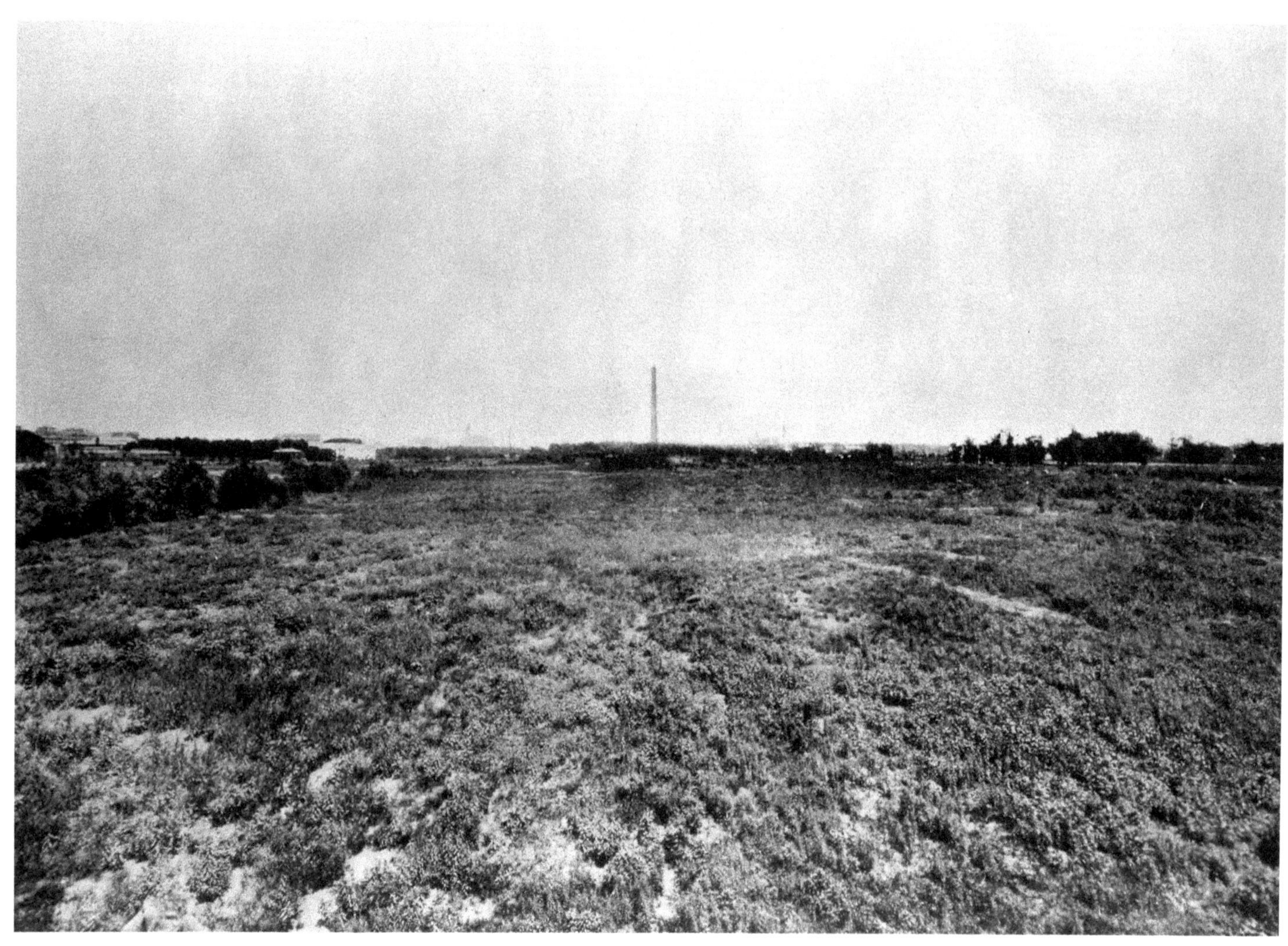

The plot of swampy land, now the National Mall, where the Lincoln Memorial was to be built. In the background stands the stately Washington Monument. Although a memorial to the sixteenth president was proposed in the 1860s, it was not until 1911 that President Taft and Congress approved the bill for the structure.

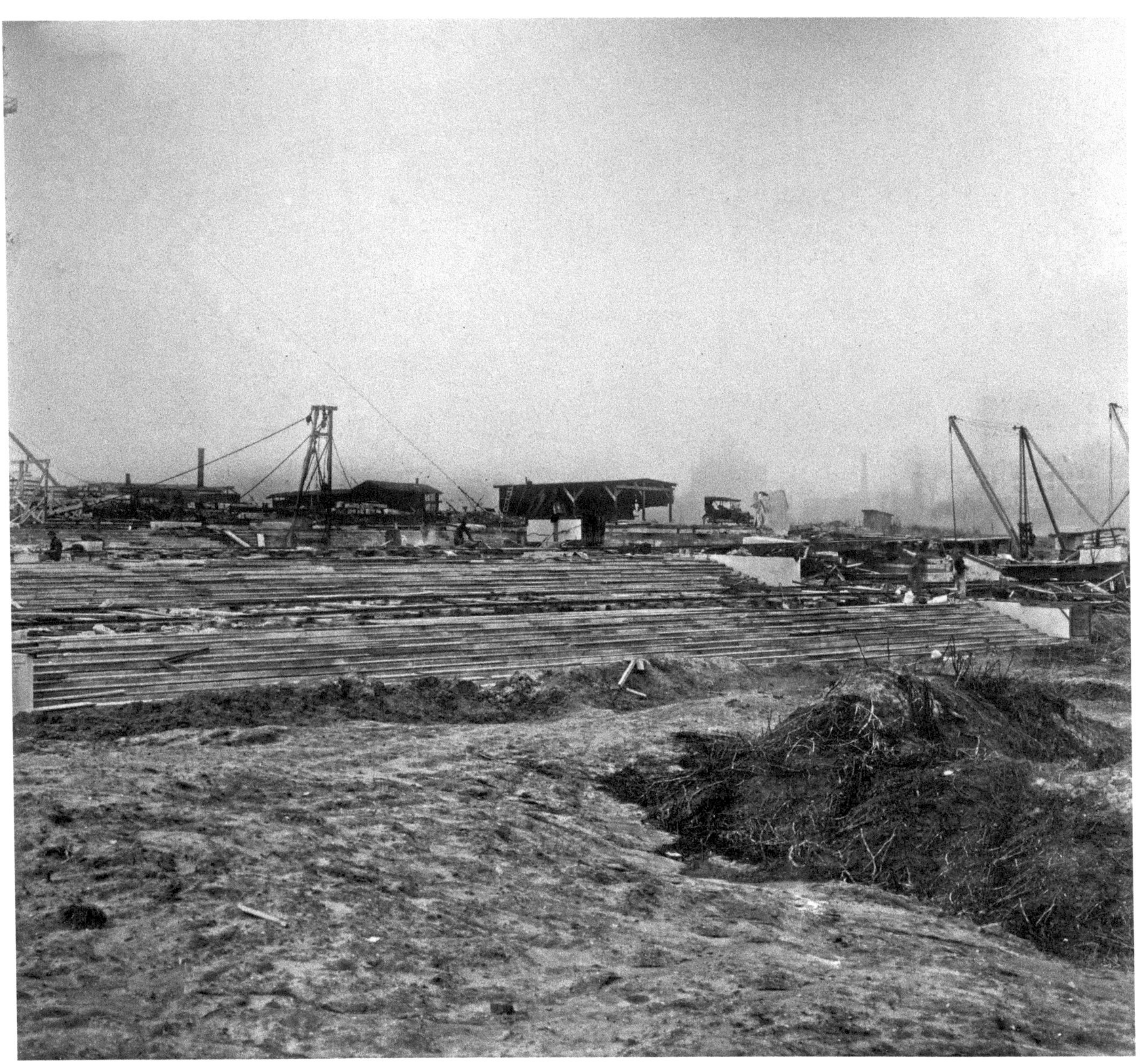

Construction begins: Workers clear the land and begin building the steps of the memorial.

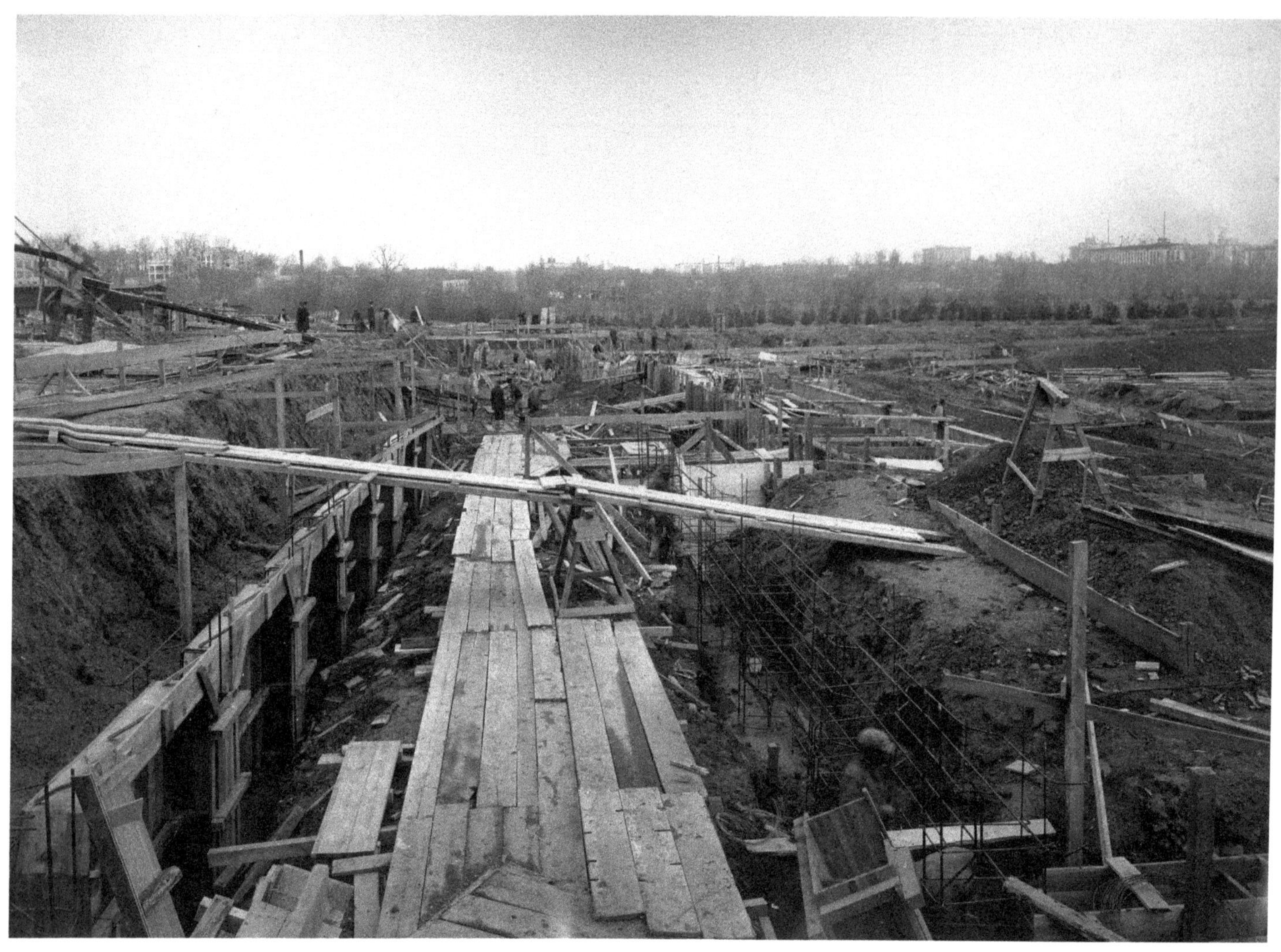

Several officials oversee the building process, while construction also takes place as seen in the background of this photo.

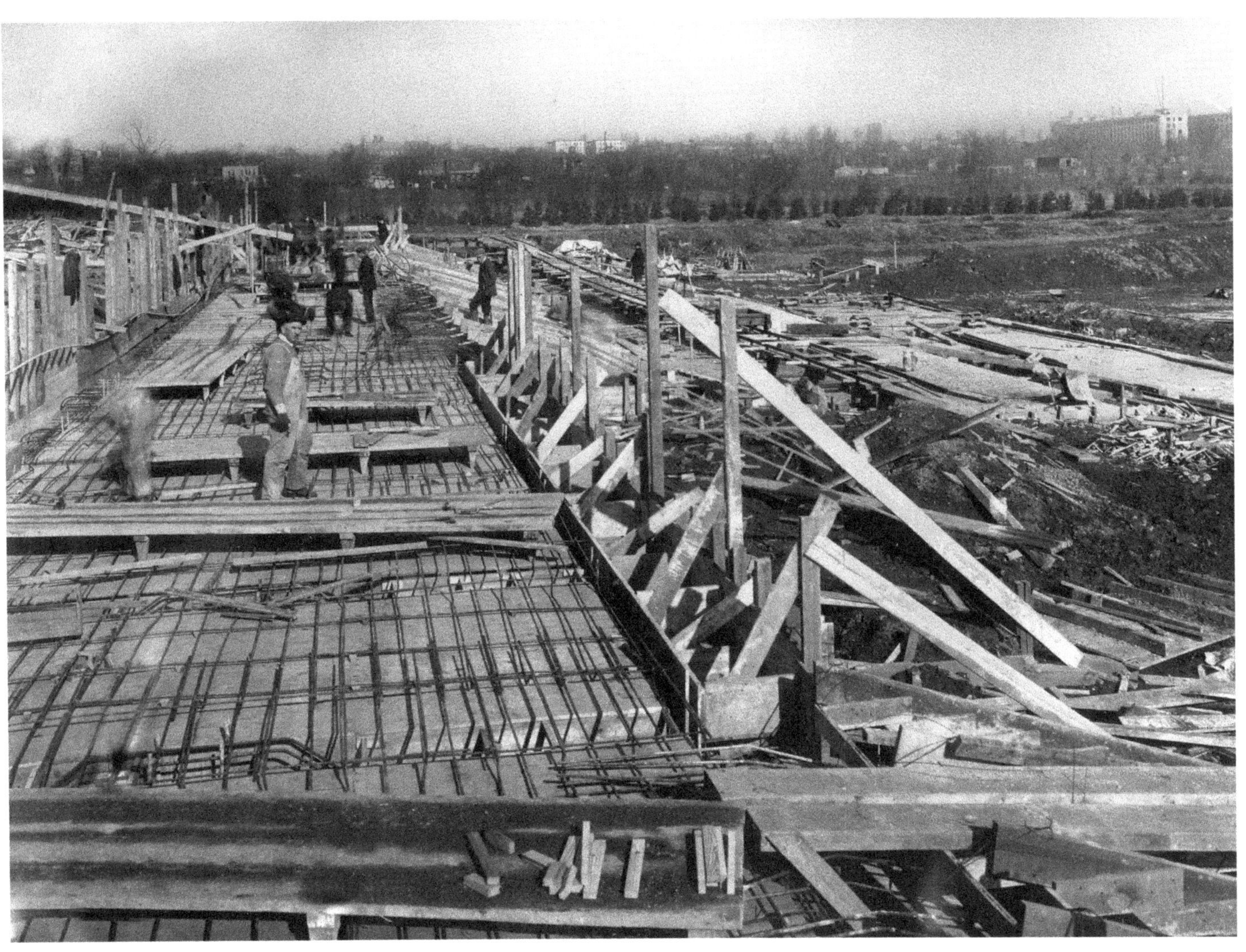

Some workers glance at the camera, but the worker in overalls seems to be the only person in this image posing for the photographer.

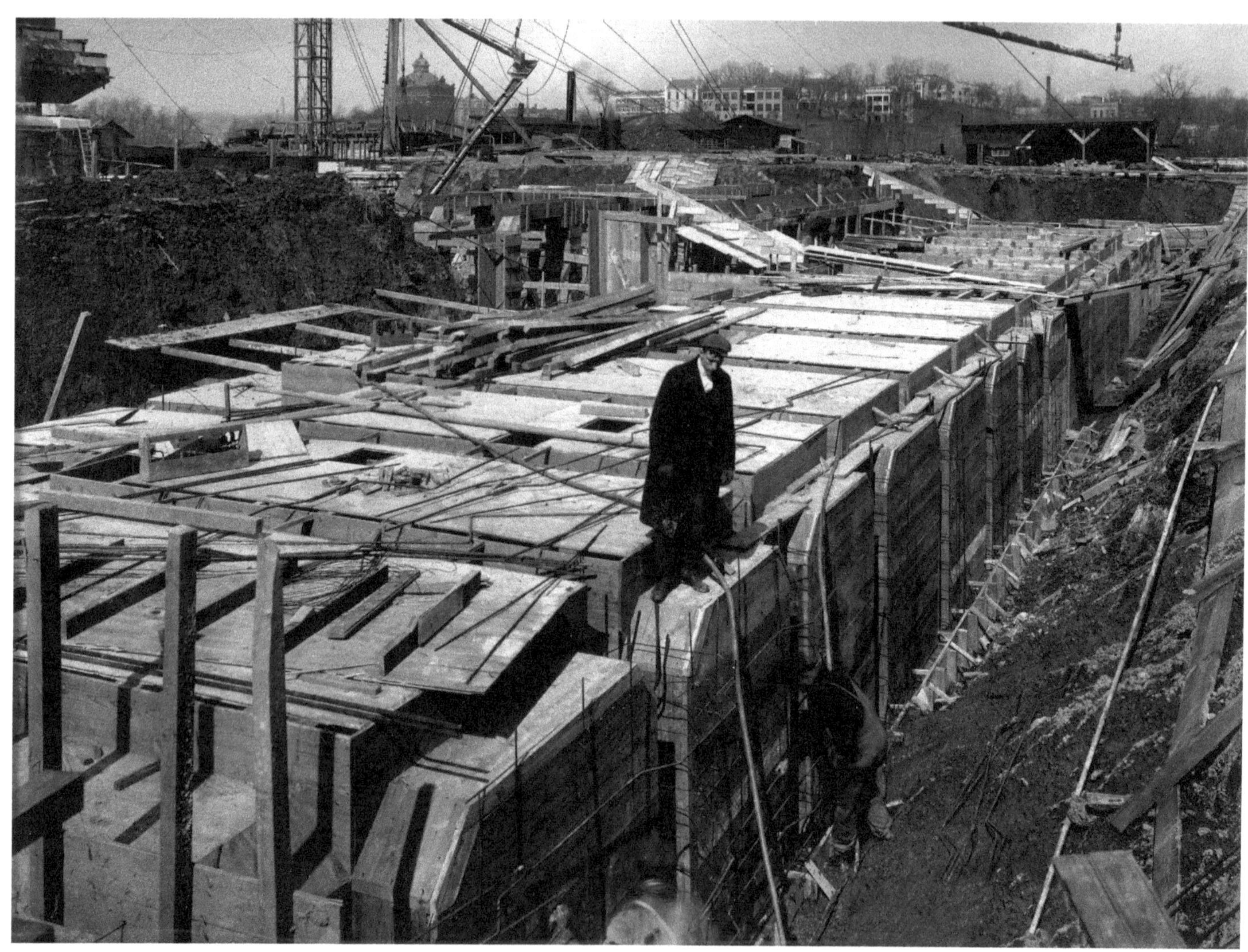

A man peers down over a mass of wooden planks during the rudimentary stage of construction.

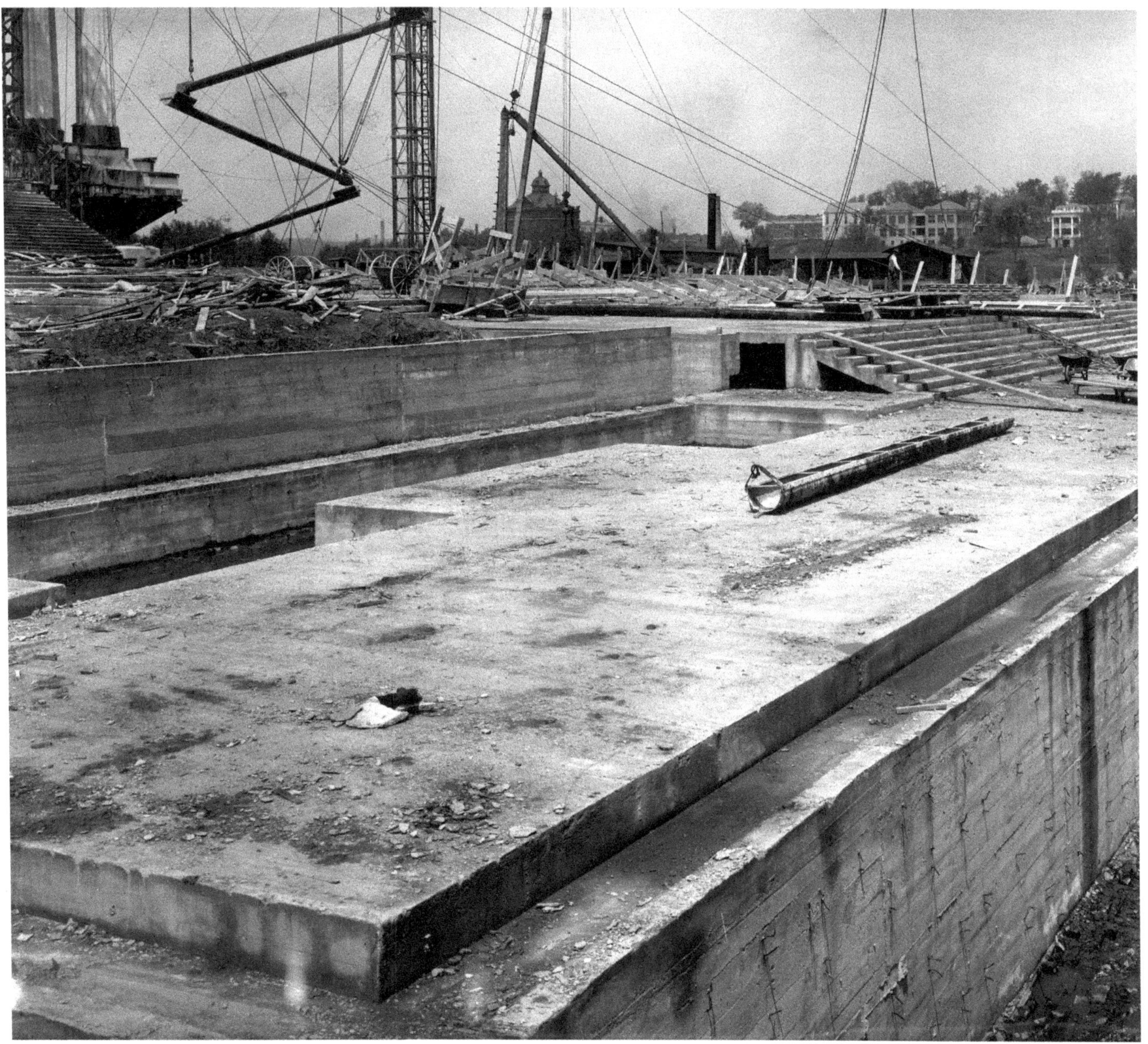

This photograph depicts construction of the Lincoln Memorial foundation and steps. A tangle of cranes, cables, and early machinery surround the construction site.

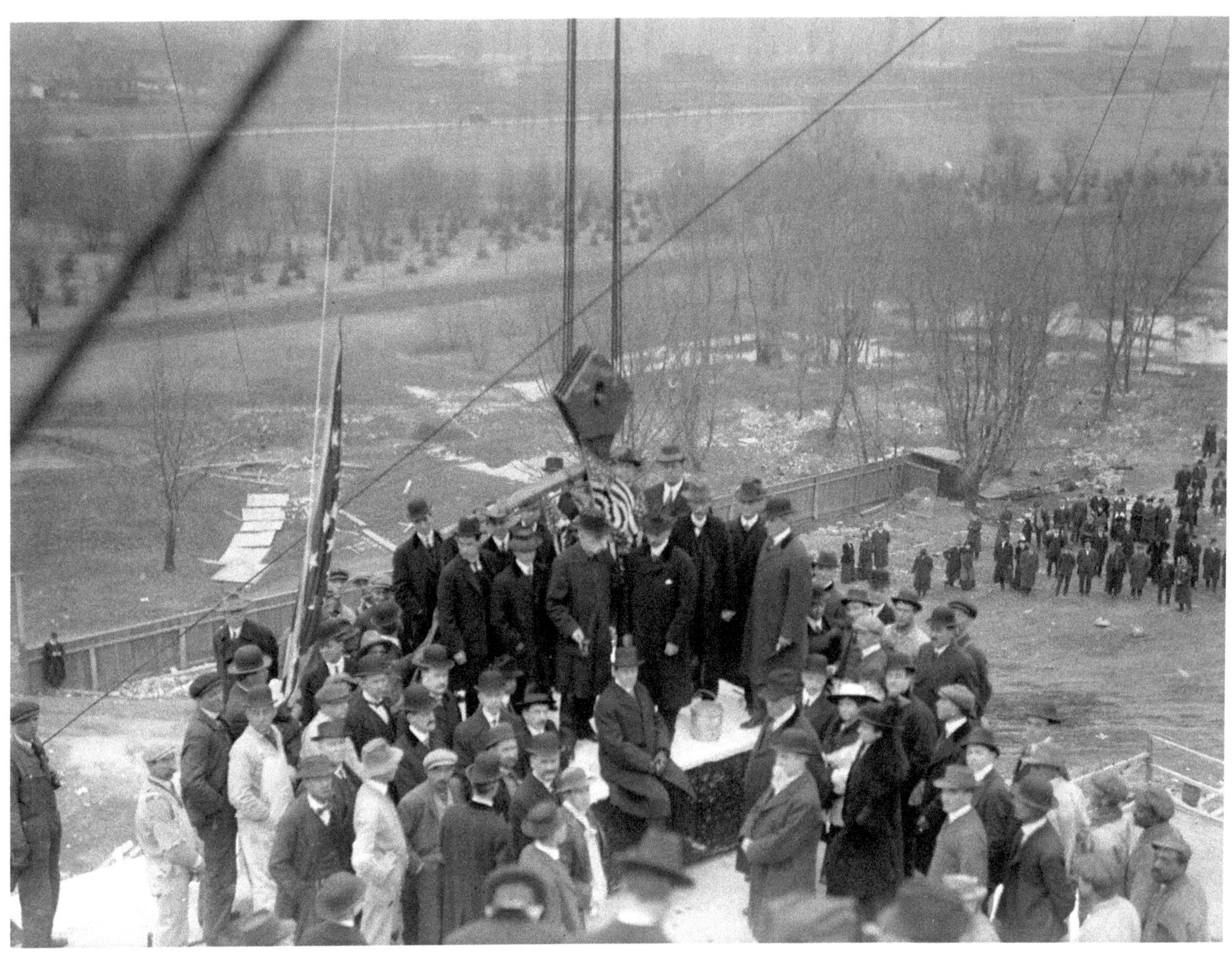

The cornerstone is laid for the Lincoln Memorial. This image was recorded on February 12, 1914, on Lincoln's birthday.

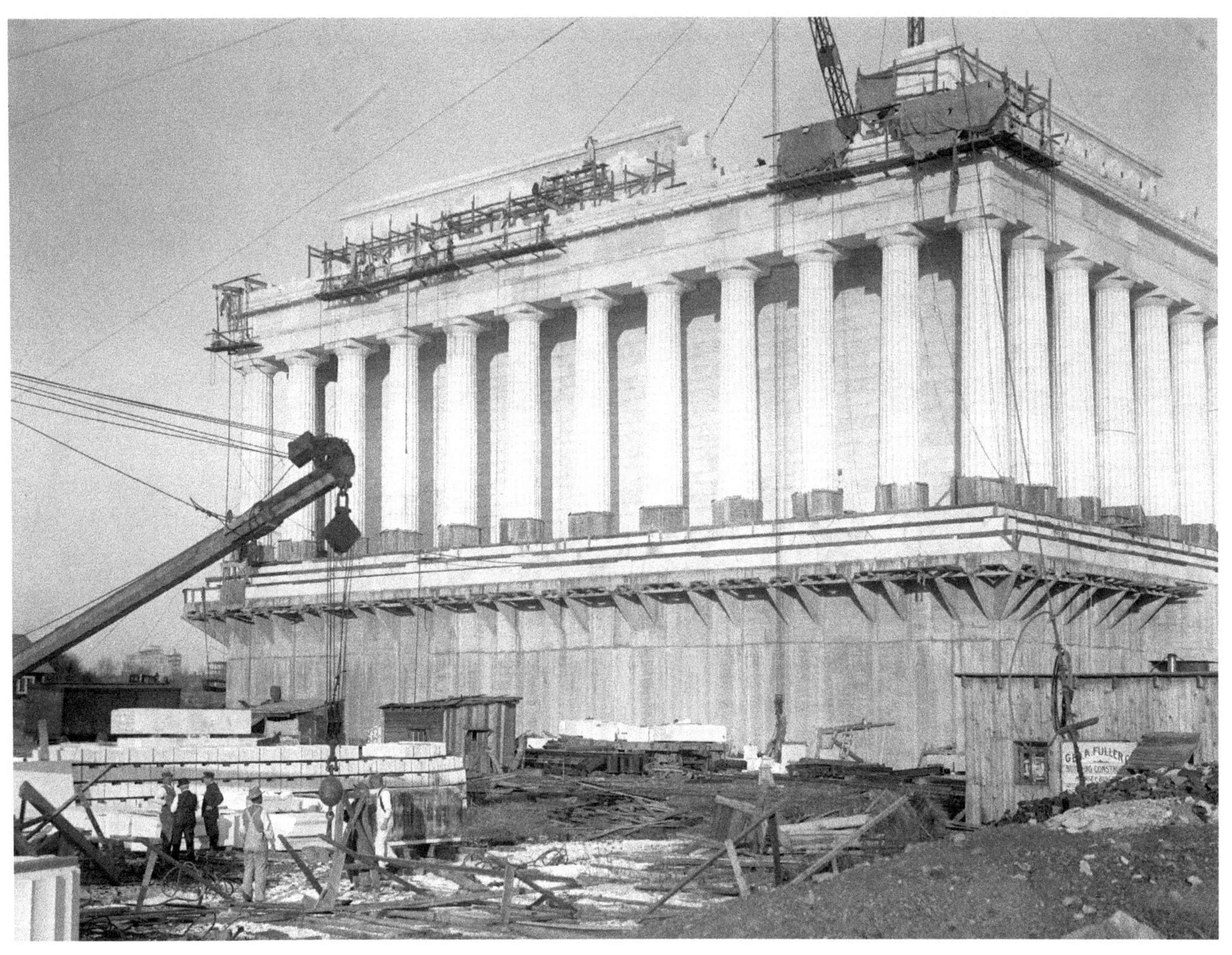

Pictured here is the Lincoln Memorial under construction in 1914. The memorial begins to resemble its Greek model, the Temple of Zeus.

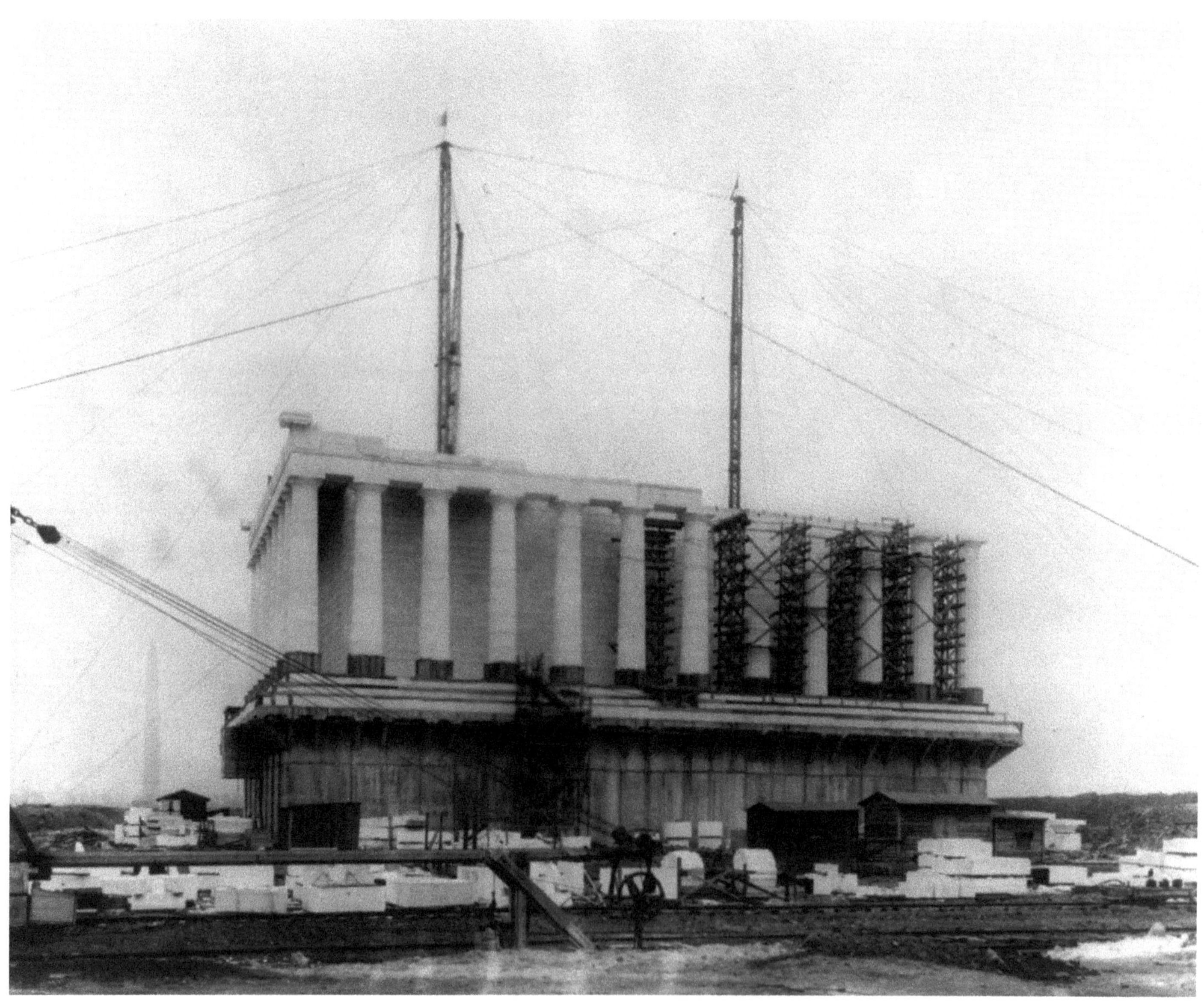

This was the scene in 1916 as construction was well under way on the Lincoln Memorial. That same year Congress passed legislation called the National Park Service Organic Act, which created the National Park Service. The NPS is a federal bureau which manages national parkland previously under the jurisdiction of the Department of the Interior.

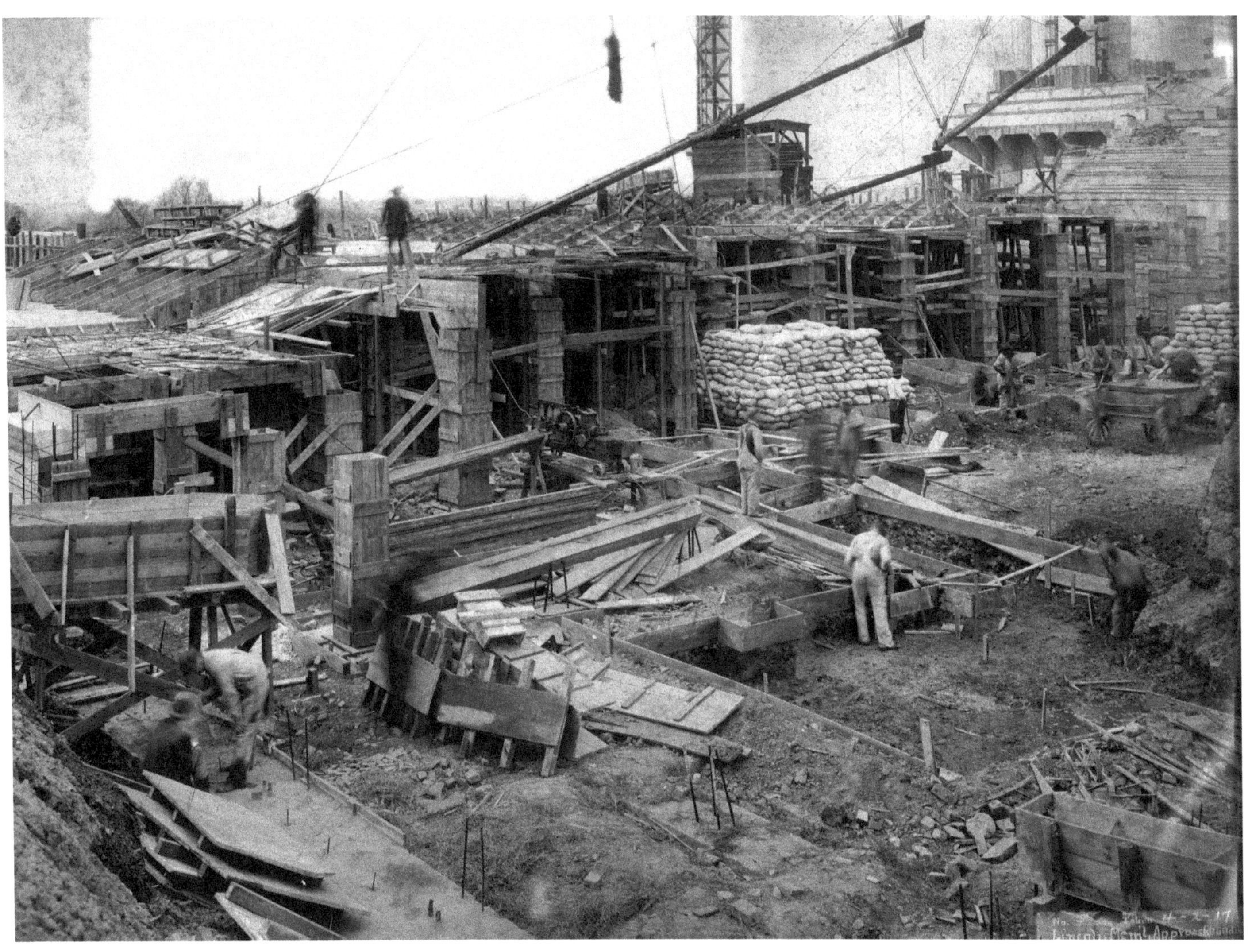

This early image shows the Lincoln Memorial under construction in 1916. Construction took place between 1914 and 1922, slowing down after the United States began fighting in World War I.

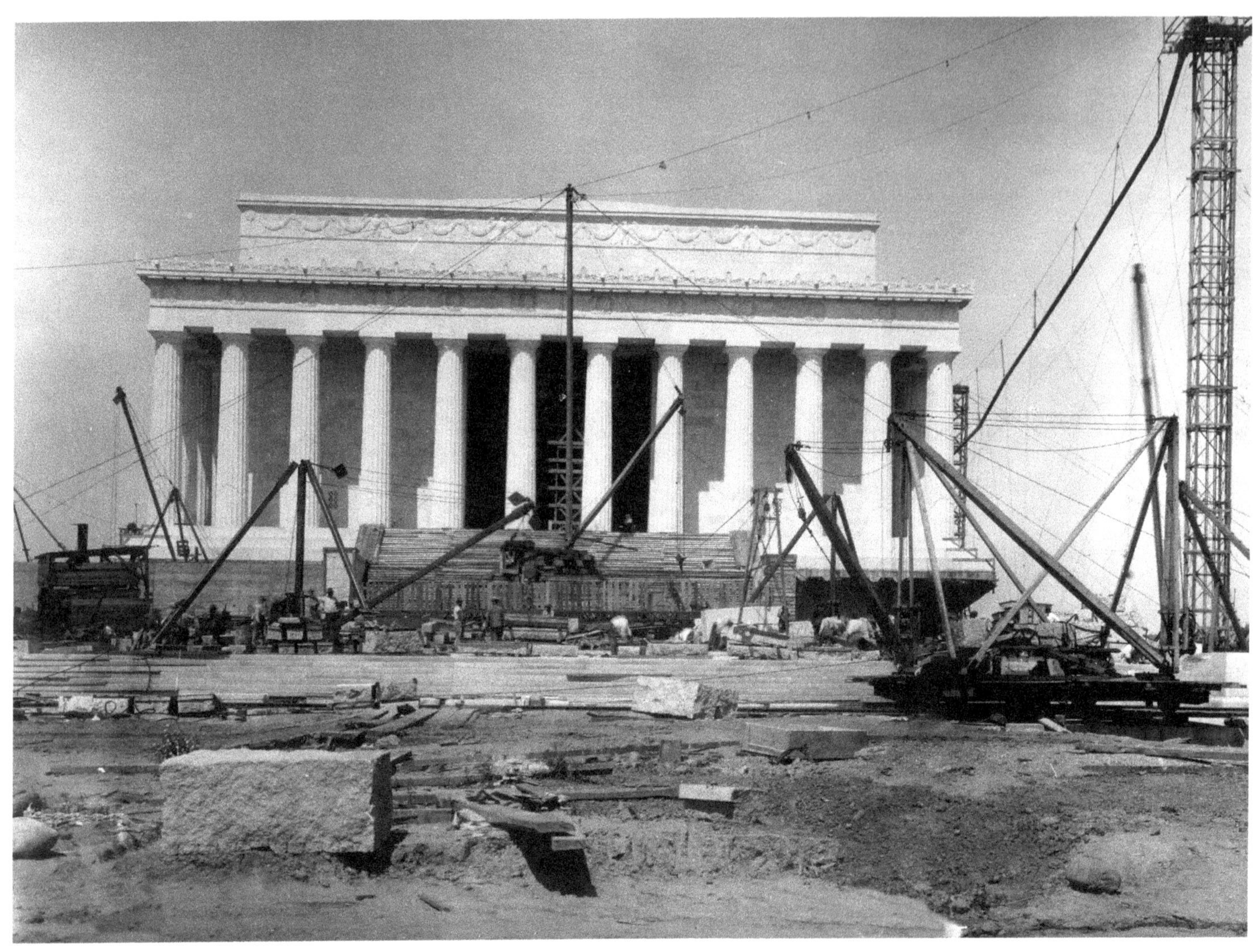

Work on the Lincoln Memorial was slowed considerably by World War I; however, most of the architectural elements were completed by April of 1917. After the war began, workers continued to move forward with the interior decorations, granite terrace, approach plaza, and grounds landscaping.

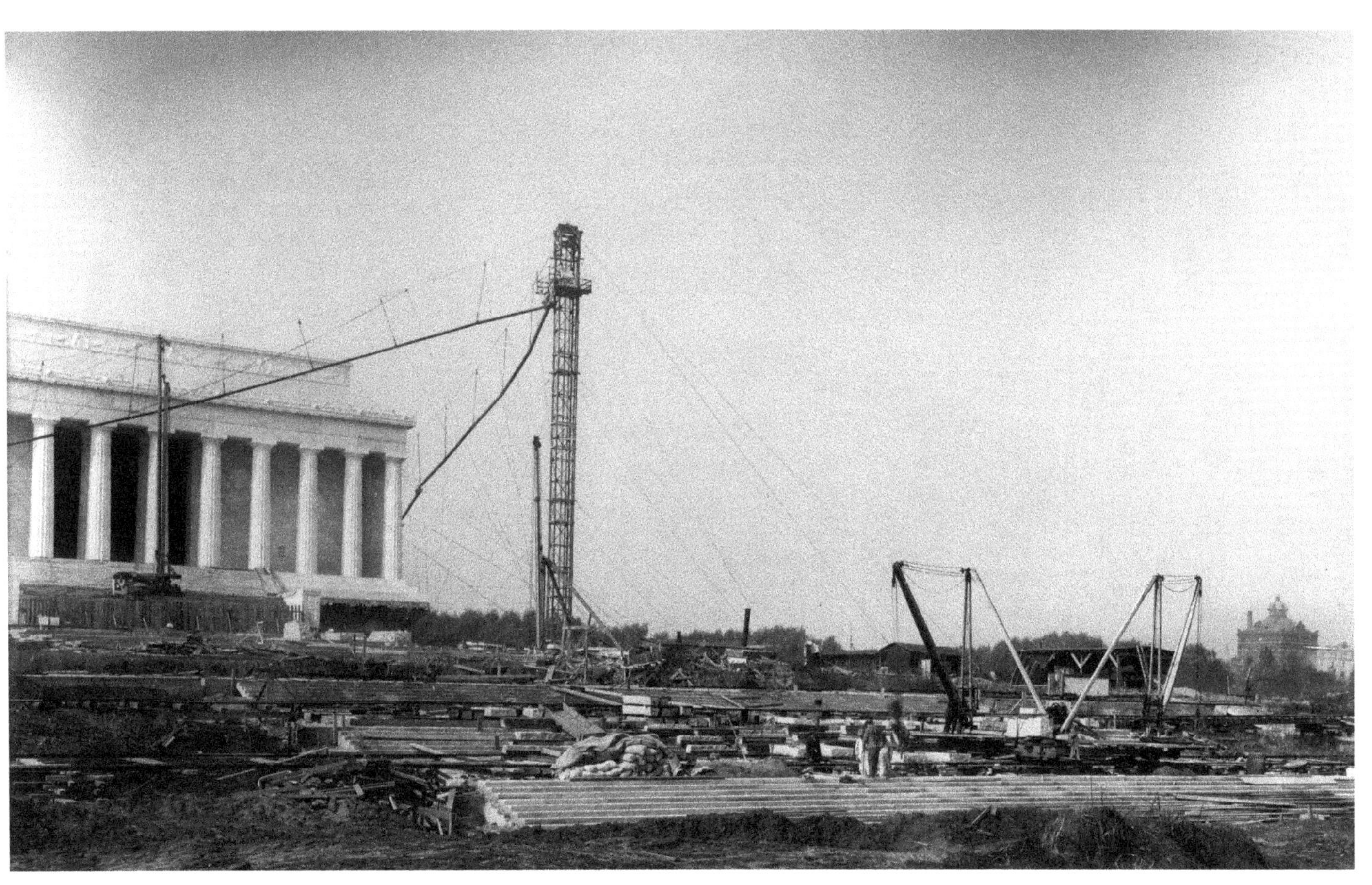

Many significant figures, including presidents, politicians, and singers, would address crowds or perform on these stairs of the Lincoln Memorial, which are under construction in this image.

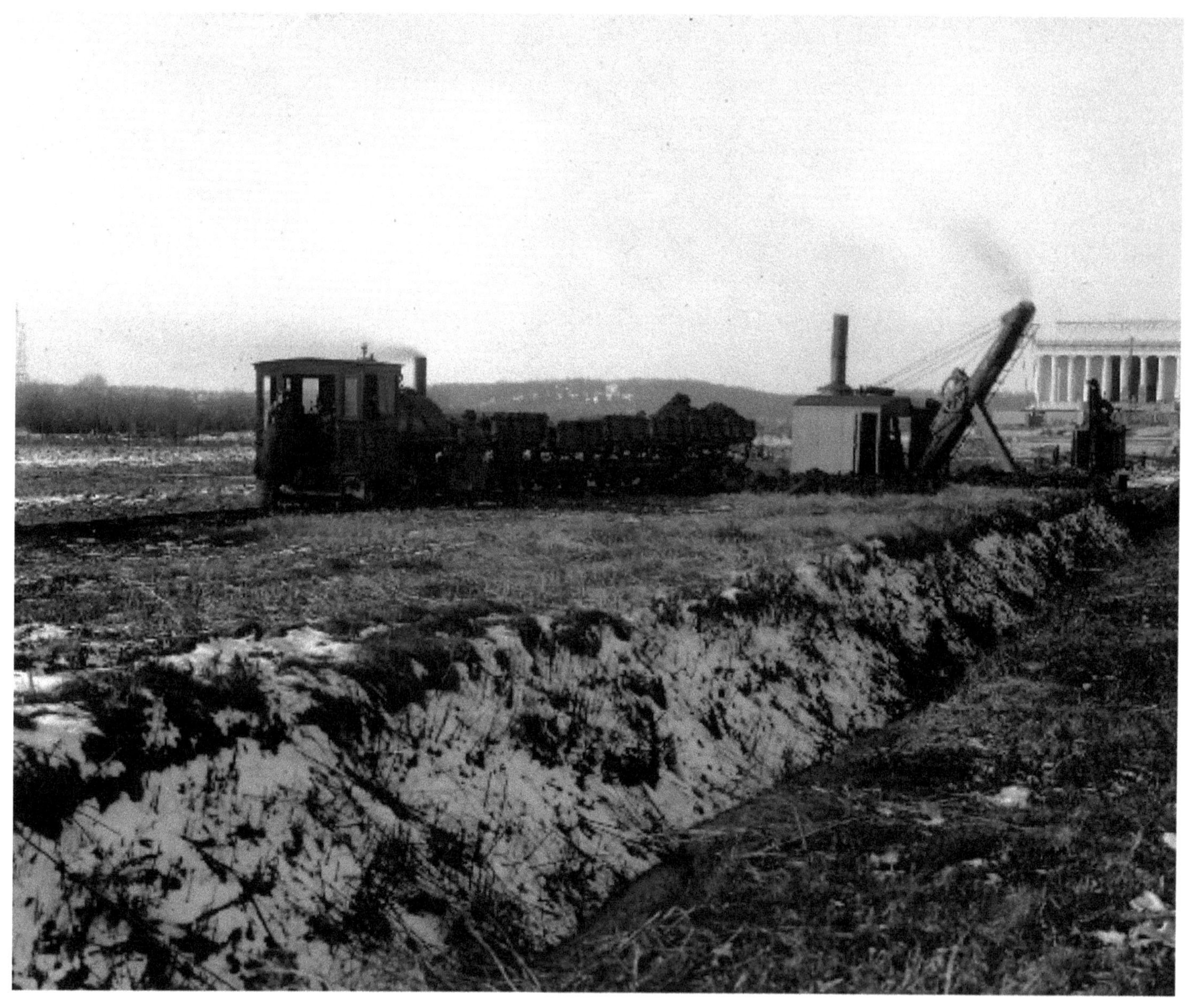

A trench is visible in front of the Lincoln Memorial prior to the Arlington Memorial Bridge construction, which began in 1926.

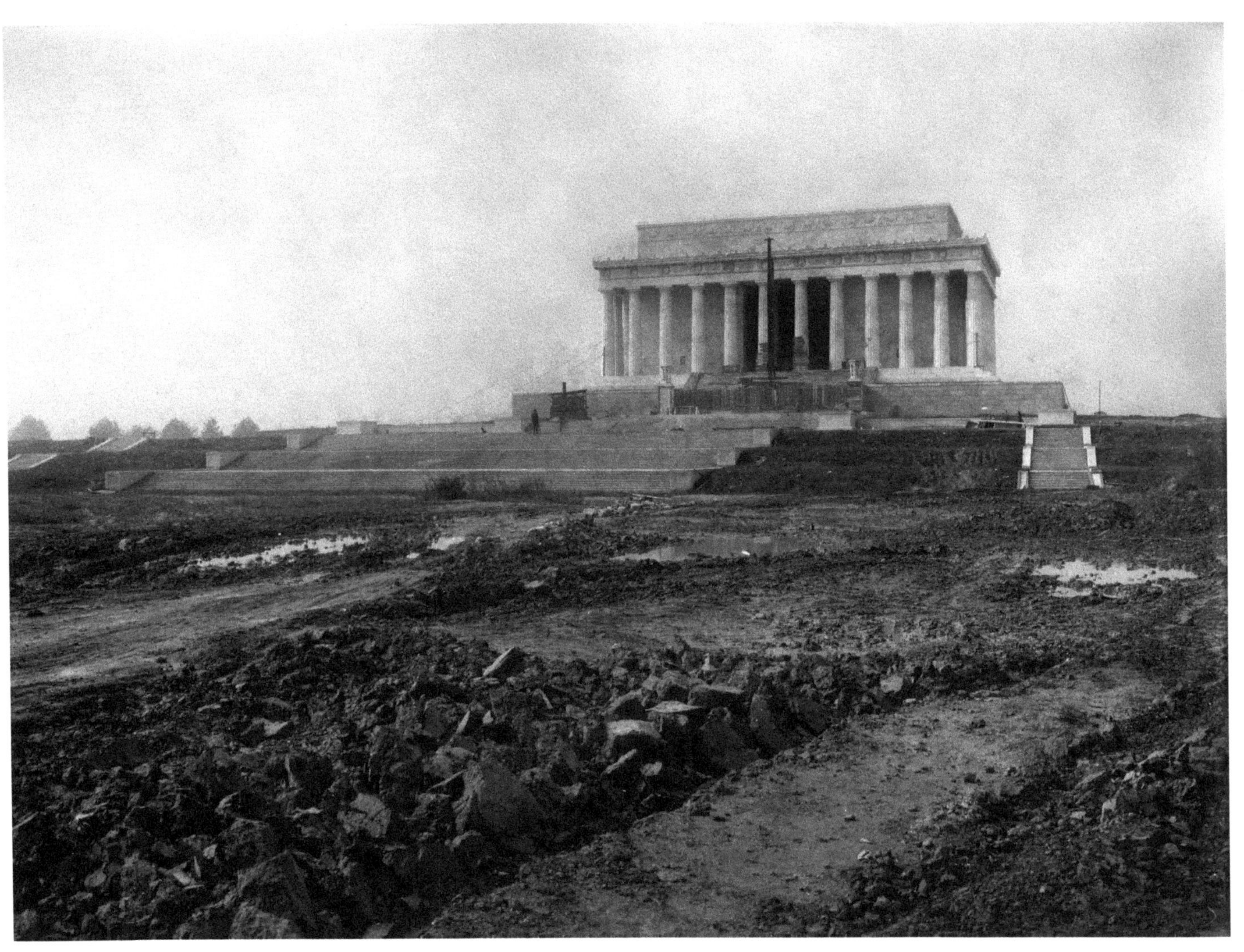

A solitary figure stands on the newly completed stairs of the memorial. In the foreground, mud and rocks replace the swampy land that existed here before the memorial was built.

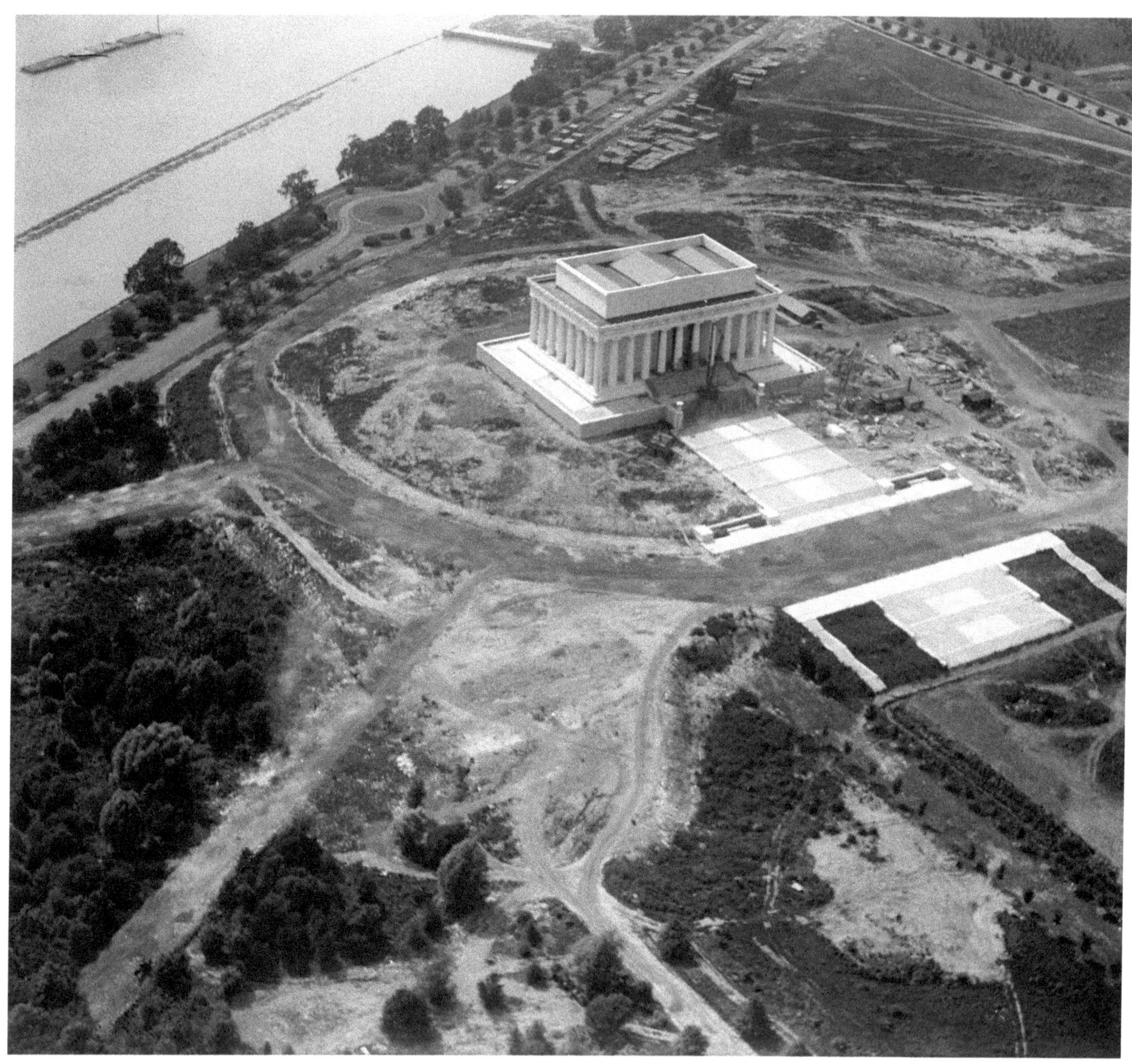

A 1919 Harris & Ewing photograph shows an aerial view of the Lincoln Memorial during construction.

The pedestal on which the sculpture of Abraham Lincoln will rest is assembled.

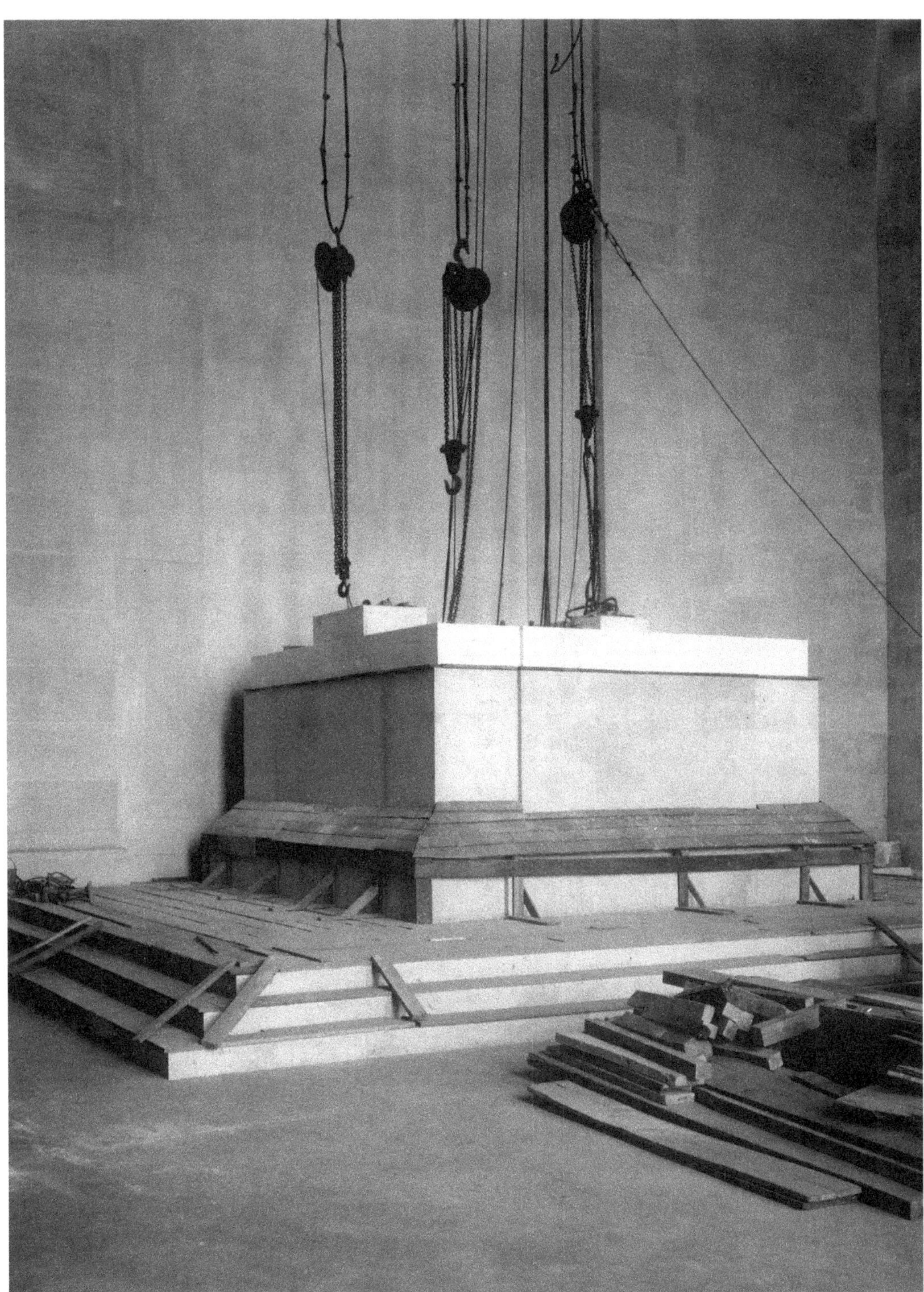

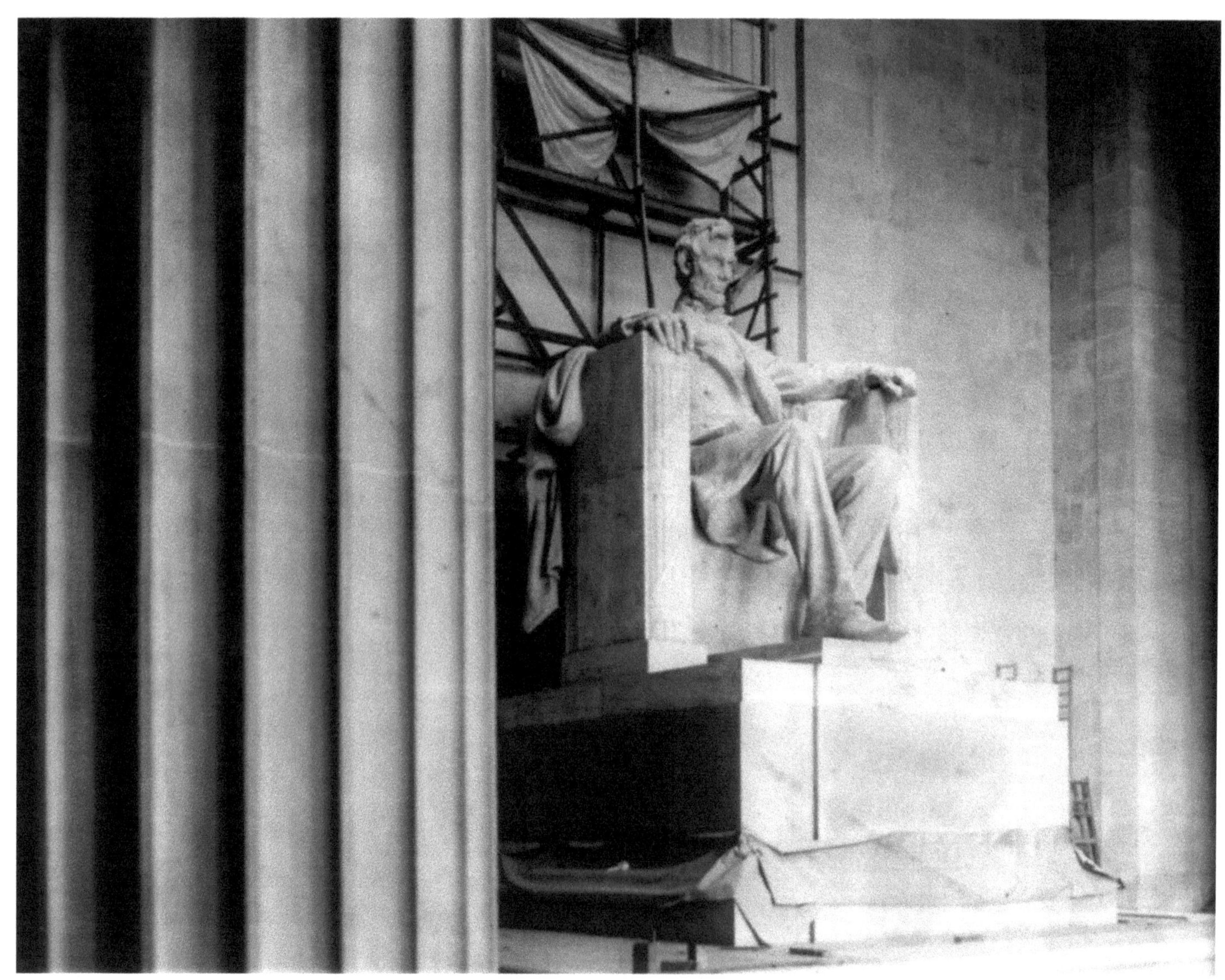

Twenty-eight pieces of Georgia marble were used to construct the Lincoln Memorial statue.

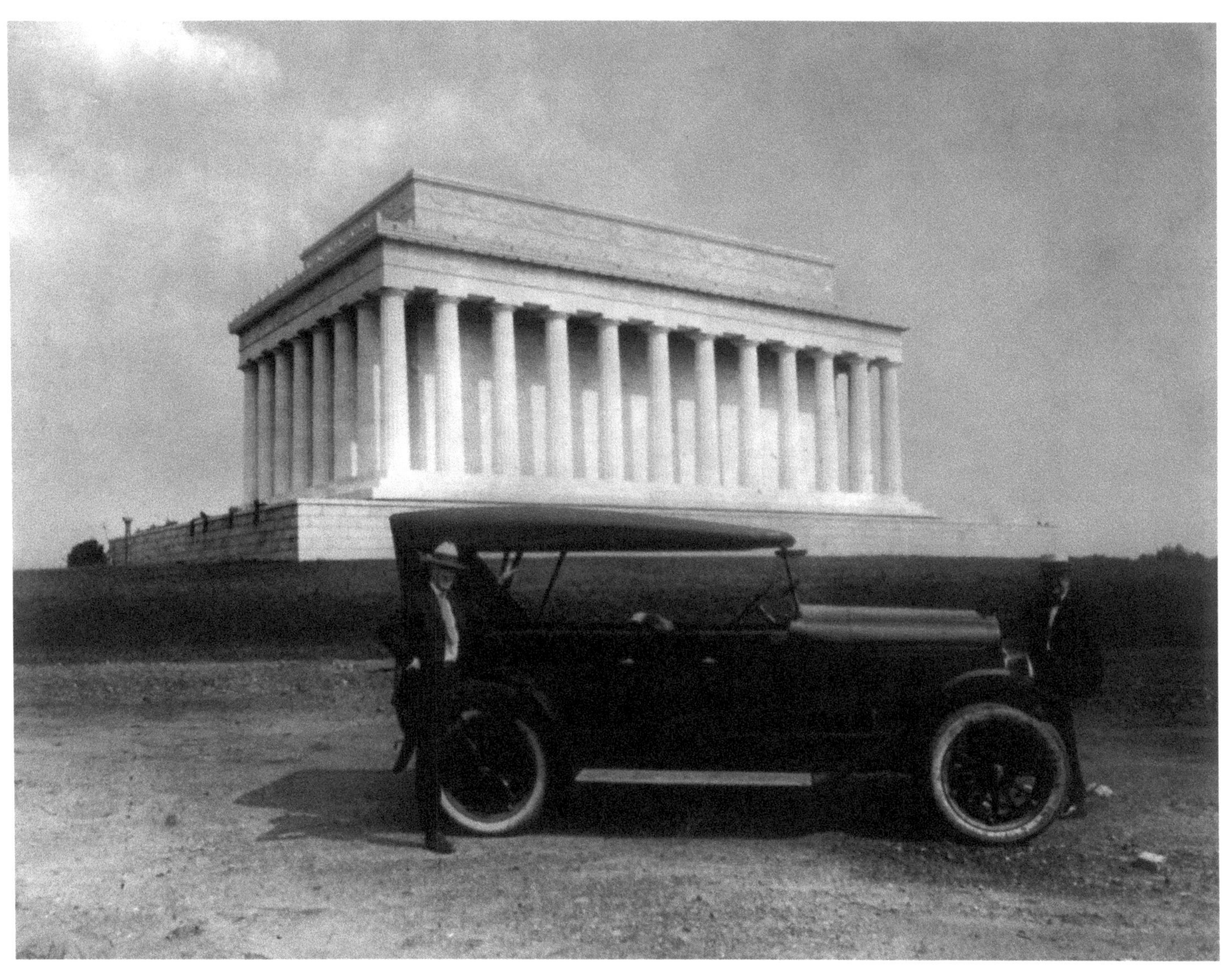

Pictured here are two gentlemen posing near a King car, with the Lincoln Memorial in the background. Charles King, an engineer with Northern Motor Car Company, developed the King car. He was the first person to design, build, and drive a car in Detroit.

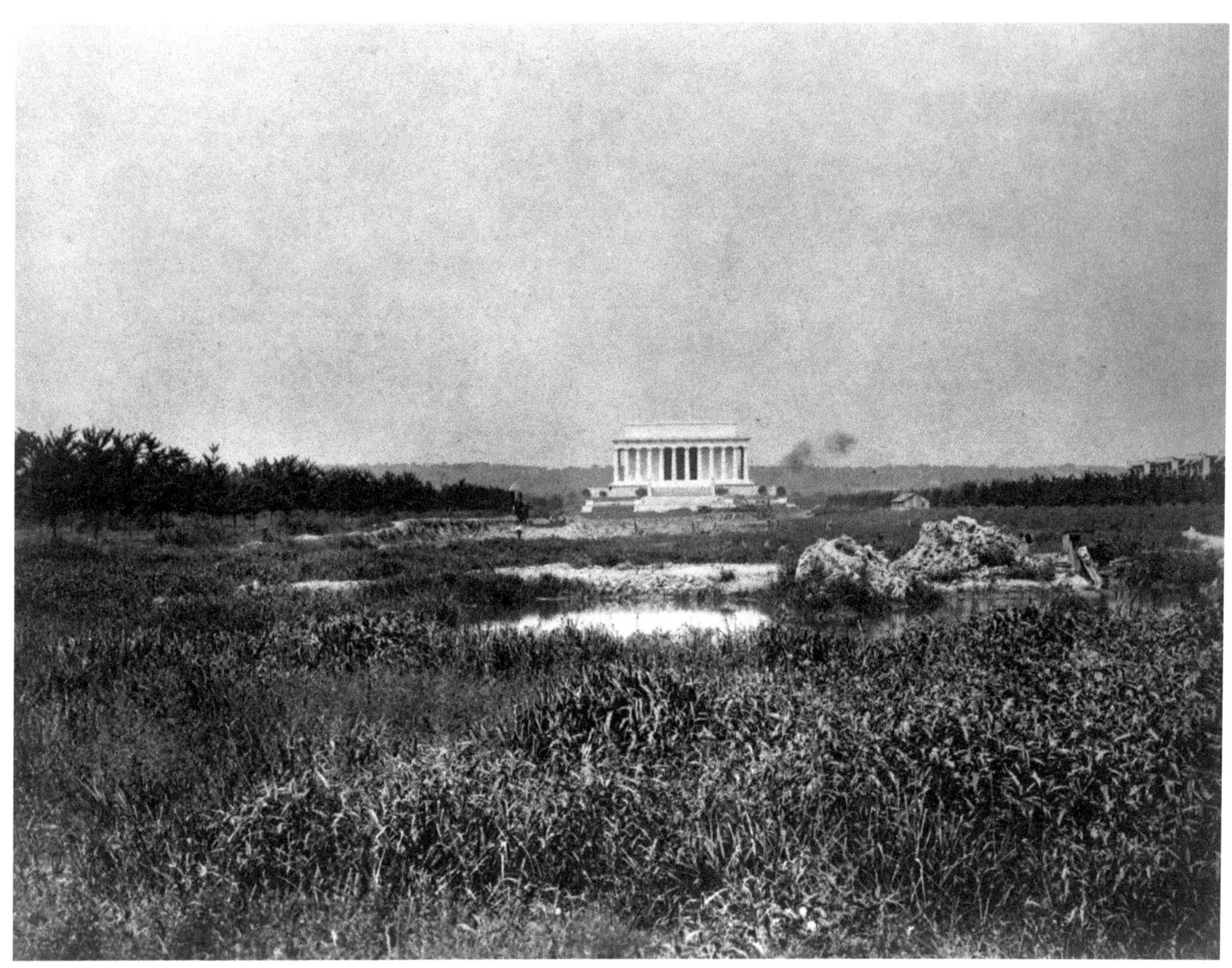

An early photograph of the Lincoln Memorial with marsh in the foreground.

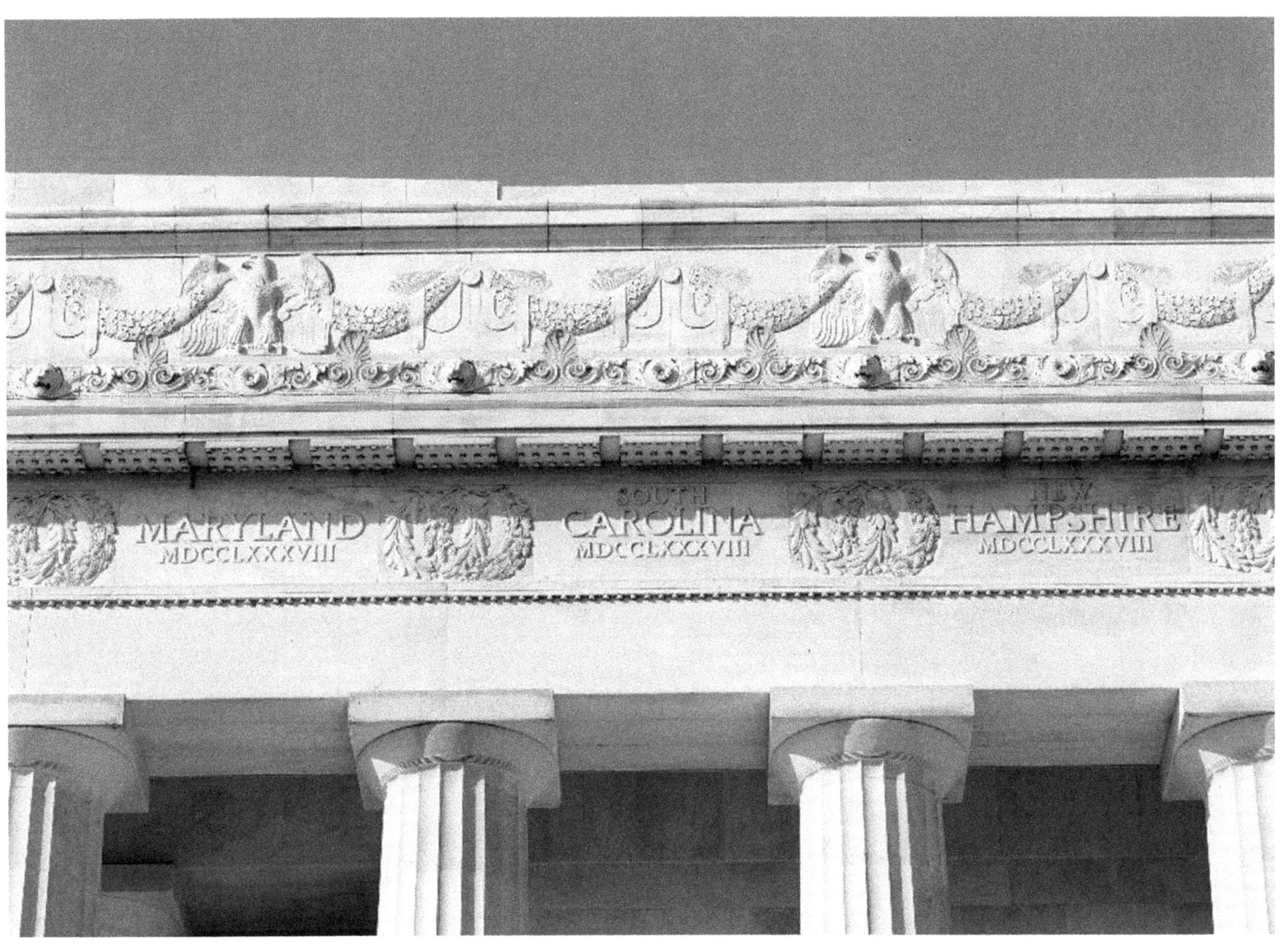

This photograph shows the detail on the east entablature (top moldings) of the Lincoln Memorial's facade.

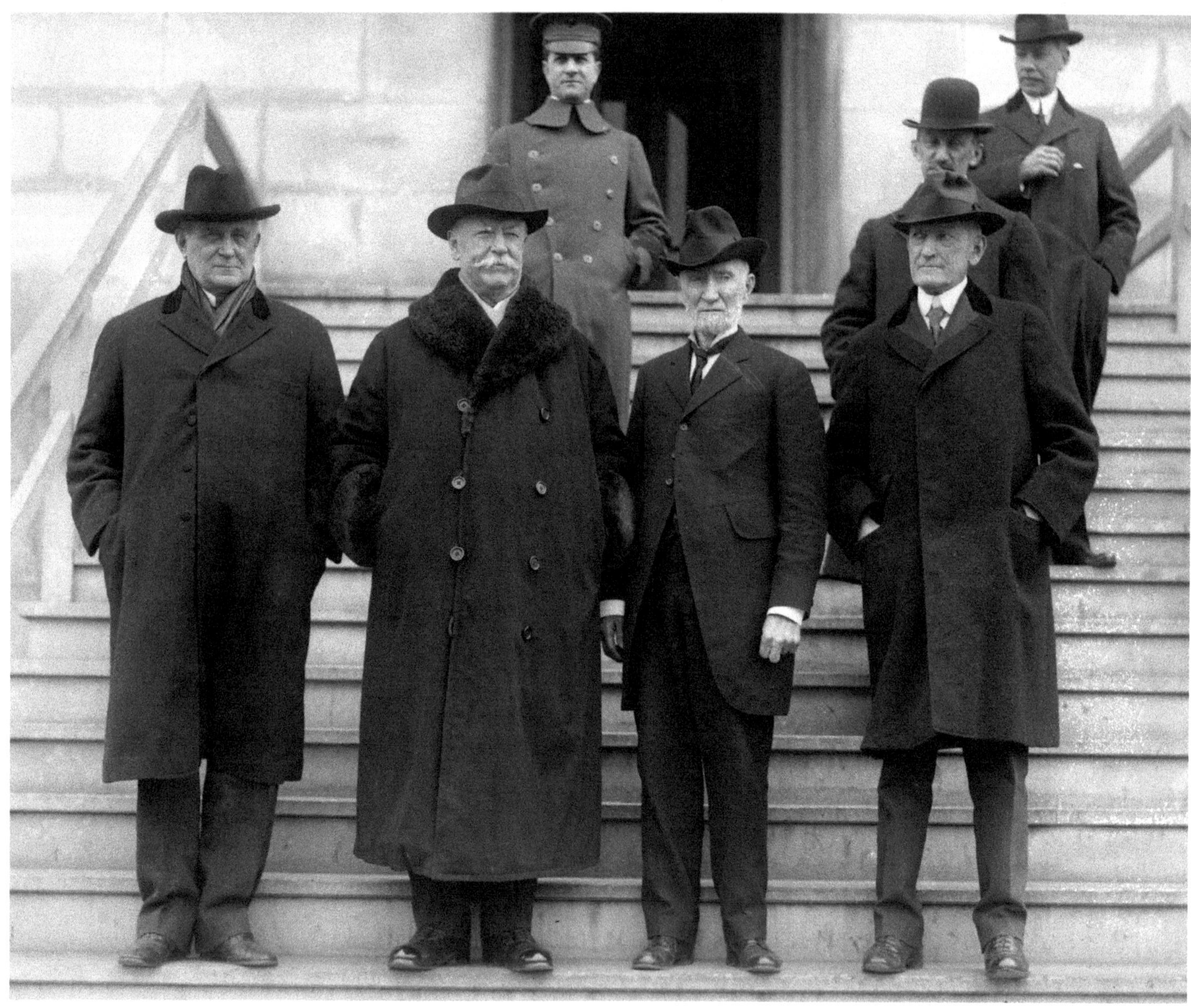

James Beauchamp (Champ) Clark, President Taft, Joseph G. Cannon, and former Massachusetts governor Samuel W. McCall posed for this photo. The members of the Lincoln Memorial Commission were to hold a meeting at the Capitol in Washington, D.C., to decide on a Lincoln Memorial dedication ceremony date.

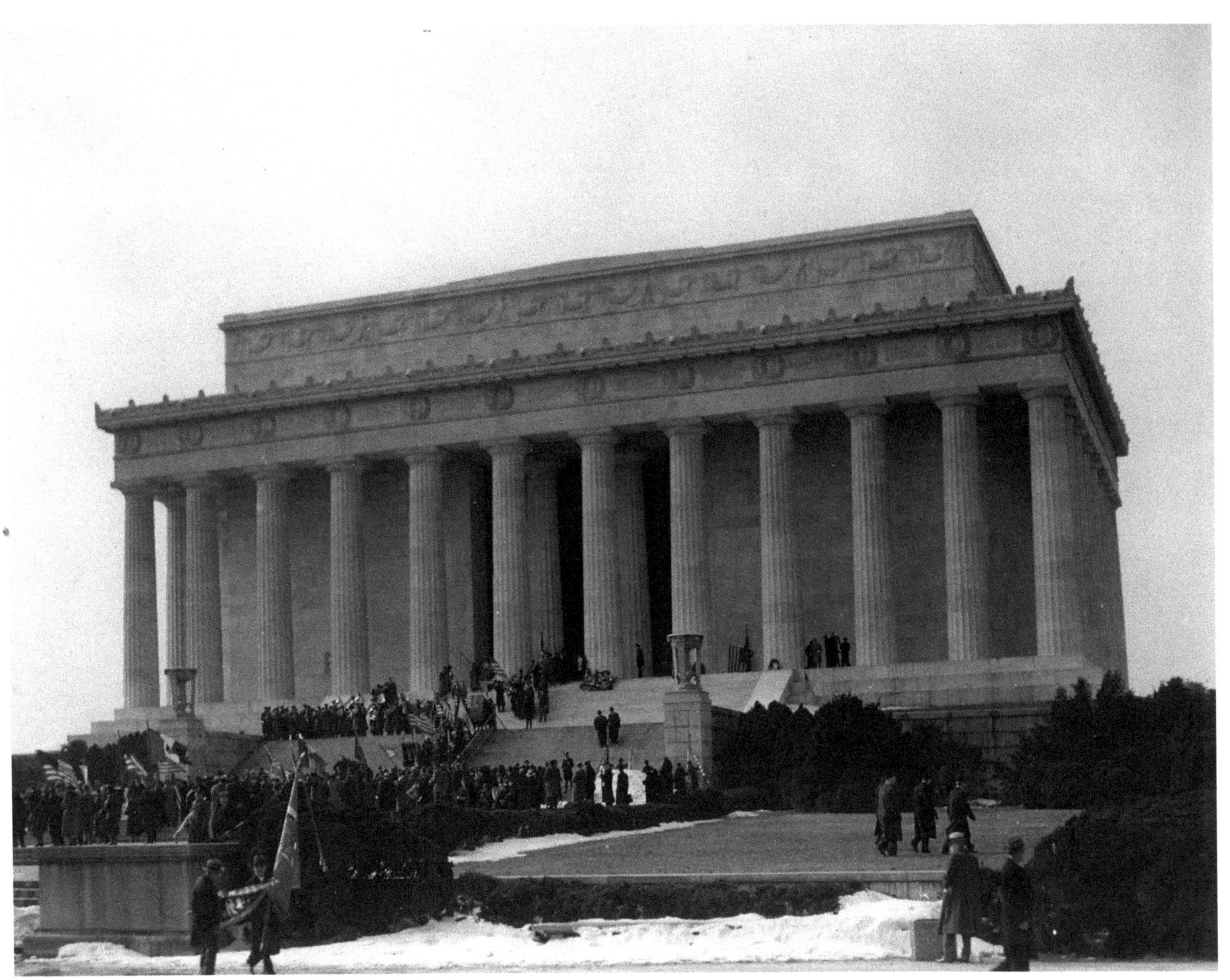

Lincoln Memorial visitors may notice the structure comprises numerous kinds of stone, including granite (lower steps), Colorado marble (columns, facade, and upper steps), Alabama marble (ceiling tiles), and pink Tennessee marble (the floor).

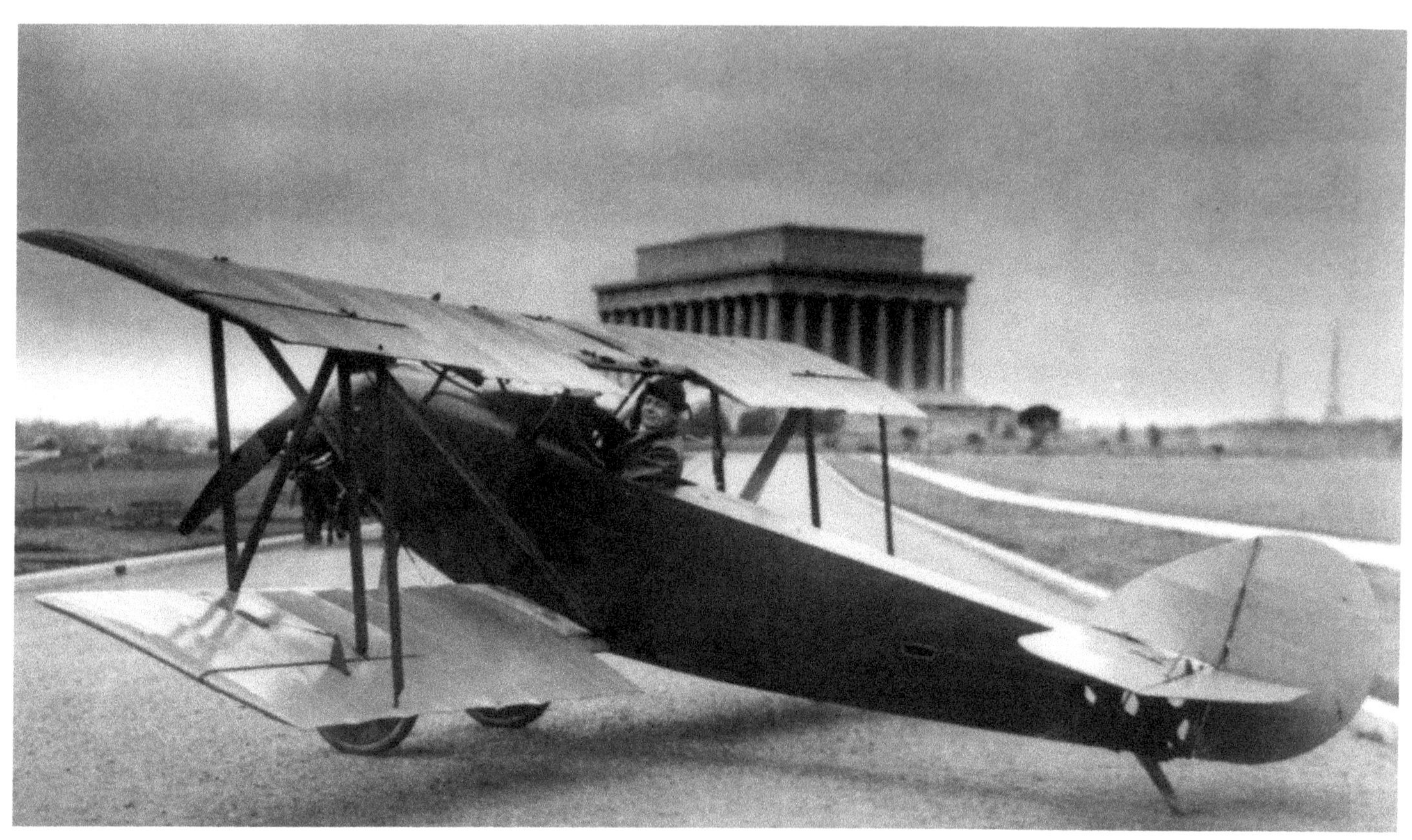

Lawrence Perry landed his plane near the Lincoln Memorial on March 22, 1922. According to the annotation on the original photograph, Perry claimed his craft would be the "Fliver" of the air. The plane was capable of flying 100 M.P.H. and landing in small spaces.

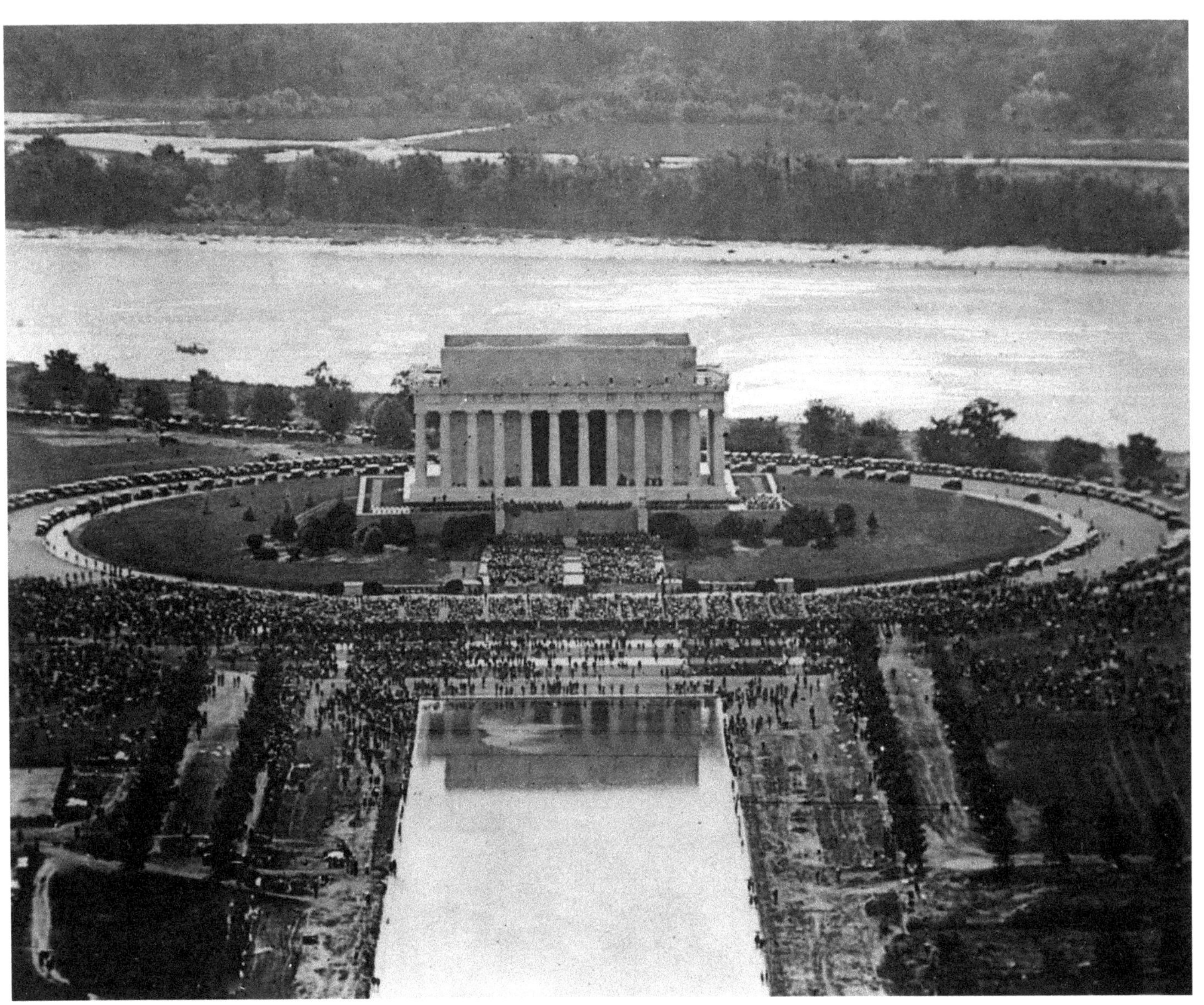

Masses of people attend the dedication of the Lincoln Memorial on May 30, 1922. On that day, President Abraham Lincoln's only surviving son, Robert Todd Lincoln, was present.

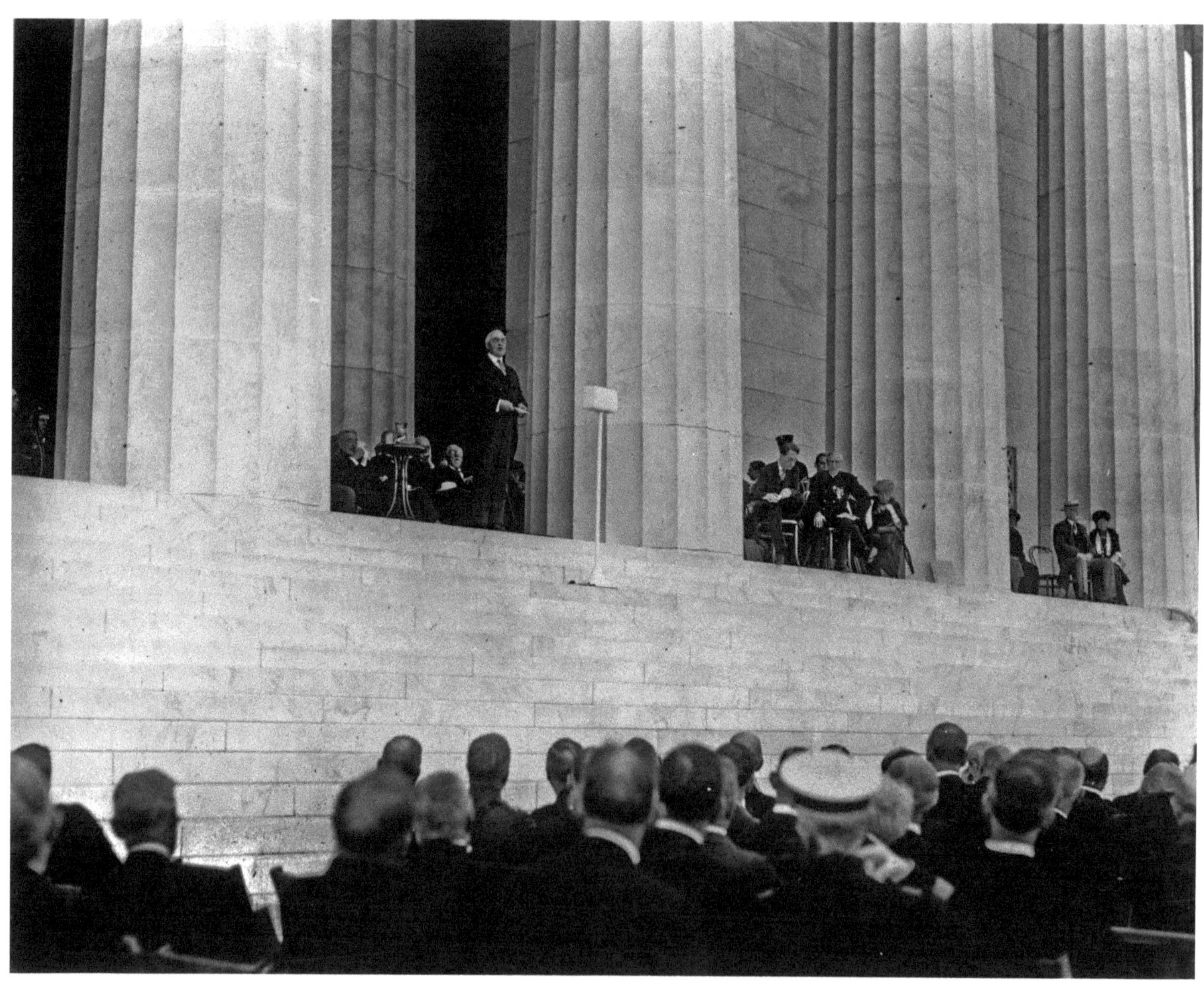

President Warren G. Harding makes dedication remarks on May 30, 1922, on the steps of the Lincoln Memorial. Although Harding delivered the dedication speech, President William Howard Taft signed the bill in February of 1911 to create the memorial. By the time of the dedication, Taft was Chief Justice of the Supreme Court and officiated at the Lincoln Memorial dedication ceremony.

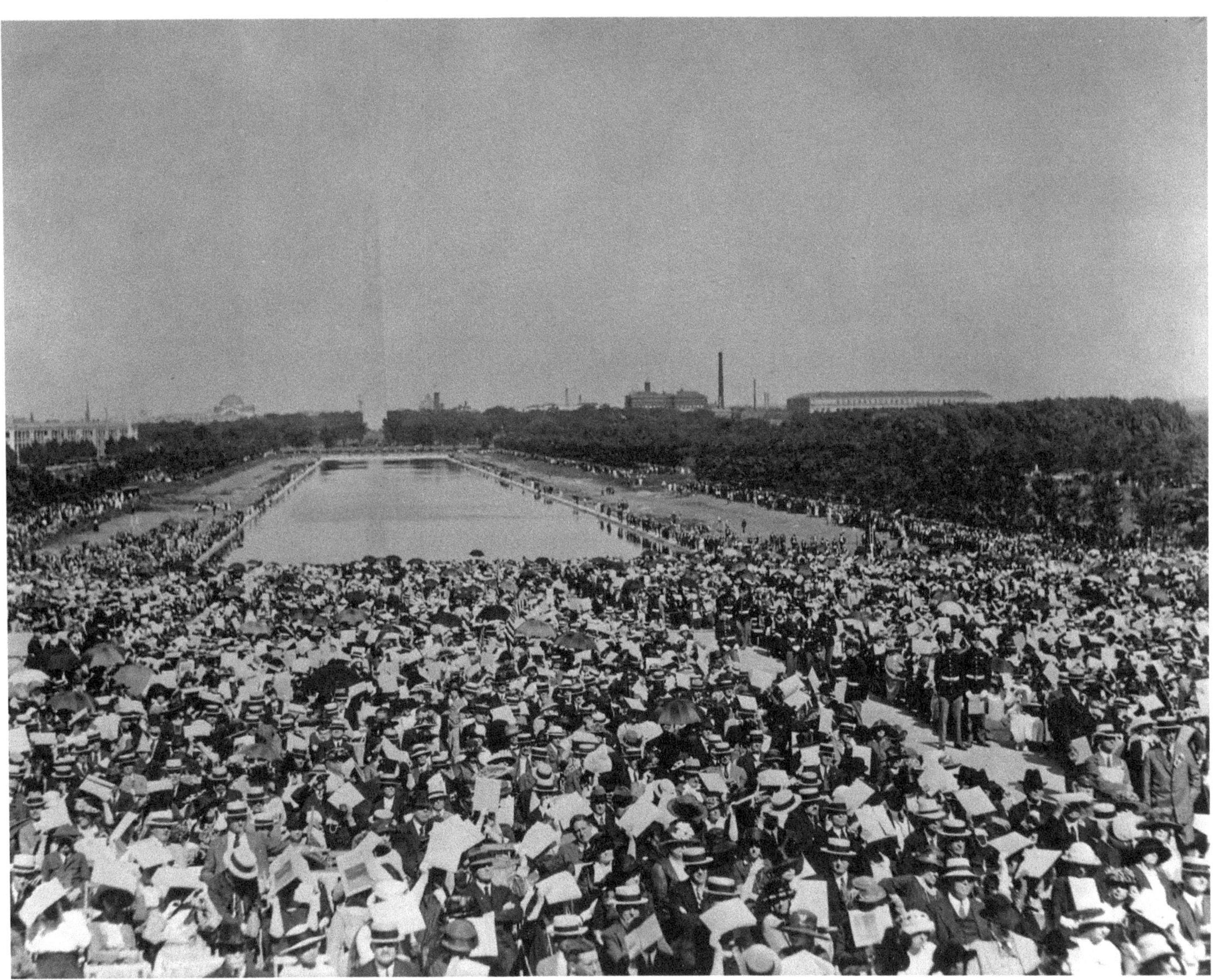

This photo shows crowds around the reflecting pool attending the monument dedication ceremony on May 30, 1922. The National Park Service continues to honor the sixteenth president by marking his birthday with an annual ceremony in the chamber. The ceremony is attended by dignitaries, diplomats, and the public.

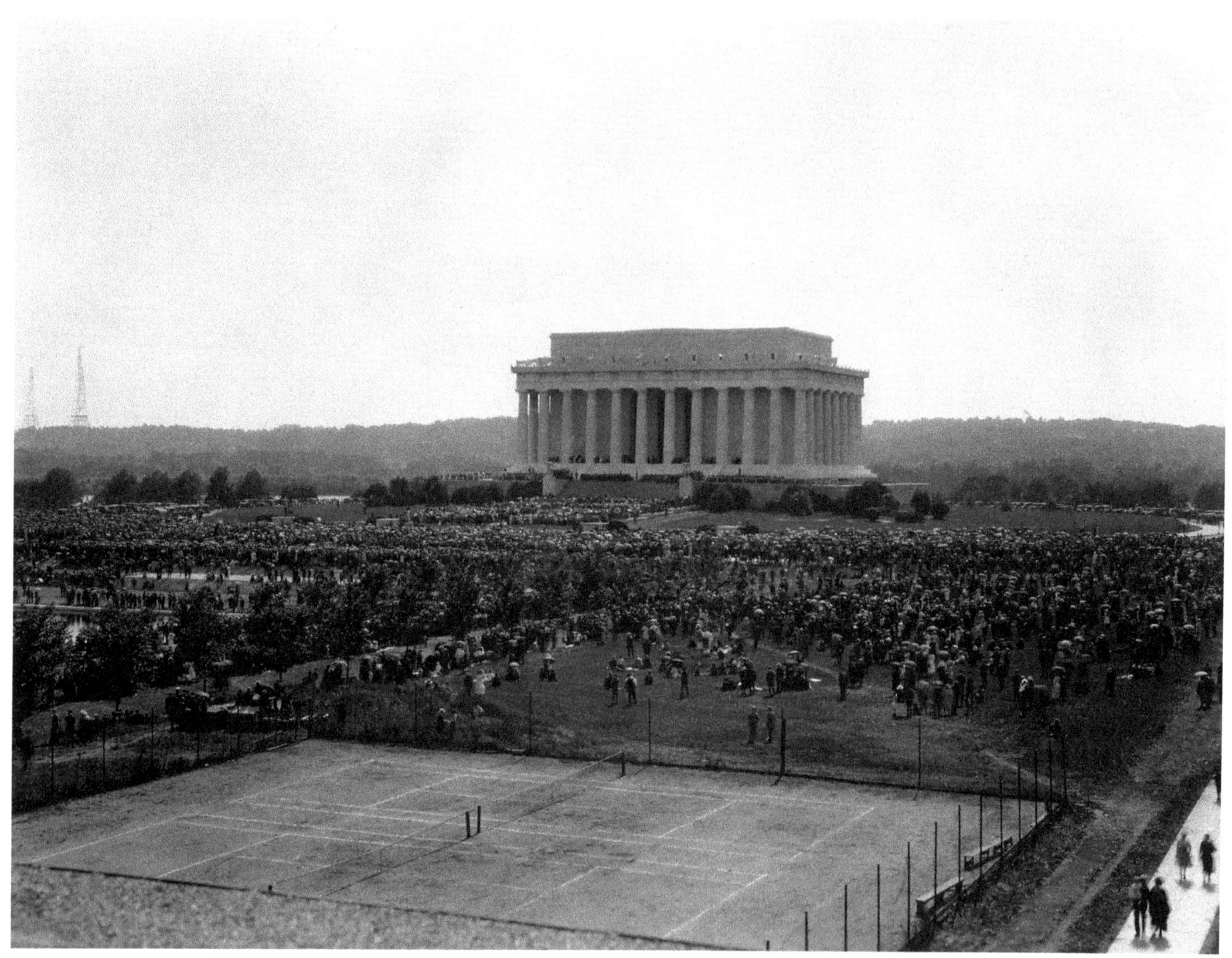

On the eve of the Lincoln Memorial dedication, a *New York Times* reporter wrote, "Thousands will gather tomorrow for the dedication ceremony with which the new Lincoln Memorial will pass from the custody of the Memorial Commission to the Government." According to the article, some 2,000 guests were formally invited to the event, but as evidenced in this Army Signal Corps photograph, thousands more would attend.

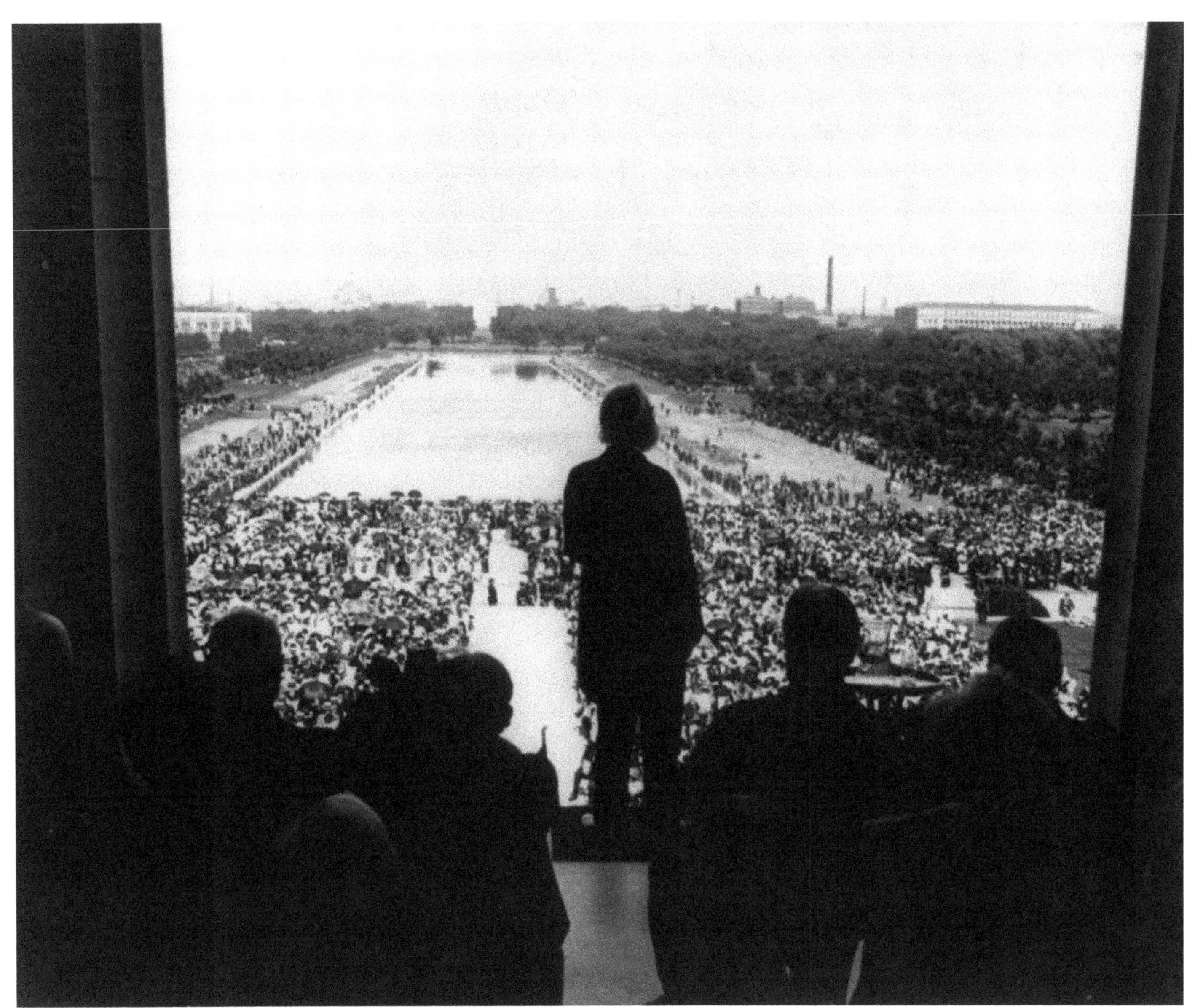

One of the speakers for the Lincoln Memorial dedication included poet Edwin Markham. Markham recited a poem during the ceremony.

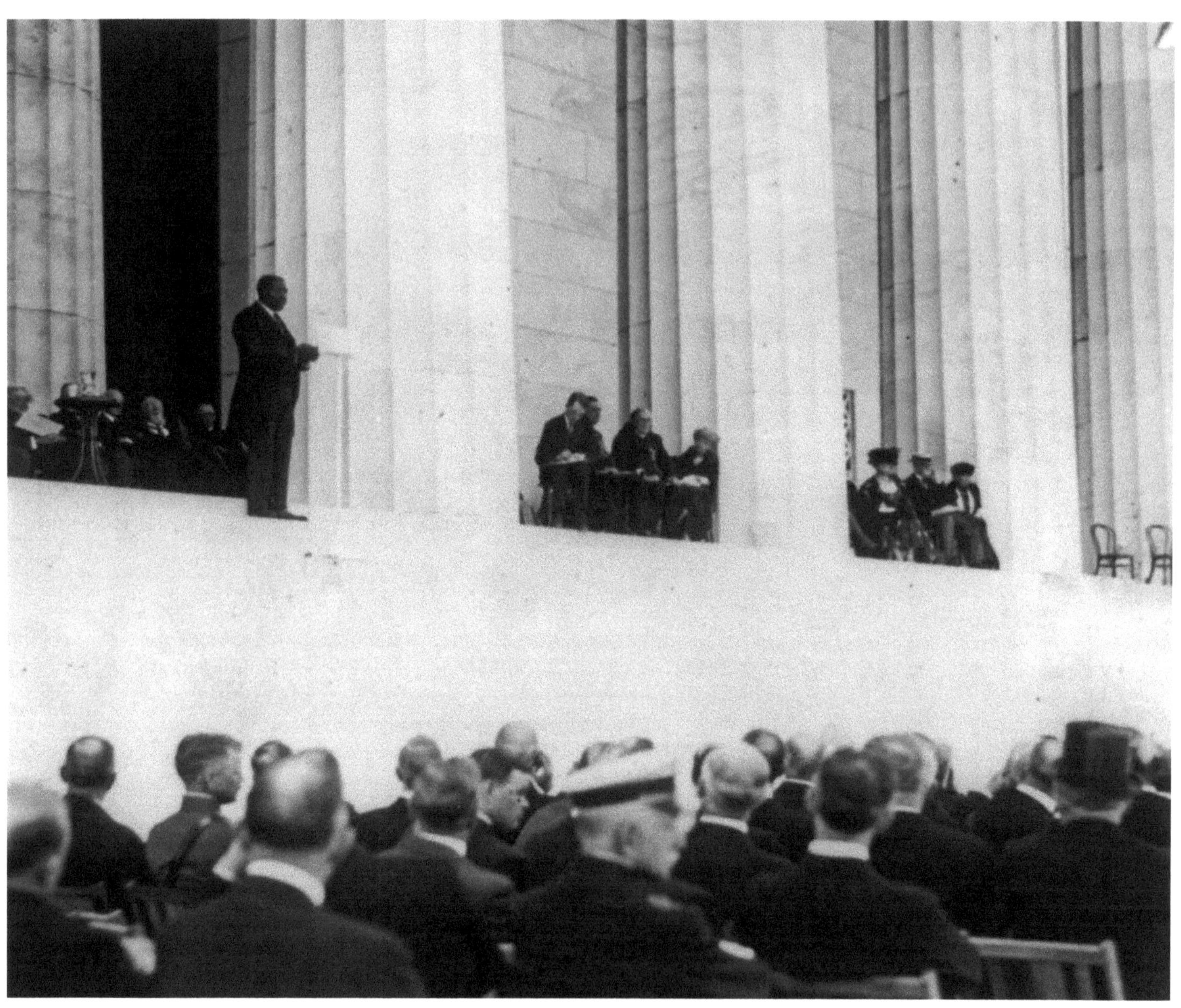

Improving race relations in America was one of the themes discussed during the dedication. Dr. Robert Moton, second president of the Tuskegee Institute in Alabama, delivered the keynote address. Although his speech was concerned with promoting racial equality, the audience during the dedication was largely segregated.

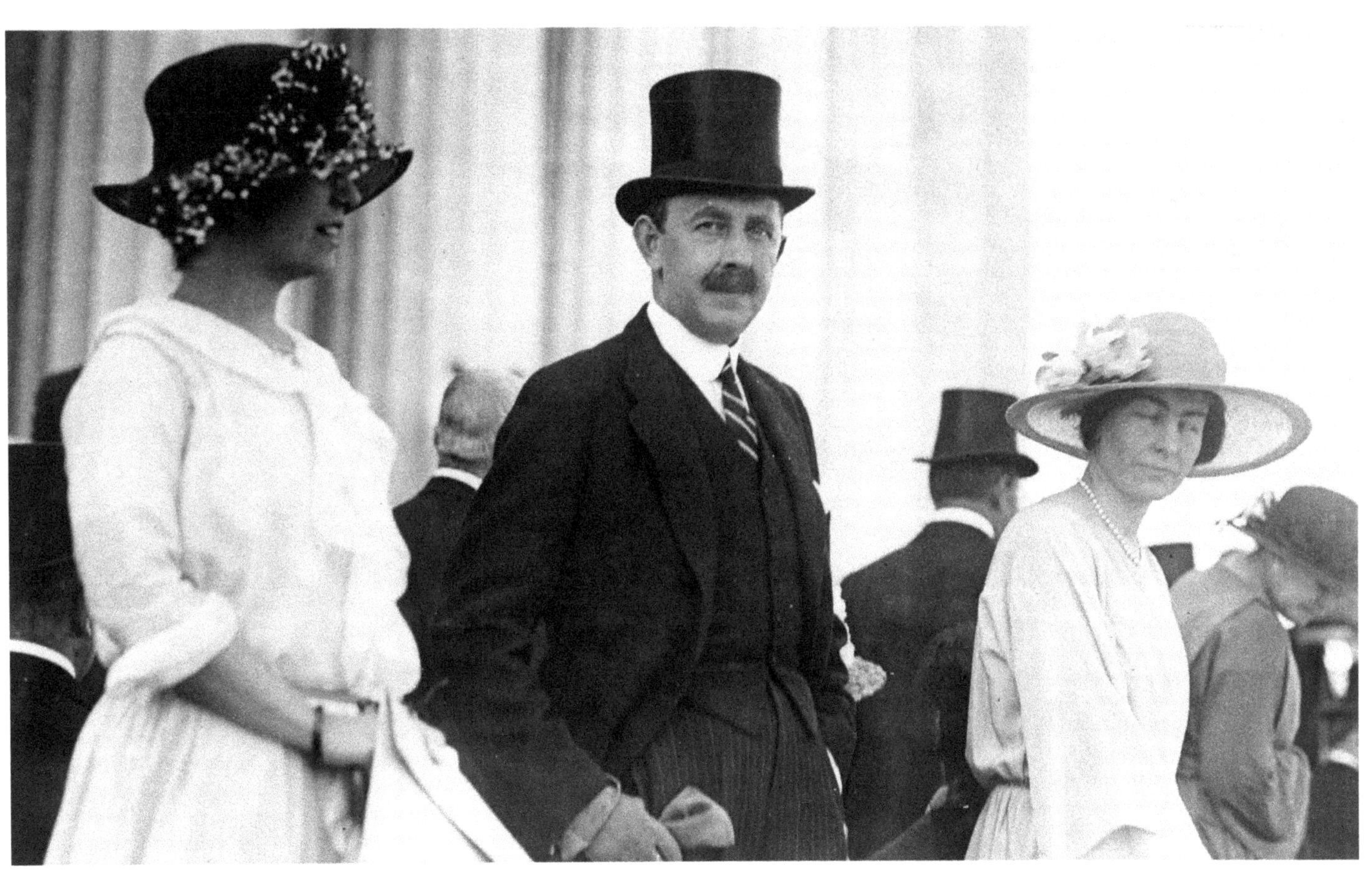

Madame Széchenji, Count Lásló Széchenji, and Alice Roosevelt Longworth are photographed during the dedication of the Lincoln Memorial on May 30, 1922.

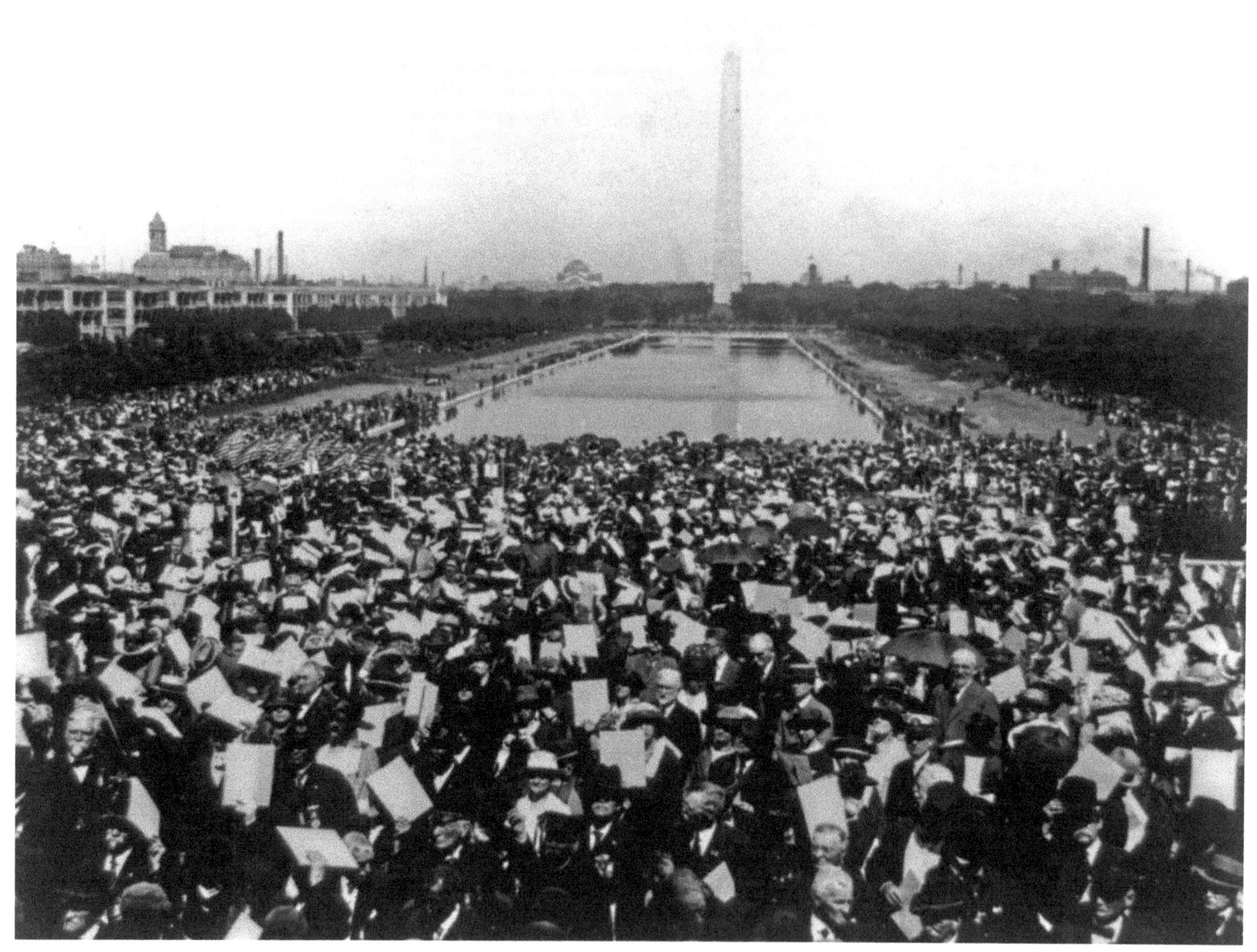

This image features a view of the Mall from the east side of the Lincoln Memorial.

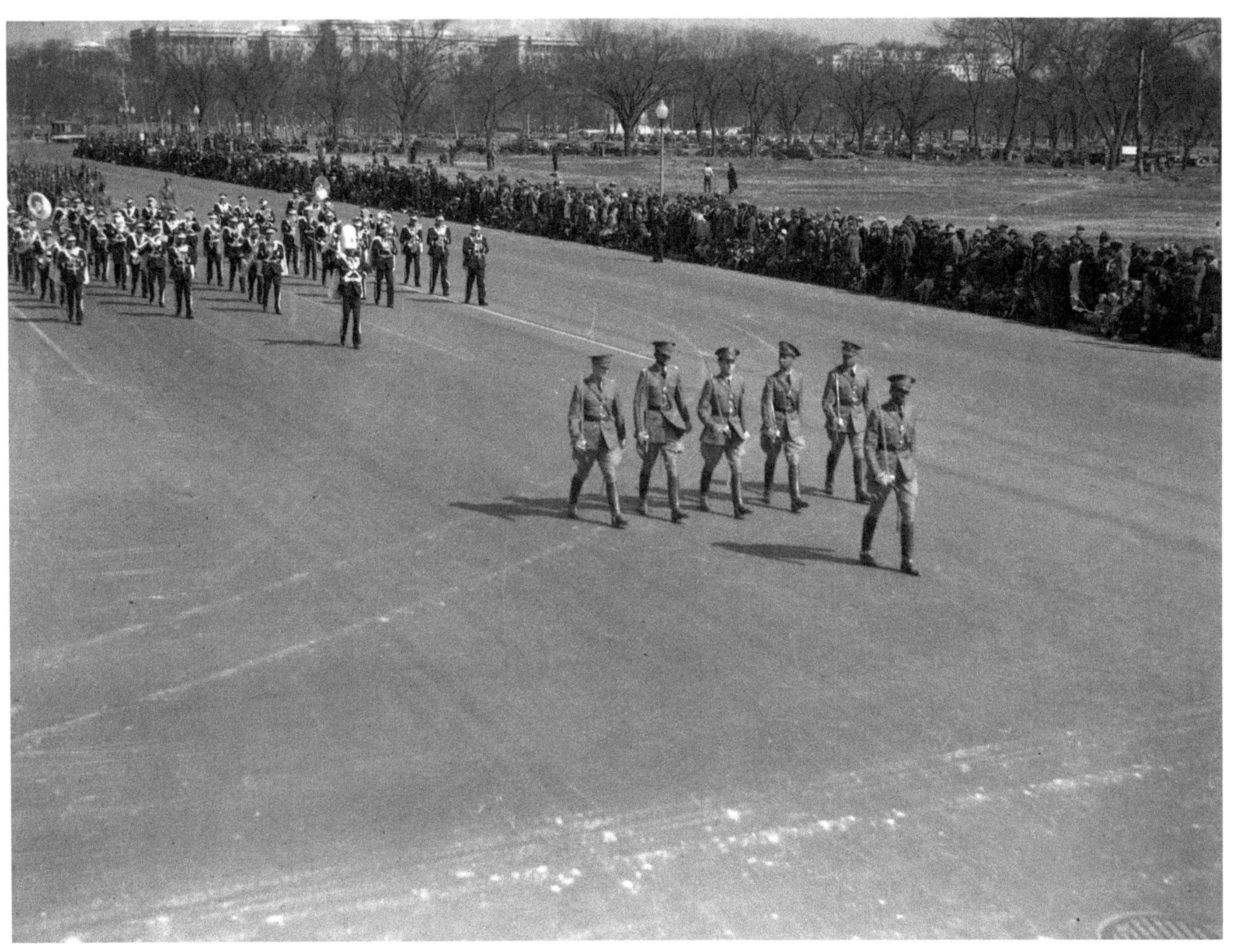

Pomp and circumstance is not unusual at monument sites in Washington, D.C. Shown here, a marching band is in action near the Lincoln Memorial.

A view of the Washington Monument through the Lincoln Memorial columns, and farther still, the nation's Capitol.

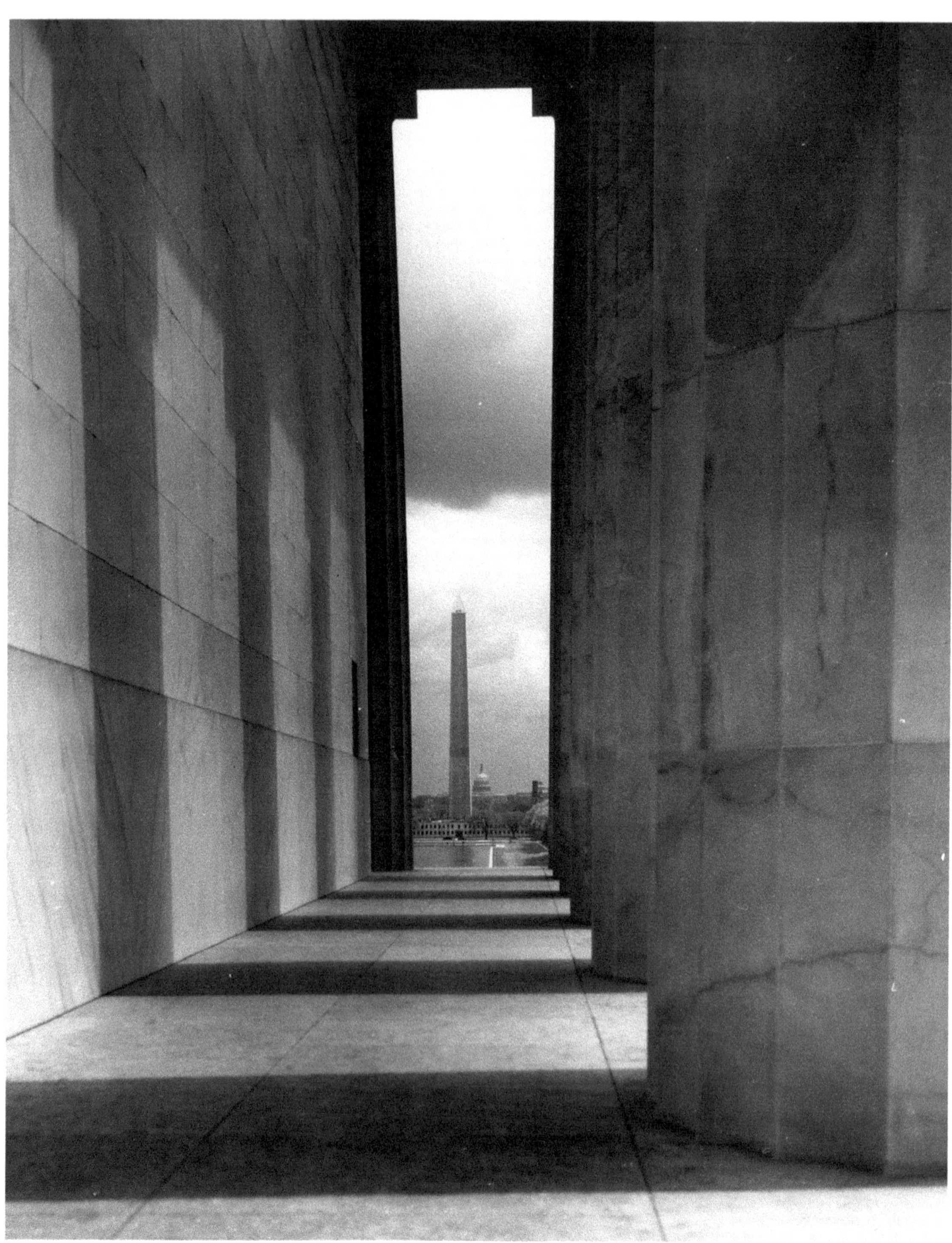

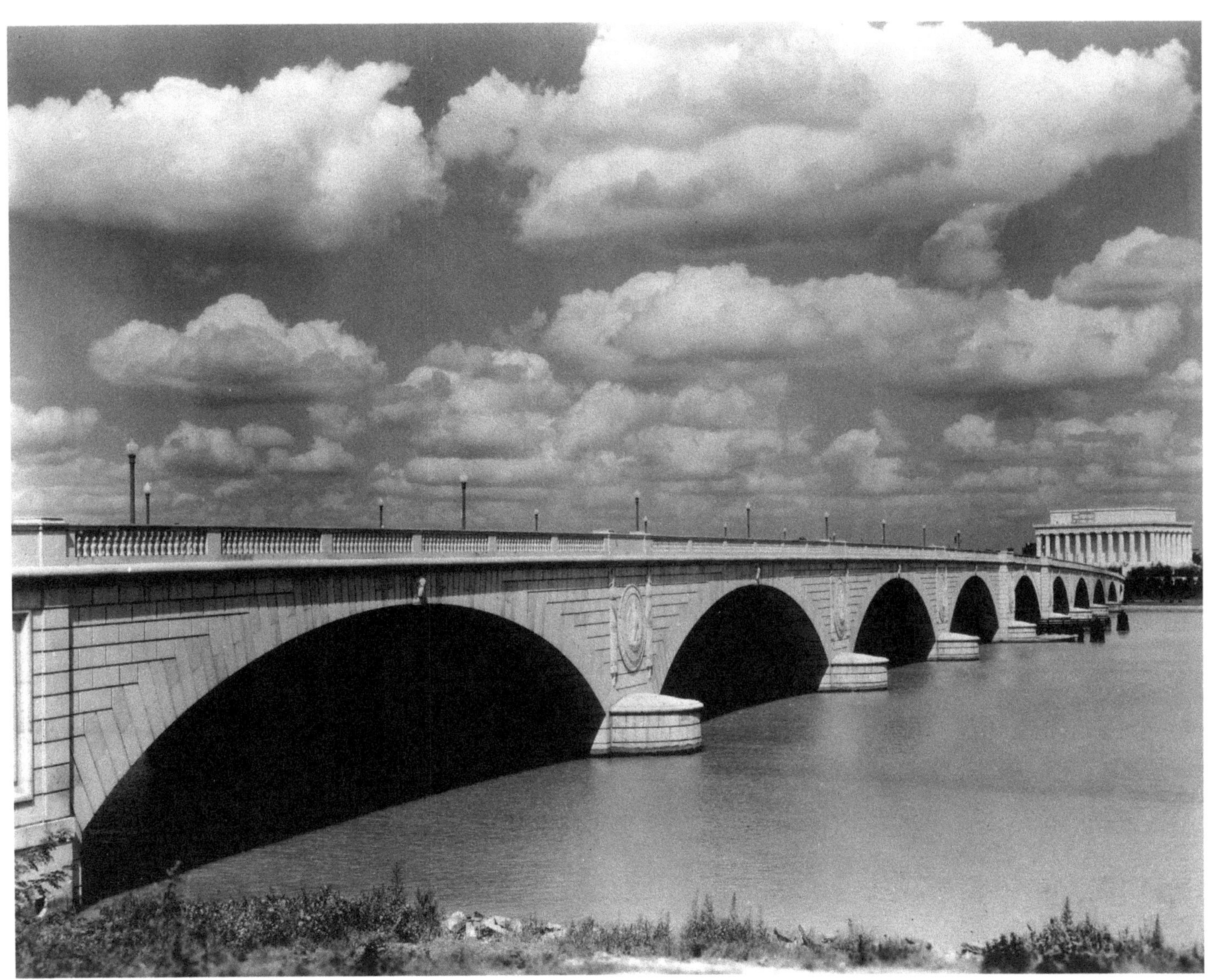

A view of the Lincoln Memorial from the Arlington Memorial Bridge. The bridge connects the Lincoln Memorial and Arlington National Cemetery.

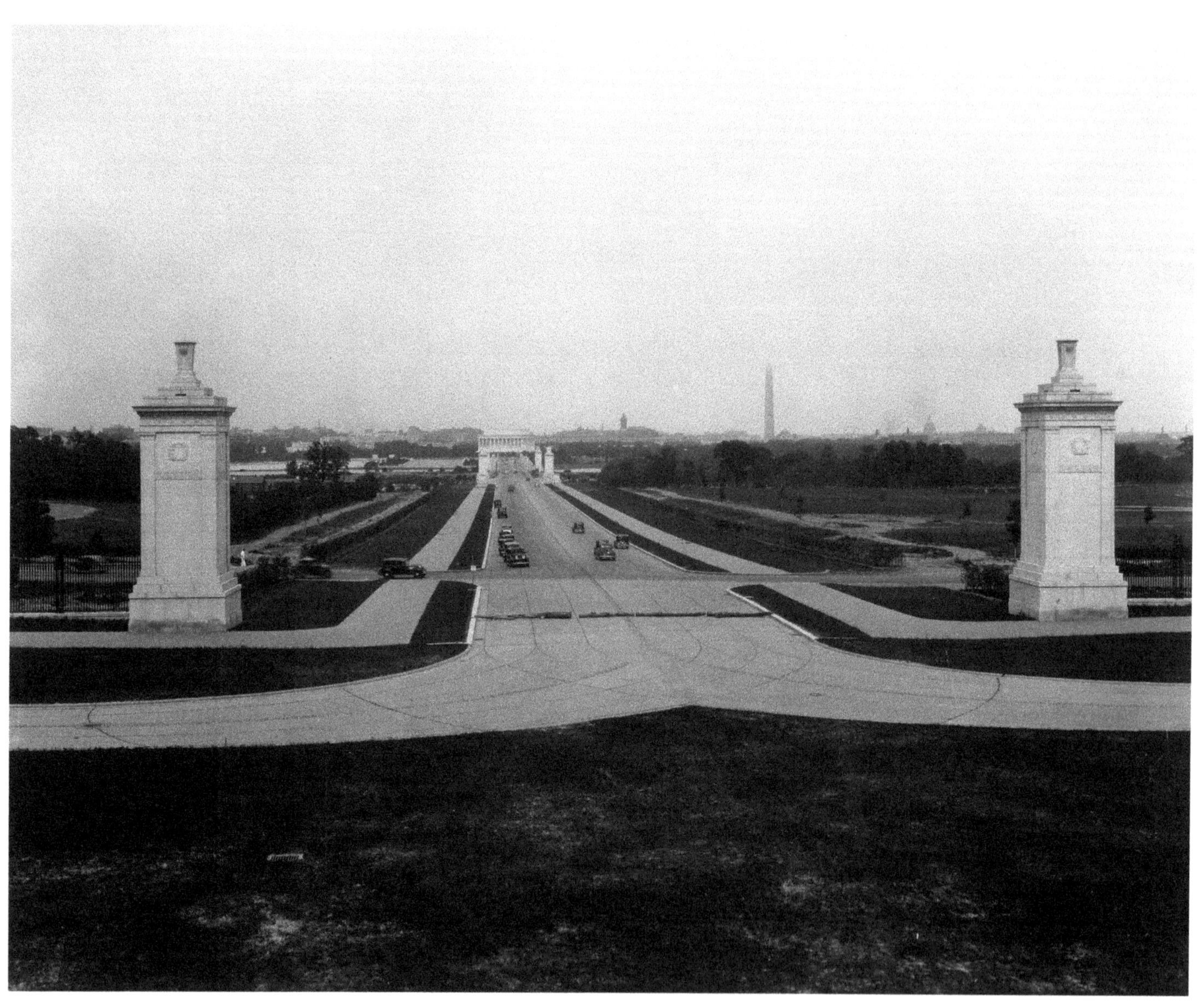

Built February 24, 1925, the Arlington Memorial Bridge symbolizes the end of the conflict between the North and the South, and the states coming together to form one unified country.

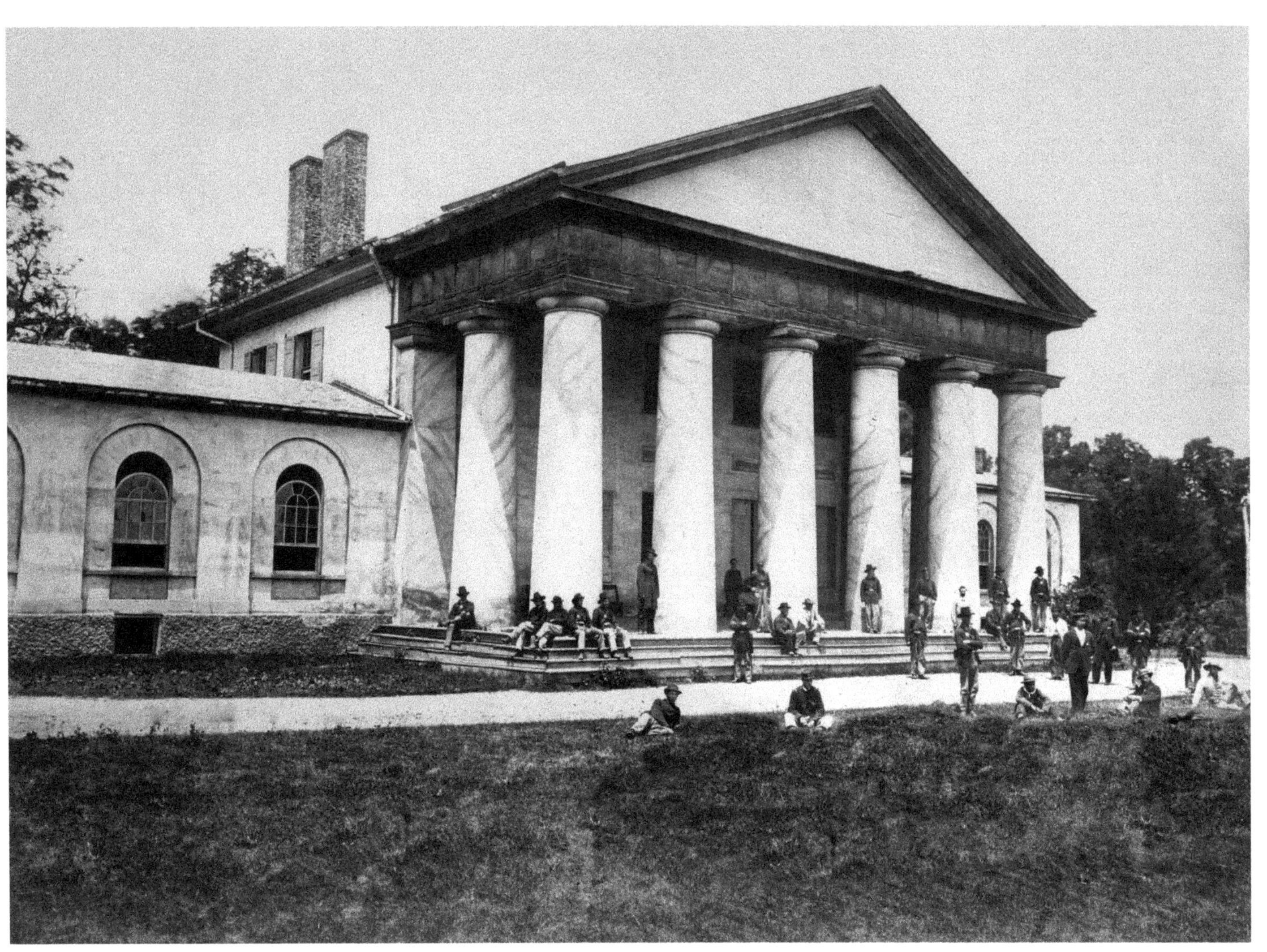

The Arlington House, located in Arlington, Virginia, was the home of Robert E. Lee before the Civil War.

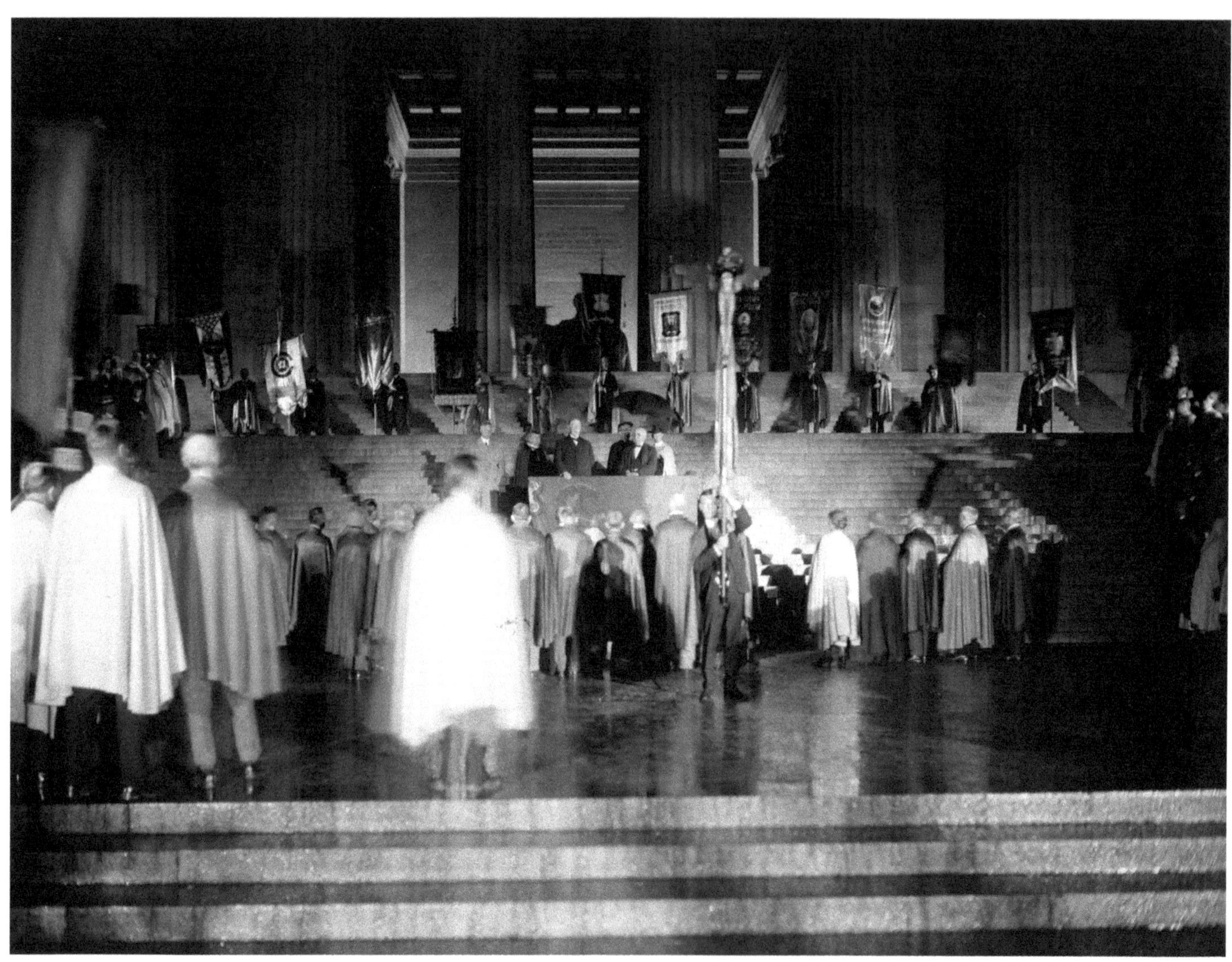

This picture, dated 1923, was a gift to the Library of Congress from Herbert A. French in 1947. The same year this photograph was taken, Henry Bacon was honored by his peers with a gold medal for his Lincoln Memorial design. The medal is the most prestigious honor that the American Institute of Architects awards.

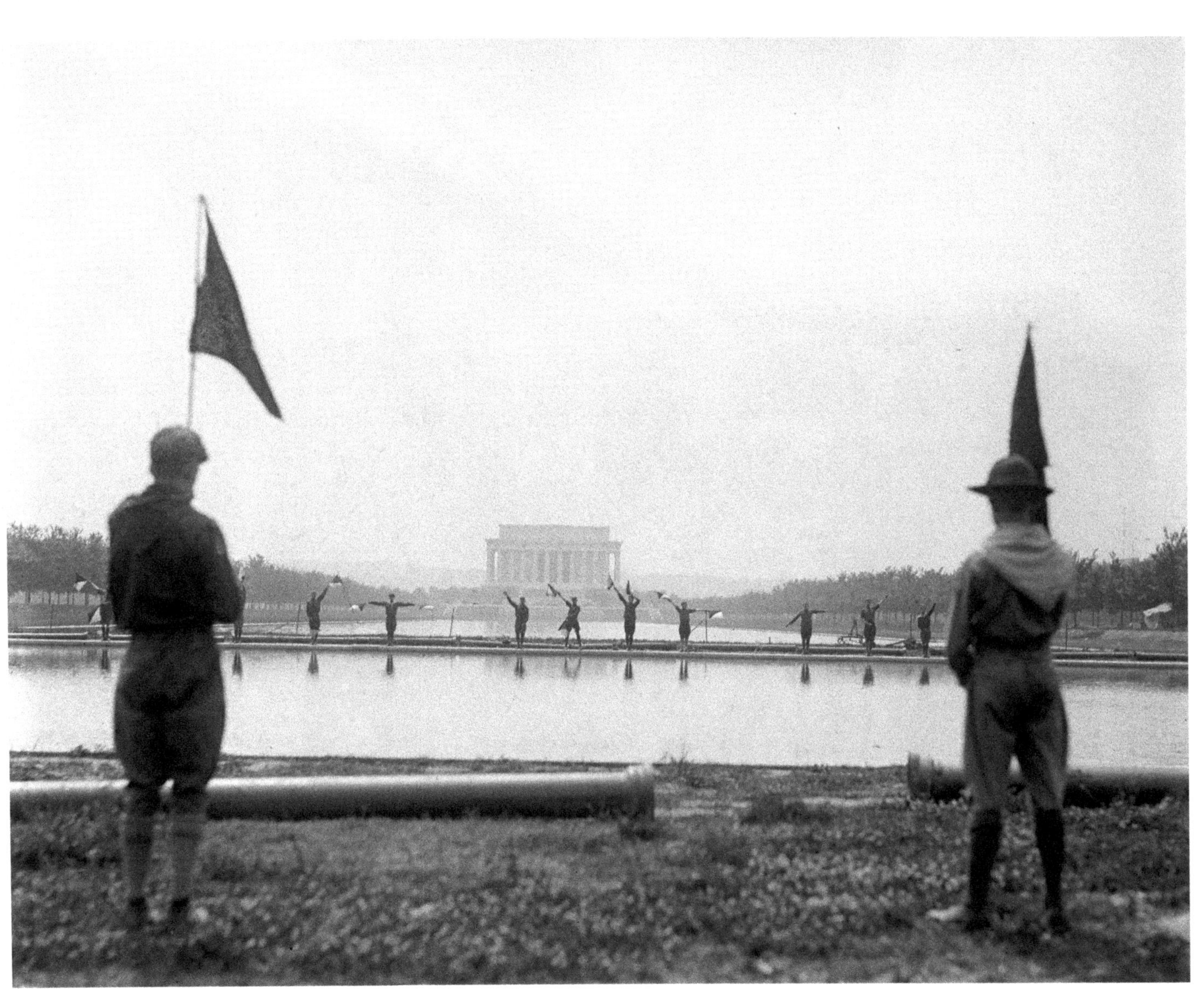

On June 16, 1923, this photo of Boy Scouts bearing signal flags was taken at the Lincoln Memorial.

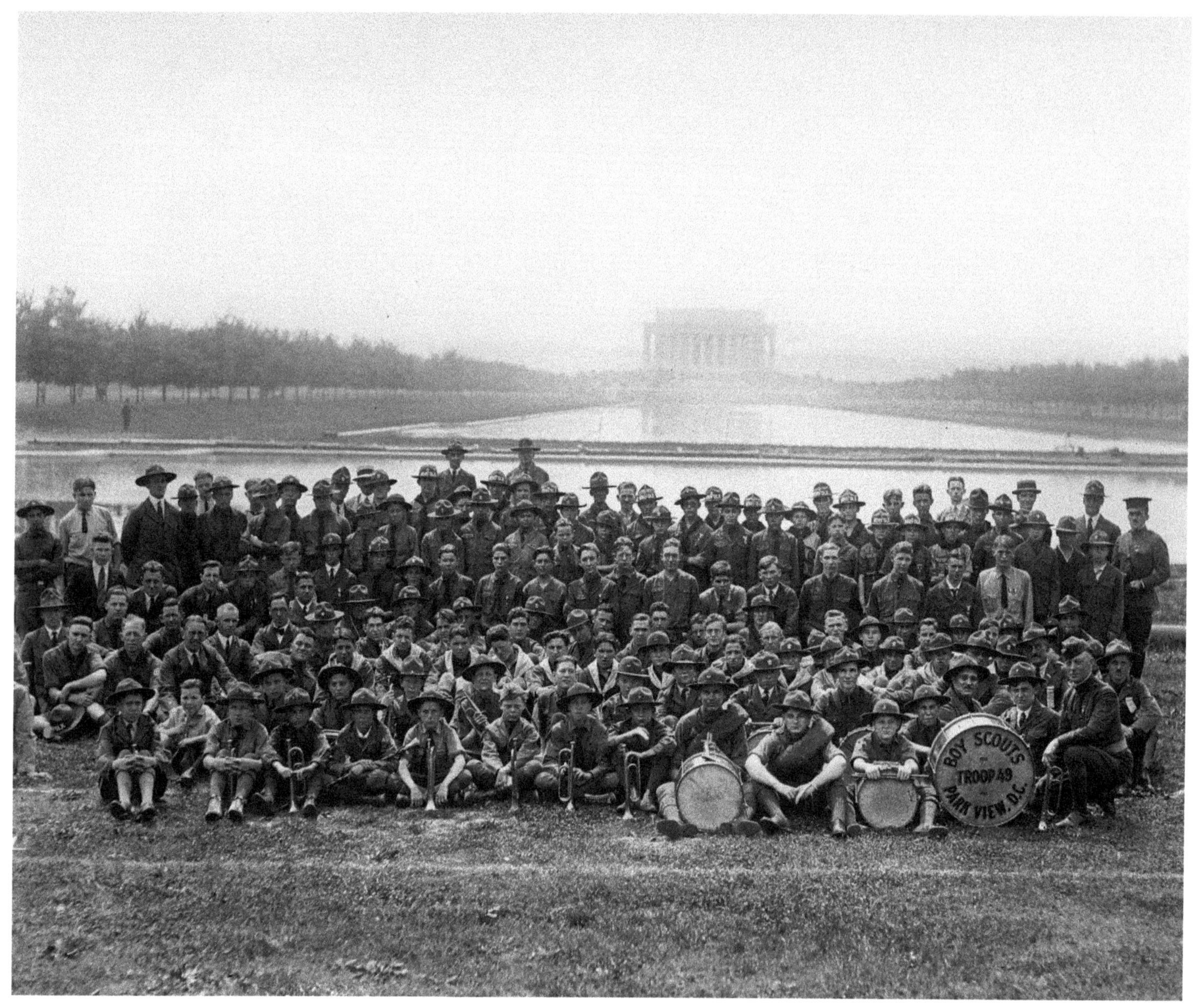

A group photo of Boy Scouts taken in 1923. Founded in 1910, the Boy Scouts of America is one of the largest and most active youth organizations in the United States.

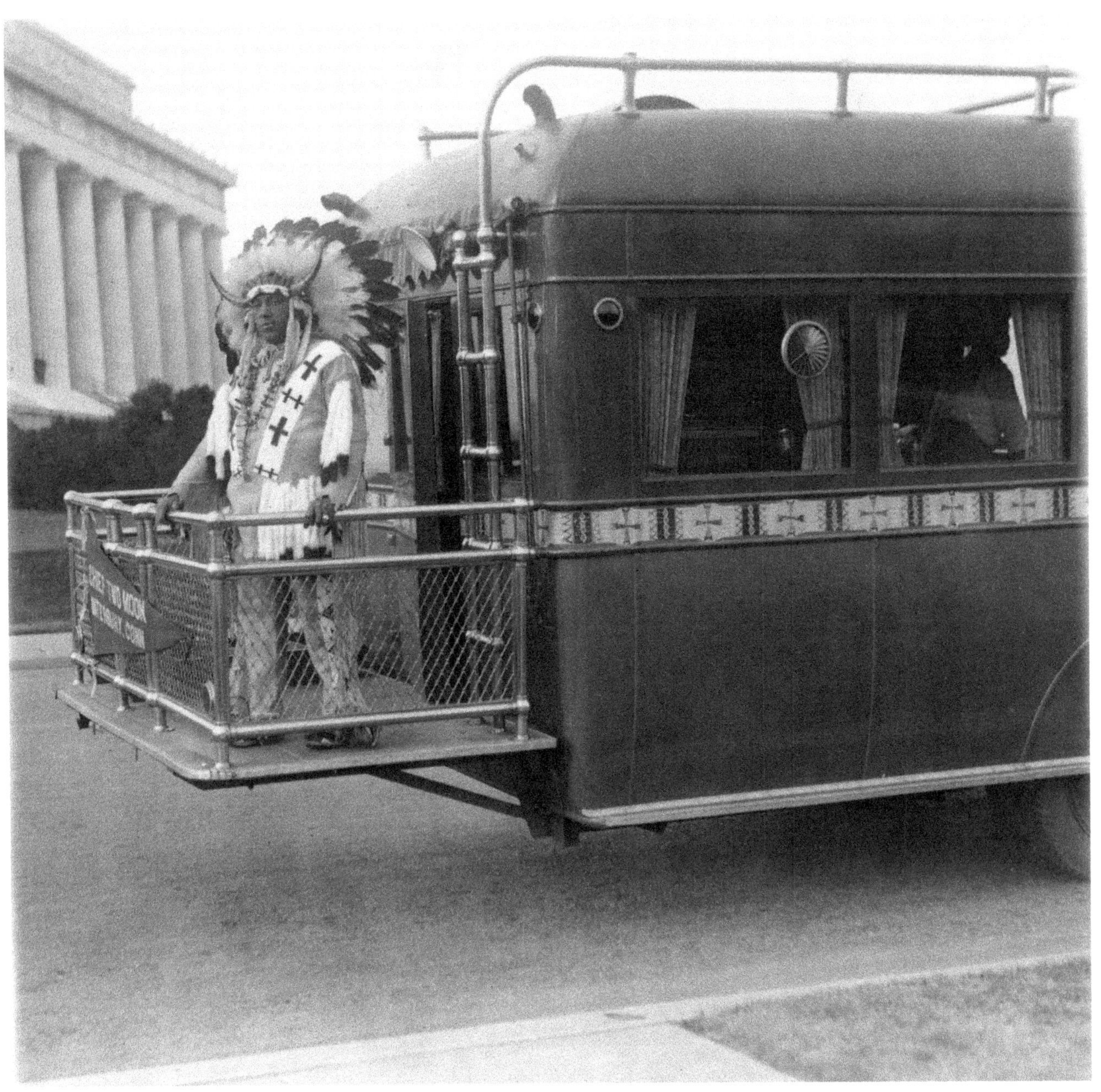

On a visit to the Lincoln Memorial, Chief Two Moon, a wealthy Native American medicine man from Waterbury, Connecticut, poses for posterity from his tour bus.

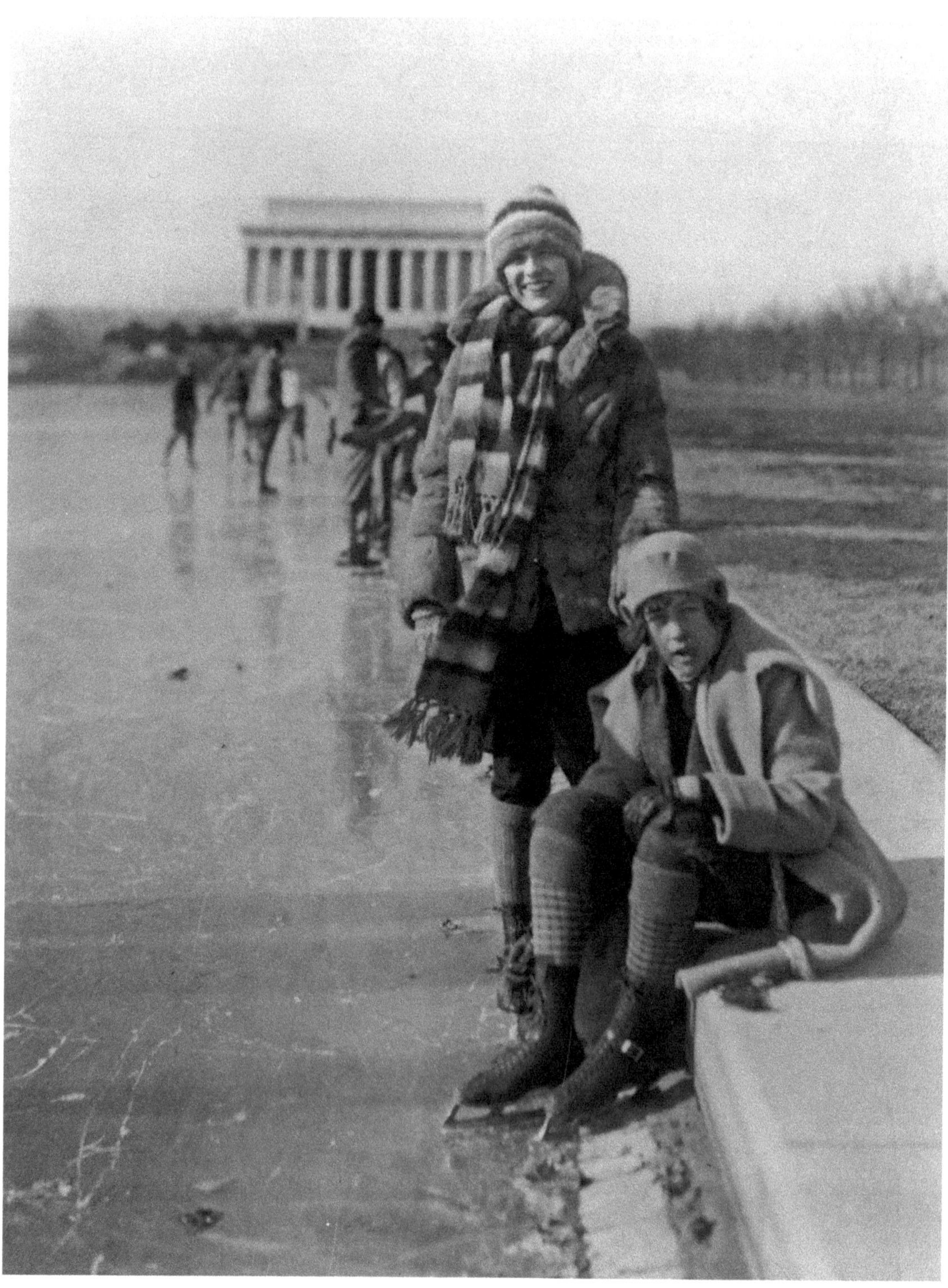

Abbey Jackson (seated) and Celene DuPuy take a brief break from ice skating on the Reflecting Pool. The Lincoln Memorial is visible in the background.

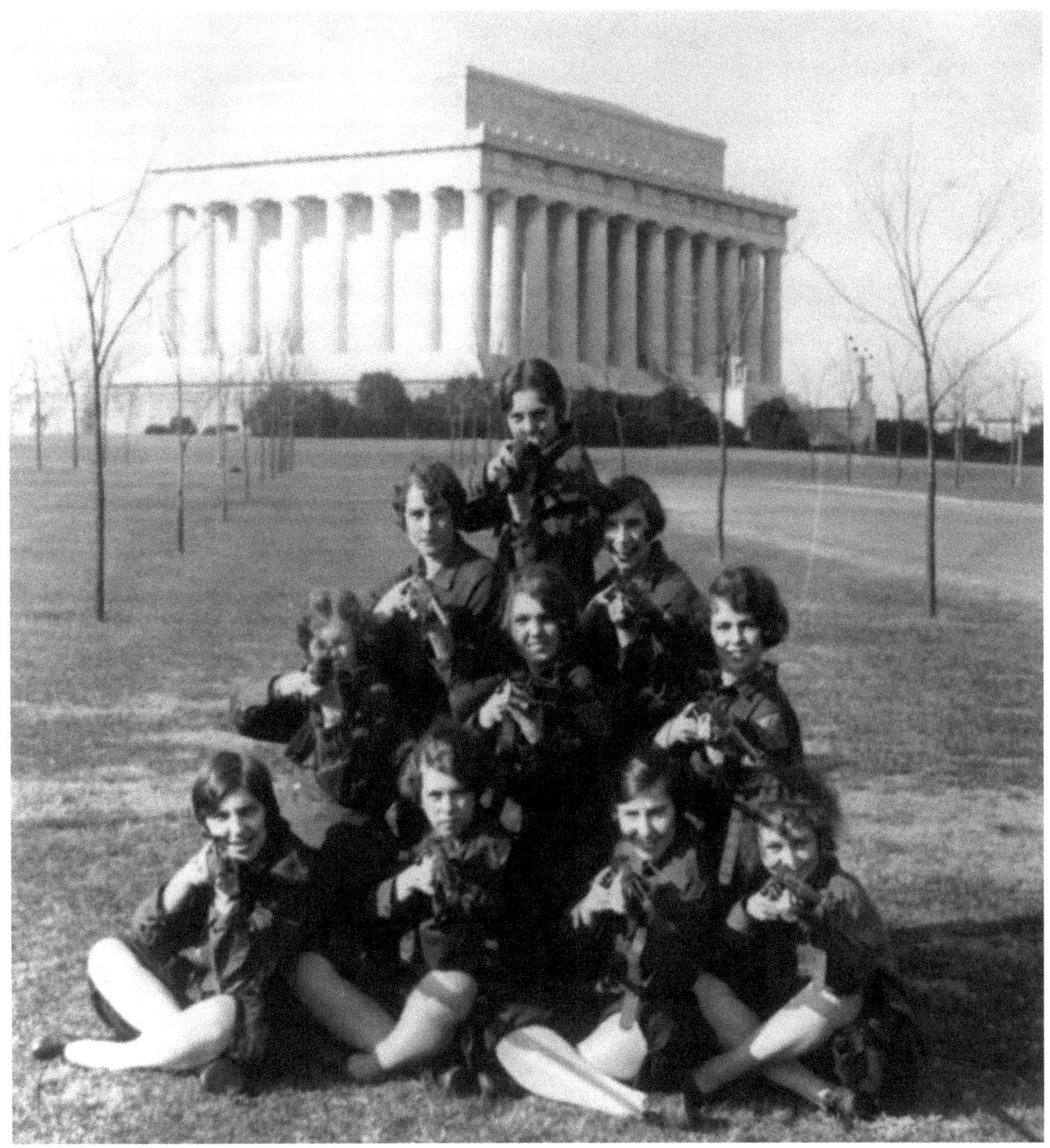

Ten girls from the George Washington University Rifle Team pose with rifles on February 2, 1927, with the Lincoln Memorial as a backdrop.

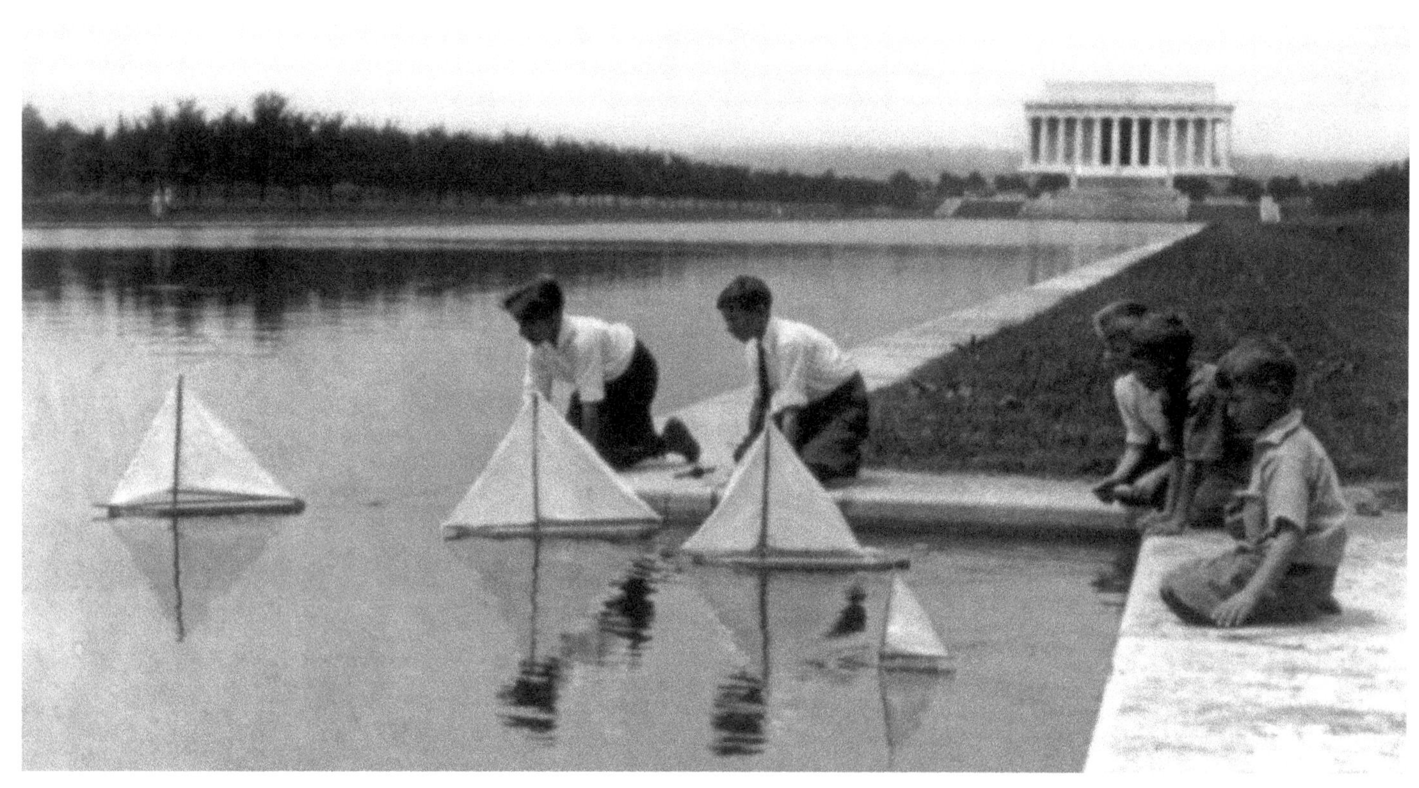

In this 1920s photo, children sail their boats on the waters of the Reflecting Pool. The Lincoln Memorial can be seen in the background.

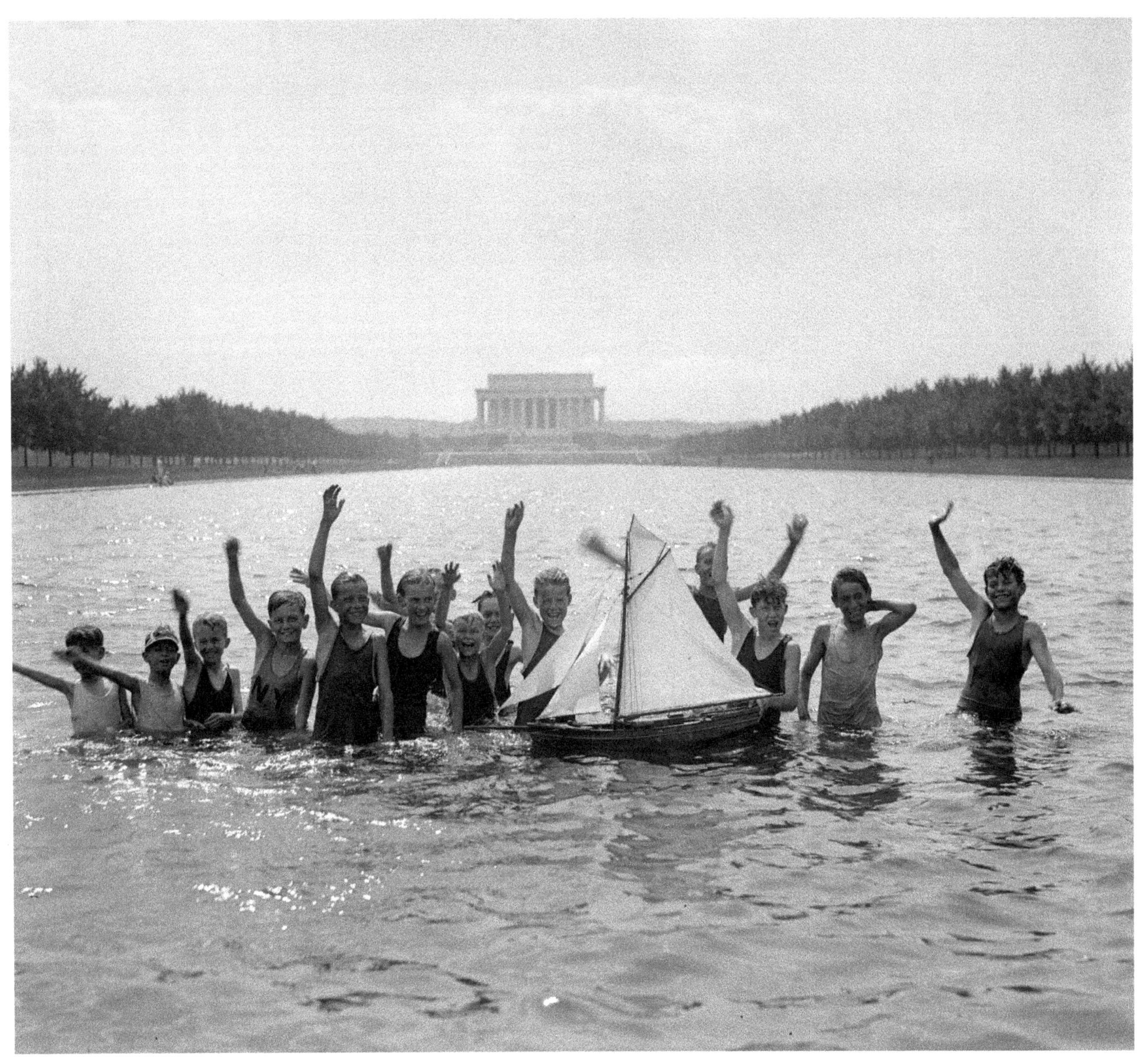

A group of swimmers pose on July 16, 1926, with the Lincoln Memorial in view.

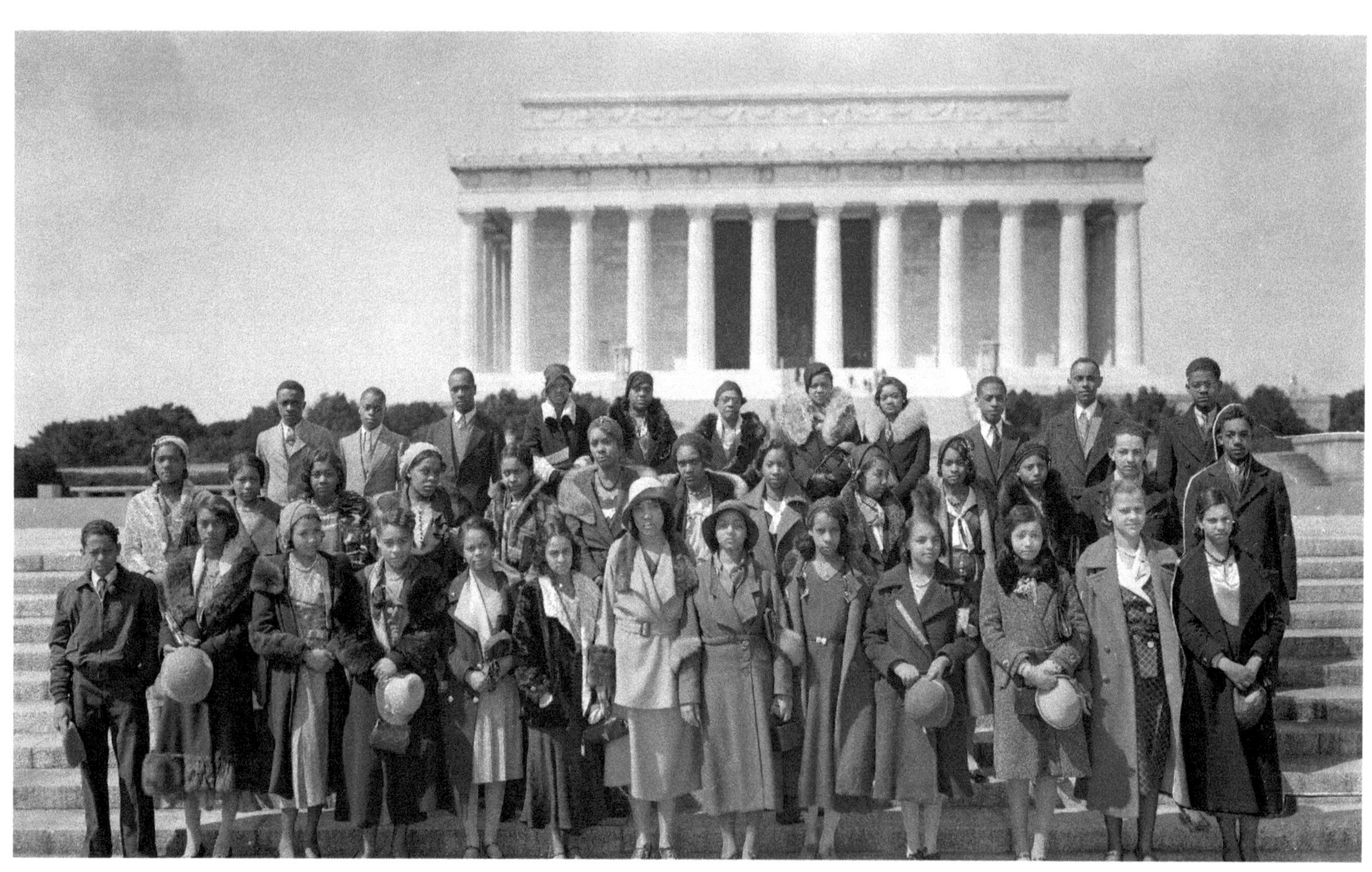

In 1932 this unidentified group of men and women pose for Washington, D.C., photographer Addison Scurlock in front of the Lincoln Memorial.

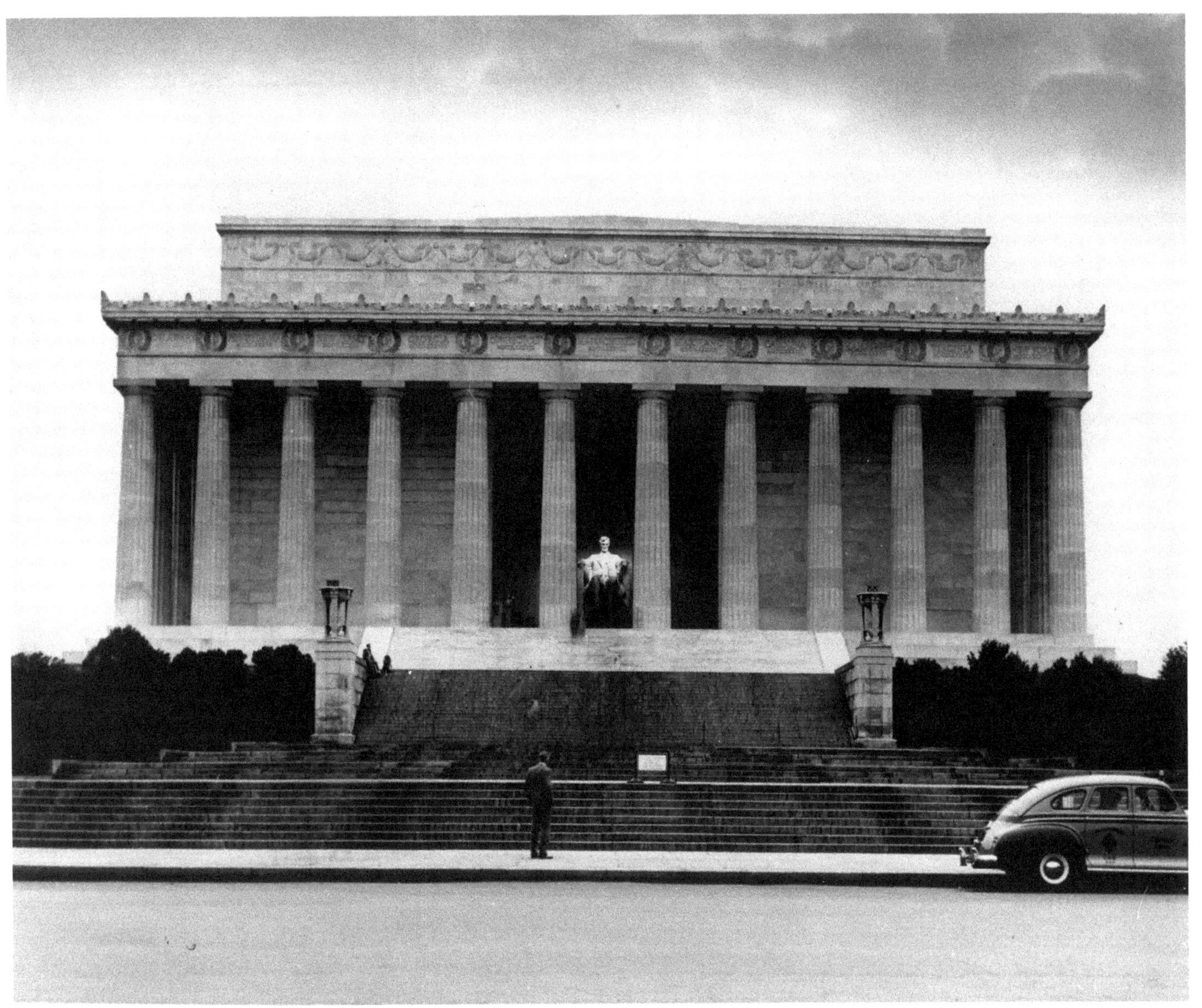

This memorial is an artistic interpretation of much more than Abraham Lincoln's legacy. Architect Henry Bacon used stone from different quarries around the country to symbolize how the states formed a unified nation.

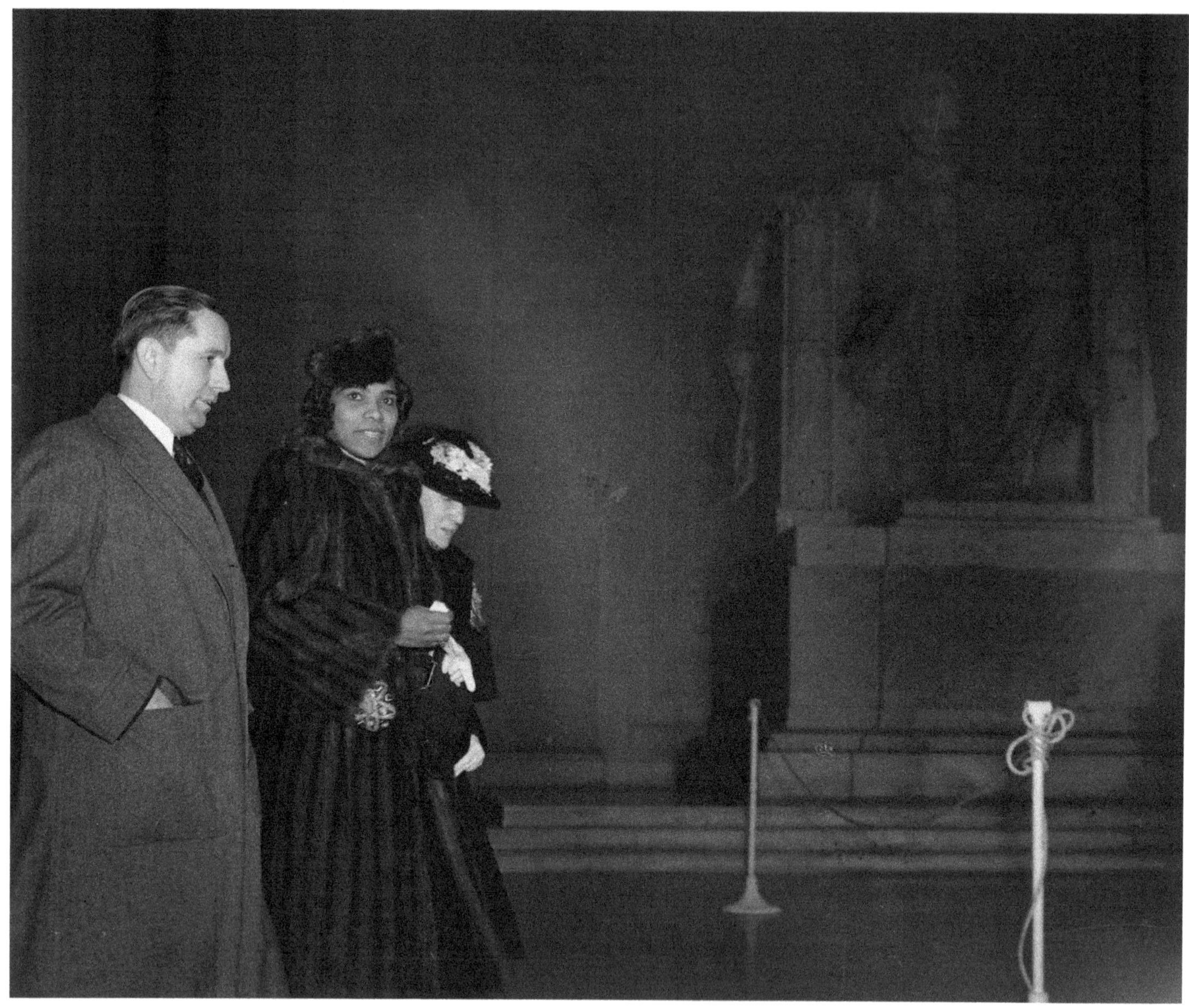

In 1939, the Daughters of the American Revolution declined a performance by singer Marian Anderson at DAR Constitution Hall. When Eleanor Roosevelt heard of this, she arranged for Anderson to sing at the Lincoln Memorial. This image shows Anderson walking through the memorial. Years later, Anderson would perform at Constitution Hall for a humanitarian benefit to aid China.

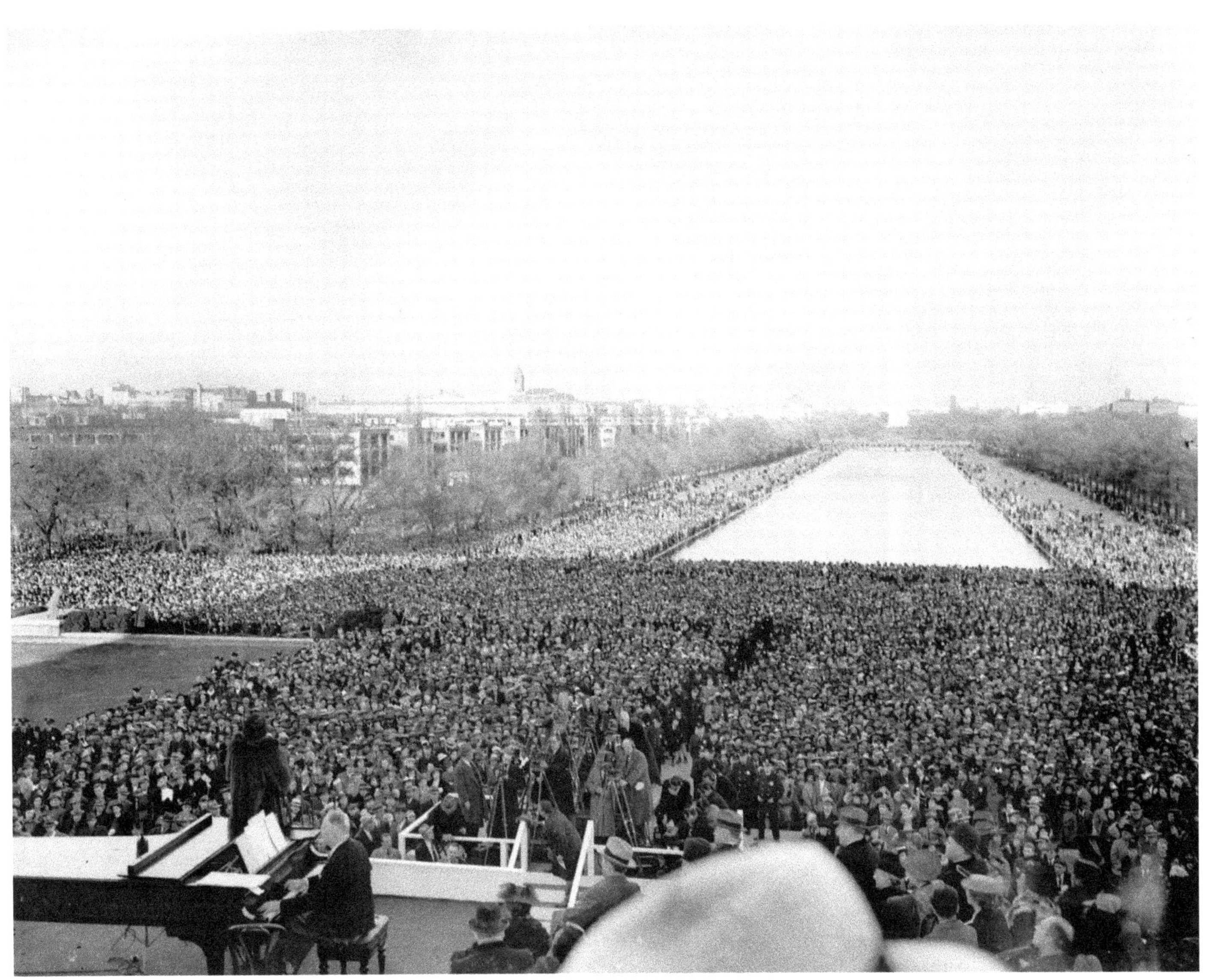

On Easter Sunday 1939, Marian Anderson mesmerizes the crowds during her concert on the steps of the Lincoln Memorial.

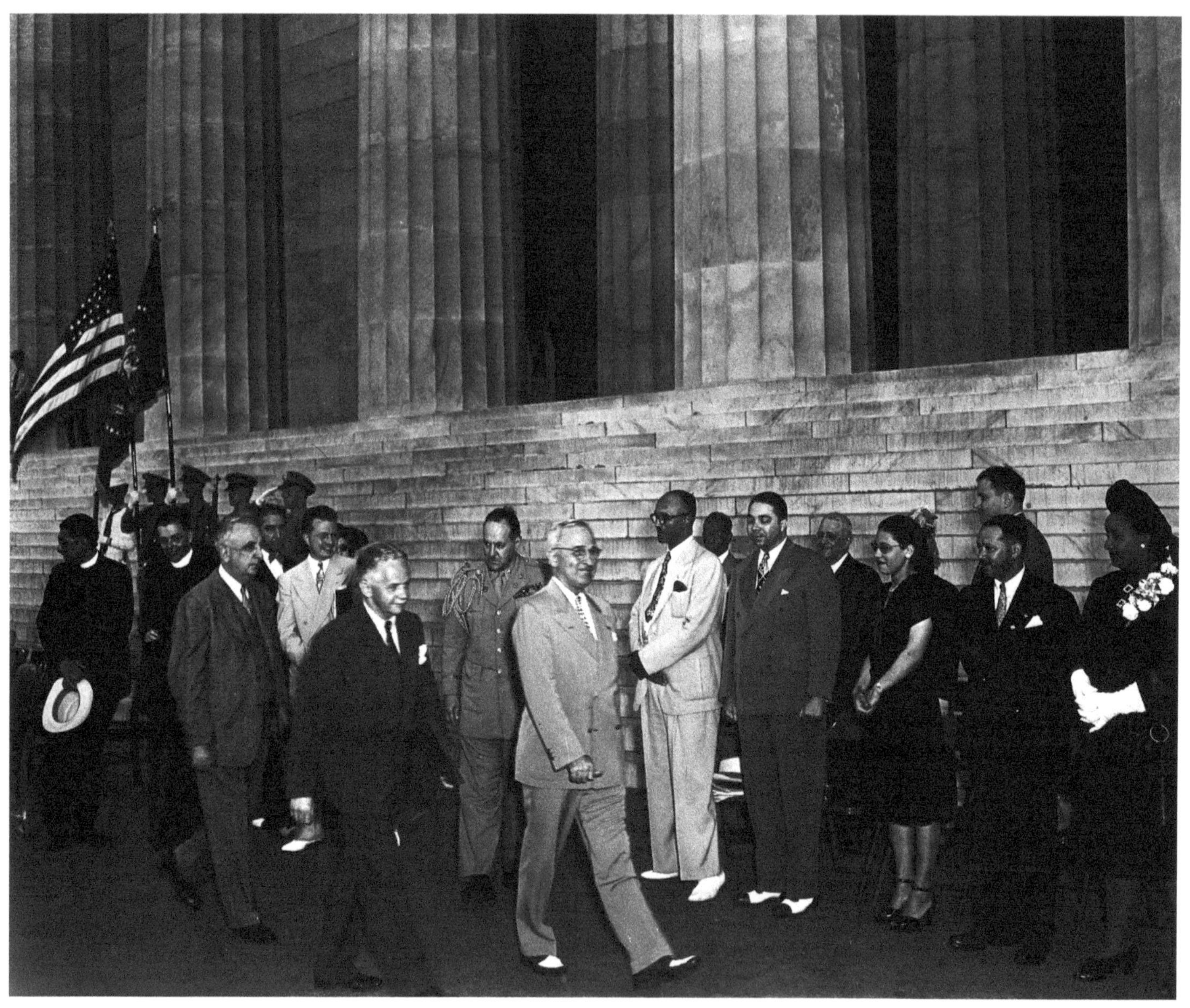

President Harry Truman leaves after giving a speech at the NAACP conference held in 1947 at the Lincoln Memorial.

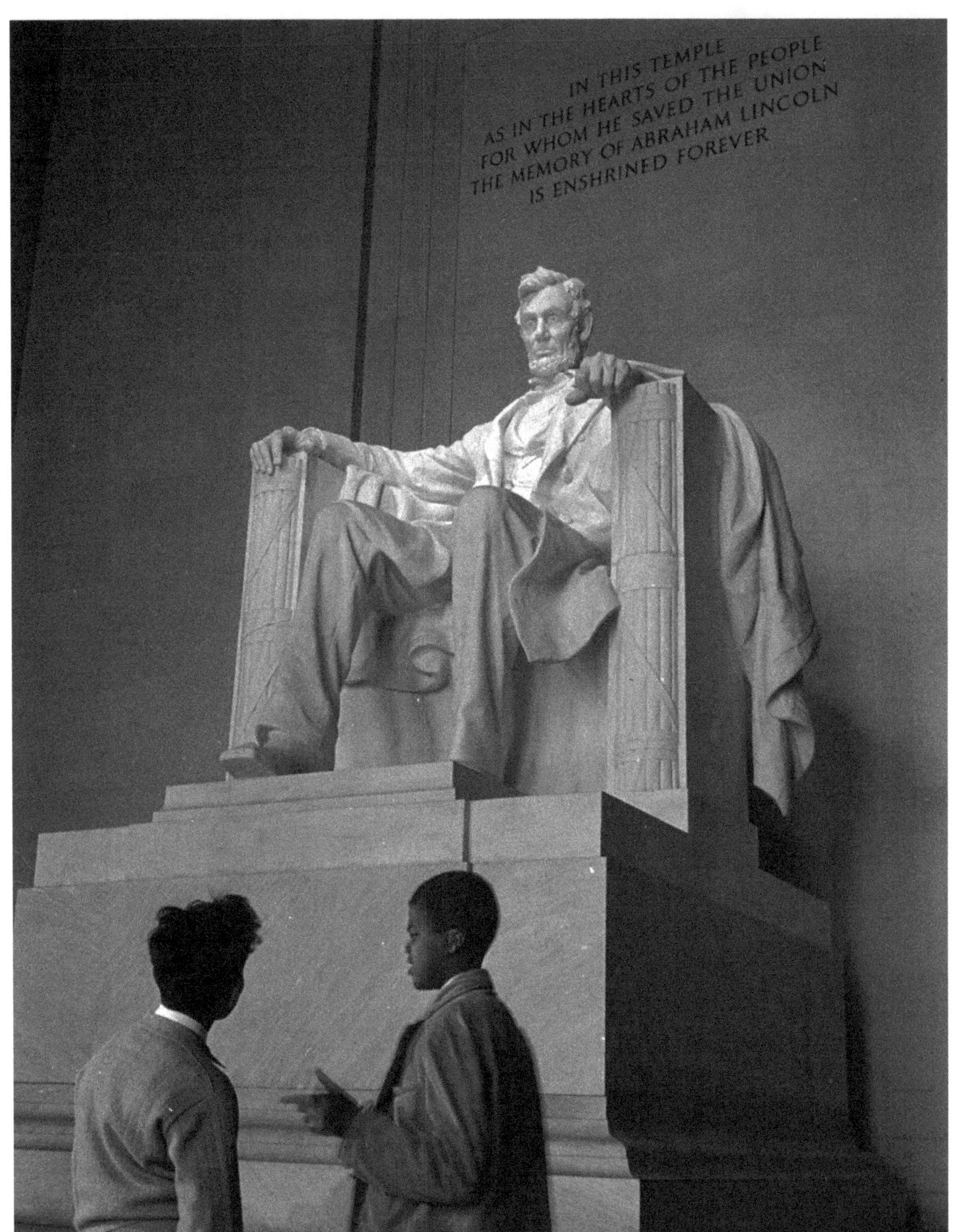

In the spring of 1942, these unidentified young men admire the Lincoln Memorial.

Following Spread: This photo was taken by the U.S. Navy from the top of the Washington Monument on September 12, 1944. The view faces west, toward the Lincoln Memorial.

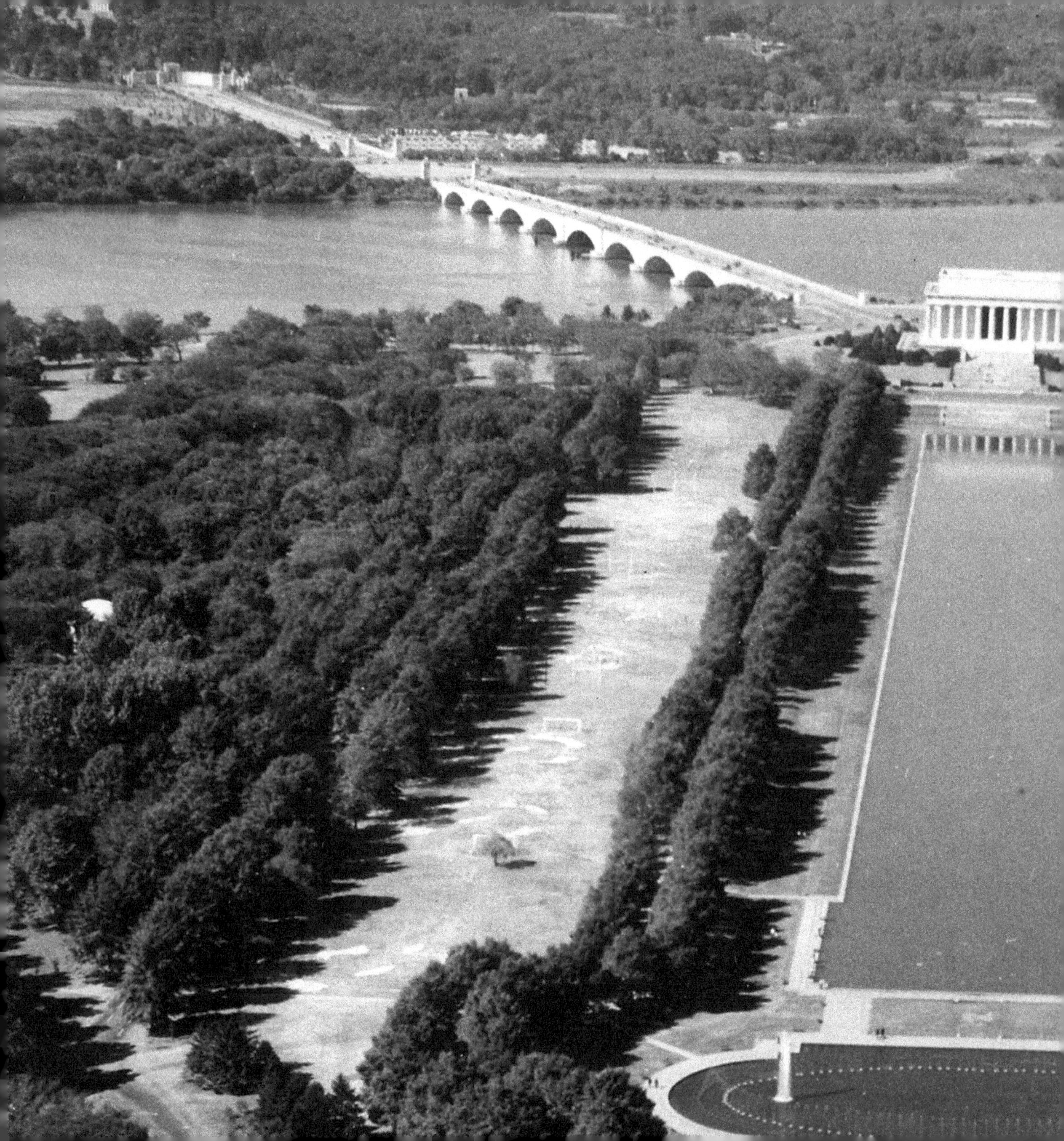

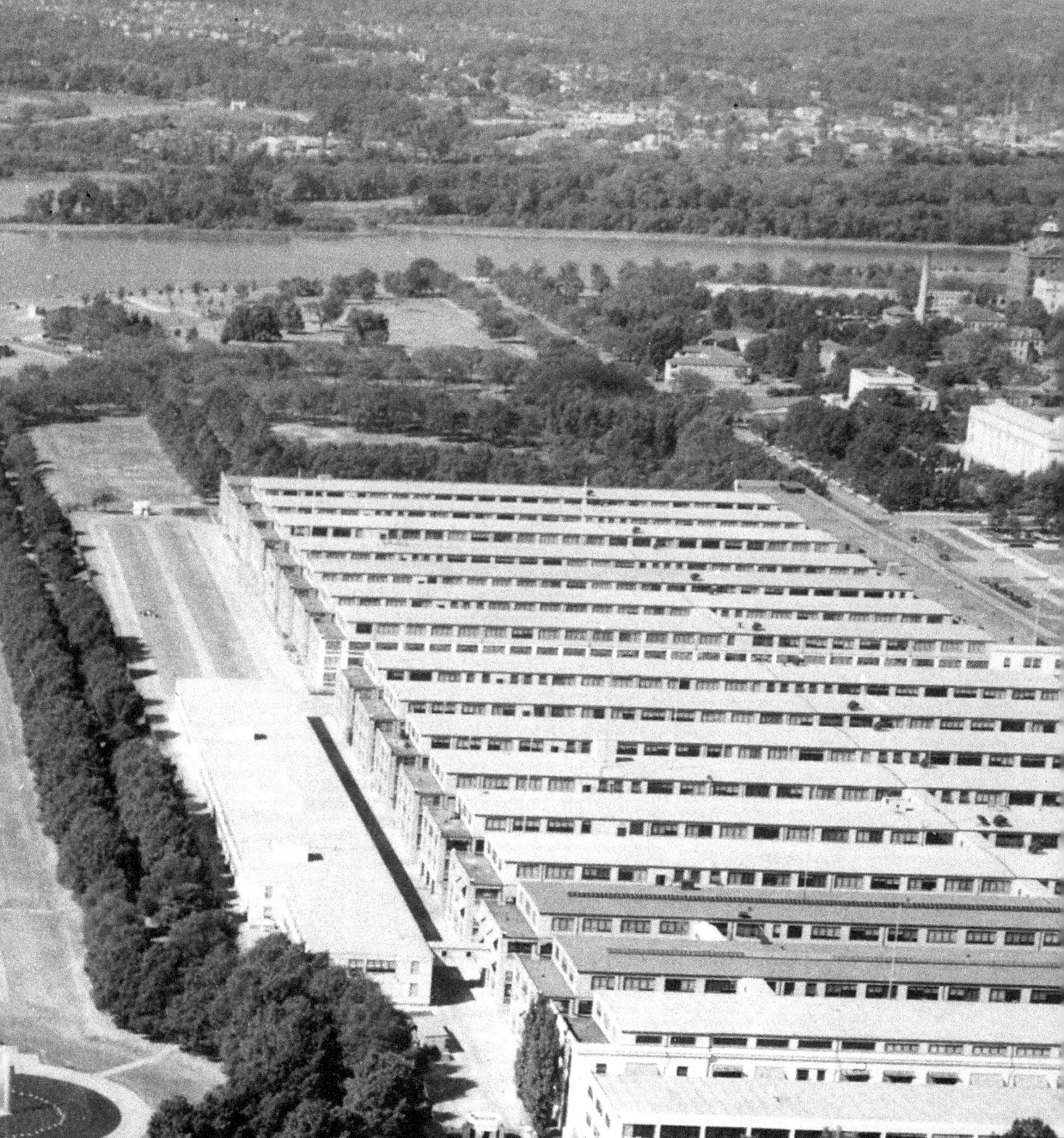

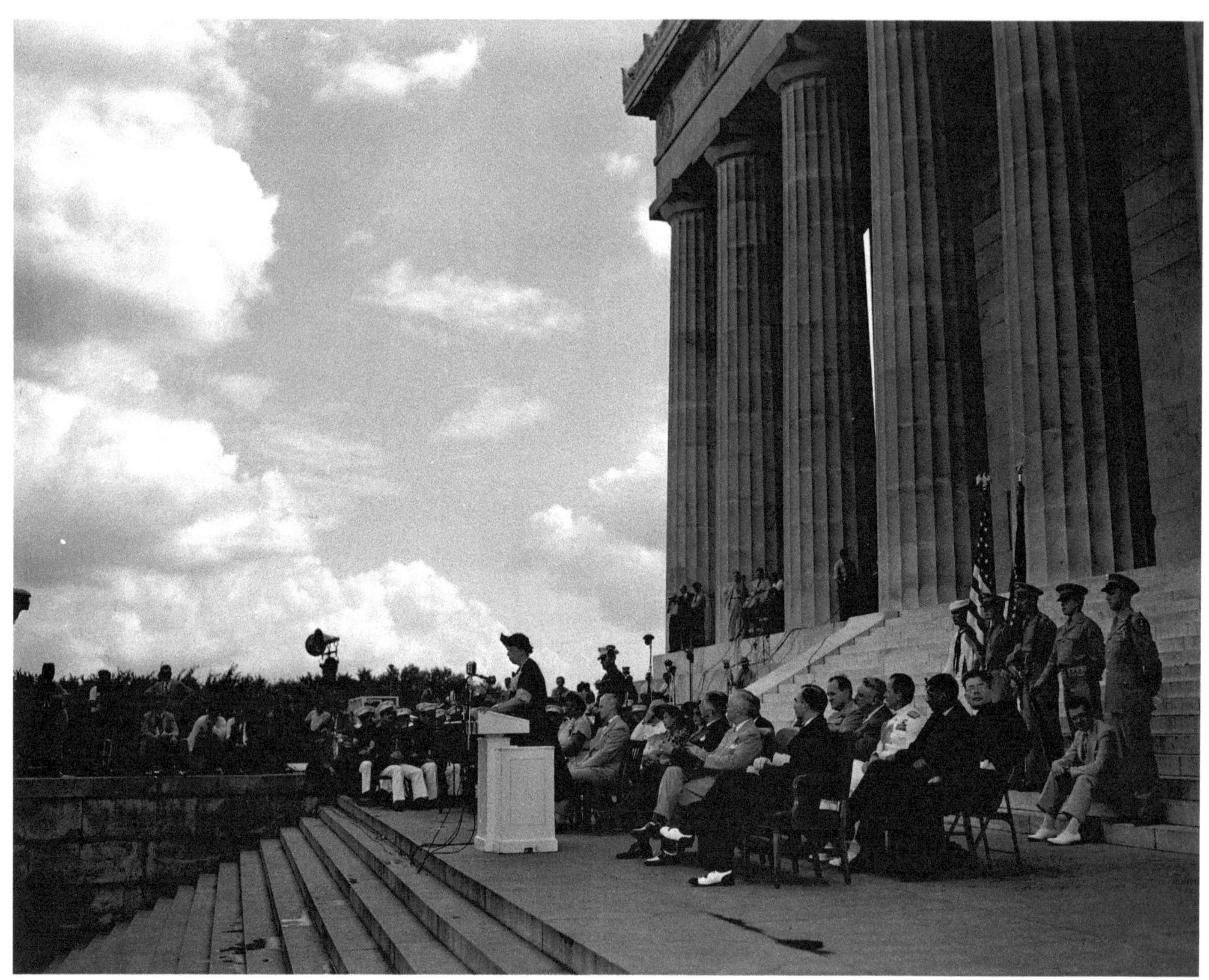

First Lady Eleanor Roosevelt attends an NAACP rally at the Lincoln Memorial in 1947.

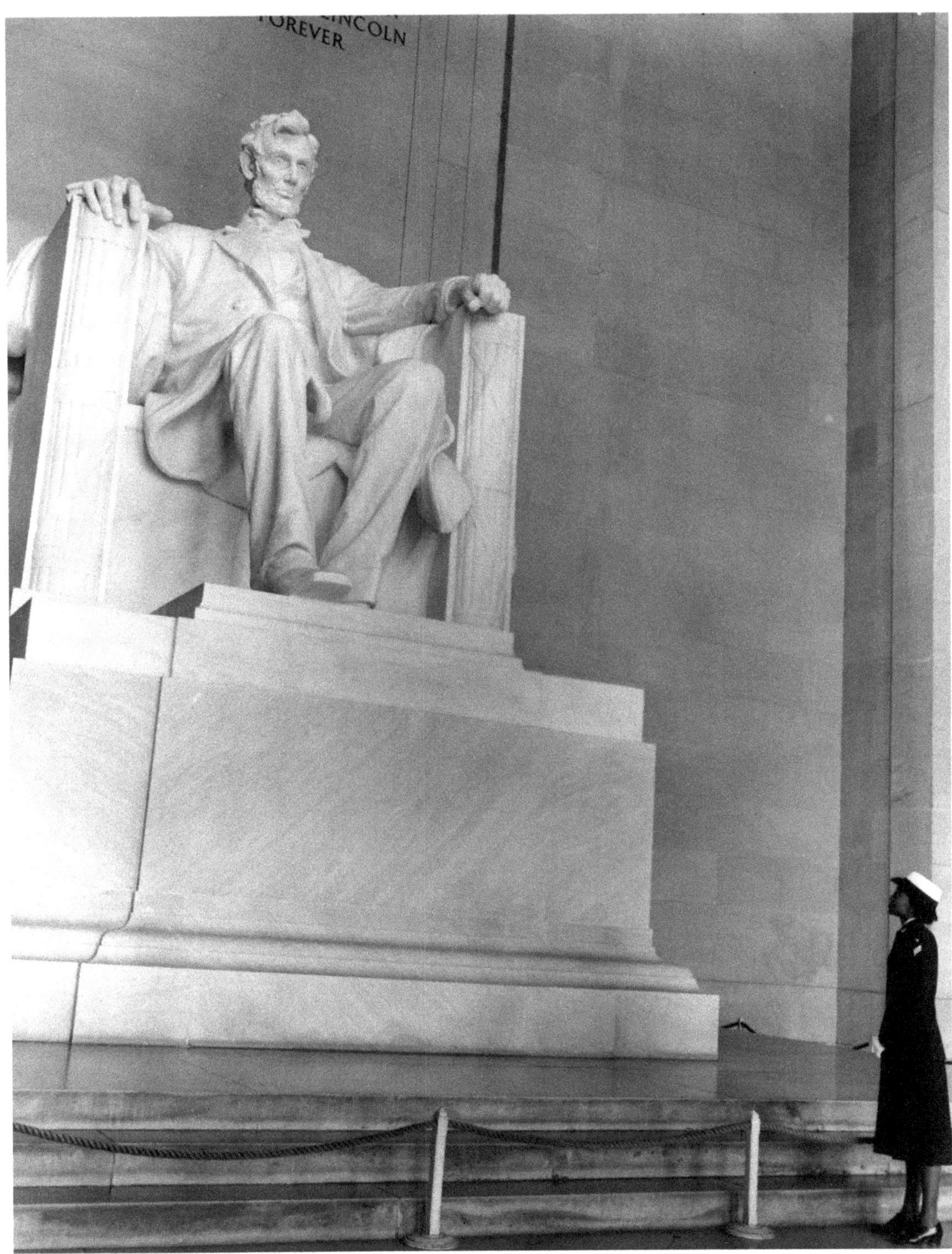

A U.S. service member gazes up at the statue of Abraham Lincoln in 1952.

President Abraham Lincoln's second inaugural address is engraved on the north wall of the Lincoln Memorial.

THE OTHER WOULD ACCEPT WAR RATHER
LET IT PERISH · AND THE WAR CAME ·
EIGHTH OF THE WHOLE POPULATION WERE
SLAVES NOT DISTRIBUTED GENERAL-
OVER THE UNION BUT LOCALIZED IN THE
PART OF IT · THESE SLAVES CONSTI-
A PECULIAR AND POWERFUL INTEREST ·
KNEW THAT THIS INTEREST WAS SOMEHOW
CAUSE OF THE WAR · TO STRENGTHEN PER-
AND EXTEND THIS INTEREST WAS THE
FOR WHICH THE INSURGENTS WOULD
THE UNION EVEN BY WAR WHILE THE GOV-
CLAIMED NO RIGHT TO DO MORE
TO RESTRICT THE TERRITORIAL ENLARGE-
OF IT · NEITHER PARTY EXPECTED FOR
WAR THE MAGNITUDE OR THE DURATION
IT HAS ALREADY ATTAINED · NEITHER
THAT THE CAUSE OF THE CONFLICT
CEASE WITH OR EVEN BEFORE THE CON-
ITSELF SHOULD CEASE · EACH LOOKED FOR
TRIUMPH AND A RESULT LESS FUN-
AND ASTOUNDING · BOTH READ THE
BIBLE AND PRAY TO THE SAME GOD AND
INVOKES HIS AID AGAINST THE OTHER ·
SEEM STRANGE THAT ANY MEN SHOULD
TO ASK A JUST GOD'S ASSISTANCE IN
THEIR BREAD FROM THE SWEAT OF
FACES BUT LET US JUDGE NOT
WE BE NOT JUDGED · THE PRAYERS OF BOTH
NOT BE ANSWERED – THAT OF NEITHER
BEEN ANSWERED FULLY · THE ALMIGHTY
HIS OWN PURPOSES: "WOE UNTO THE WORLD
OF OFFENSES FOR IT MUST NEEDS BE
OFFENSES COME BUT WOE TO THAT MAN
WHOM THE OFFENSE COMETH."
IF WE SHALL SUPPOSE THAT AMERICAN
SLAVERY IS ONE OF THOSE OFFENSES
WHICH IN THE PROVIDENCE OF GOD MUST
NEEDS COME BUT WHICH HAVING CON-
TINUED THROUGH HIS APPOINTED TIME HE
NOW WILLS TO REMOVE AND THAT HE
GIVES TO BOTH NORTH AND SOUTH THIS
TERRIBLE WAR AS THE WOE DUE TO THOSE BY
WHOM THE OFFENSE CAME SHALL WE DIS-
CERN THEREIN ANY DEPARTURE FROM
THOSE DIVINE ATTRIBUTES WHICH THE
BELIEVERS IN A LIVING GOD ALWAYS ASCRIBE
TO HIM. FONDLY DO WE HOPE – FERVENTLY
DO WE PRAY – THAT THIS MIGHTY SCOURGE
OF WAR MAY SPEEDILY PASS AWAY · YET IF
GOD WILLS THAT IT CONTINUE UNTIL ALL
THE WEALTH PILED BY THE BONDSMAN'S
TWO HUNDRED AND FIFTY YEARS OF UN-
REQUITED TOIL SHALL BE SUNK AND
UNTIL EVERY DROP OF BLOOD DRAWN WITH
THE LASH SHALL BE PAID BY ANOTHER
DRAWN WITH THE SWORD AS WAS SAID THREE
THOUSAND YEARS AGO SO STILL IT MUST
BE SAID "THE JUDGMENTS OF THE LORD
ARE TRUE AND RIGHTEOUS ALTOGETHER."
WITH MALICE TOWARD NONE WITH CHARITY
FOR ALL WITH FIRMNESS IN THE RIGHT AS
GOD GIVES US TO SEE THE RIGHT LET US
STRIVE ON TO FINISH THE WORK WE ARE IN
TO BIND UP THE NATION'S WOUNDS TO CARE
FOR HIM WHO SHALL HAVE BORNE THE BAT-
TLE AND FOR HIS WIDOW AND HIS ORPHAN-
TO DO ALL WHICH MAY ACHIEVE AND CHER-
ISH A JUST AND LASTING PEACE AMONG
OURSELVES AND WITH ALL NATIONS ·

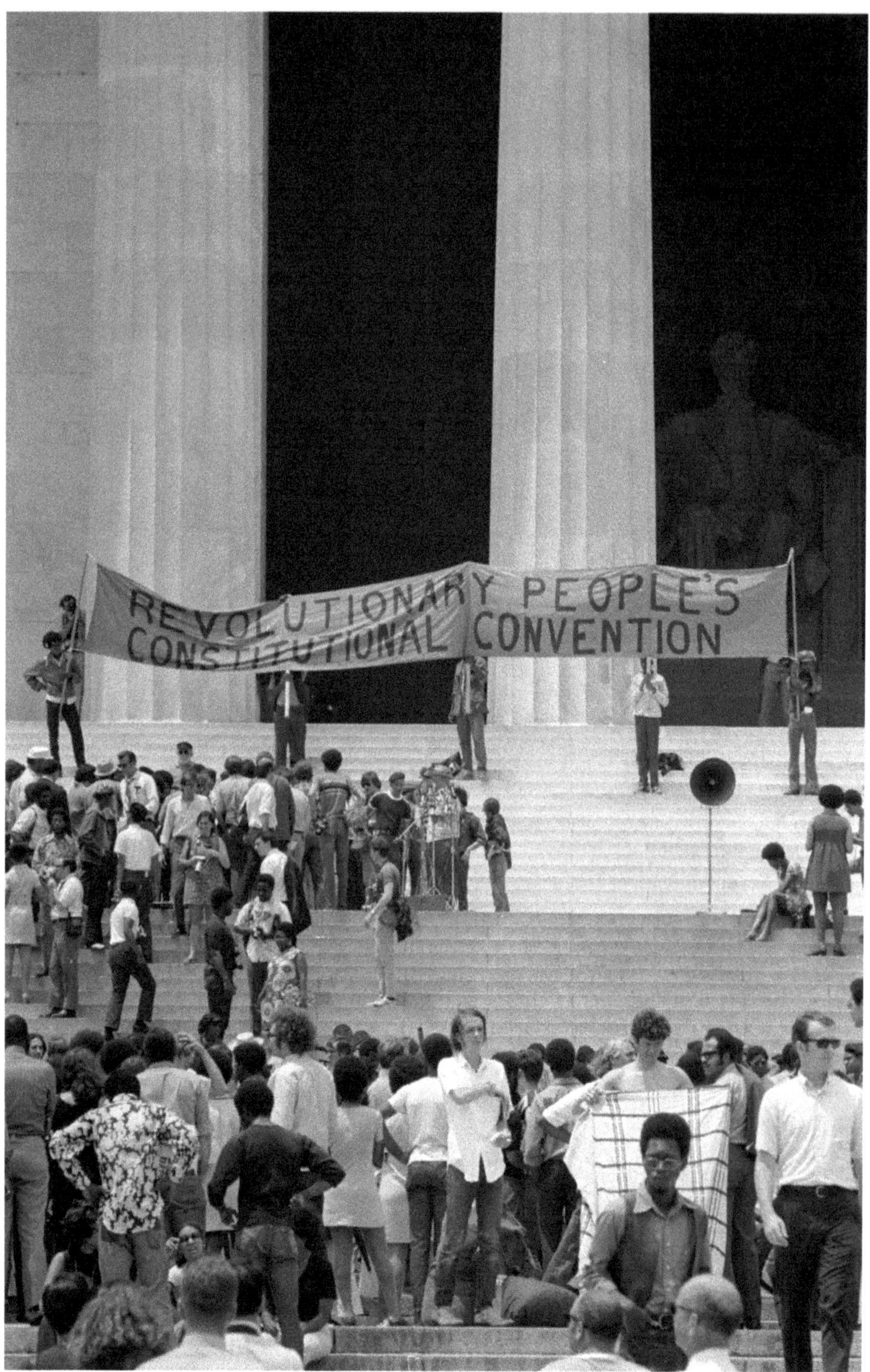

In this photograph taken in June 1970, a Black Panther convention is under way on the steps of the Lincoln Memorial. The Black Panther Party for Self Defense was a radical militant organization committed to Marxist answers for the social and economic grievances of some Americans.

Important Monuments Around Washington, D.C. (1851–2001)

Extraordinary service to this country—that's the commonality shared by the significant historical figures who are immortalized in the monuments passed by every day in Washington, D.C. This section explores the stories behind popular and lesser-known monuments, significant sculptures, sites, and memorials in the city. Some structures, such as the *Statue of Freedom* atop the United States Capitol, have existed for more than a hundred years, while others, including the Dwight D. Eisenhower Memorial and Dr. Martin Luther King, Jr., Stone of Hope, are burgeoning ideas that have yet to take shape as full-fledged memorials.

Images from controversial movements that spawned great change in this country, such as the 1963 March on Washington, are included in this chapter, as are other important events that have taken place at the city's monuments.

Because members of the military continue to uphold the values of this land by risking their lives in service to the country, a large portion of the monuments in this chapter, such as the Tomb of the Unknown Soldier, represent them and their invaluable contribution.

Finally, the contributions of people famous and relatively unknown who have been honored in monuments around Washington, D.C., can best be summed up in the words of civil rights leader Dr. Martin Luther King: "Everyone has the power for greatness because greatness is determined by service." These monuments of great people will continue to live on as they are admired by D.C. residents and visitors alike.

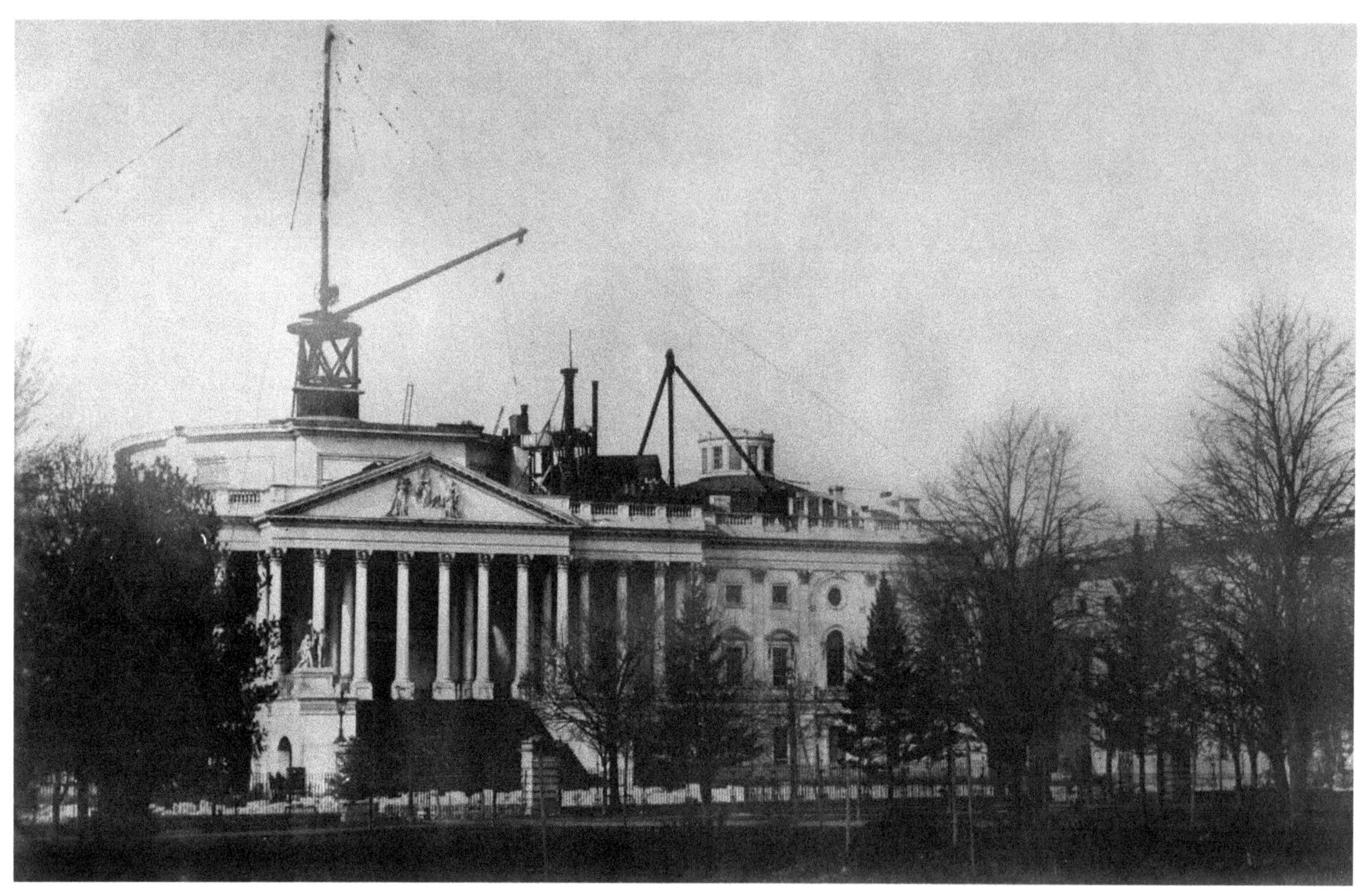

This is how the United States Capitol looked in 1851. The Capitol building has been through several renovations, restorations, and additions since construction began in 1793.

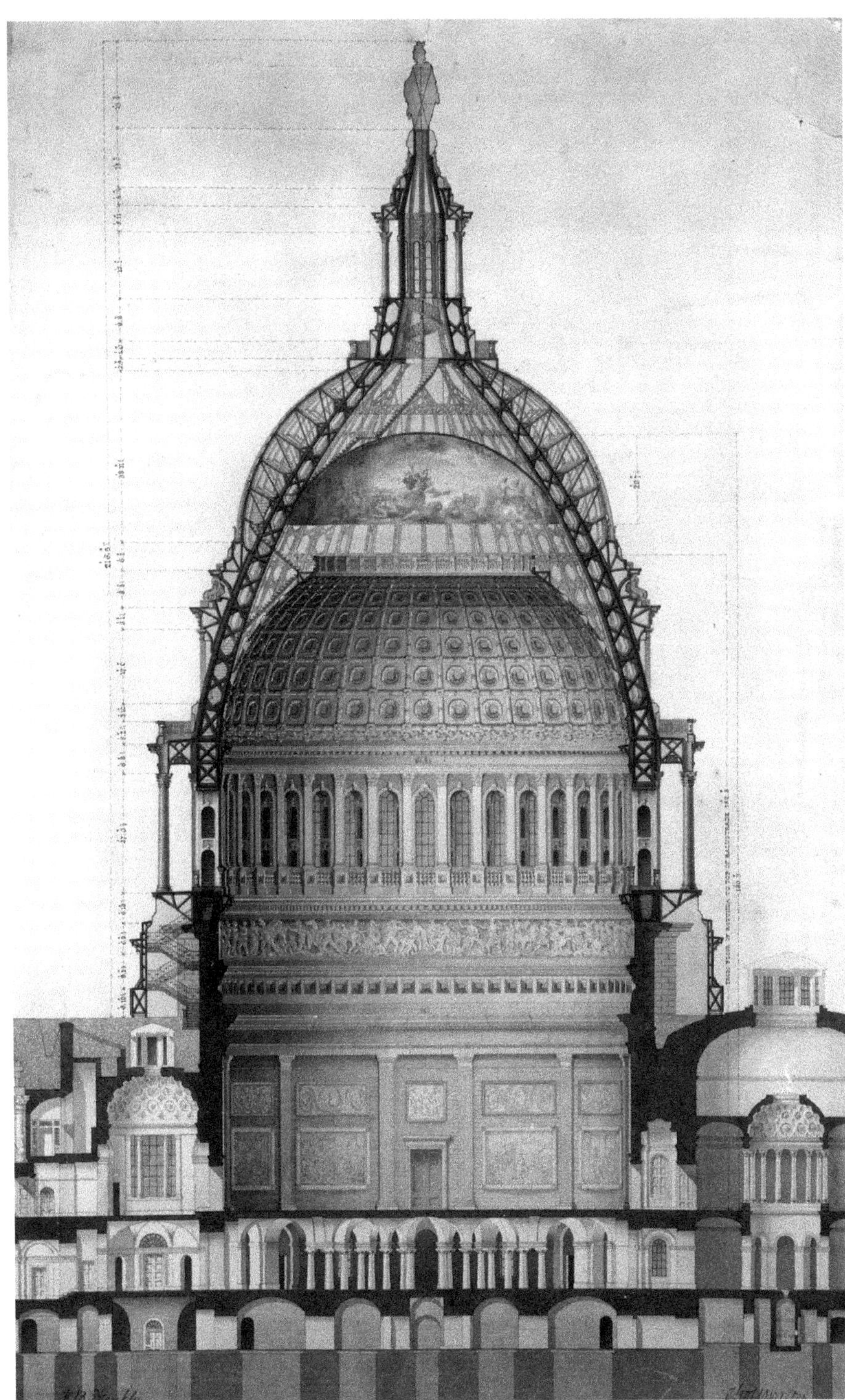

On December 9, 1859, Thomas Ustick Walter created this cross-section drawing of the U.S. Capitol Dome and supporting structure.

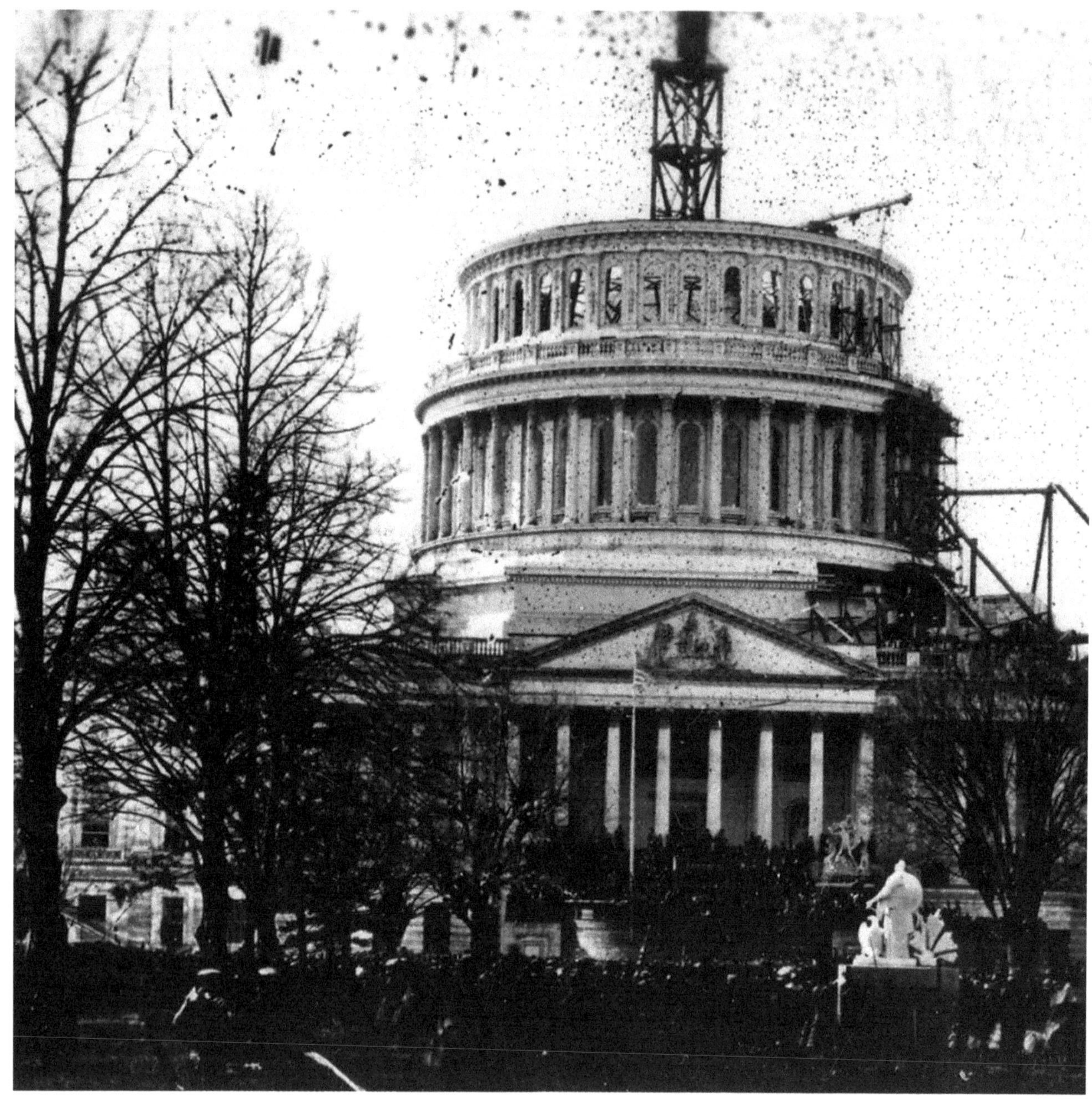

The Capitol was under construction in the 1800s, and the new Capitol Dome was completed in 1863. Slave labor was used to help build the Capitol among other Washington buildings, including the White House.

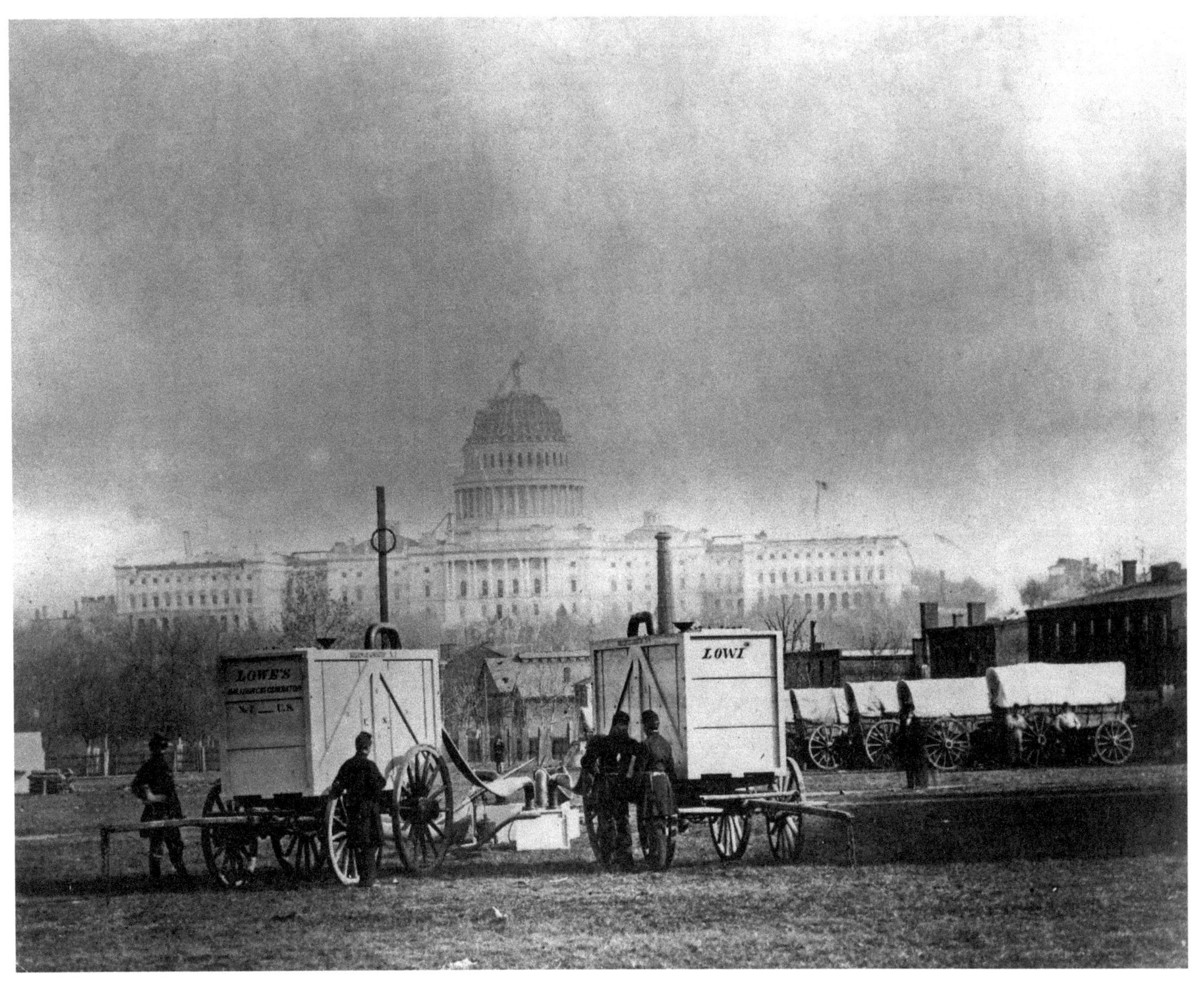

Union soldiers with their Conestoga wagons appear in front of the Capitol in this 1865 photograph.

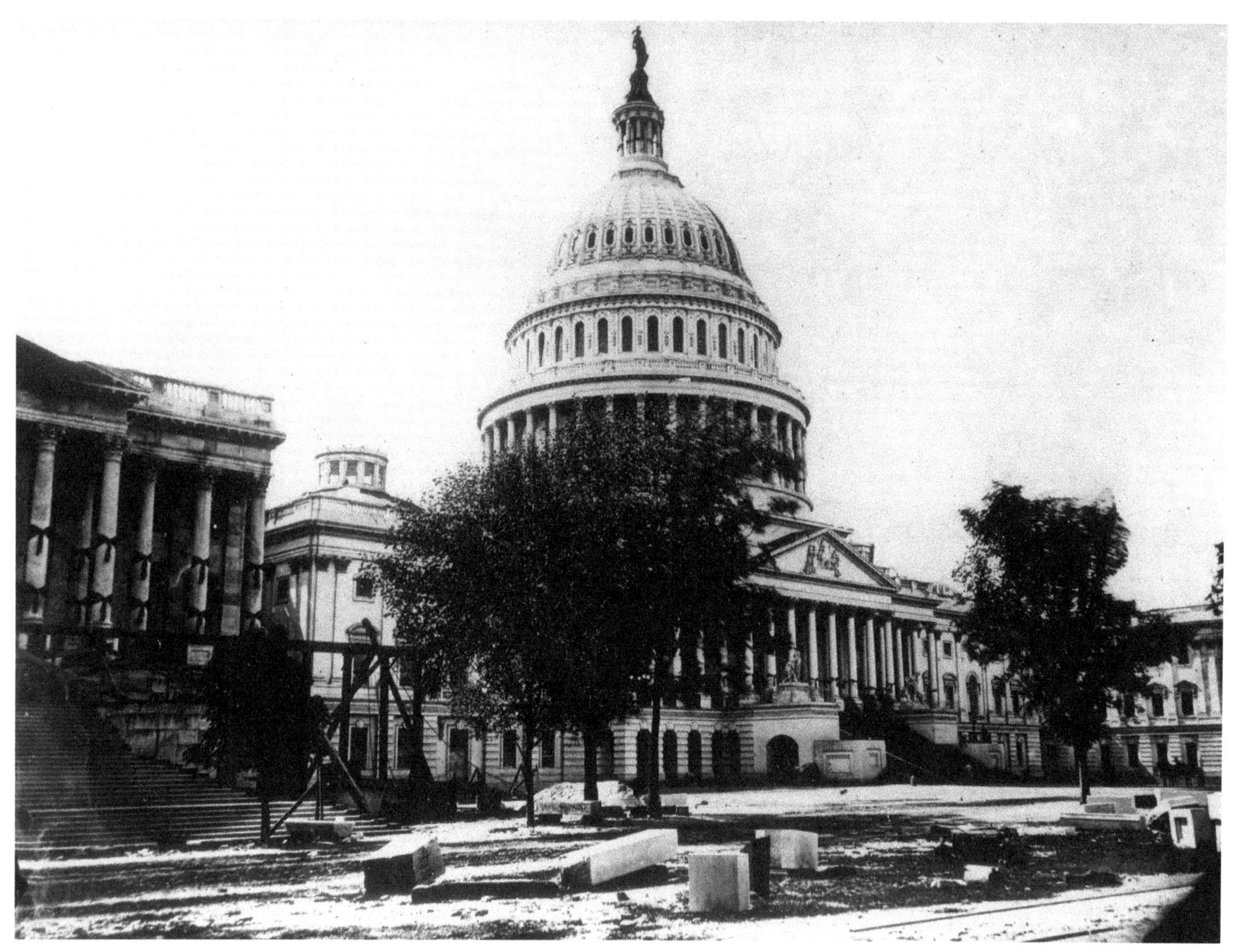

This image shows how the Capitol building looked after the dome was completed, with bows adorning the columns.

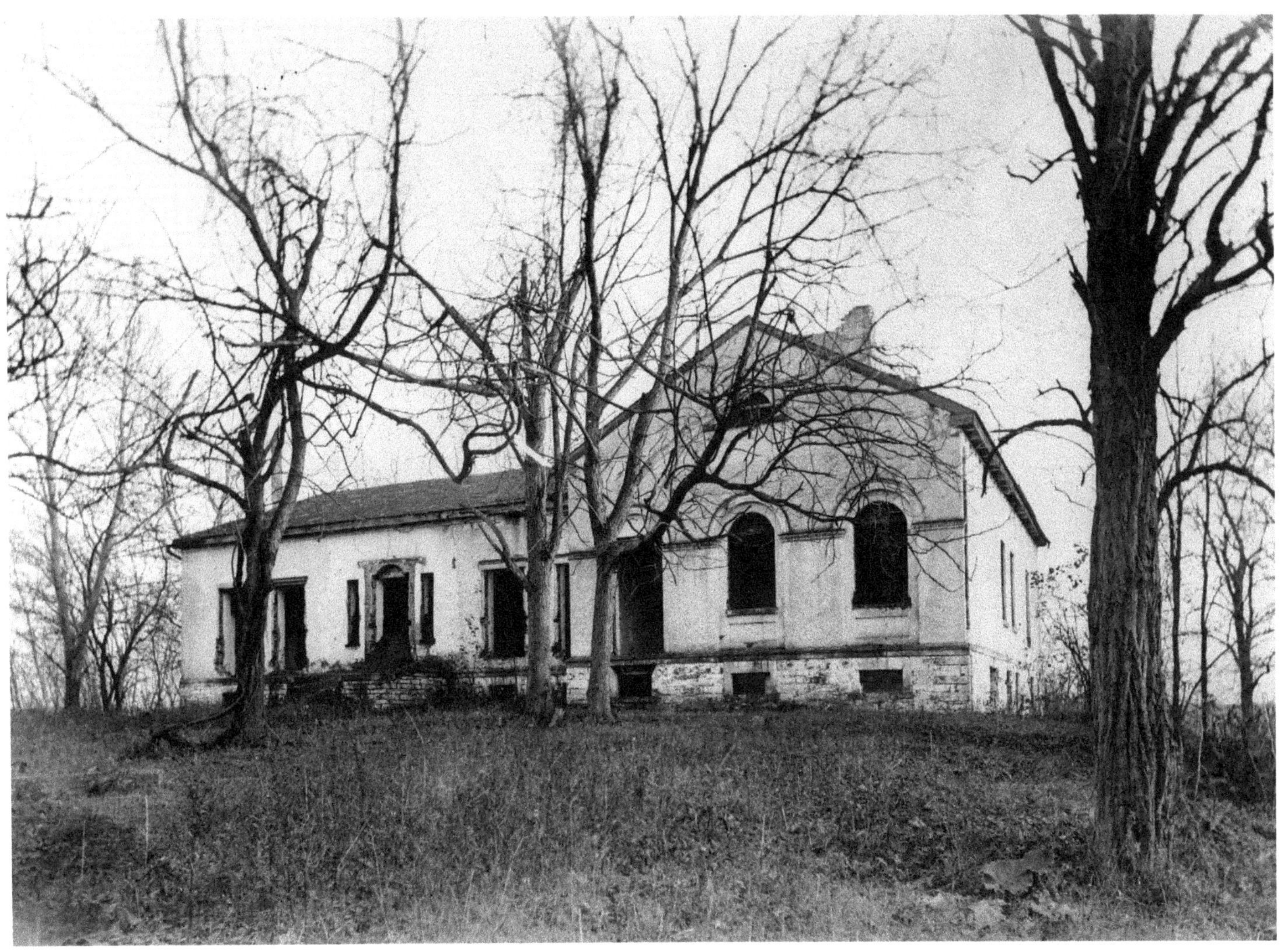

During the Civil War, African-American soldiers were housed and trained on Analostan Island, now known as Theodore Roosevelt Island. This rare photo shows the house of General John Mason on Analostan Island, memorialized in 1932.

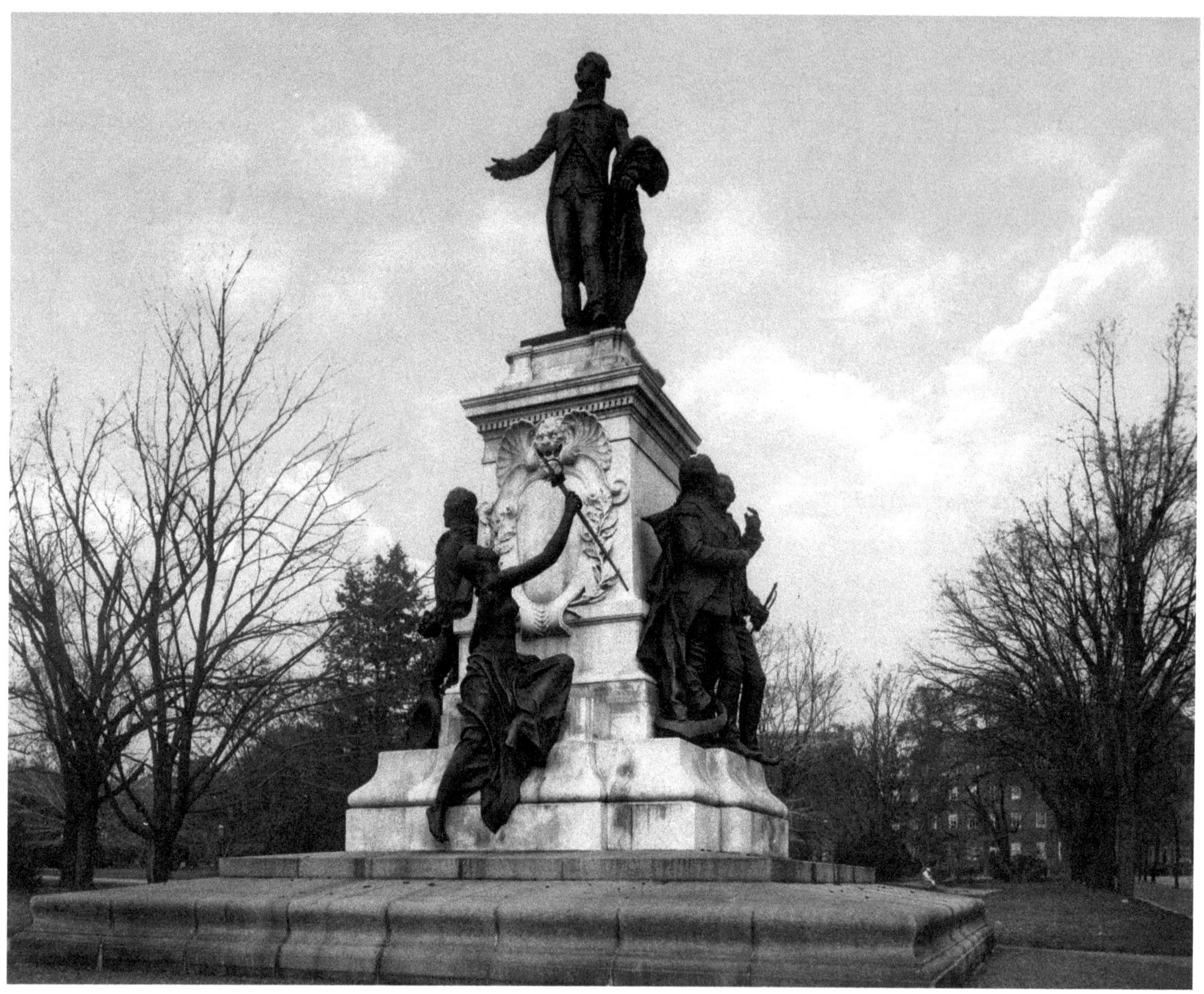

Members of the Sons of the Revolution attended a wreath-laying ceremony at the statue of Gilbert de Lafayette, the French military officer who served under George Washington during the Revolutionary War. This 1924 ceremony marked Lafayette's September 6, 1757 birthday. Attending was the great-grandson of Lafayette, Count de Chambrun; Lieutenant Labat; General George Rickard; and Assistant Secretary of the Navy Franklin Roosevelt, who delivered a speech. Lafayette Park Memorial is located in Lafayette Park on Pennsylvania Avenue in front of the White House.

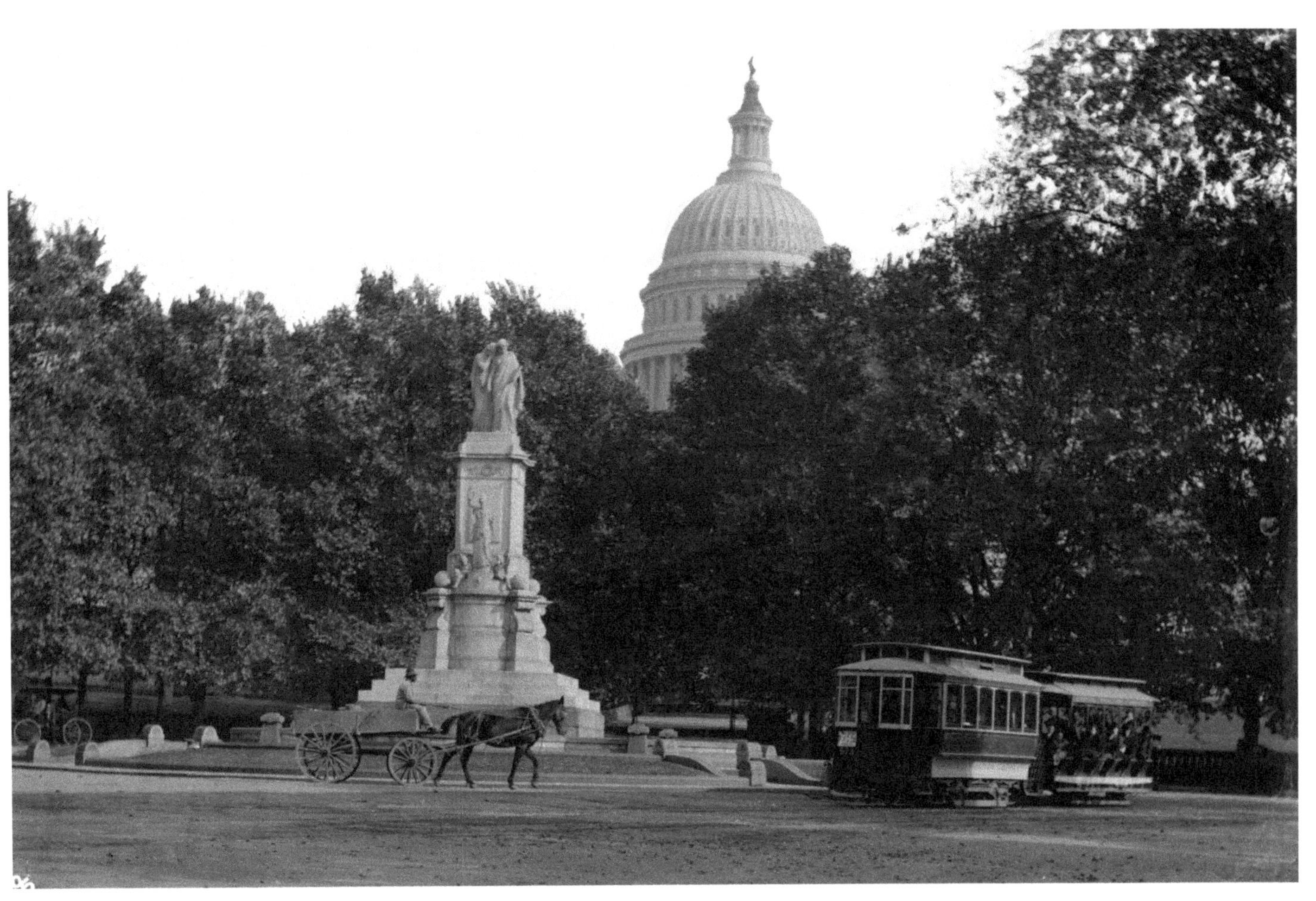

There may be vigorous—sometimes contentious—debate among members of Congress inside the Capitol, but outside the Capitol this sculpture stands as a monument to peace. Located in Peace Circle at First Street and Pennsylvania Avenue, the Peace Monument, sometimes called the Naval Monument or Civil War Sailors Monument, honors navy service members who died in the Civil War. Constructed of white marble in 1877, the 44-foot-tall sculpture depicts a woman weeping over History's shoulder. The statue is part of a group of Peace Circle monuments, including the James A. Garfield Monument and the Ulysses S. Grant Memorial.

West Potomac Park is also the home of the John Paul Jones Memorial. Jones is touted as the father of the United States Navy. He received a Congressional Gold Medal for his efforts in the American Revolutionary War, and is perhaps best known for saying "I have not yet begun to fight!" This photo was taken on the day of the John Paul Jones Memorial dedication, April 17, 1912.

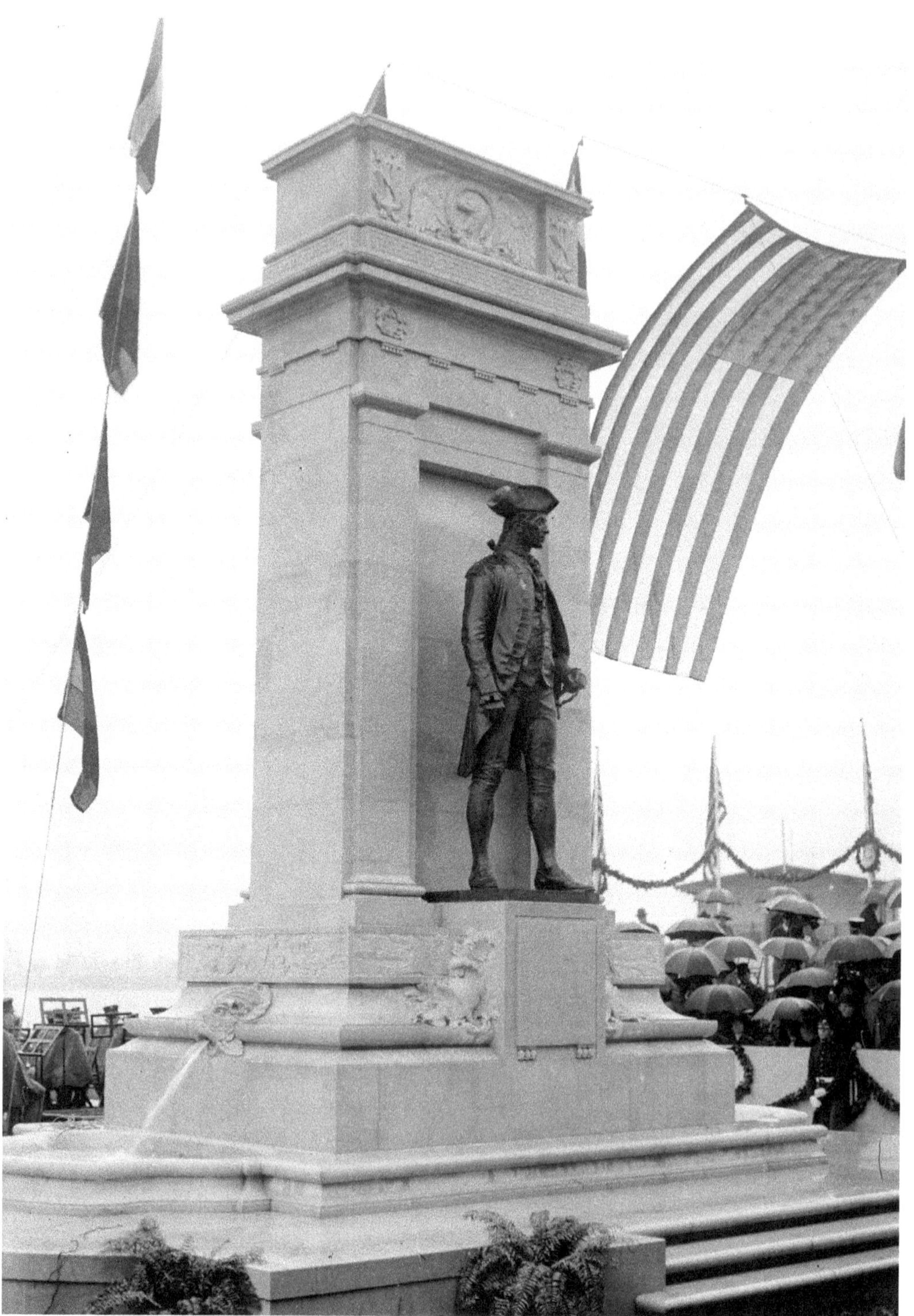

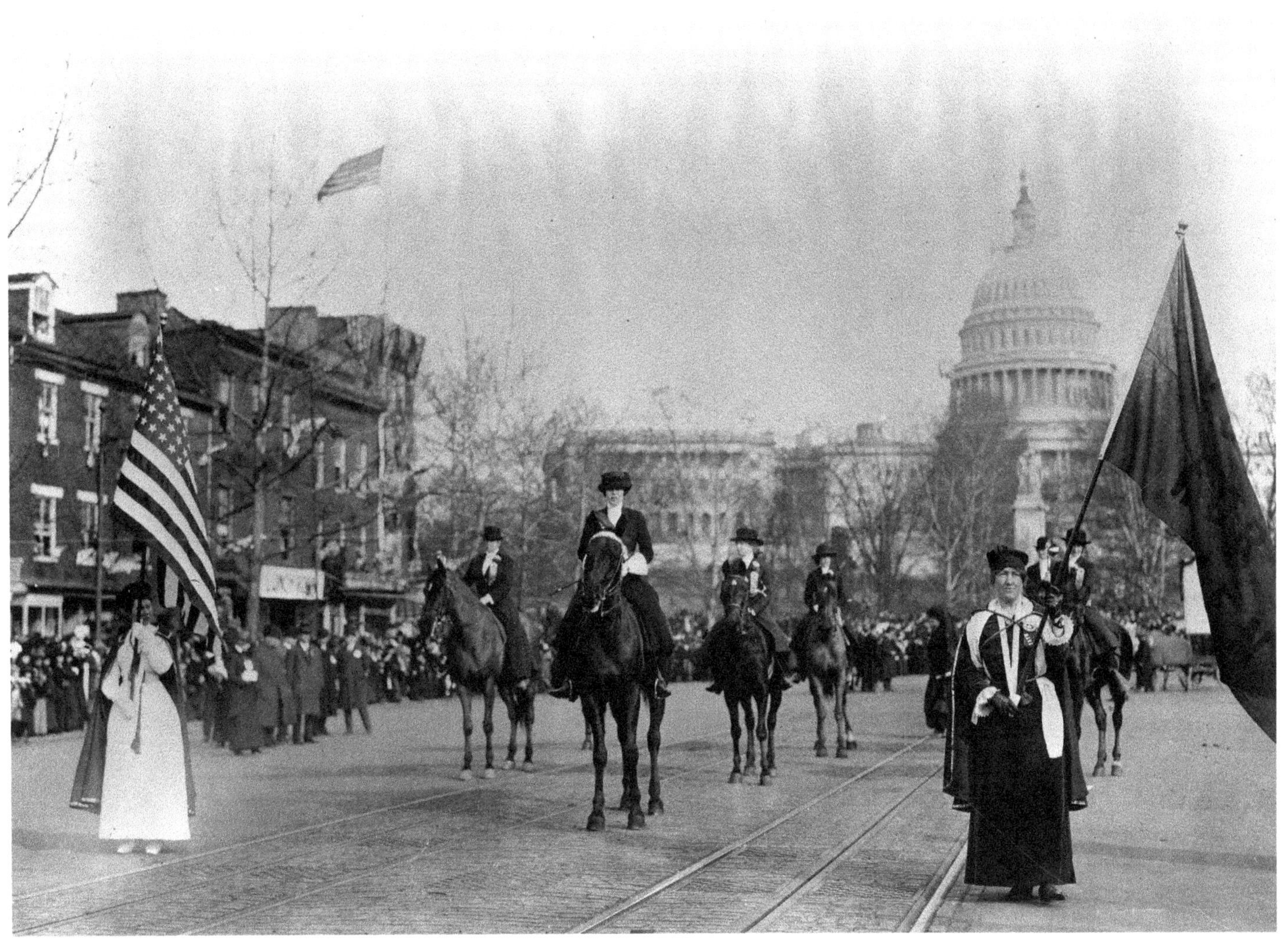

Several significant rallies took place near the Capitol grounds. Here, women suffragists participate in a parade down the streets of Washington, D.C., on March 3, 1913. The nation's Capitol is in view.

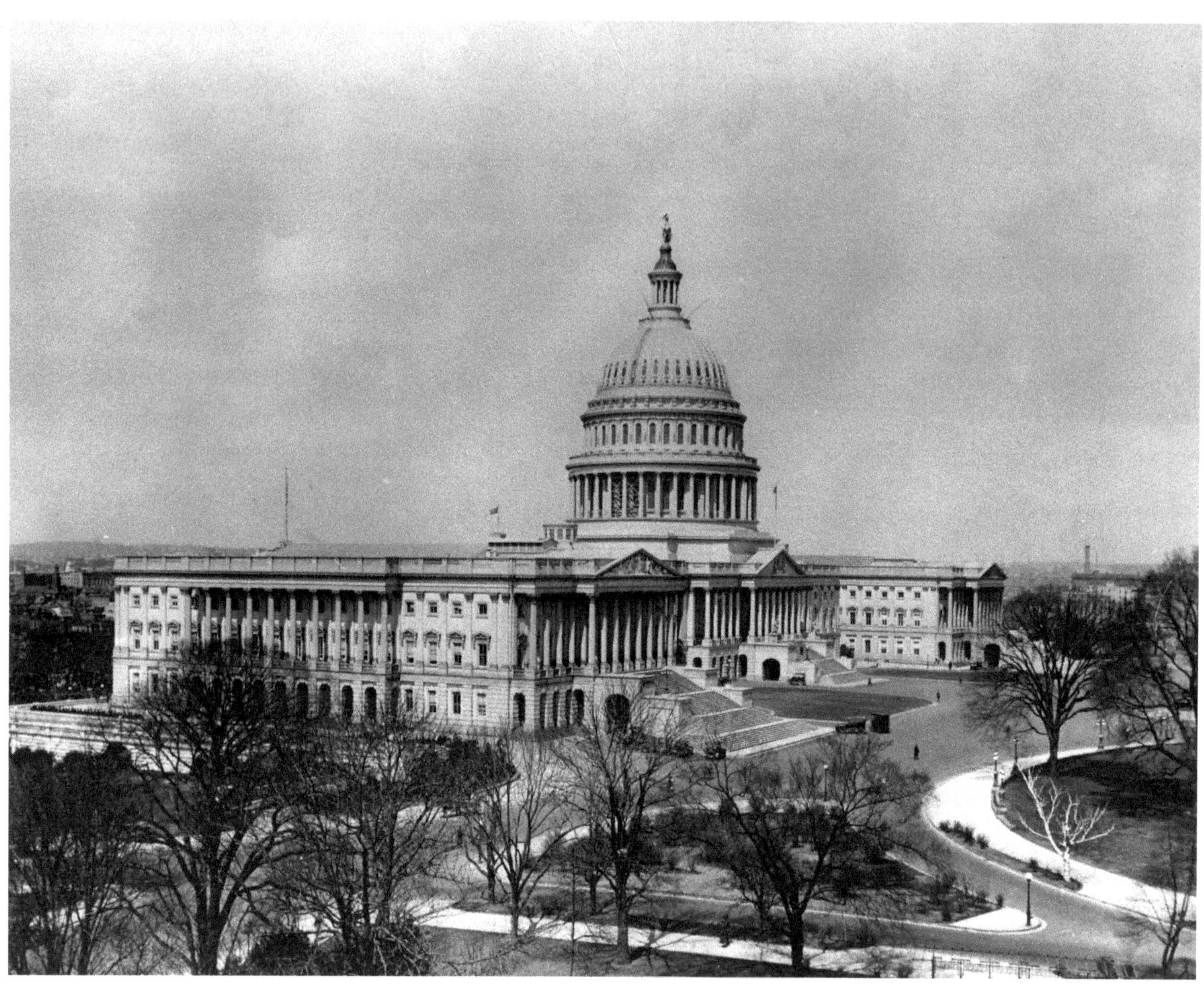

With flags perched high on the dome of the Capitol, this 1915 view of the U.S. Capitol exterior is similar to a present-day view of the building.

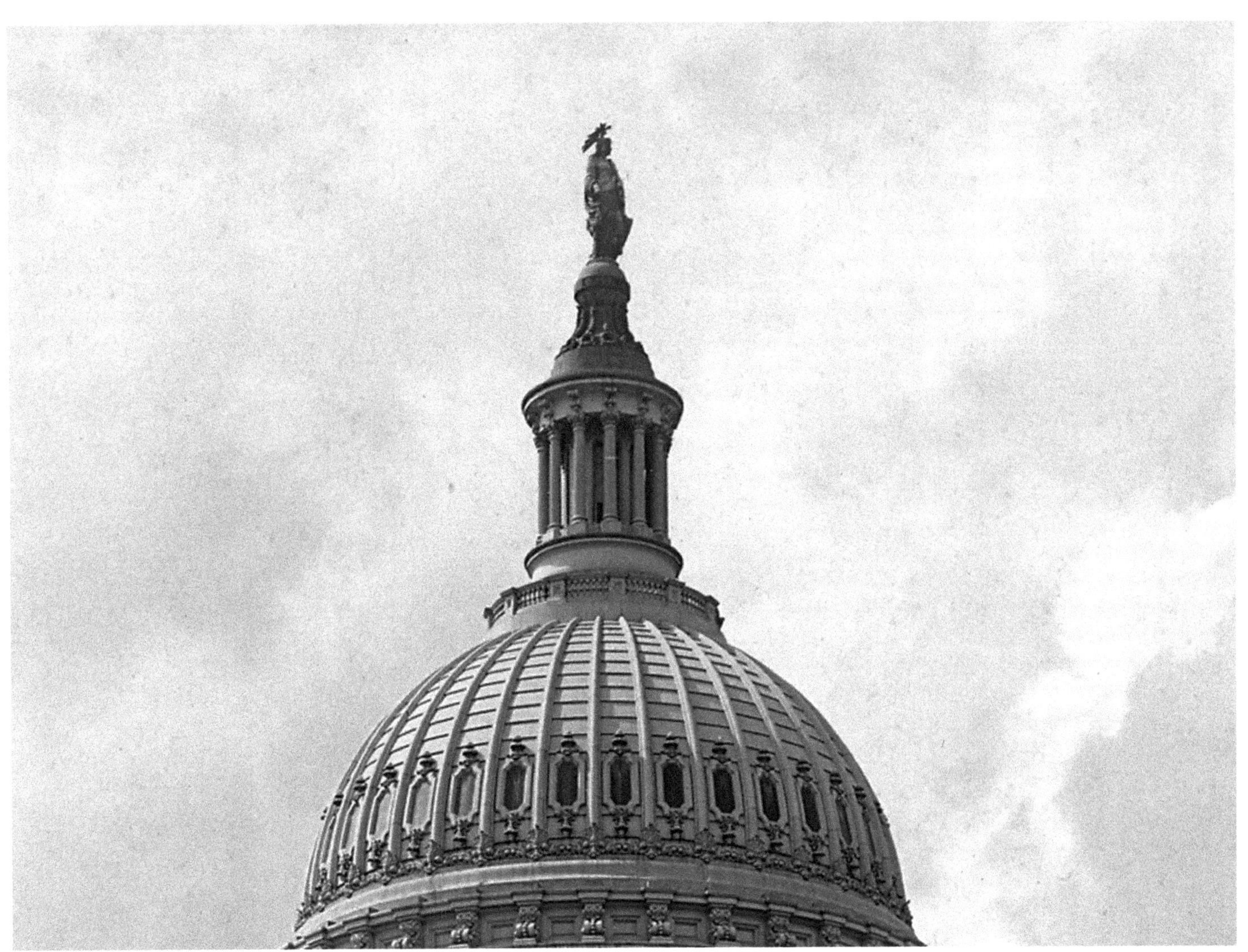

The Capitol Dome sculptor, in an attempt to get a raise, decided he would deliberately withhold information needed by workers to raise the statue to its perch. Instead of the sculptor getting the extra funds, a slave, Philip Reid, took his place. Reid completed work on the statue and implemented a pulley system that allowed it to be elevated to the top of the dome. Thus, he was credited with solving the *Statue of Freedom* dilemma.

This image captures a fire at the Capitol in 1930, which did extensive damage to the House Document Room. Tall ladders extend from the fire trucks as fire fighters attempt to extinguish the fire.

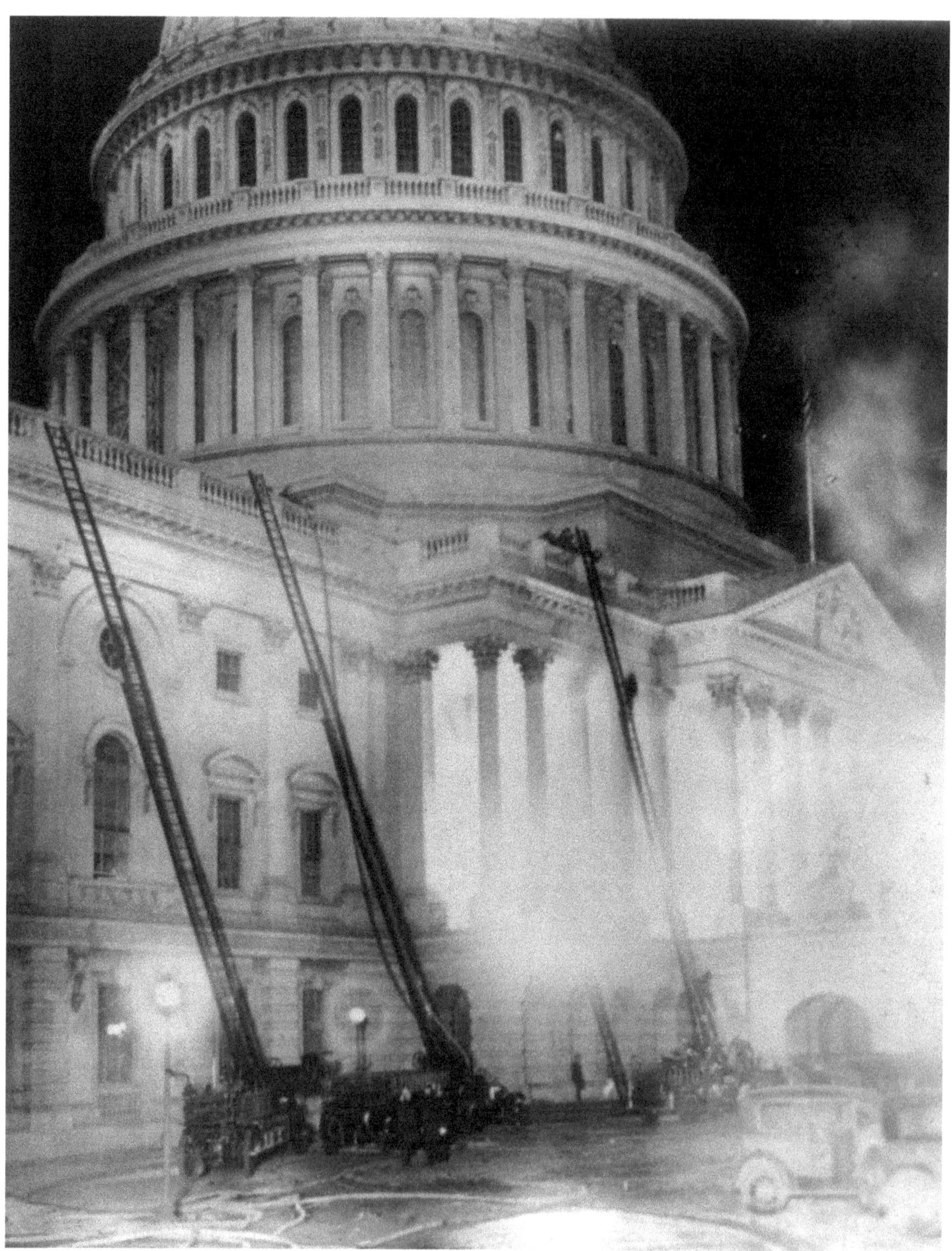

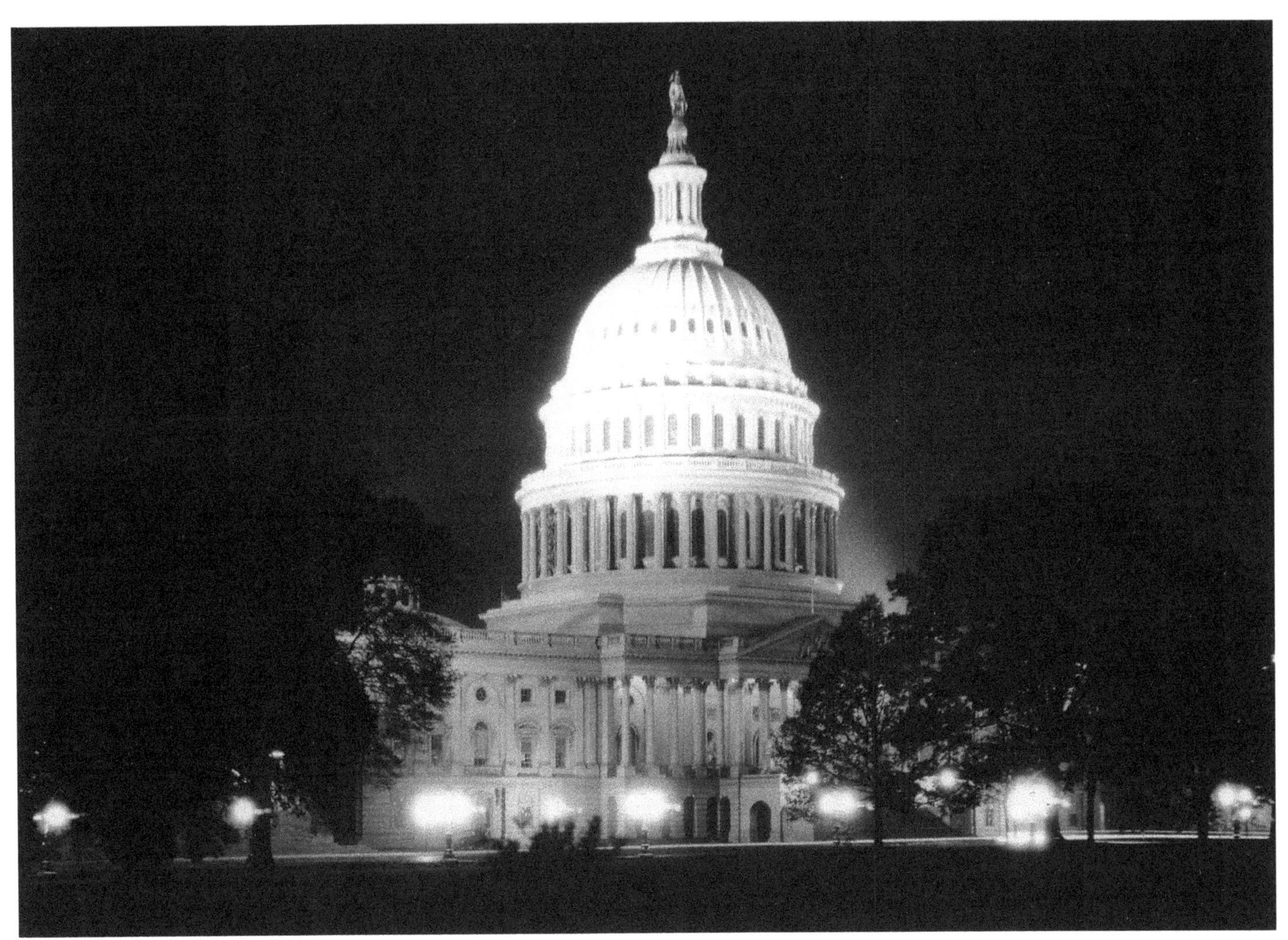

Pictured here is a night view of the illuminated Capitol exterior.

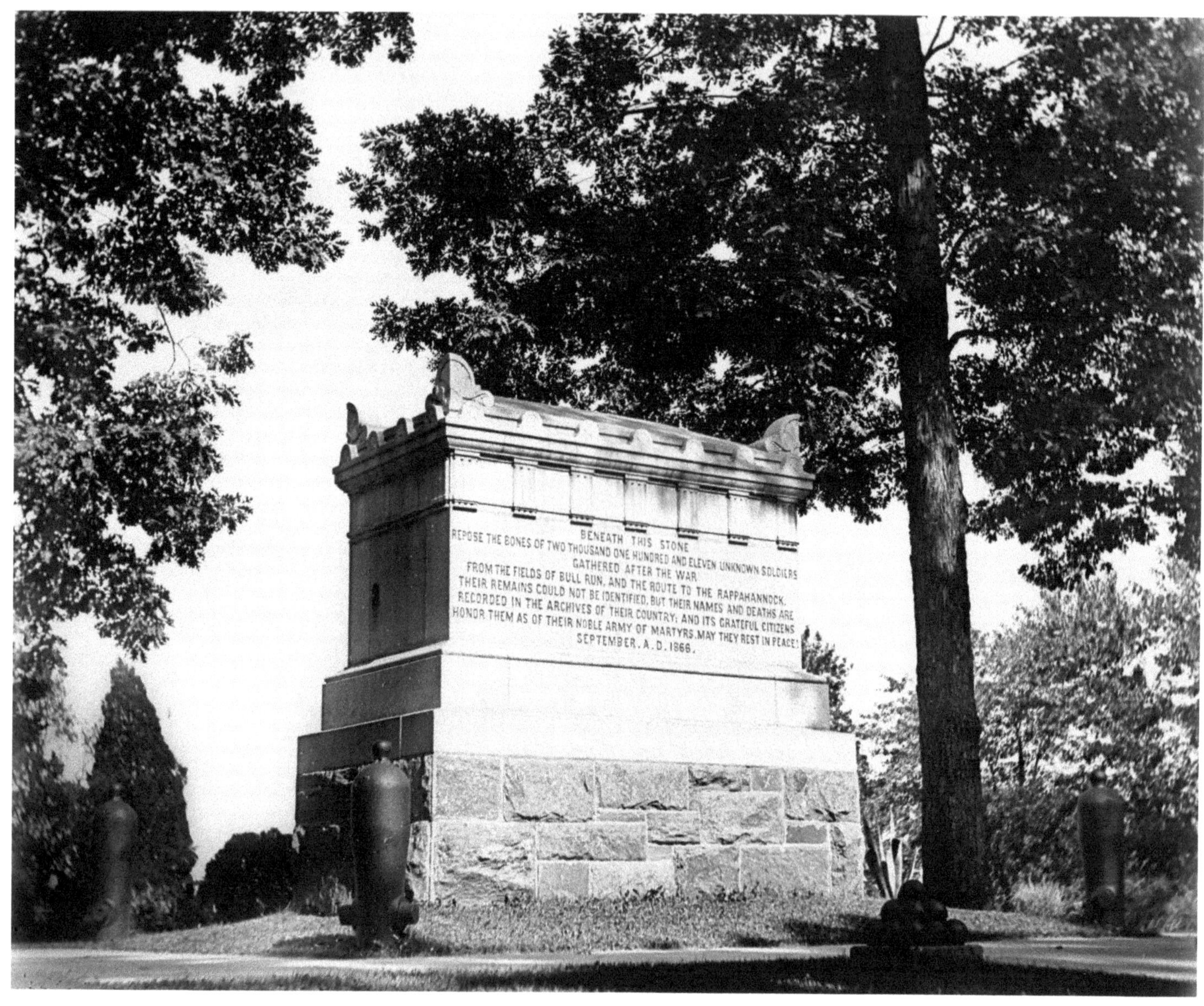

"Beneath this stone repose the bones of two thousand one hundred and eleven unknown soldiers. Gathered after the war from the fields of Bull Run and the route to Rappahannock, their remains could not be identified. . . ." These words from 1866, describing the sacredness of this Civil War monument, are engraved on the face of the Memorial to the Unknown Dead at Arlington National Cemetery.

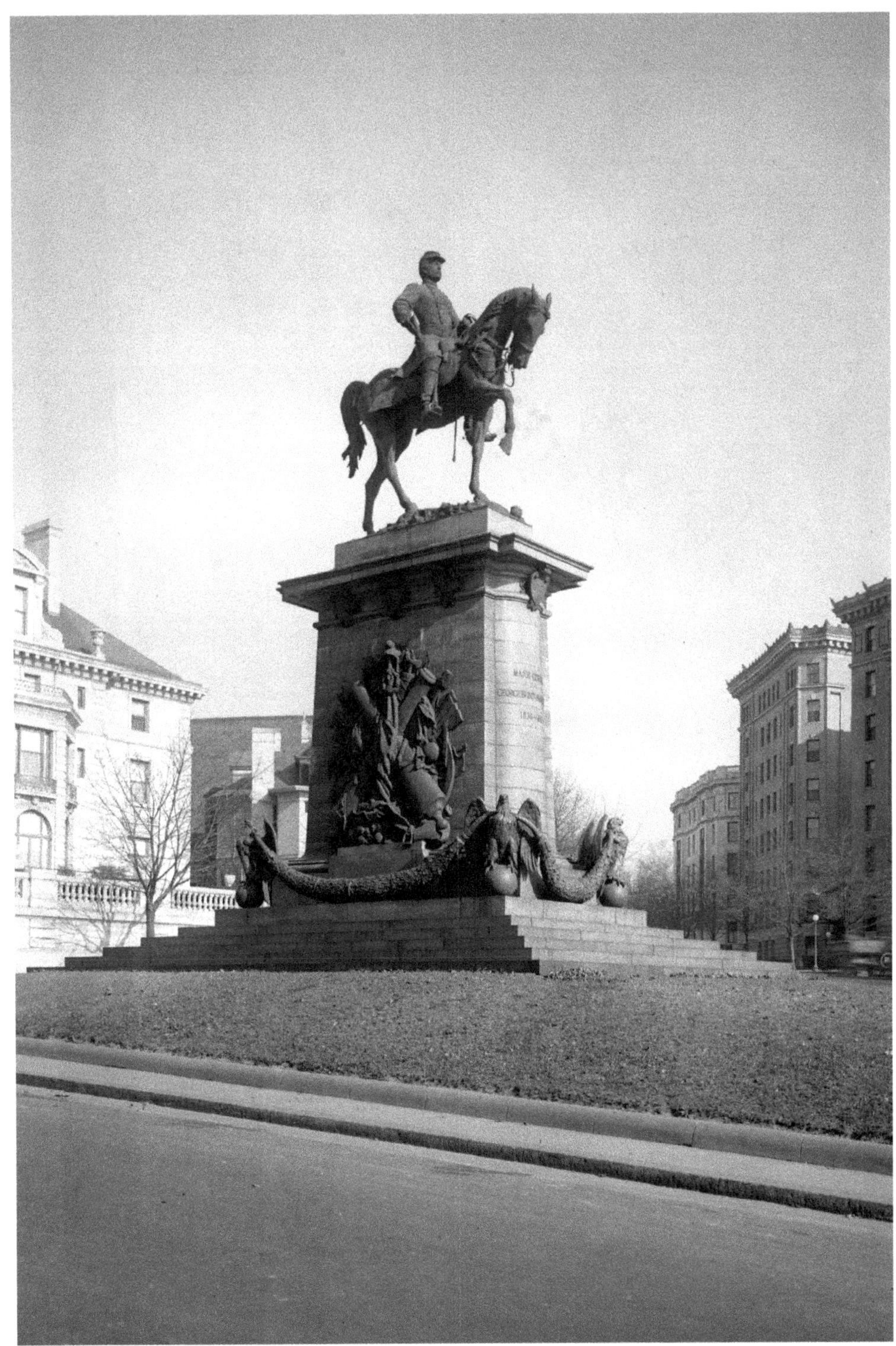

Major General George B. McClellan will forever be remembered as a Union hero. A statue honoring the General-in-Chief of the Union army and organizer of the Army of the Potomac can be found on Connecticut Avenue NW, a mile and a quarter northwest of the White House.

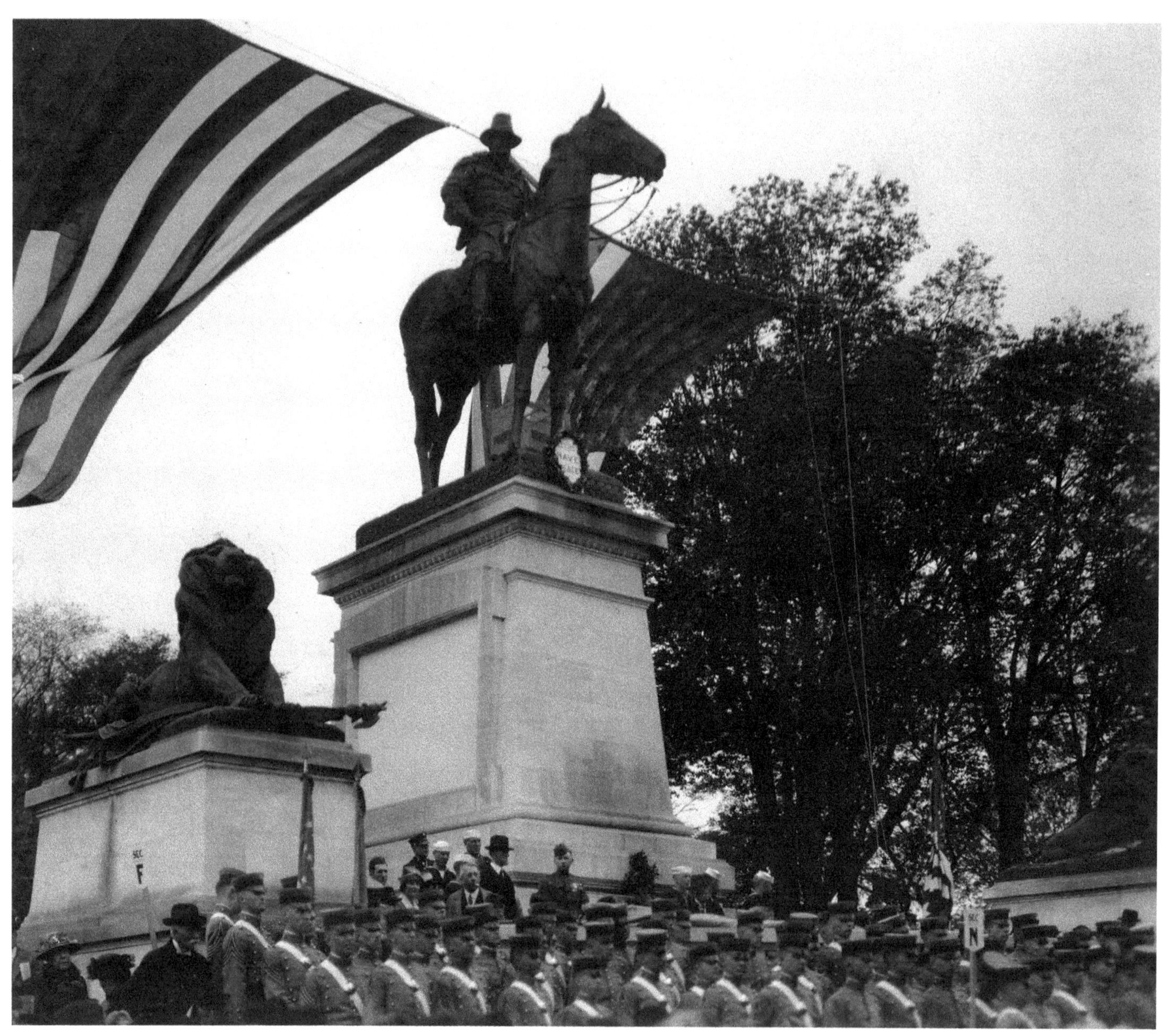

This more than 17-foot-tall statue on a 22-foot pedestal is the second-largest equestrian statue in the United States, and at the time of its completion in 1921, the third-largest in the world. Designated the Ulysses S. Grant Memorial, the statue depicts the eighteenth president on a horse. Visitors will find it at Union Square, the Mall at First Street, between Pennsylvania and Maryland avenues.

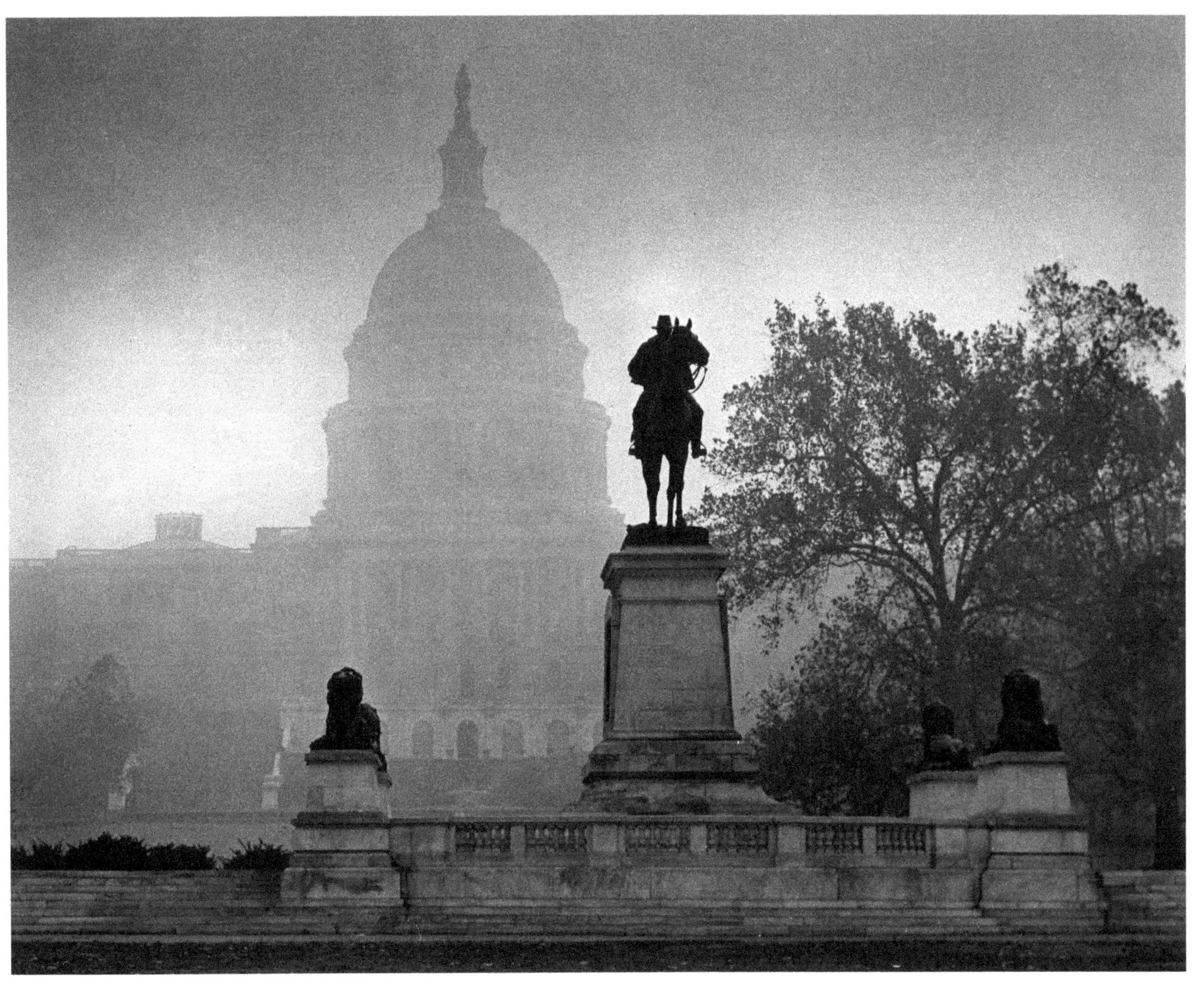

Pictured here is the Ulysses S. Grant Memorial with the Capitol towering in the background.

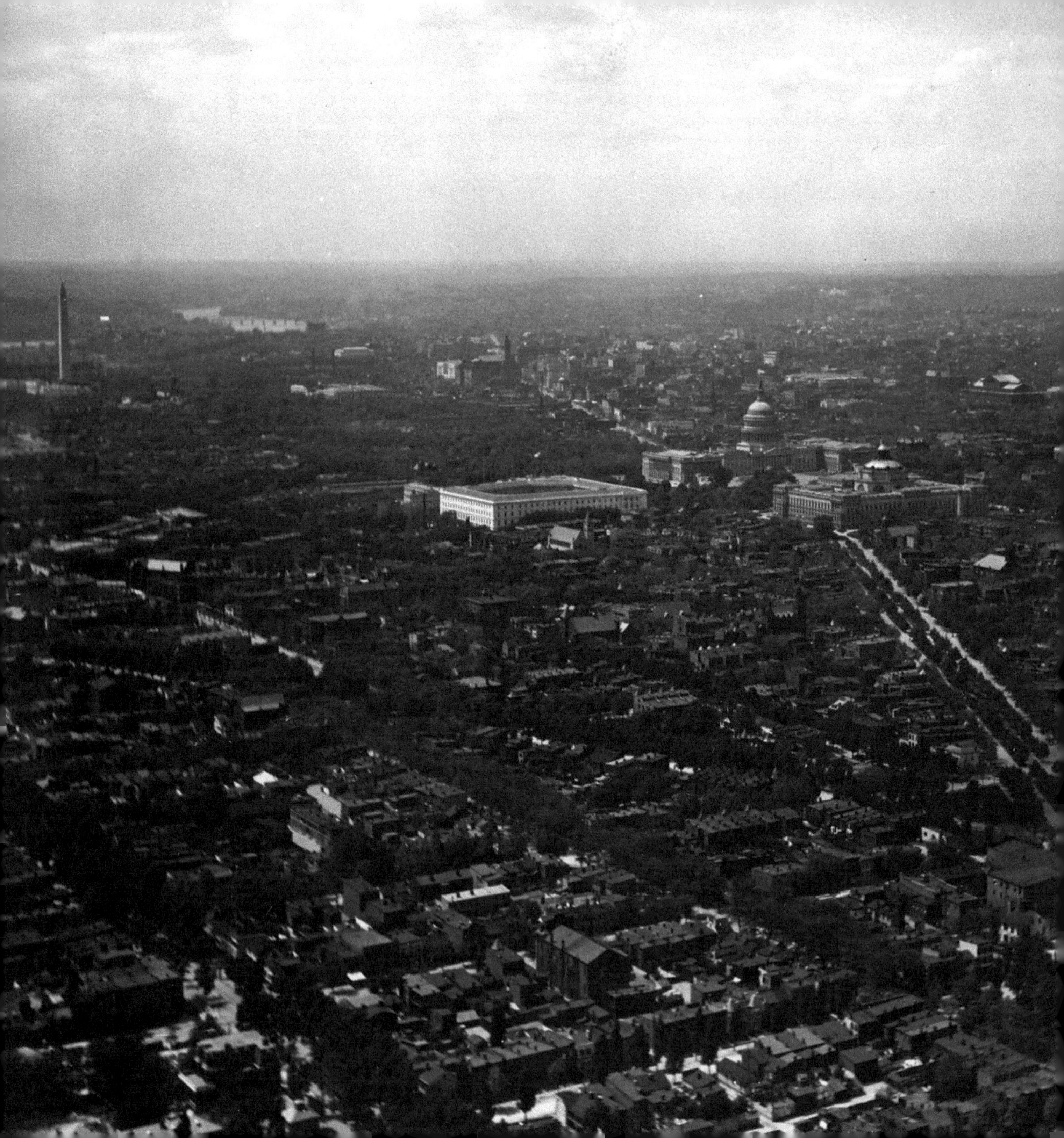

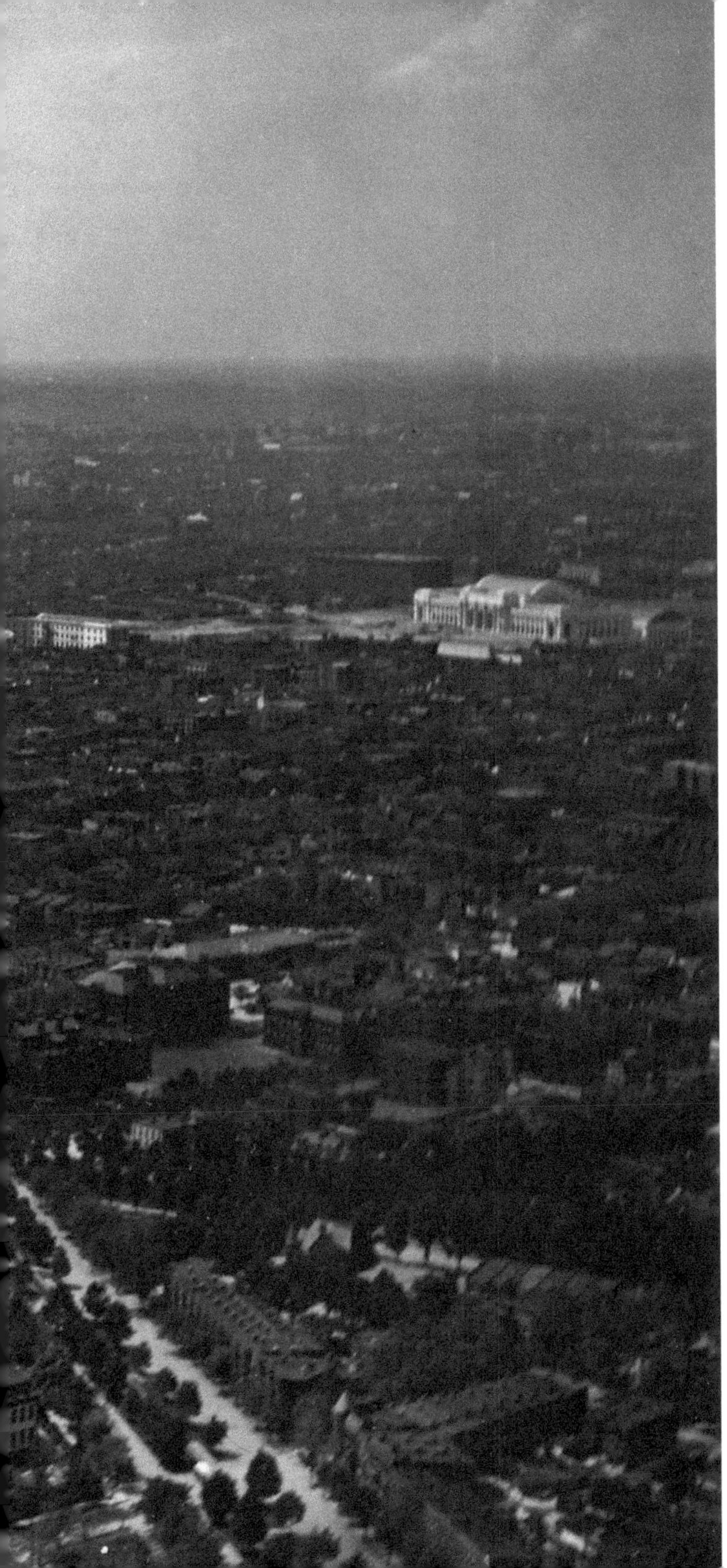

An aerial view of the nation's capital. The United States Capitol building and the Washington Monument are prominent among the seemingly endless landscape of buildings and topography.

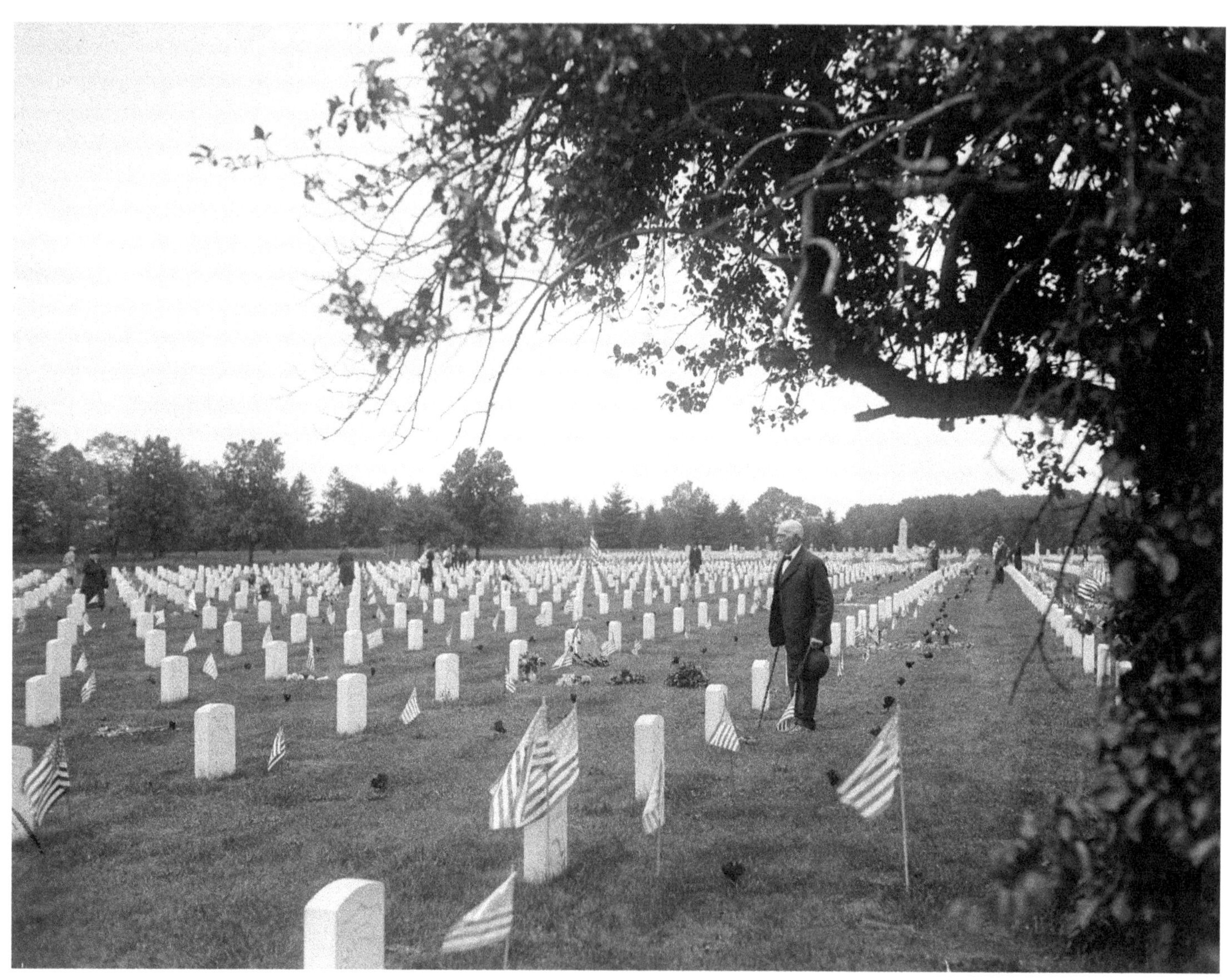

Every week approximately 25 funerals are held daily at Arlington National Cemetery. In this 1924 photograph, pristine rows of alabaster grave markers line the lawn. Presidents Taft and Kennedy are buried at the cemetery.

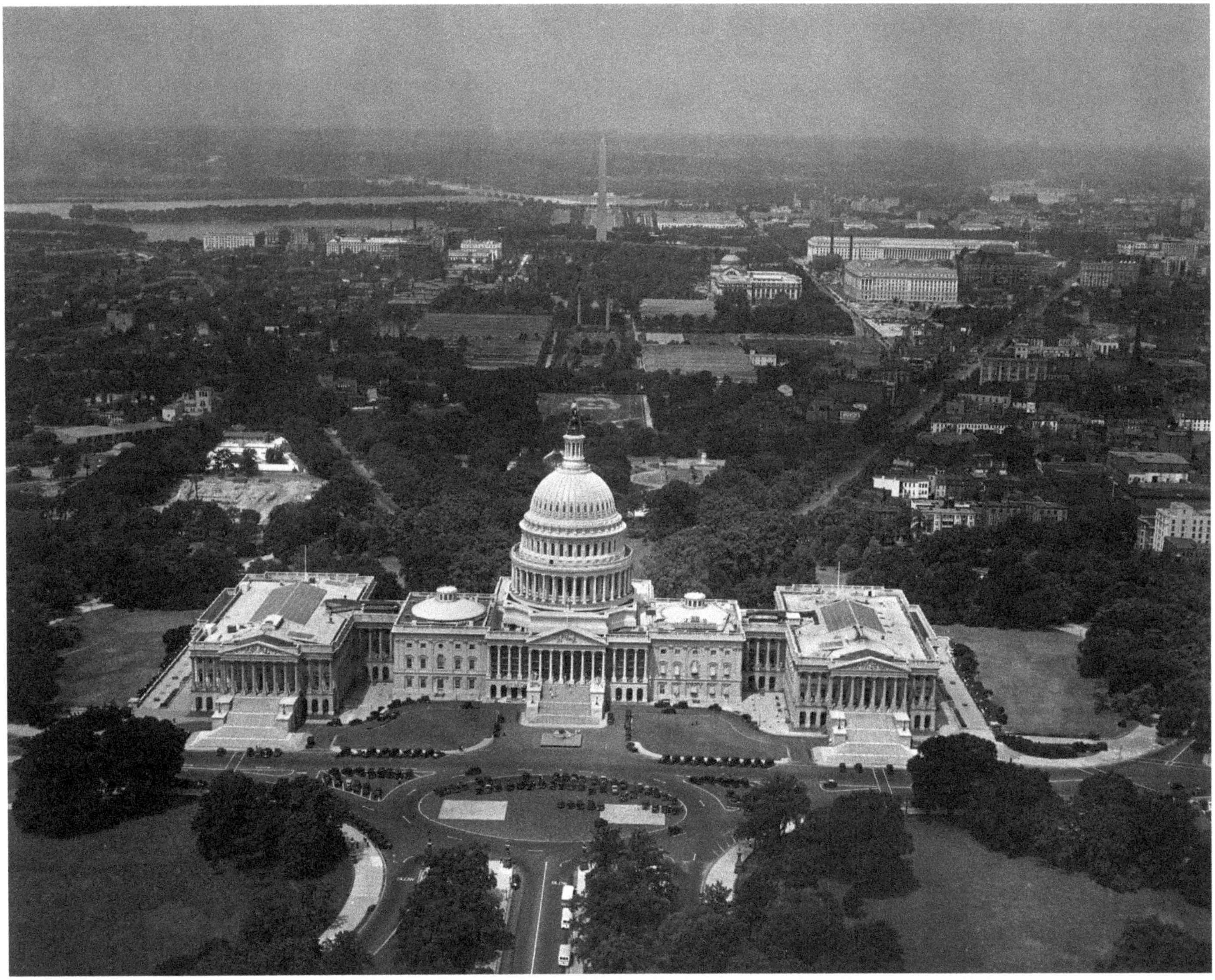

An aerial image of the United States Capitol with its surrounding areas and buildings. The U.S. Botanic Garden, the National Garden, Smithsonian Institution buildings, the National Mall, the Washington Monument, and the Lincoln Memorial are present among other notable structures in this image.

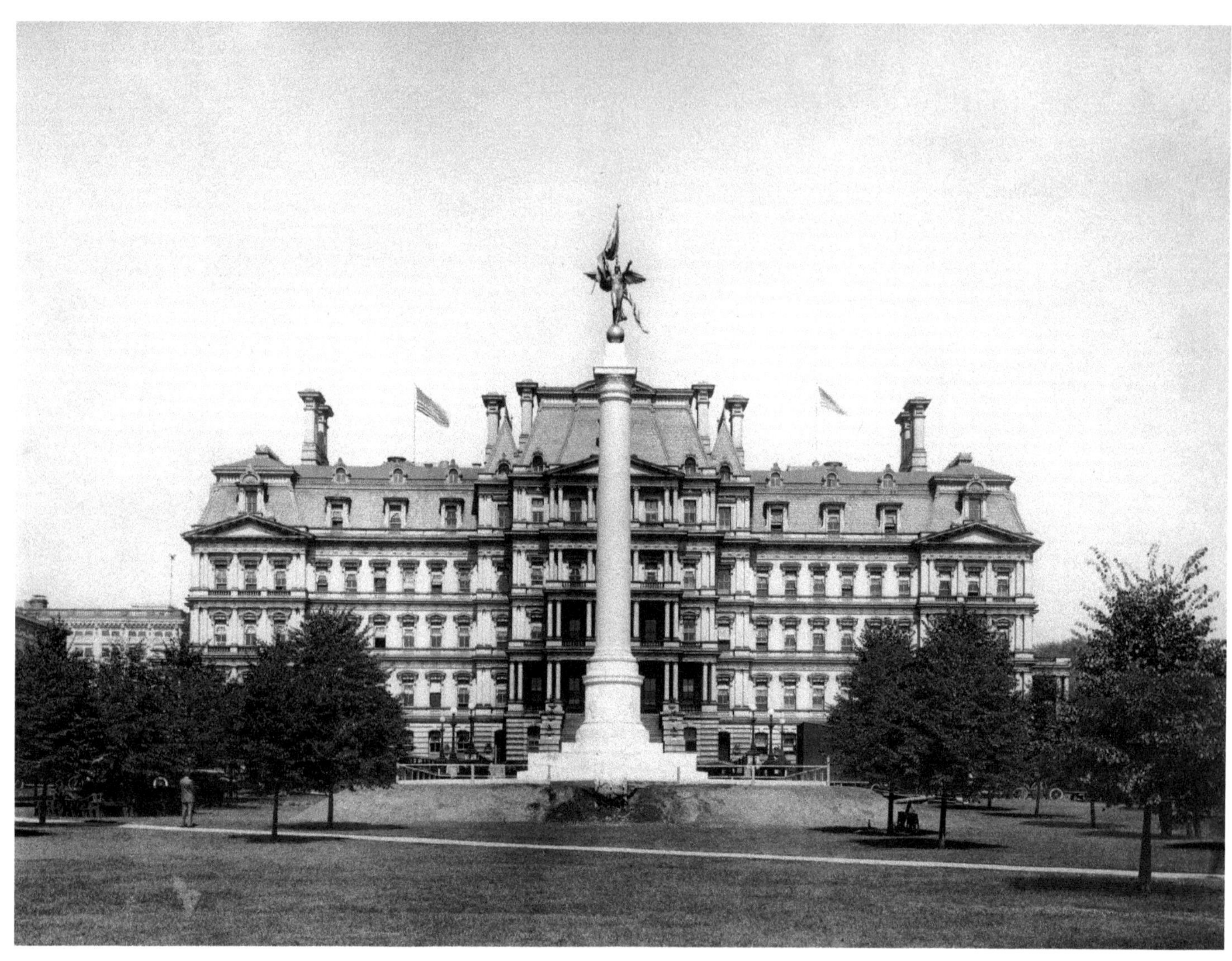

Sculptor Daniel Chester French's First Division Memorial is visible in front of the Eisenhower Executive Office Building. Constructed in 1924 and set in President's Park, the monument honors First Division service members who died in World War I. The building behind the monument was formerly known as the Old Executive Office Building but renamed for Dwight D. Eisenhower. A memorial commemorating President Eisenhower will be sited on a four-acre parcel on Independence Avenue between Fourth and Sixth streets in southwest Washington, D.C.

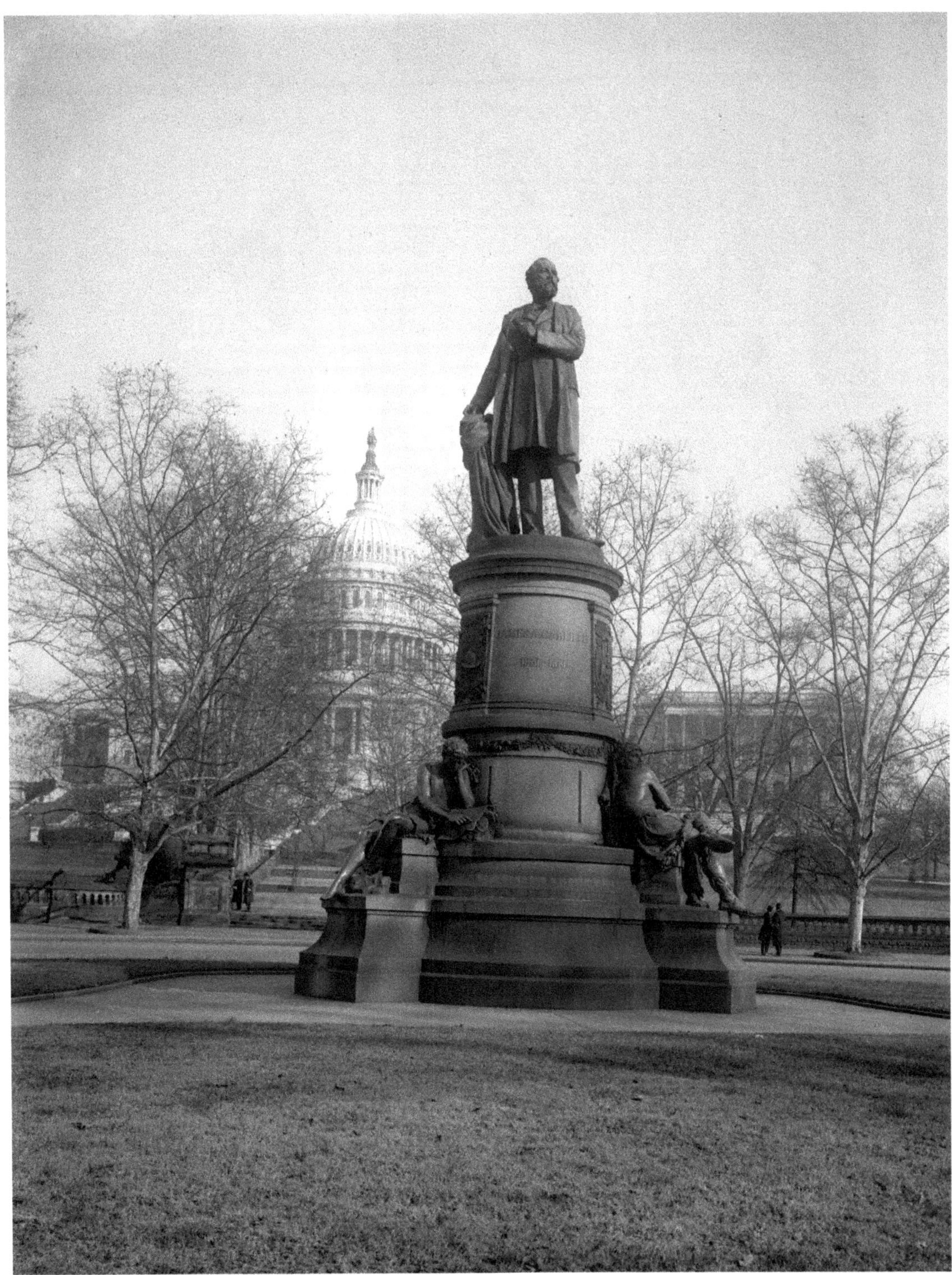

Elected in 1880 and assassinated a year later, President James Garfield is immortalized by this statue, located on the grounds of the United States Capitol in the circle at First Street, SW, and Maryland Avenue. Garfield was in office only four months of his term before he was shot. He died two months later.

This contemplative sculpture could be a character from a Tolkien novel. The piece, known as the Adams Memorial, was commissioned by author and historian Henry Adams in tribute to his late wife Clover Hooper Adams. Located in Rock Creek Cemetery, the Augustus Saint-Gauden bronze sculpture is allegorical. Adams conveyed his wish to the artist to incorporate elements of Buddhist devotional art into this work.

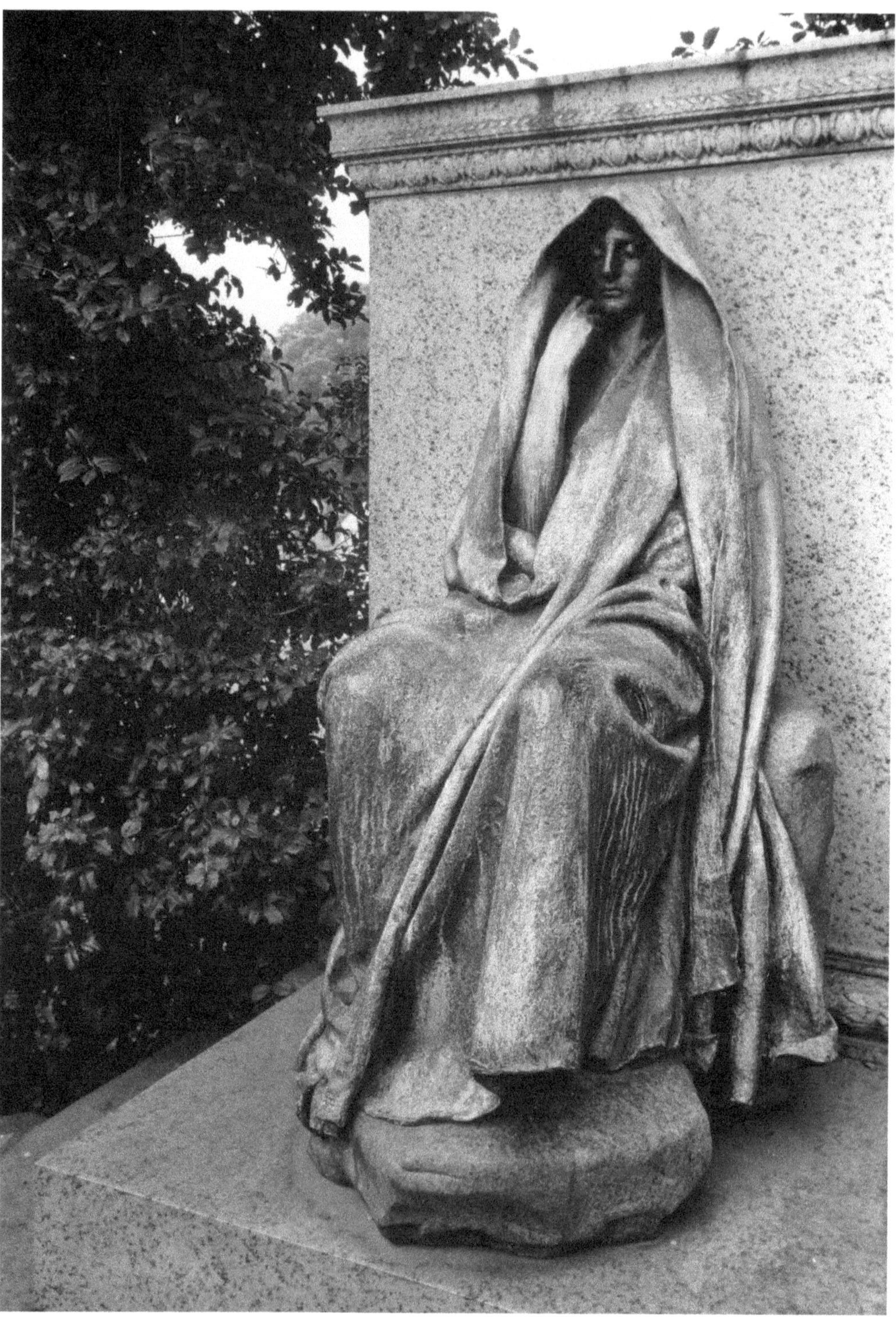

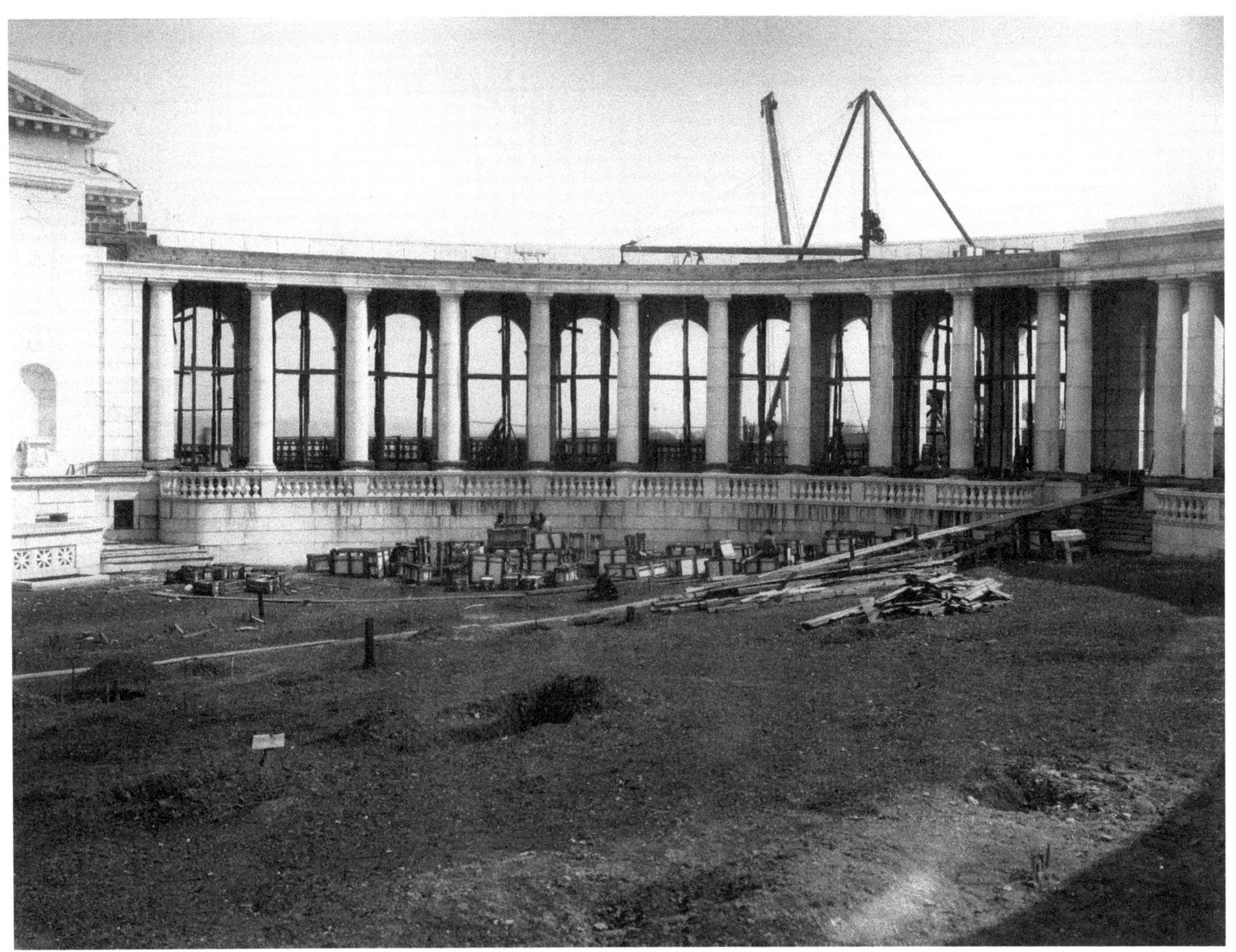

The Arlington Memorial Amphitheater, designed by architect Thomas Hastings, began construction in 1913.

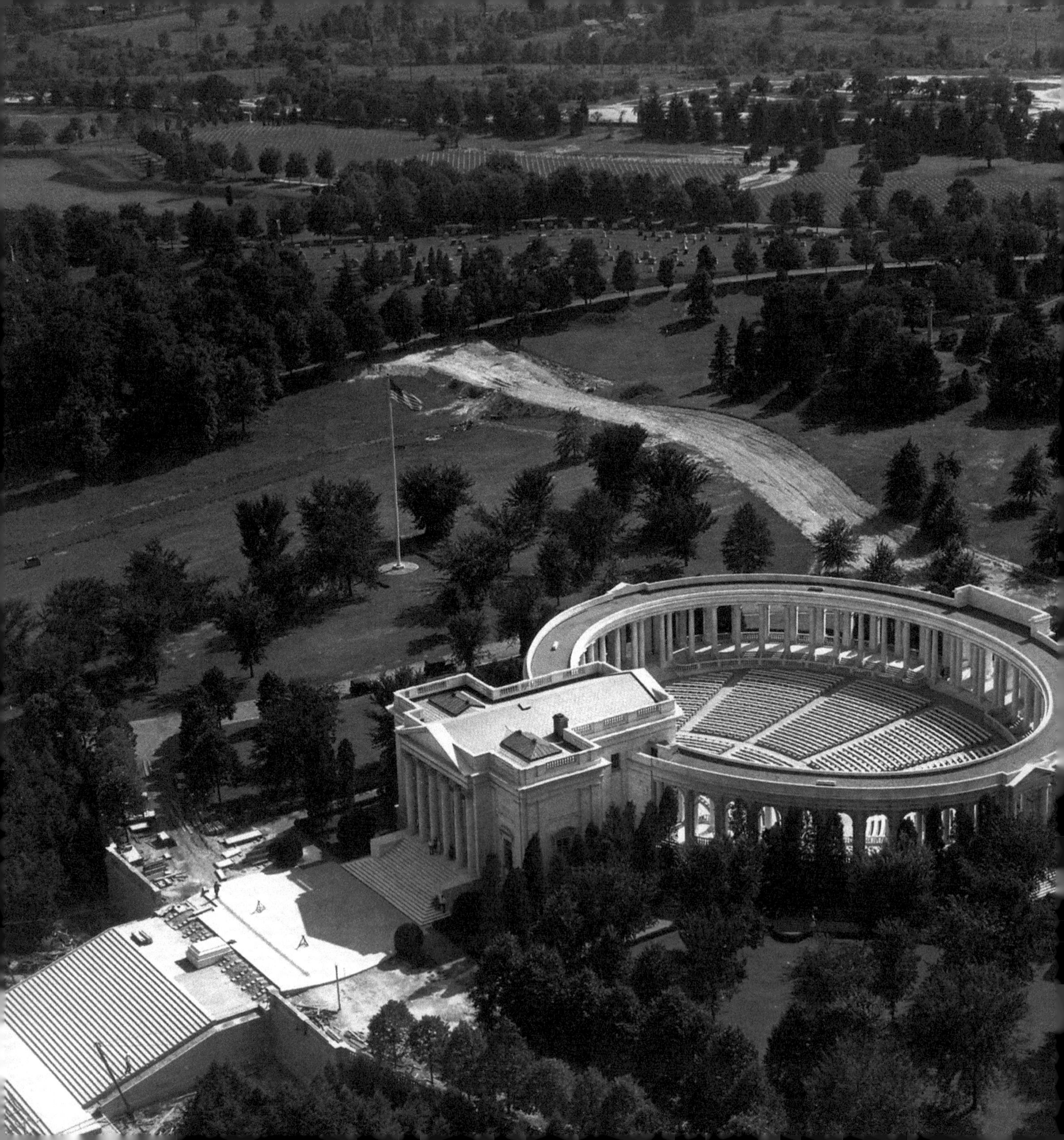

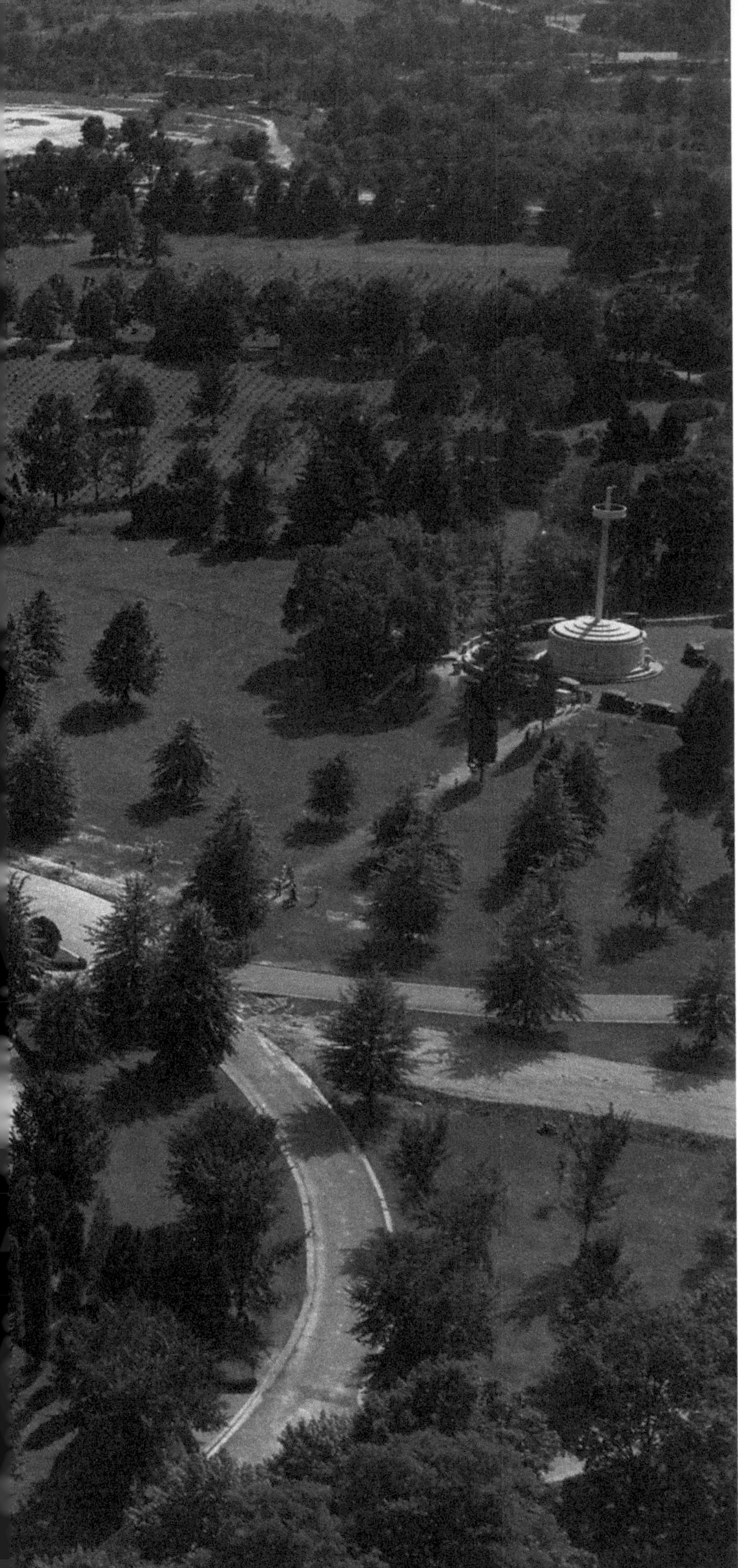

The Tomb of the Unknown Soldier is located at the Arlington Memorial Amphitheater. In the background of this aerial view is the cemetery, where many soldiers are buried after their funerals are held at the amphitheater.

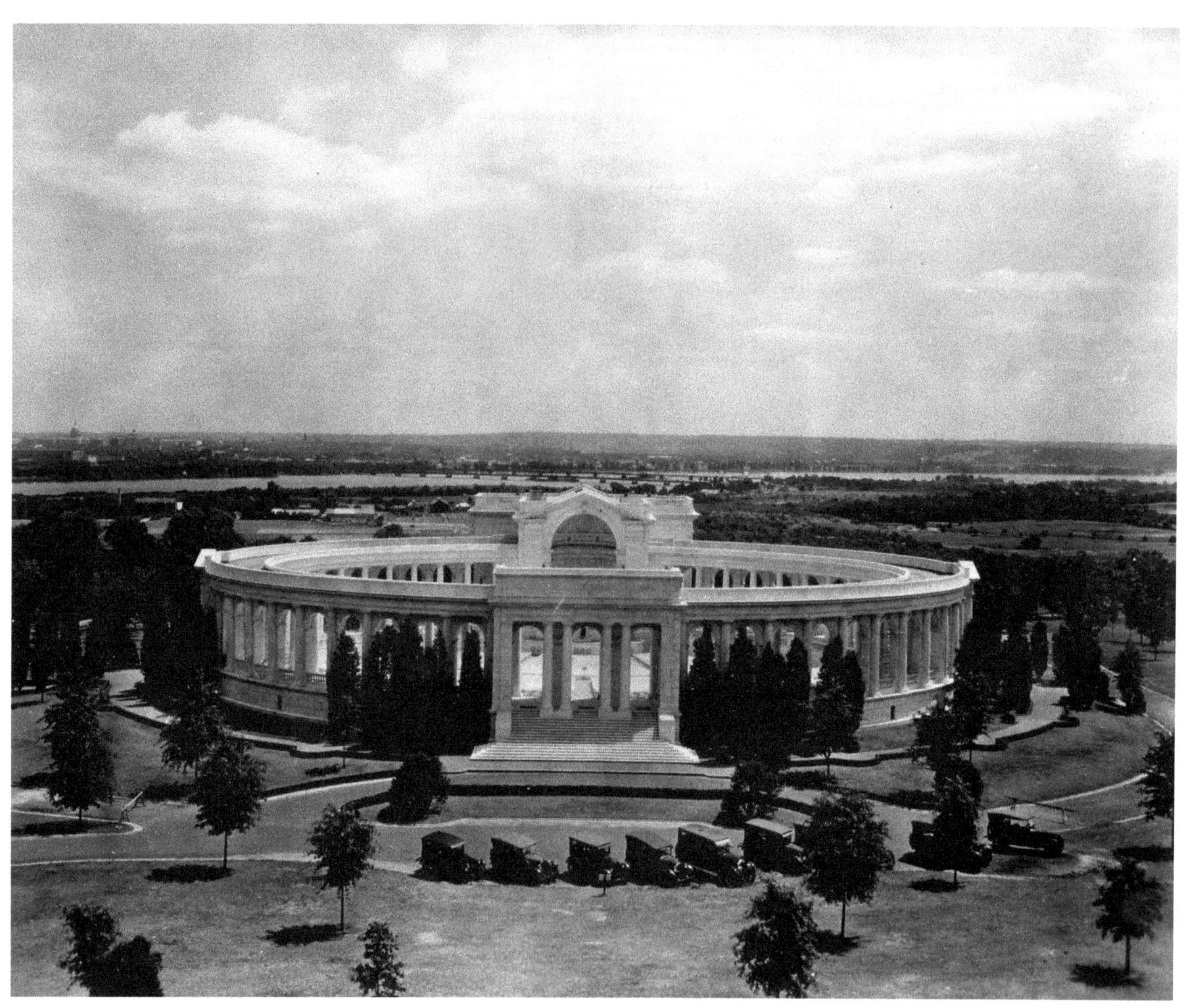

Constructed of marble and modeled after Greek architecture, the Arlington Memorial Amphitheater stands completed in the Arlington National Cemetery. Although approval to build the memorial was enacted by Congress during President Taft's term, it was President Wilson who placed the cornerstone in 1915.

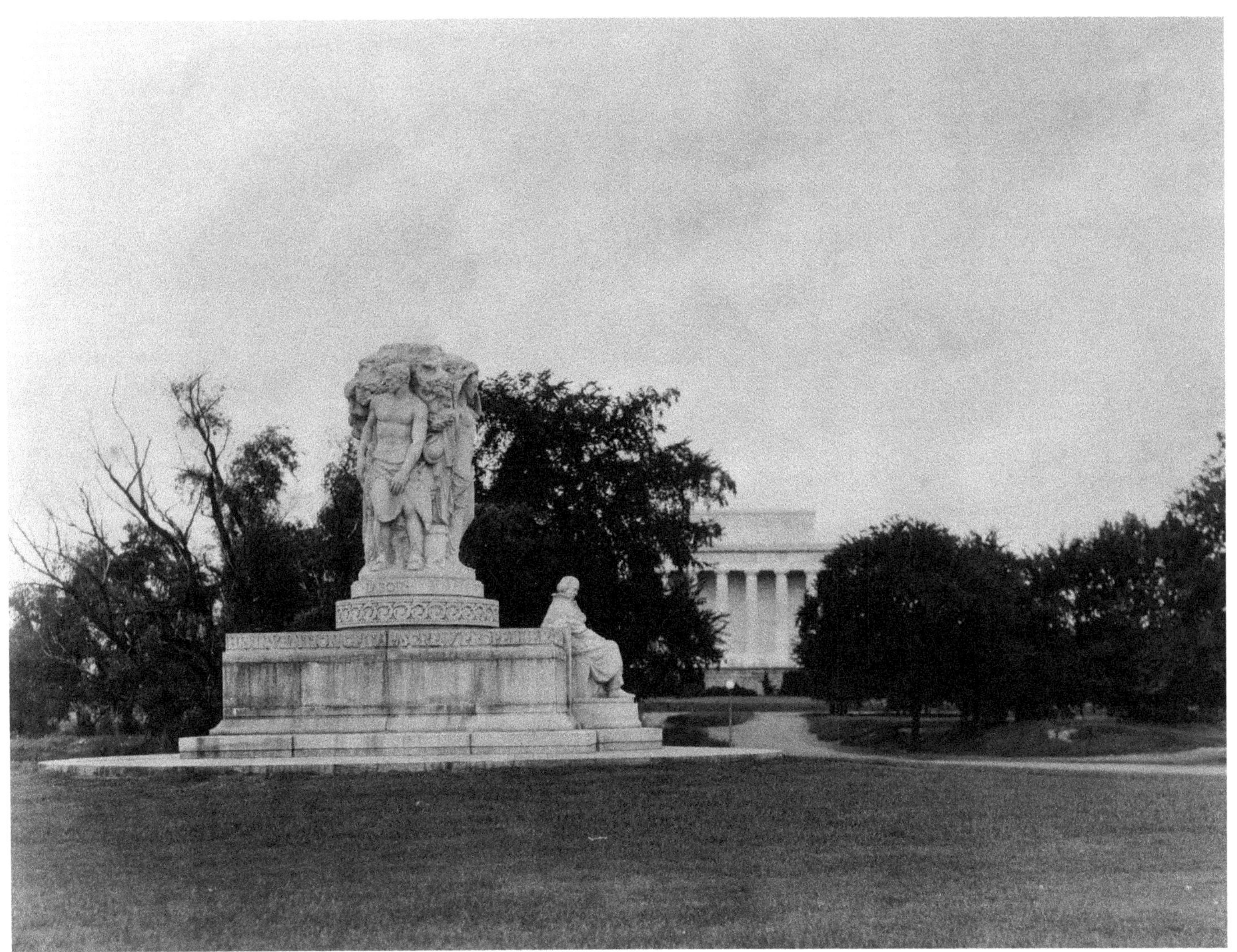

John Ericsson, an engineer of Swedish descent, used his considerable technological expertise to design the U.S. naval vessel USS *Monitor*. What made this ship different from others was the use of iron in its design. Ericsson is credited with developing technological advances that helped the Union forces prevail in the Civil War. The memorial in his honor, pictured in this 1930s photograph, can be found in West Potomac Park near the Lincoln Memorial.

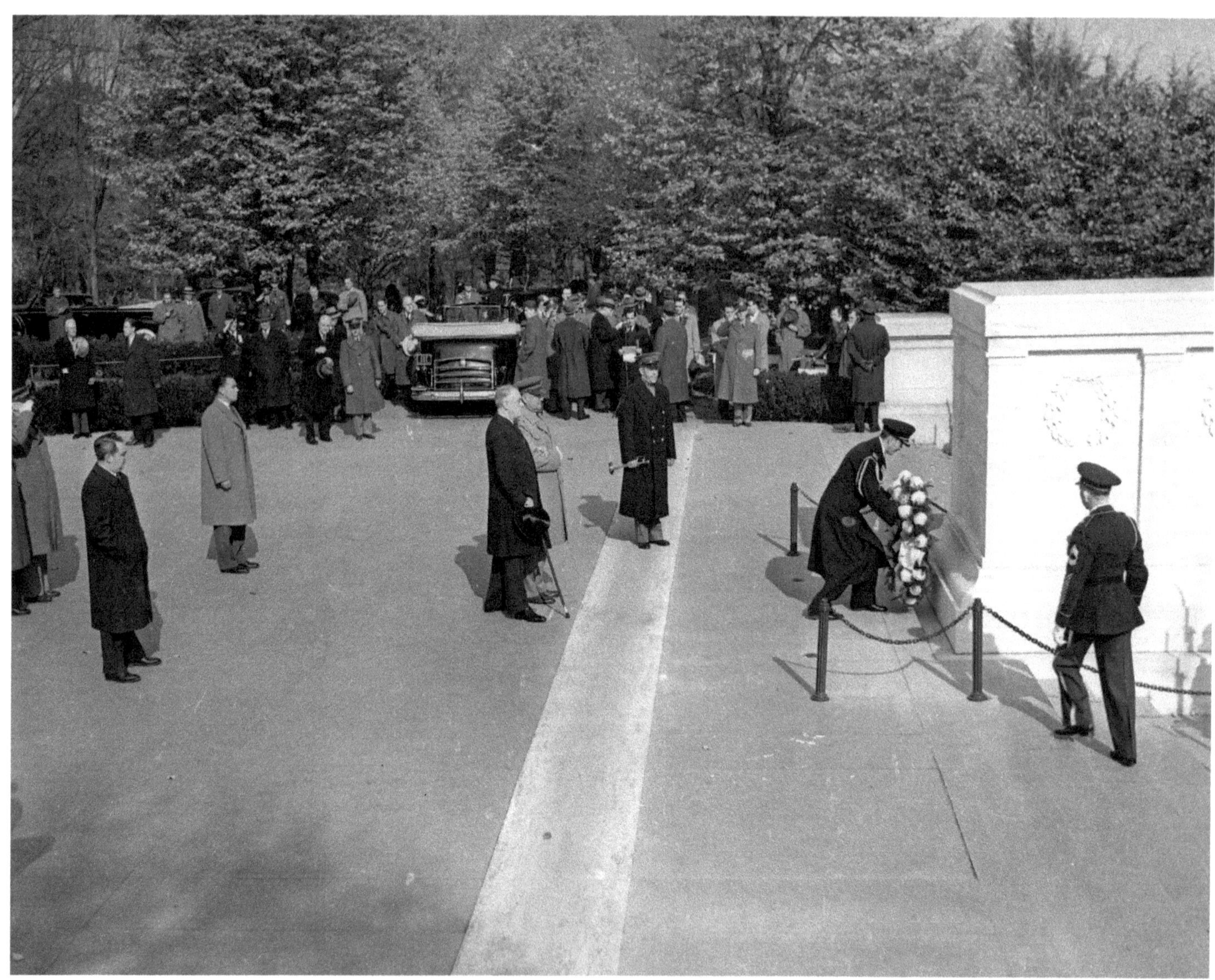

The Tomb of the Unknown Soldier in Arlington National Cemetery is a popular tourist attraction but also the setting for many solemn occasions. On Veterans Day in 1946, a crowd gathers at the site to pay homage to military men and women who sacrificed their lives for the country.

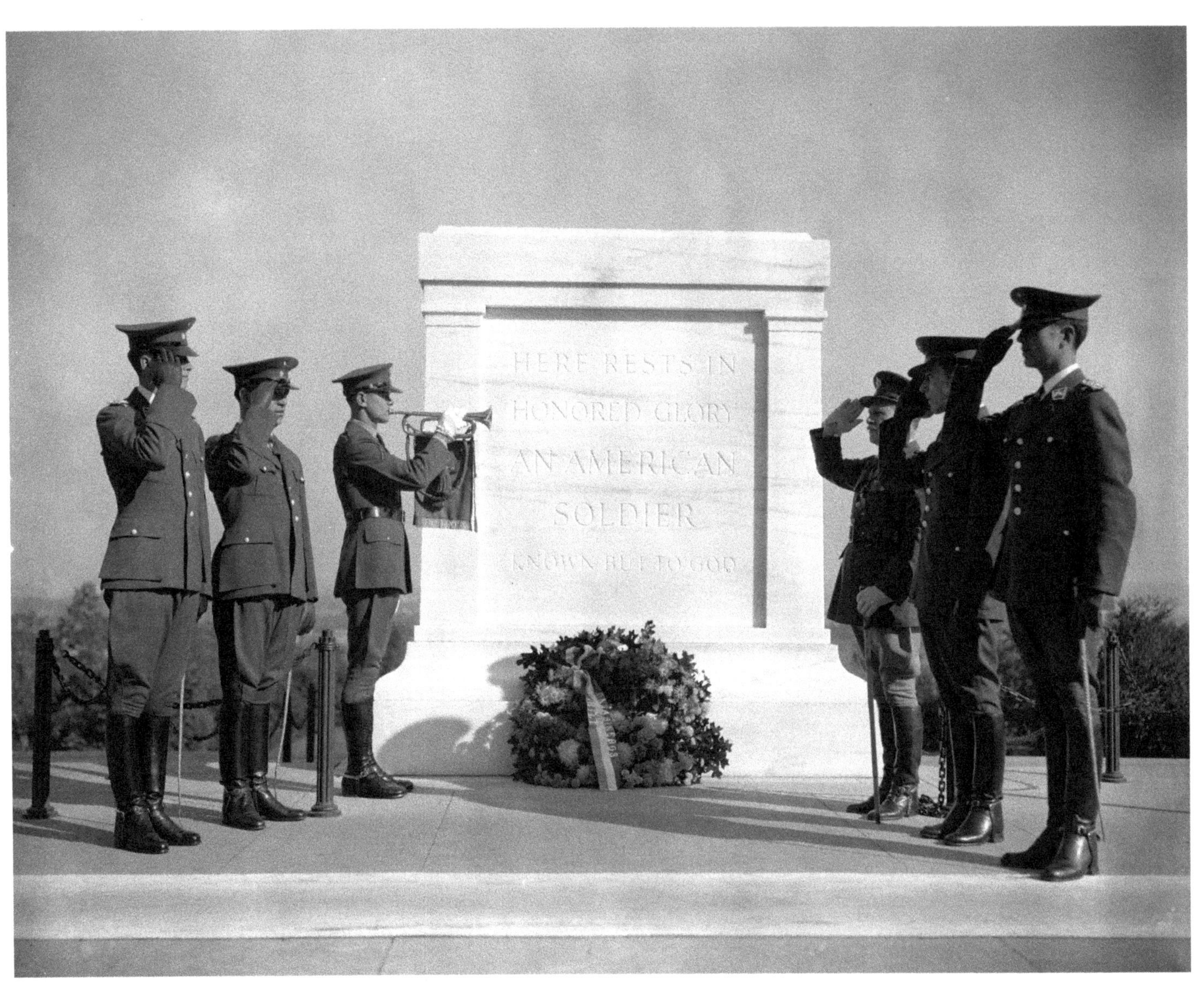

Located at the center of Arlington National Cemetery, this tomb is guarded around the clock. Each of the unknown service members interred here received a medal of honor.

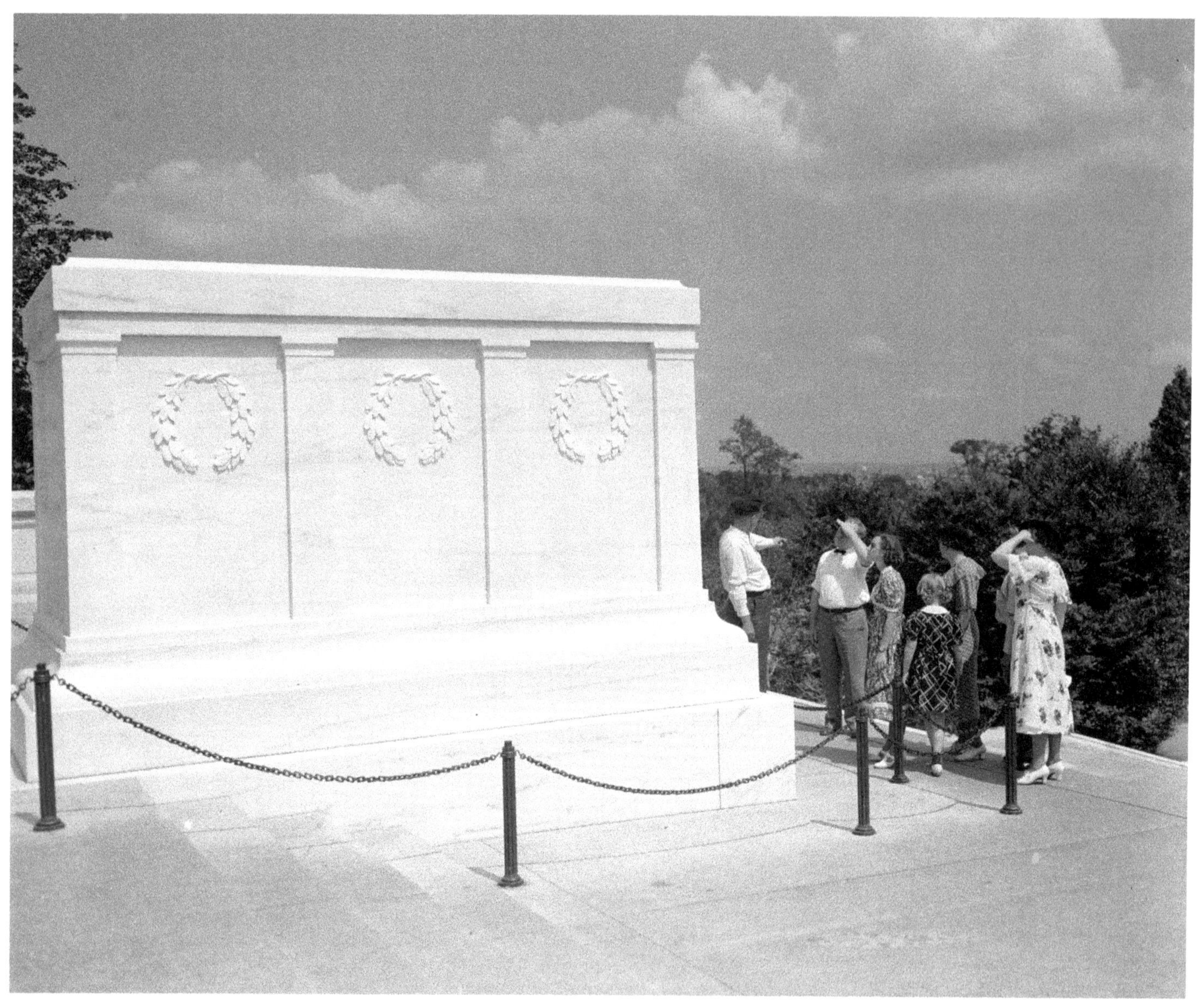

Just as the Tomb of the Unknown Dead bears the remains of soldiers from the Civil War, the Tomb of the Unknown Soldier is the final resting place for unidentified service members of World War I, World War II, the Korean War, and the Vietnam War. Here, visitors from Capitol City Transit tour the memorial.

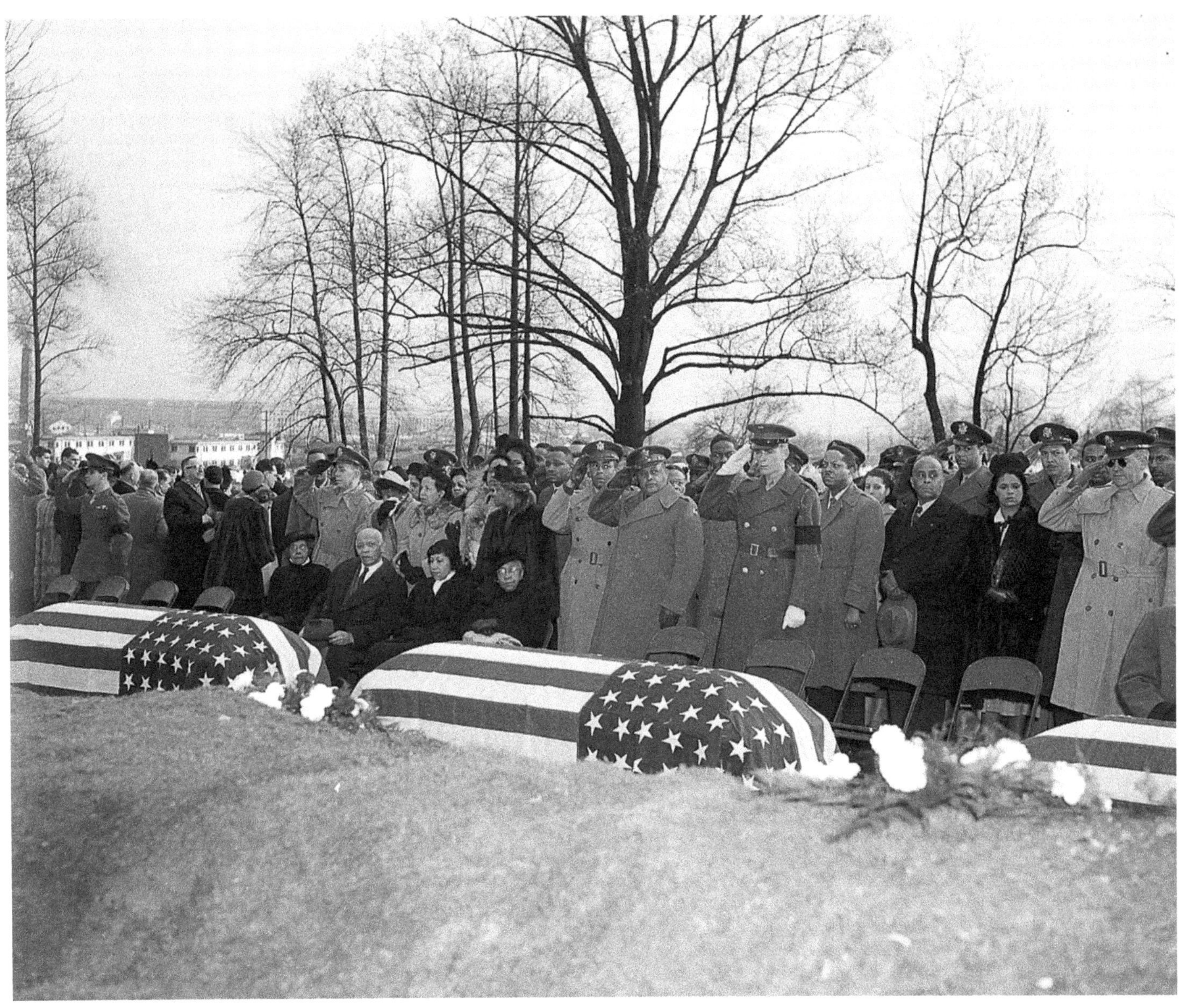

Renowned Washington, D.C., photographer Addison Scurlock captured this scene of burials at Arlington National Cemetery in January of 1949.

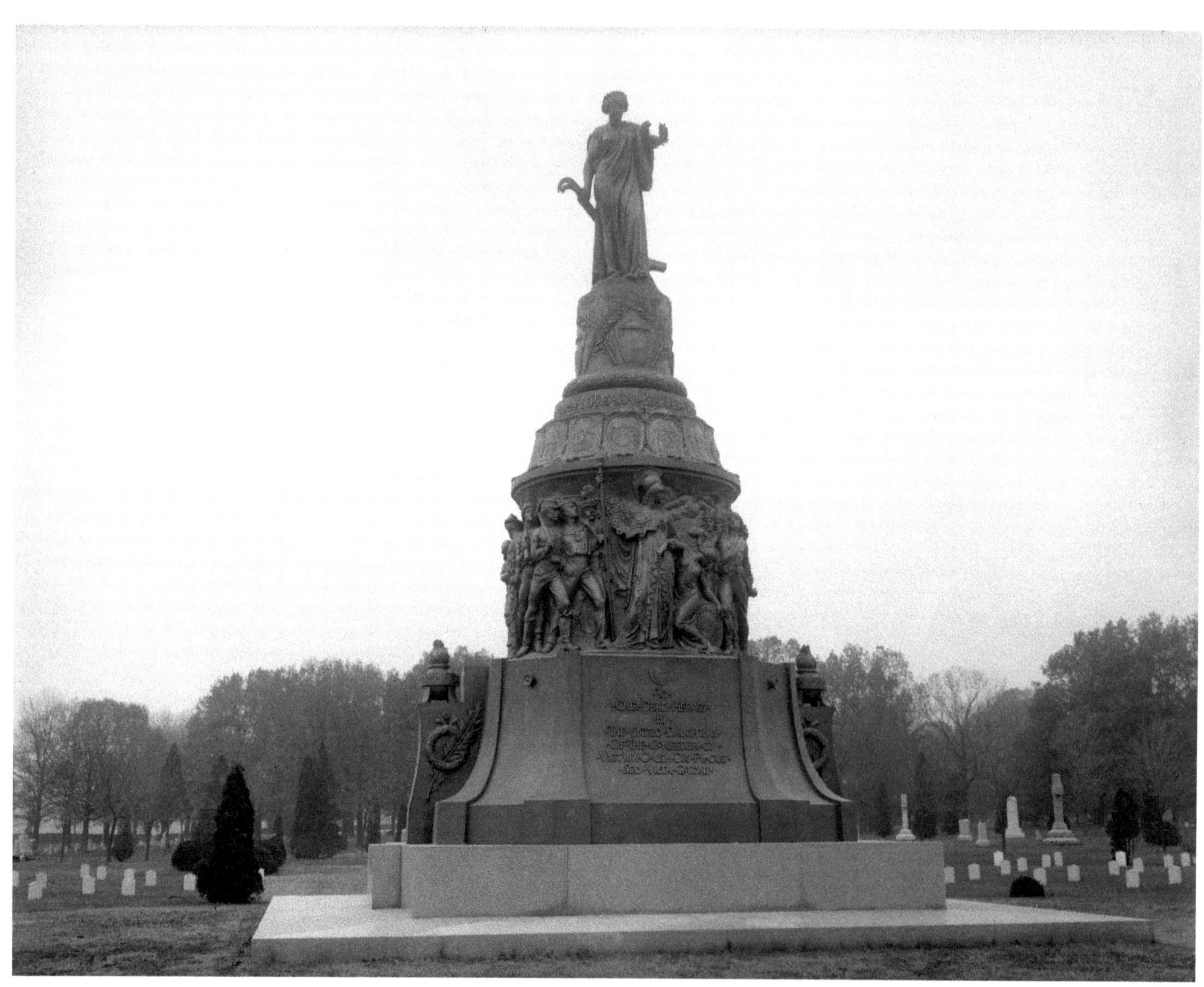

The inscription on one side of the Confederate memorial reads, "Not for fame or reward, not for place or rank, not lured by ambition or goaded by necessity, but in simple obedience to duty as they understood it. These men suffered for all, sacrificed all, dared all and died." After the Civil War ended and the schism between the North and the South was mended, hundreds of Confederate soldiers were laid to rest at Arlington National Cemetery.

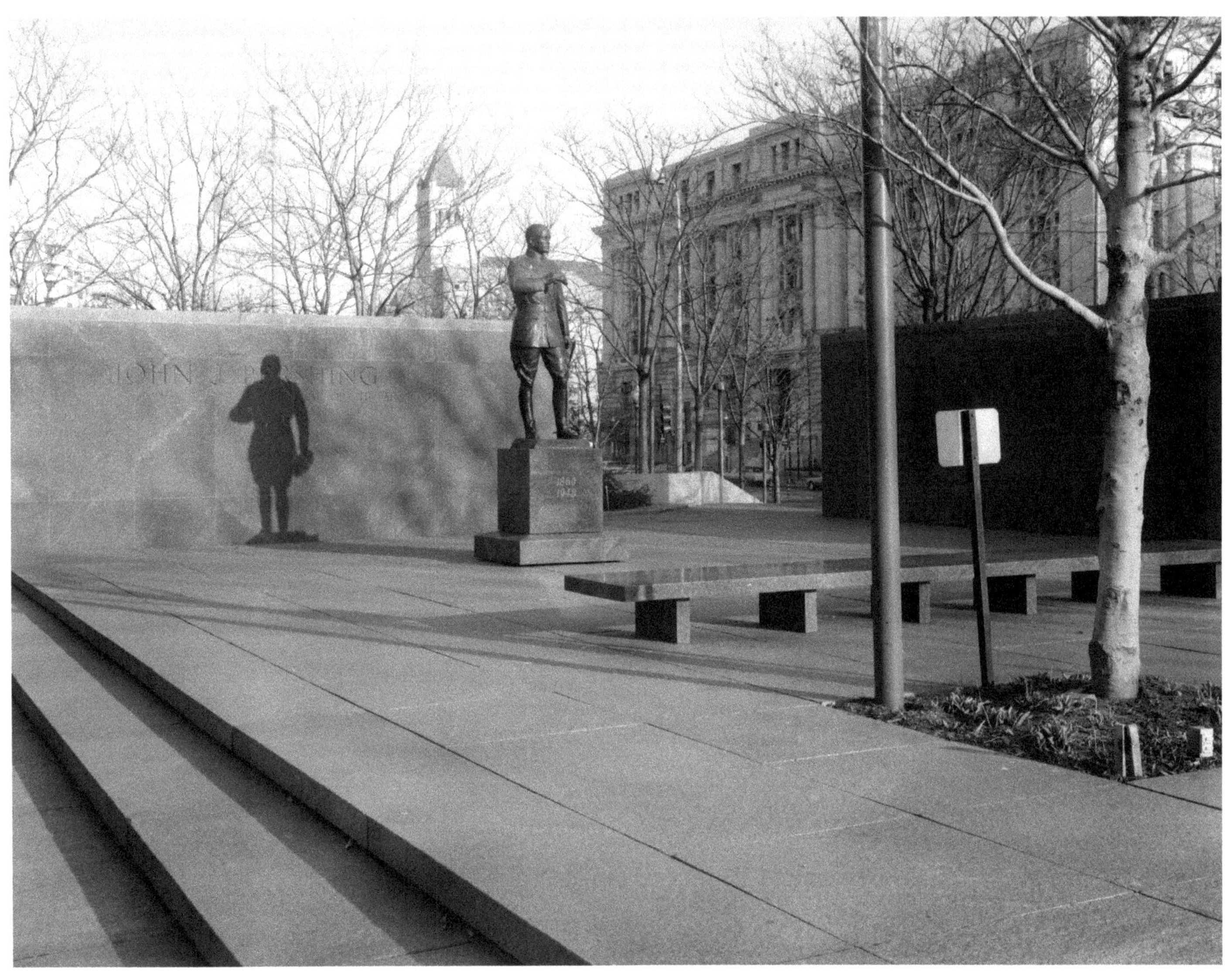

Army general John Joseph Pershing (September 13, 1860–July 15, 1948) was known during his time at West Point as "Lord God Almighty." His career would later lead him back to the military academy as a tactical instructor. A commanding presence, Pershing would later acquire the nickname "Black Jack"—an officer who rose to the top rank of General of the Armies. He served in the Russo-Japanese War, the Mexican Expedition, World War I, and as a mentor to World War II generals. The John Pershing Memorial is located at E and 14th streets NW, in Pershing Park.

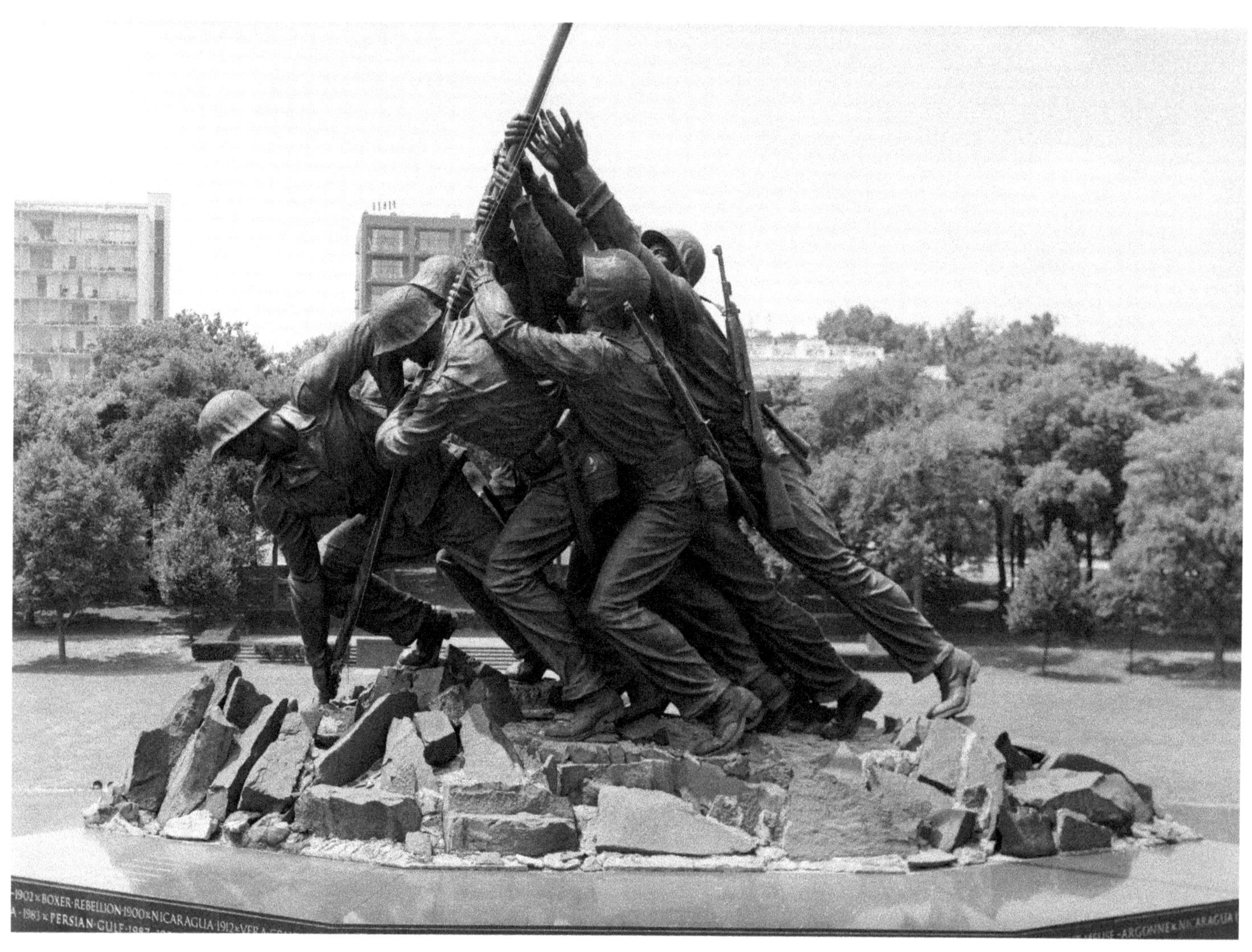

The Iwo Jima flag raising is one of the most familiar images burned into the consciousness of American memory. The bronze sculpture appears to be moving as four service members struggle to raise an American flag at Iwo Jima. Modeled after the Joe Rosenthal photograph, the famous memorial stands near Arlington Cemetery and the Netherlands Carillon in Arlington, Virginia. The Felix de Weldon design was dedicated by President Dwight D. Eisenhower on November 10, 1954.

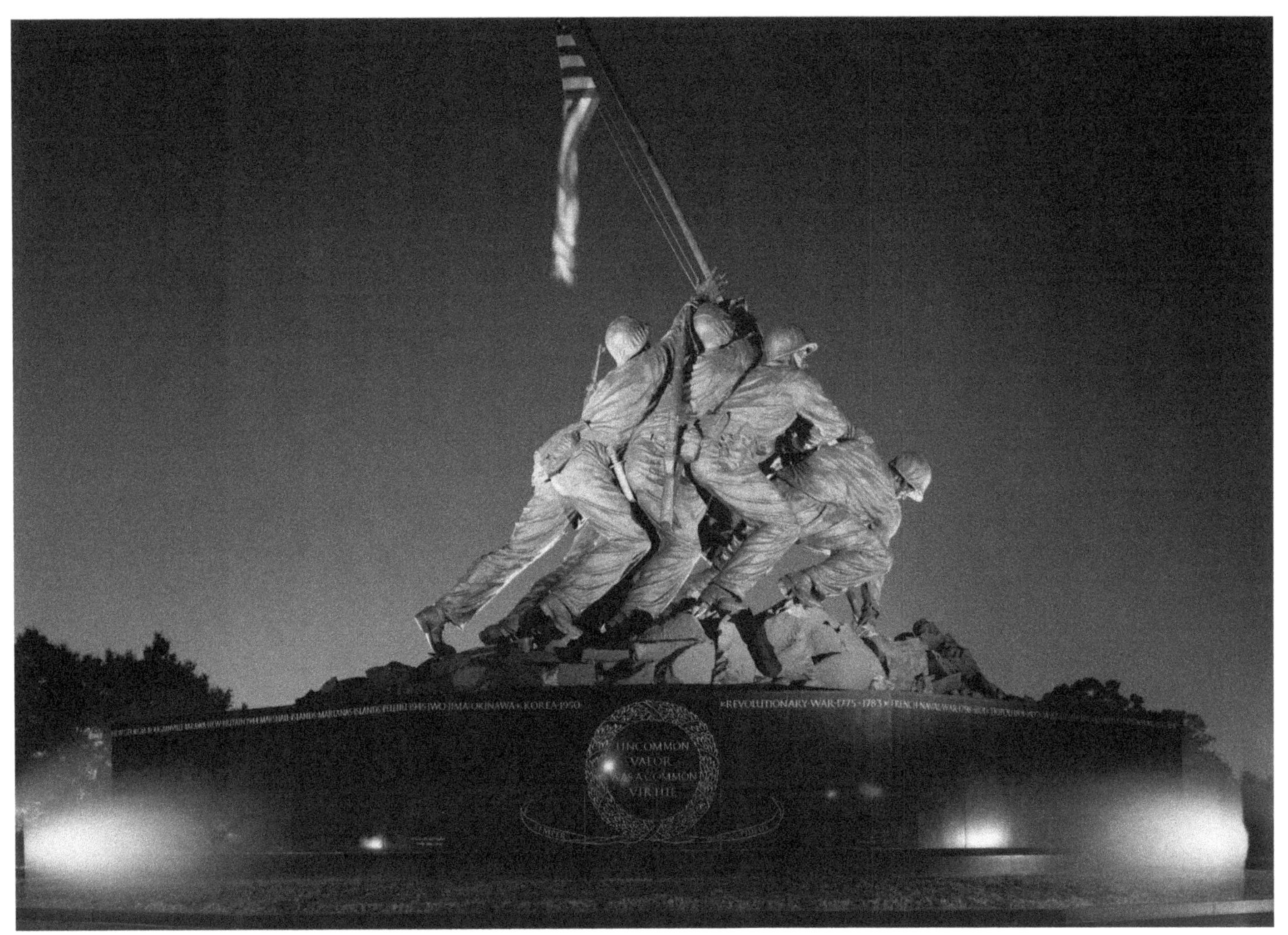

A night view of the Iwo Jima Memorial, also known as the USMC (United States Marine Corps) Memorial. The real life subjects in this sculpture are Sergeant Michael Strank, USMC; Corporal Harlon Block, USMC; Private First Class Franklin Sousley, USMC; Private First Class Rene Gagnon, USMC; Private First Class Ira Hayes, USMC; and PM2 John Bradley, Hospital Corpsman U.S. Navy.

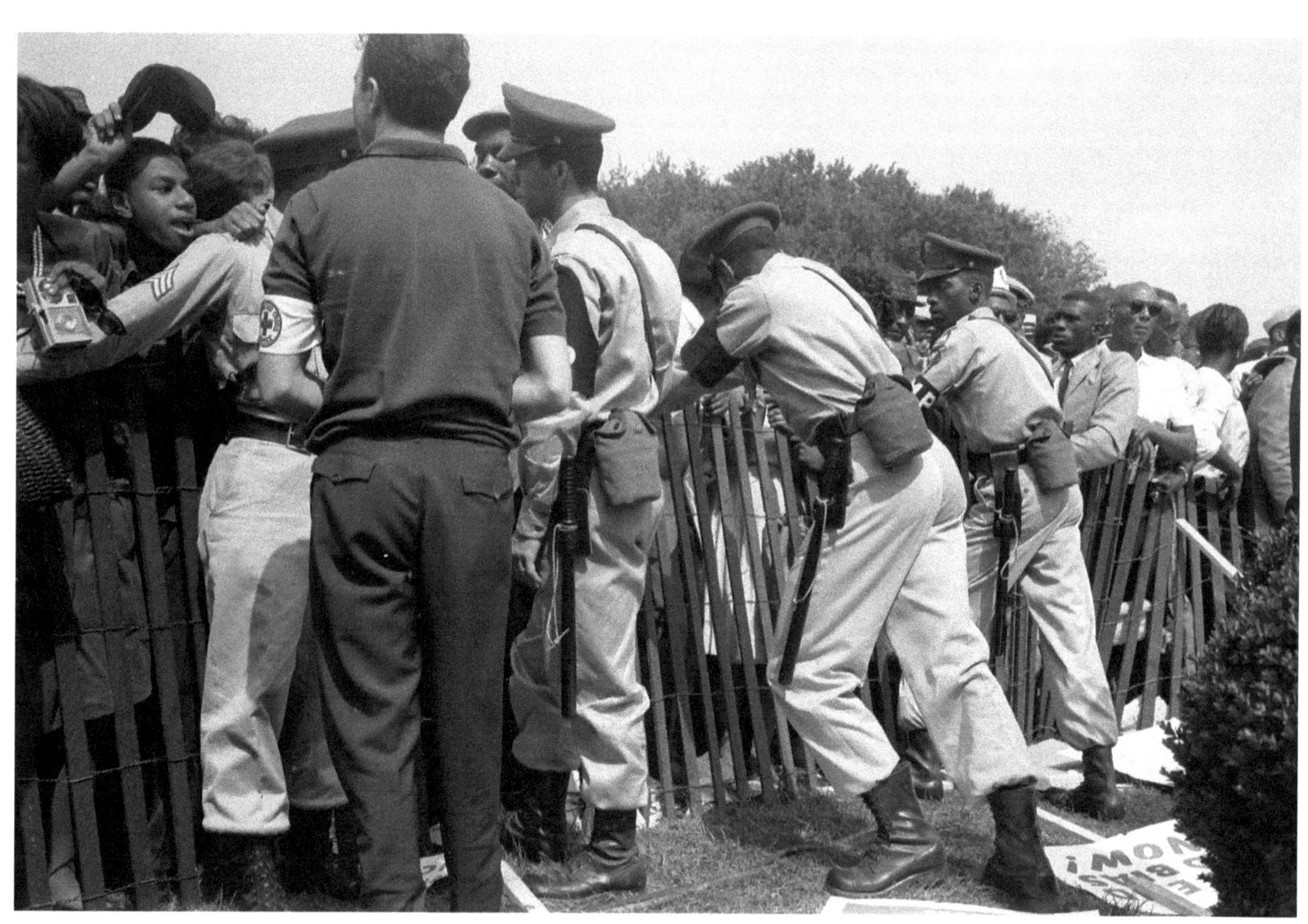

Police secure a fence at the National Mall during Dr. Martin Luther King, Jr.'s 1963 March on Washington.

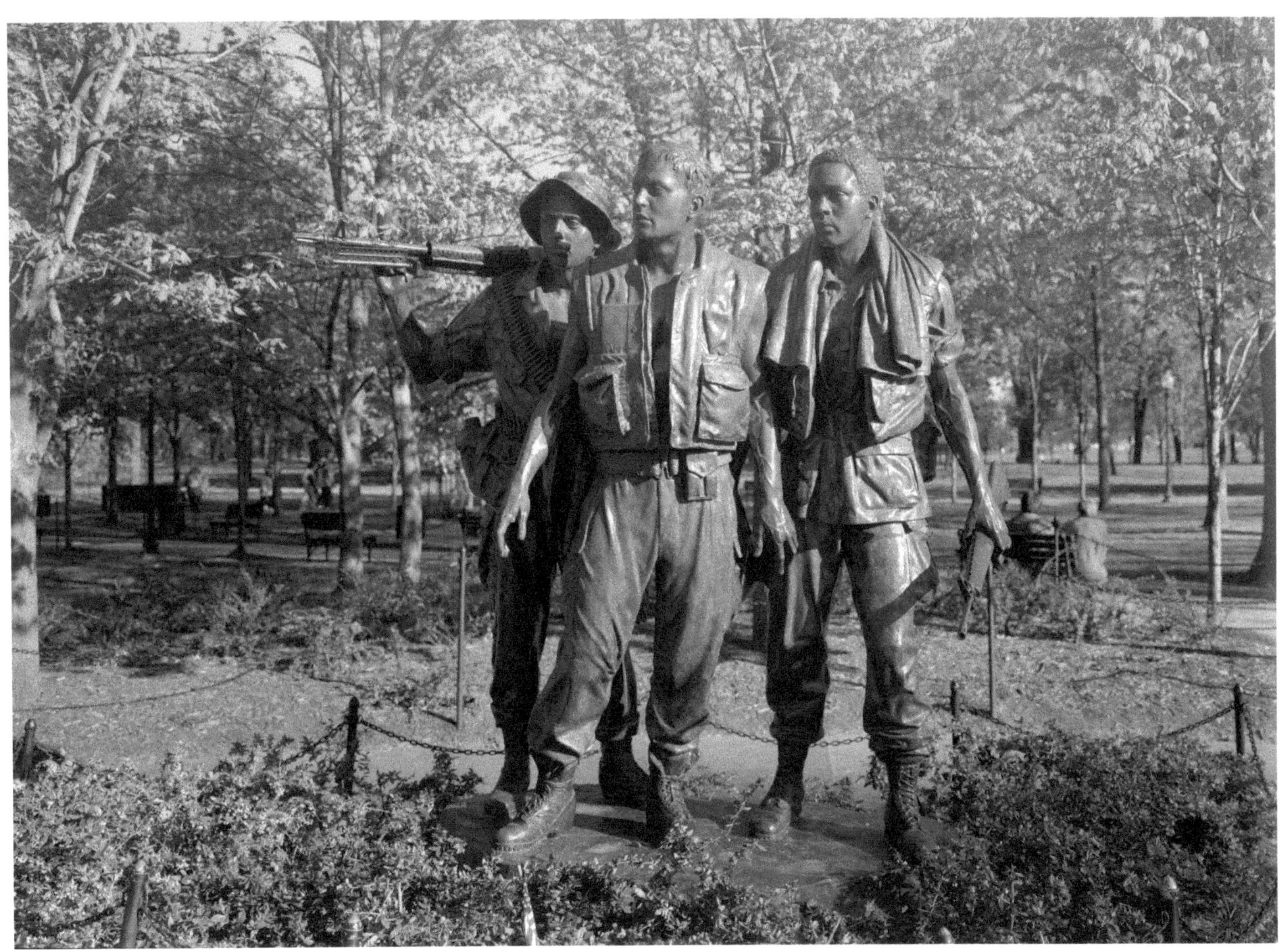

Presented to the world on Veterans Day in 1984, this bronze sculpture of the *Three Soldiers,* also known as the *Three Servicemen,* honors the veterans of the Vietnam War. This statue complements the Vietnam Memorial Wall at which the soldiers direct their gazes.

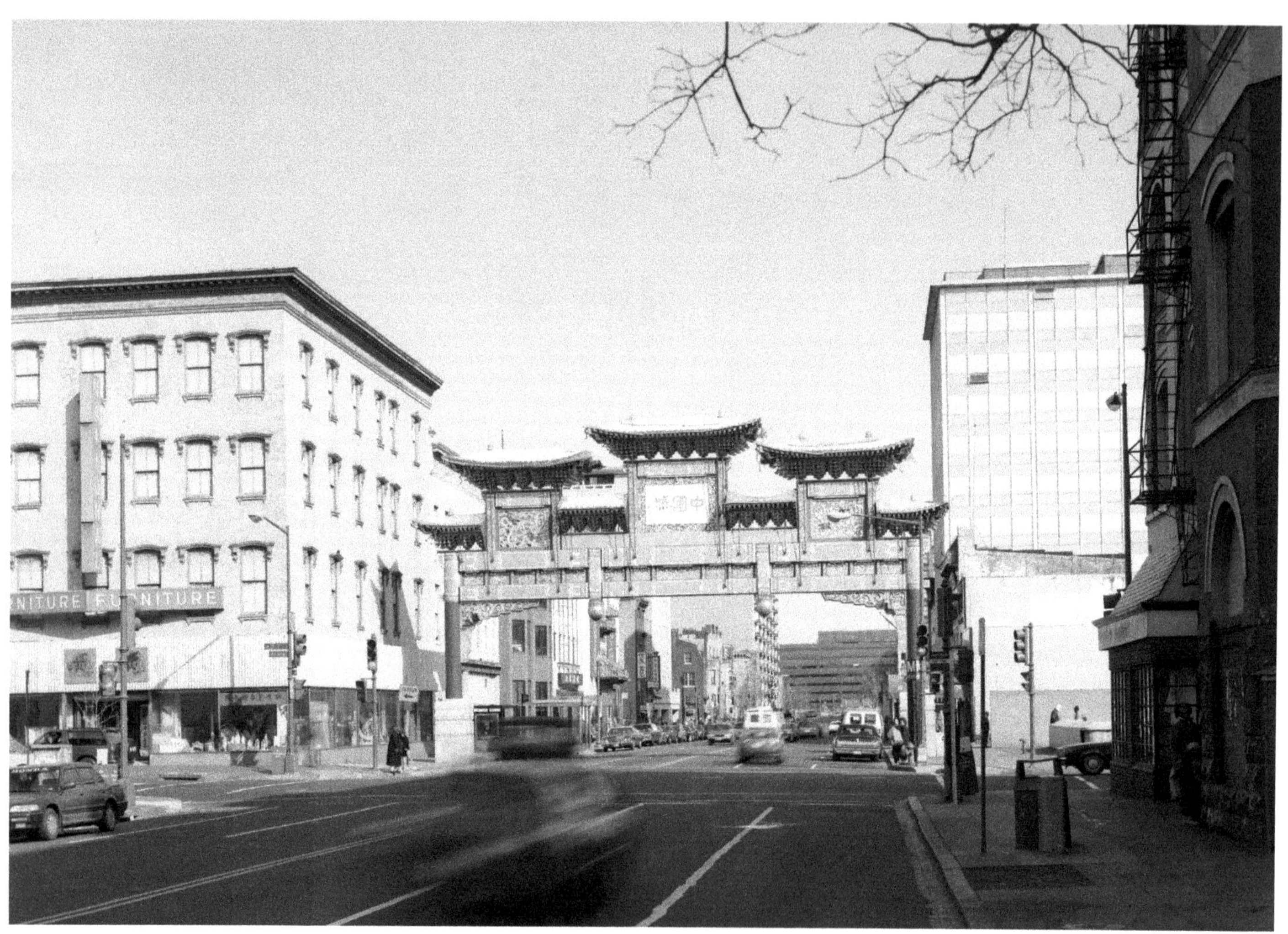

This photograph features a view of H Street, with the Chinatown Arch facing east from Seventh Street, NW. Built in 1896, the arch is still there today; however, many old family-run businesses have been replaced by new businesses bolstered by the presence of the Verizon Center, formerly the MCI Center.

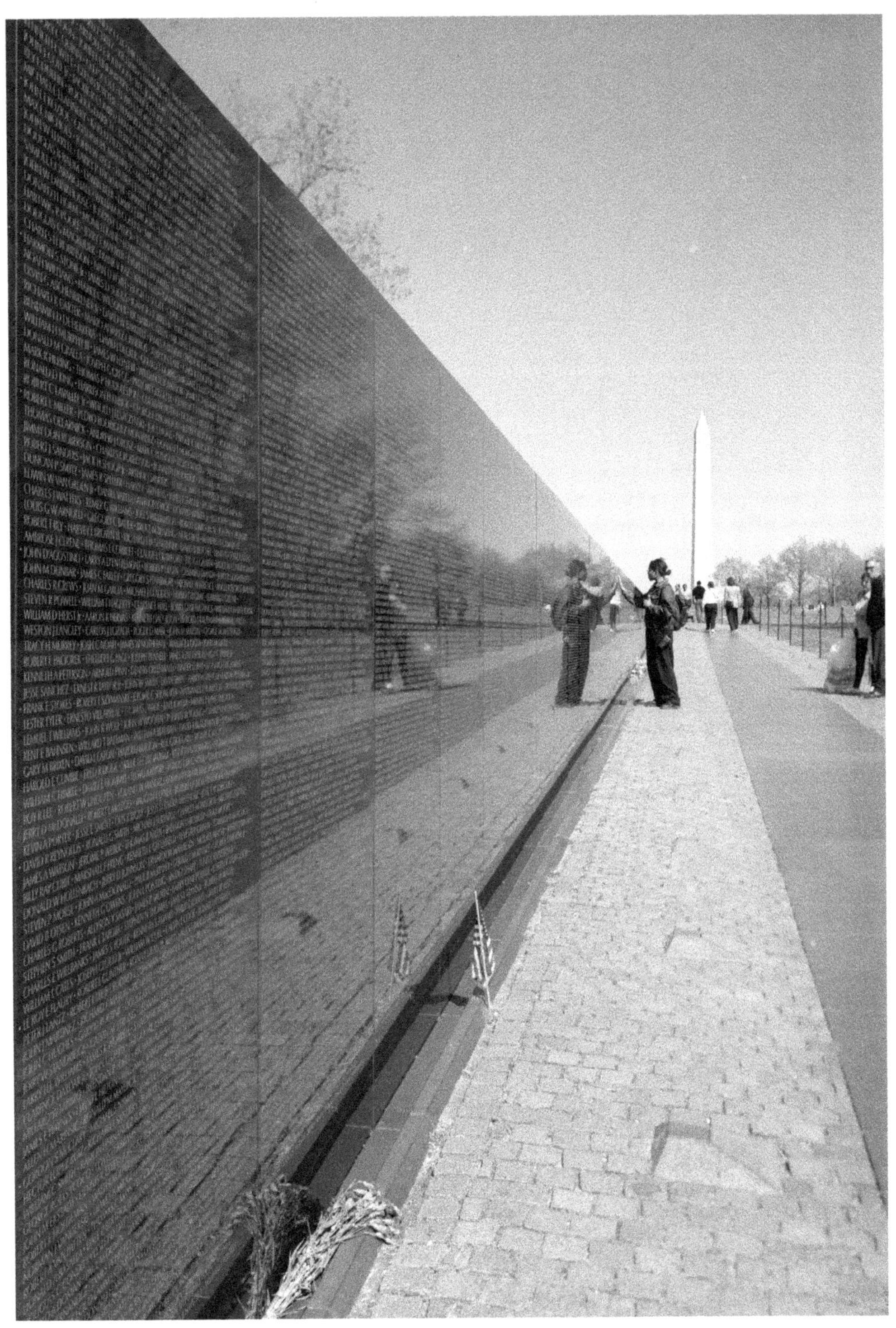

The Vietnam War (1959–1975) was both long and intractable, and the collective human impact is arguably still being felt today. This view of the Vietnam Memorial shows the apex directed toward the Washington Monument, with a small flag left by a visitor at the base of the wall. The wall is located at the western end of the National Mall, adjacent to the Lincoln Memorial in West Potomac Park. It also rests just north of the Korean War Veterans Memorial, across from the Reflecting Pool. On some days the emotions at "the Wall" from visitors who lost loved ones are palpable.

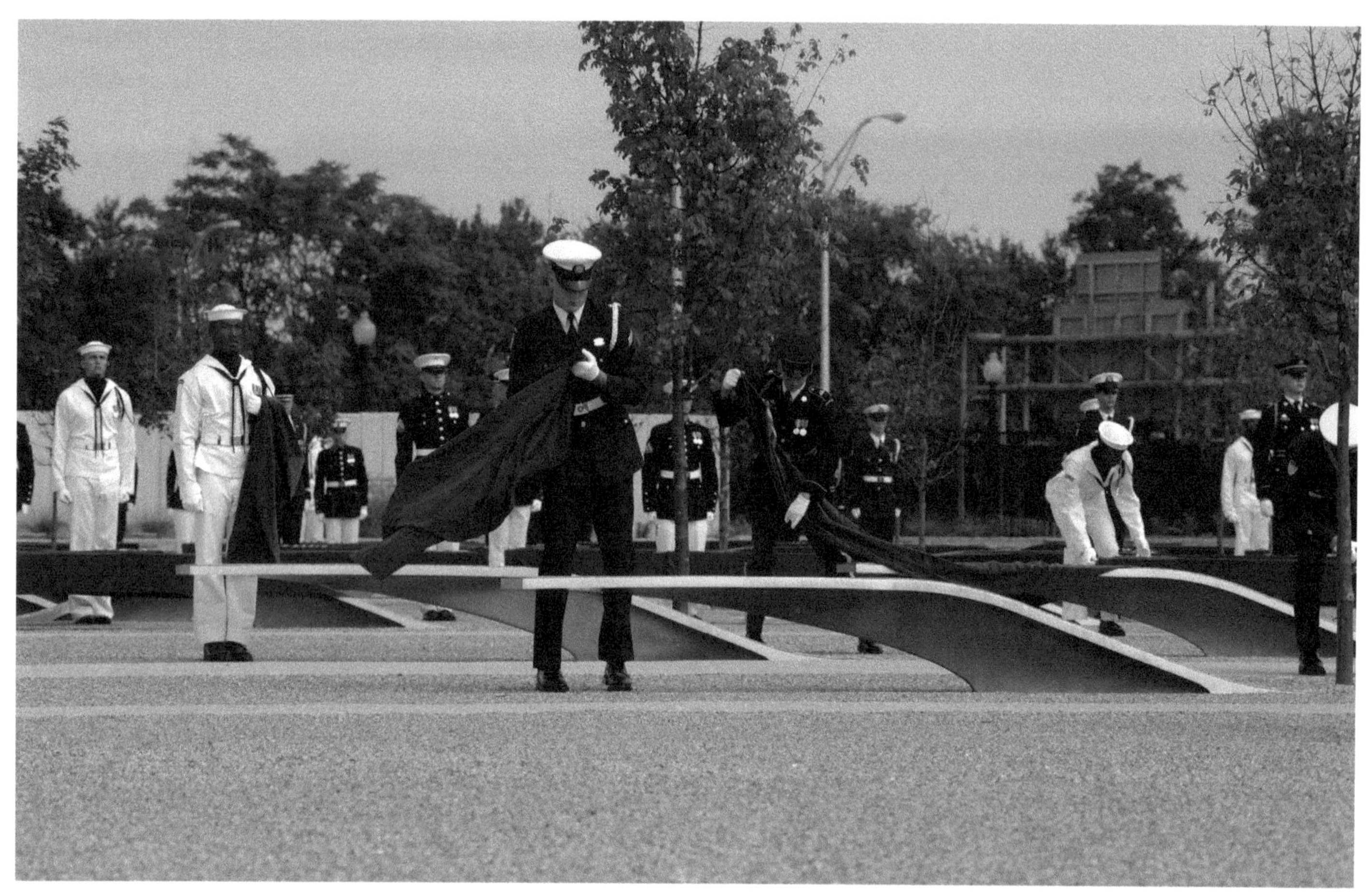

Service members unveil the engraved benches dedicated to the 184 who lost their lives at the Pentagon during the terrorist attacks of September 11, 2001.

Notes on the Photographs

These notes, listed by page number, attempt to include all aspects known of the photographs. Each of the photographs is identified by the page number, photograph's title or description, photographer and collection, archive, and call or box number when applicable. Although every attempt was made to collect all data, in some cases complete data may be unavailable due to the age and condition of some of the photographs and records.

ii **Drawing of the National Mall**
National Archives and Records Administration
RG66DC-21004

vi **Two Presidents Remembered**
Library of Congress
LC-G613-T01-43404

x **Bird's-eye Panorama of Washington, D.C.**
National Archives
RG66DC-009

2 **The Father of the Nation**
Library of Congress
LC-DIG-pga-02503

3 **Mills' Original Monument Sketch**
Library of Congress
LC-USZ62-11312

4 **Washington Monument Under Construction**
National Archives and Records Administration
111-B-90238

5 **The Scene in 1860**
Library of Congress
LC-DIG-cwpbh-03249

6 **Rooftop View of Construction in Progress**
National Archives and Records Administration
RG66DC-26-003

7 **The Monument Nearly Complete**
National Archives and Records Administration
111-B-90239

8 **Setting the Capstone, 1884**
Library of Congress
LC-USZ62-135828

9 **The Monument and Camp George, 1887**
Library of Congress
LC-USZ62-77140

10 **Lock House at Constitution Avenue**
National Archives and Records Administration
RG42-SPB049

11 **Lock House at Constitution Avenue No. 2**
National Archives and Records Administration
RG42-SPB023

12 **Dedication of Camp Roosevelt on the Monument Grounds**
Library of Congress
LC-DIG-ppmsca-15939

13 **The View from Tidal Basin**
Library of Congress
LC-USZ62-105477

14 **1902 Aerial View of the City**
National Archives and Records Administration
RG42PR-7-007

15 **Performance at the Sylvan Theatre**
Library of Congress
LC-USZ62-88075

16 **The View from Arlington Cemetery**
National Archives and Records Administration
RG64-AC2923

17 **Towering Above the Trees**
Library of Congress
LC-DIG-hec-07607

18 **Washington Monument, Baltimore**
Library of Congress
LC-DIG-det-4a29716

19 **Two Women and the Monument**
Smithsonian
AC0143-0019742

20 **The Monument in 1919**
National Archives and Records Administration
111SC-34420

21 **Man on Skis near the Monument**
Library of Congress
LC-USZ62-93060

23 **Aerial View of the Monument, 1919**
Library of Congress
LC-DIG-hec-12303

24 **Ongoing Construction Around the Monument**
Library of Congress
LC-DIG-hec-13719

25 **The Scene at Night**
National Archives and Records Administration
RG66DC-26-004

26 **Early View of the Monument at Evening**
National Archives and Records Administration
111SC-240981

27 **Night View from the Department of Treasury**
Library of Congress
LC-USZ62-85784

28 **Lighting of the National Christmas Tree**
Library of Congress
LC-DIG-npcc-25152

29 **The Washington Monument and Blimps**
Library of Congress
LC-USZ62-104731

30 **Stocking the Potomac near the Monument**
Library of Congress
LC-USZ62-113055

31 **View of the Nation's Capitol from the Monument Deck**
National Archives and Records Administration
RG66DC-006

32 **Fashionable Young Ladies at Tidal Basin**
Library of Congress
LC-USZ62-97817

33 **View of the Monument from the Capitol**
National Archives and Records Administration
RG66DC-007

34 **Spectacular Night View**
National Archives and Records Administration
RG111-WDC-99217

35 **50th Birthday Repairs**
National Archives and Records Administration
RG30-N-45-464

36 **Laus Deo Inscription**
National Archives and Records Administration
RG111-WDC-315301

37 **The Monument and Hains Point from the Air**
Library of Congress
LC-USZ62-135450

38 **On a Snowy Day, 1939**
National Archives and Records Administration
RG66DC-26-006

39 **Contemplating the Monument on a Sunny Day**
Library of Congress
LC-USF33-015611-M1

40 **An Event on the Grounds**
National Archives and Records Administration
111SC-240961

41 **Military Helicopter on the Grounds**
National Archives and Records Administration
RG79-D7476

42 **Cherry Blossoms and the Monument at Night**
Smithsonian
AC0618.004.0000432

43 **Gold Star Wives**
Smithsonian
AC0618.004.0000888

44 **Independence Day Fireworks Display**
National Archives and Records Administration
RG79-6676H

46 **A View from the White House, 1949**
Library of Congress
HABS DC,WASH,635-5

47 **During the War Years**
National Archives and Records Administration
111SC-240984

48 **Robert Mills Headstone Inscription**
Library of Congress
200693pu

49 **President Truman and Guests Inside the Monument**
National Archives and Records Administration
RG79-AR-566E

50 **A View from the Tidal Basin in Spring**
National Archives and Records Administration
111-SC-571726

51 **Ceremony with Men in Uniform**
National Archives and Records Administration
RG79-AR-512D

52 **The Monument and Environs**
National Archives and Records Administration
RG79-4500B

53 **President Truman at Centennial Ceremonies**
National Archives and Records Administration
RG79-D7609

54 Protest March 1963
Smithsonian
618ps0237231-01jp

55 Papal Visit and Address
National Archives and Records Administration
RG79-AR-27961

56 The Mall Facing West
Library of Congress
HABS DC,WASH,615-9

58 Future Site of Jefferson Memorial
Smithsonian
AC0143-0019746

59 A View of the Jefferson Memorial
National Archives and Records Administration
RG66DC-11001

60 Architect John Russell Pope
Library of Congress
LC-DIG-ggbain-38375

61 Columns of the Jefferson Memorial
Library of Congress
LC-G613-T01-41213

62 Placid Reflection
Library of Congress
LC-USZ62-89370

63 Temple of the Scottish Rite
Library of Congress
LC-DIG-npcc-08918

64 Monumental Storm
Library of Congress
LC-G613-T-41198

65 Majestic Exterior of the Memorial
Library of Congress
LC-USF347-014552

67 A View from the Northwest
National Archives and Records Administration
RG79-DC004

68 Dedication of the Memorial, 1943
National Archives and Records Administration
RG79-AR-157D

69 Inside the Memorial Rotunda
Library of Congress
LC-G613-T-43400

70 Bronze Statue of Jefferson
Library of Congress
LC-G613-T-43397

71 Potomac River View
Library of Congress
LC-USF347-014552

73 A Memorial View During the World War II Era
Library of Congress
LC-G613-T-43414

74 Against Choppy Waters
National Archives and Records Administration
RG111-WDC-315308

75 Portrayal of Jefferson Inside the Memorial
National Archives and Records Administration
RG79-AR157-1

76 Revolutionary War Reenactors at the Memorial
National Archives and Records Administration
RG79-AR157

77 Jefferson Memorial Cherry Blossoms
Library of Congress
LC-G613-T01-43411

78 Cyclists and the Memorial, 1945
Library of Congress
LC-USZ62-102193

79 Crowd at the Memorial in Springtime
Library of Congress
LC-USZ62-68082

80 On the Portico
National Archives and Records Administration
RG79-AR-770C

81 Servicemen and Other Visitors at the Memorial
National Archives and Records Administration
RG66DC-11002

82 Aerial View of the Memorial and Grounds
Library of Congress
LC-USW31-058717-B

83 History of the Cherry Trees
Library of Congress
LC-USZ62-123168

85 Jefferson Memorial from the Air, 1953
National Archives and Records Administration
RG111-WDC-168080

86 On a Clear Day
National Archives and Records Administration
RG111-WDC-422571

87 The Memorial Facade
Library of Congress
LC-G613-T-43408

88 The Jefferson Memorial and Washington Monument
National Archives and Records Administration
RG79-DC005

89 National City Christian Church
Library of Congress
HABS DC,WASH, 453-684-1

90 Inside Look at Marble Details
Library of Congress
HABS DC,WASH,453-11

91 National Archives and Records Administration
Library of Congress
HABS DC,WASH,493-1

92 **1630 Crescent Place**
Library of Congress
00001a

94 **Abraham Lincoln with Cabinet, 1862**
Library of Congress
LC-DIG-pga-02502

95 **Lincoln with Sojourner Truth**
Library of Congress
LC-USZ62-16225

96 **Lincoln's Second Inaugural Address**
Library of Congress
LC-USA7-16837

97 **The Emancipation Memorial**
Library of Congress
LC-USZ62-53278

98 **Site of the Lincoln Memorial**
National Archives and Records Administration
RG66DC-12010

99 **Early Stage of Construction**
National Archives and Records Administration
RG121-LM012

100 **Building the Foundation**
National Archives and Records Administration
RG121-LM010

101 **Construction Workers at Work**
National Archives and Records Administration
RG121-LM009

102 **A View of the Foundation**
National Archives and Records Administration
RG121-LM016

103 **A Tangle of Cranes and Cables**
National Archives and Records Administration
RG121-LM002

104 **Laying the Cornerstone**
Library of Congress
LC-DIG-hec-05427

105 **Later Stage of Construction**
Library of Congress
LC-DIG-hec-03444

106 **Later Stage of Construction no. 2**
Library of Congress
LC-USZ62-77389

107 **Progress as of 1916**
National Archives and Records Administration
RG121-LM001

108 **World War I Delays**
National Archives and Records Administration
RG121-LM003

109 **Later Stage of Construction no. 3**
National Archives and Records Administration
RG121-LM007

110 **Trenchworks**
National Archives and Records Administration
RG66DC-12011

111 **Newly Completed Memorial Stairway**
National Archives and Records Administration
RG121-LM022

112 **Aerial View of the Memorial During Construction**
Library of Congress
LC-DIG-hec-12314

113 **Installing the Lincoln Statue Pedestal**
National Archives and Records Administration
RG121-LM006

114 **Marble Statue of Abraham Lincoln in Place**
Library of Congress
LC-USZ62-59028

115 **Visitors Posing with Charles King Car at the Memorial**
Library of Congress
LC-USZ62-59226

116 **Early View of the Completed Memorial**
Library of Congress
LC-USZ62-111420

117 **Detail of East Entablature**
Library of Congress
HABS DC,WASH,462-24

118 **The Lincoln Memorial Commission**
Library of Congress
LC-DIG-npcc-01186

119 **The Memorial's Granite and Marble**
National Archives and Records Administration
RG111-WDC-A101766

120 **Lawrence Perry Plane at the Memorial**
Library of Congress
LC-USZ62-42050

121 **Aerial View of the Dedication, 1922**
National Archives and Records Administration
111SC74859

122 **President Harding Dedicatory Remarks**
Library of Congress
LC-USZ62-110537

123 **Crowd at Reflecting Pool During the Dedication**
National Archives and Records Administration
111SC74851

124 **Eve of the Dedication**
National Archives and Records Administration
111SC74845

125 **Edwin Markham at the Dedication**
Library of Congress
LC-USZ62-64974

126 **Moton Keynote Address at the Dedication**
Library of Congress
LC-USZ62-99406

127 Dedication Dignitaries
Library of Congress
LC-USZ62-110538

128 A View of the Mall from the Lincoln Memorial
Library of Congress
LC-USZ62-99405

129 Pomp and Circumstance
Smithsonian
AC0618.004.0000134

130 Colonnade Perspective
National Archives and Records Administration
RG111-WDC-315304

131 View from the Arlington Memorial Bridge
National Archives and Records Administration
RG66DC-12001

132 Symbolism of the Bridge
National Archives and Records Administration
RG66DC-12020

133 The Arlington House
Library of Congress
LC-DIG-ppmsca-07322

134 A Memorial Event
Library of Congress
LC-F81-24388

135 Boy Scouts at the Lincoln Memorial
Library of Congress
LC-DIG-npcc-08887

136 Boy Scouts of America Group Shot
Library of Congress
LC-DIG-npcc-08886

137 Chief Two Moon at the Memorial
Library of Congress
LC-USZ62-114534

138 Reflecting Pool Ice-skaters
Library of Congress
LC-USZ62-116308

139 University Rifle Team at the Memorial
Library of Congress
3b26822u

140 Tykes with Toy Sailboats at the Reflecting Pool
Library of Congress
LC-USZ62-55111

141 Reflecting Pool Swimmers
Library of Congress
LC-DIG-npcc-16087

142 Group of Memorial Visitors
Smithsonian
618ns0177506bp

143 Architect Henry Bacon's Marble Symbolism
National Archives and Records Administration
RG111-WDC-319374

144 Marian Anderson at the Memorial
Smithsonian
618ns0227133-01jp

145 The Anderson Concert
Smithsonian
618ns0227136-01jp

146 Harry Truman at the Lincoln Memorial
Smithsonian
618ns0178934jp

147 The Memorial During World War II, 1942
Library of Congress
LC-USW38-001603-E

148 Perspective from the Washington Monument Deck
National Archives and Records Administration
RG111-WDC-123145

150 Eleanor Roosevelt at Memorial NAACP Rally
Smithsonian
618ns0178935jp

151 Service Member at the Statue of Lincoln
National Archives and Records Administration
RG80-G-447868

152 Engraving of Lincoln's Second Inaugural Address
Library of Congress
HABS DC,WASH,462-39

154 Black Panther Rally at the Memorial
Library of Congress
LC-DIG-ppmsca-04303

156 Construction of the Nation's Capitol
Library of Congress
HABS DC,WASH,1-1

157 Walter Drawing of the Capitol
National Archives and Records Administration
RG66DC-61664

158 New Capitol Dome Under Construction, 1860s
National Archives and Records Administration
111-B-1444

159 Union Soldiers at the Capitol, 1865
National Archives and Records Administration
RG16AD002

160 The New Dome with Statue of Freedom
National Archives and Records Administration
111-B711

161 House of General John Mason
Library of Congress
HABS DC,WASH,131-10

162 Monument to the Marquis de Lafayette
Library of Congress
LC-DIG-ppmsca-18017

163 The Civil War Sailors Monument
Library of Congress
LC-DIG-npcc-18814

164 The John Paul Jones Memorial
Library of Congress
LC-DIG-hec-00914

165 Suffragists at Nation's Capitol
Library of Congress
LC-USZ62-22262

166 The Capitol, 1915
National Archives and Records Administration
RG111-WDC-6687

167 The Statue of Freedom
National Archives and Records Administration
RG16-FLS002

168 Capitol Fire, 1930
Library of Congress
LC-USZ62-52246

169 The Illuminated Capitol at Night
National Archives and Records Administration
RG30-N-35-2245

170 Memorial to the Unknown Dead
Library of Congress
LC-DIG-npcc-00017

171 Monument to General George B. McClellan
Library of Congress
LC-DIG-npcc-30413

172 The Ulysses S. Grant Memorial
National Archives and Records Administration
111SC74816

173 The Grant Memorial with a Capitol Backdrop
National Archives and Records Administration
RG79-AR-2222A

175 Aerial View of the Nation's Capital
National Archives and Records Administration
RG66DC-005

176 Arlington National Cemetery
Library of Congress
LC-DIG-npcc-25791

177 Aerial Close-up of the Capitol
National Archives and Records Administration
RG66DC-1-17028

178 First Division Memorial to World War I Fallen
Smithsonian
00021403

179 Monument to President Garfield
Library of Congress
LC-DIG-npcc-30148

180 The Adams Memorial in Rock Creek Cemetery
Library of Congress
HABS DC,WASH,384-4

181 Arlington Memorial Amphitheater Under Construction
National Archives and Records Administration
RG121-LM023

183 Aerial View of the Amphitheater
National Archives and Records Administration
RG66DC-1-17082

184 Arlington Memorial Amphitheater Completed
National Archives and Records Administration
111SC80805

185 John Ericsson Memorial
Library of Congress
LC-USZ62-128859

186 Ceremony at the Tomb of the Unknown Soldier, 1946
National Archives and Records Administration
RG79-AR-38B048

187 Ceremony at the Tomb no. 2
Library of Congress
LC-DIG-hec-25203

188 Visitors at the Tomb of the Unknown Soldier
Library of Congress
LC-DIG-hec-23601

189 Burial Service at Arlington National Cemetery, 1949
Smithsonian
618ns0242250sc

190 Confederate Memorial at Arlington National Cemetery
Library of Congress
LC-DIG-hec-13525

191 The John Pershing Memorial
Library of Congress
HABS DC,WASH,628-1

192 The Iwo Jima (United States Marine Corps) Memorial
Library of Congress
HALS VA-9-13

193 Night View of the Iwo Jima Memorial
Library of Congress
HALS VA-9-18

194 Scene at the March on Washington
Library of Congress
LC-DIG-ppmsca-03191

195 The Three Soldiers Memorial
Library of Congress
HABS DC,WASH,643-4

196 The Chinatown Arch
Library of Congress
HABS-DC,WASH,612-28

197 The Vietnam Memorial
Library of Congress
HABS DC,WASH,643-13

198 Pentagon 9-11 Memorial Benches
Department of Defense
080911-D-7203C-014
RG48-RC11014Q007

HISTORIC PHOTOS OF WASHINGTON D.C. MONUMENTS

What makes Washington, D.C., so attractive to so many people? Locals and visitors in the nation's capital may respond with a range of generic answers, but one top response will always be the great monuments. From Washington, D.C.'s historic beginnings in the 1790s, these prominent structures soon became an important identifying feature of the district and a way to preserve its past.

This book examines a number of significant monuments, memorials, and historic sites through stunning black-and-white photographs spanning a century and a half. *Historic Photos of D.C. Monuments* highlights chapter-by-chapter the Washington Monument, the Jefferson Memorial, the Lincoln Memorial, and other monuments receiving significantly less foot traffic—but ones that are no less significant. The memorialized figures, the architects and artists behind the structures, and captivating historical facts are further explored in accompanying captions. Each chapter also looks at historical events that took place at these monuments, including political rallies, civil rights demonstrations, and speeches given by those who helped shape the nation.

It is hoped that readers of Washington D.C. Monuments—from D.C. residents and visitors to art enthusiasts, history buffs, and architecture lovers—will visit these hallowed places and see for themselves why people love Washington, D.C.

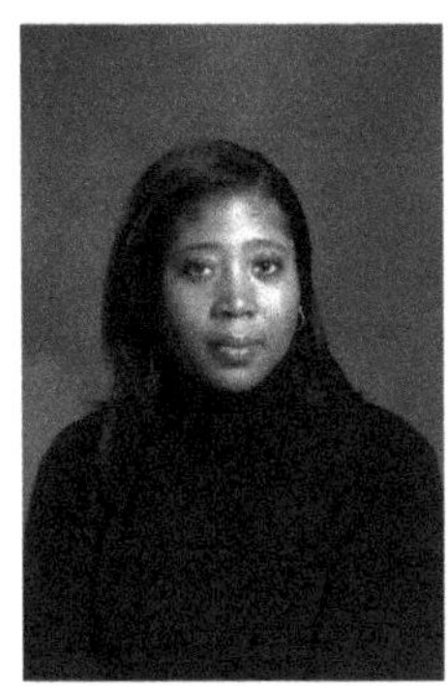

Tracey Gold Bennett has written and produced news for numerous radio and television stations around the country and has also worked as a columnist for the *Washington Examiner.* This is her fourth book on Washington, D.C.

WWW.TURNERPUBLISHING.COM

www.ingramcontent.com/pod-product-compliance
Lightning Source LLC
LaVergne TN
LVHW060608110826
845154LV00003B/51
* 9 7 8 1 6 8 4 4 2 0 7 3 5 *